Blended Practices for Teaching Young Children in Inclusive Settings

Second Edition

by

Jennifer Grisham-Brown, Ed.D.
Interdisciplinary Early Childhood
Education Program
University of Kentucky
Lexington

and

Mary Louise Hemmeter, Ph.D.
Department of Special Education
Vanderbilt University
Nashville, Tennessee

with Kristie Pretti-Frontczak, Ph.D., and invited contributors

·P A U L·H·
BROOKES
PUBLISHING CO.®

Baltimore • London • Sydney

Paul H. Brookes Publishing Co.
Post Office Box 10624
Baltimore, Maryland 21285-0624
USA

www.brookespublishing.com

Typeset by Absolute Service, Inc., Towson, Maryland.
Manufactured in the United States of America by Sheridan Books, Inc., Chelsea, Michigan.

The individuals described in this book are composites or real people whose situations are masked and are based on the authors' experiences. In all instances, names and identifying details have been changed to protect confidentiality. Any similarity to actual individuals or circumstances in photographs is coincidental, and no implications should be inferred.

Cover image courtesy of Photography by Katie Jane. Additional photos are used by permission and courtesy of Jennifer Grisham Brown. Chapters 4 and 5 opener photos and Section III photo is courtesy of BiShaune Battle.

Library of Congress Cataloging-in-Publication Data

The Library of Congress has cataloged the printed edition as follows:

Names: Grisham-Brown, Jennifer, author. | Hemmeter, Mary Louise, author. | Pretti-Frontczak, Kristie, author.
Title: Blended practices for teaching young children in inclusive settings / by Jennifer Grisham-Brown, Ed.D., Interdisciplinary Early Childhood Education Program, University of Kentucky, Lexington; and Mary Louise Hemmeter, Ph.D., Department of Special Education, Vanderbilt University; with Kristie Pretti-Frontczak, Ph.D., and invited contributors.
Description: Second Edition. | Baltimore, Maryland: Paul H. Brookes Publishing Co., [2017] | Includes bibliographical references and index.
Identifiers: LCCN 2016035532 (print) | LCCN 2016050593 (ebook) | ISBN 9781598576689 (Paper) | ISBN 9781598578966 (pdf) | ISBN 9781598578997 (epub)
Subjects: LCSH: Early childhood education. | Early childhood special education.
Classification: LCC LB1139.23 .G75 2017 (print) | LCC LB1139.23 (ebook) | DDC 372.21—dc23
LC record available at https://lccn.loc.gov/2016035532

British Library Cataloguing in Publication data are available from the British Library.

2021   2020   2019   2018   2017

10   9   8   7   6   5   4   3   2   1

Contents

About the Online Materials

Purchasers of this book may download, print, and/or photocopy these appendices for professional and educational use. These materials are included with the print book and are also available at http://www.brookespublishing.com/grishambrown/materials for both print and e-book buyers.

About the Authors

Jennifer Grisham-Brown, Ed.D., is a Professor in the Interdisciplinary Early Childhood Education program and Faculty Director of the Early Childhood Laboratory School at the University of Kentucky. She teaches courses in assessment and instructional design/implementation. Dr. Grisham-Brown has been named a *Teacher Who Made a Difference* on two separate occasions. Dr. Grisham-Brown coauthored the first book on blended practices as well as its companion text *Blended Assessment Practices in Early Childhood Education* (2011). She also coauthored a book titled *Reach for the Stars: Planning for the Future* (2013), which is used to support families of young children to plan for their children's future and articulate their priorities to educational team members. Dr. Grisham-Brown has directed or codirected numerous state and federal grants in the areas of personnel preparation, program evaluation, training and technical assistance, model development, and research. Her research interests include authentic assessment, tiered instruction, and inclusion of children with disabilities in inclusive preschool settings. She has authored/coauthored numerous peer-reviewed articles and book chapters related to those areas. In addition, she is frequently asked to provide professional development to state departments of education, universities, and local education agencies on topics on which she conducts research throughout the country. Dr. Grisham-Brown is a member of the Early Intervention Management and Research Group, where she is part of a team of early intervention professionals from across the country who are responsible for the development and research of the *Assessment, Evaluation, and Programming System* (AEPS®; Bricker, 2002). Dr. Grisham-Brown is cofounder of a children's home and preschool program in Guatemala City called Hope for Tomorrow. Since 2009, she has taken students from the College of Education to Guatemala for a summer education abroad experience. Dr. Grisham-Brown also works internationally in other locations to promote inclusion of young children with disabilities.

Mary Louise Hemmeter, Ph.D., is a Professor of Special Education at Vanderbilt University. She is a Faculty Director of the Susan Gray School for Children, an inclusive early childhood program. Her research focuses on effective instruction, social-emotional development and challenging behavior, and effective professional development approaches. She has been a principal investigator or co-principal investigator on numerous projects funded by the U.S. Departments of Education and Health and Human Services. Through her work on the National Center on the Social Emotional Foundations for Early Learning and the Institute of Education

Science-funded research projects, she was involved in the development of the Pyramid Model for Supporting Social Emotional Competence in Young Children and an effective model for coaching teachers to implement effective practices. She was coeditor of the *Journal of Early Intervention* and President of the Council for Exceptional Children's Division for Early Childhood. She has received the Merle B. Karnes Service to the Division Award and the Mary McEvoy Service to the Field Award from the Council for Exceptional Children's Division for Early Childhood.

About the Contributors

Kathleen Artman-Meeker, Ph.D., is an Assistant Professor at the University of Washington where she specializes in early childhood special education. She received her doctoral degree in Special Education from Vanderbilt University.

Lillian K. Durán, Ph.D., is an Associate Professor in the Department of Special Education and Clinical Sciences at the University of Oregon. She received her doctoral degree in Educational Psychology from the University of Minnesota.

Jill F. Grifenhagen, Ph.D., is an Assistant Professor at North Carolina State University. Dr. Grifenhagen earned her doctoral degree from the Peabody College of Education and Human Development at Vanderbilt University.

Anna H. Hall, Ph.D., is an Assistant Professor of Early Childhood Education in the Eugene T. Moore School of Education at Clemson University. She earned her doctoral degree in Interdisciplinary Early Childhood Education from the University of Kentucky.

Jessica K. Hardy, Ph.D., is an Assistant Professor in the Department of Special Education at the University of Louisville. She earned her doctoral degree in Early Childhood Special Education from Vanderbilt University.

Sarah Hawkins-Lear, Ed.D., is an Associate Professor at Morehead State University. She received her doctorate of education degree in Moderate to Severe Disabilities from the University of Kentucky.

Elizabeth McLaren, Ed.D., is an Associate Professor of Education in the Interdisciplinary Early Childhood Education program at Morehead State University. She earned her doctorate of education degree from the University of Kentucky.

Ragan H. McLeod, Ph.D., is an Assistant Professor in the Department of Special Education and Multiple Abilities at the University of Alabama. She received her doctoral degree in Special Education from Vanderbilt University.

Kristie Pretti-Frontczak, Ph.D., is the owner of B2K Solutions, Ltd., a company dedicated to transforming services for children from birth to kindergarten. She received her doctoral degree in Special Education-Early Intervention from the University of Oregon.

Julie Harp Rutland, Ph.D. is Assistant Professor of Early Childhood, Elementary, and Special Education at Morehead State University. She earned her doctoral degree in Interdisciplinary Early Childhood Education at the University of Kentucky.

Foreword

Anna sits at a table in her early childhood classroom, looking down at the puzzle in front of her. She frowns as she scans the pieces scattered on the table, picks one up, and moves it hesitantly in the air. Suddenly, she bangs the piece down, jumps up, and runs across the room to her cubby, where she sits sucking her thumb.

Does Anna have a disability, or is Anna a typically developing 4-year-old, perhaps with some individual, cultural, or linguistic characteristics that influence her behavior? And should the answers to these questions make a difference in how her teacher understands, plans for, and supports Anna's learning and development?

Like the first edition, this new edition of *Blended Practices for Teaching Young Children in Inclusive Settings* takes an innovative and much needed approach to preparing future and existing teachers to meet the needs of all young children. Responding to the current reality that most early childhood teachers will work in settings that include children with and without disabilities, as well as many children who are dual language learners, the authors have blended the best thinking from the fields of early childhood education, early childhood special education, and related disciplines, advocating for practices that likewise blend a variety of evidence-based, effective approaches to instruction. While recognizing the need to differentiate teaching to meet individual needs, this book repeatedly makes the point that the same features of early childhood environments and the same teaching strategies that promote positive development in typically developing children also benefit children with disabilities and other special learning and developmental needs.

Echoing the approach taken in *Blended Practices*, we comment on the book's strengths and distinctive features from our blended points of view. Although we have collaborated, written, and presented together, we come from what often seems like different worlds: that of general early childhood education and that of early childhood special education. Like the fields from which we come, we recognize how much we have in common and also see the continuing challenges of efforts to integrate these diverse perspectives. In this new edition, Jennifer Grisham-Brown and Mary Louise Hemmeter move us forward toward a shared vision for effective blended practices and blended professional development in several important ways.

Timing

The second edition of *Blended Practices for Teaching Young Children in Inclusive Settings* is as timely, if not more so, than the first edition. The spotlight on early childhood teacher education programs is even more intense than it was when the first edition was published. Influential national reports on the early child-hood workforce are recommending that all early childhood teachers should have a Bachelor of Arts (BA) degree. In keeping with these recommendations, the most recent benchmarks established by National Institute for Early Education Research (NIEER) for assessing the quality of state early childhood prekindergarten (pre-K) programs include a benchmark suggesting whether or not states require teachers to have a BA degree. At the same time, there is recognition that not all teacher preparation programs are of adequate quality; simply having a BA degree does not guarantee competence in early childhood teaching. Deficits in programs include lack of emphasis on clinical practice, weak student teaching experiences, includ-ing lack of standards for clinical practica, and inadequate coverage of key content areas such as inclusion.

There have been concerted efforts to help faculty address these gaps through the development of high-quality, practice-focused resources. Many of the resources are directly aligned with the Division for Early Childhood's Recommended Prac-tices, revised in 2014 and designed to give guidance to faculty on specific practices that should be the central focus of their personnel preparation programs. These professional development resources include demonstration videos of high-quality inclusive practices being implemented, tools that support coaching and perfor-mance feedback, and student- and consumer-friendly early childhood research and policy summaries. The need for an excellent textbook on blended practices to undergird these resources has never been stronger.

The federal agency commitment to inclusion across all early childhood sec-tors is at historic levels. The U.S. Departments of Education and Health and Human Services have developed a series of policy statements that reflect their investment in an integrated and holistic system of supports for young children, especially those suspected or identified as having disabilities under IDEA, and their fami-lies. Most notably is the 2015 Policy Statement on Inclusion of Children with Dis-abilities in Early Childhood Programs. The statement provides common language and a shared vision across all early childhood programs and funding streams for "build[ing] a nationwide culture of inclusion." The new Head Start Performance Standards (2016) build on this policy statement by including a new requirement for programs to provide individual services and supports to the maximum extent pos-sible to children awaiting determination of IDEA eligibility. This essentially rein-forces the notion that providing support to each and every child, including those with suspected or identified disabilities under IDEA, is a shared responsibility and priority across all early childhood sectors. It is no longer possible for anyone to say or think that inclusion is a special education issue that will be solved by special educators. The spillover is apparent from the strong messages on inclusion from federal agencies to national, regional, and state professional organizations, techni-cal assistance networks, and local agencies.

We increasingly recognize that *all* young children, whether officially identi-fied as having a disability or not, benefit from multiple well-planned, intentional learning opportunities throughout the day that respond to their developmental, linguistic, cultural, and individual characteristics. And we have come face to face with the realization that not all early childhood teachers are prepared to provide that kind of high-quality teaching nor do they necessarily have the skills to partner with parents and other colleagues to ensure an integrated and holistic approach to supporting children. This book is designed to meet that need in a timely way.

Questions from Teachers and Teacher Educators

This practical new edition addresses the day-to-day dilemmas that teachers often face in inclusive settings. Today, early childhood professionals are expected to influence positive outcomes for all children within contexts that reflect our country's rapidly increasing diversity, bringing richness as well as new challenges.

As they get ready to meet new and higher expectations, future teachers, practicing teachers, and teacher educators ask urgent, relevant questions:

I will be student teaching in a class where six children have been identified as having significant disabilities: Can I really teach them the mathematics content that is in our state standards?

I'm preparing to be an early childhood special educator: How do I work collaboratively with regular classroom teachers?

Is it possible to use direct instruction within a developmentally appropriate approach?

How should I involve the diverse families of the children in my program?

My biggest worry is how I will manage the children's behavior—what are effective strategies?

What kinds of learning environments will engage all children: those with and without disabilities and those with diverse strengths, learning needs, and cultural experiences?

I taught for years before returning to college; my program now includes many more immigrant and refugee families with young children. What can I do to meet their needs more effectively?

How can I balance the needs of a few children with those of the entire class?

As a teacher educator, how on earth do I coordinate attention to the many learning standards, program standards, and curriculum expectations that my students will need to address?

As a teacher educator, how do I keep myself current on these complex issues when my own professional background has become increasingly outdated?

Blended Practices is not a cookbook, and the authors do not claim to serve up easy answers to these kinds of questions, but much help will be found in these pages. In response to their questions, readers will find rich, engaging information and practical suggestions that invite reflection, dialogue with colleagues, and informed consideration of evidence-based practices.

Organization and Special Features

The second edition of *Blended Practices* is well organized to promote readers' understanding of key concepts and instructional strategies in what can be a very complex field. The book's organization supports this understanding by initially describing a comprehensive conceptual framework whose components are designed to be effective for all children. The authors next focus on outcomes for young children and propose a set of foundational practices (such as embedding instruction within developmentally appropriate activities) related to those outcomes—practices that are important at all levels or tiers of instruction and in all content areas. The concept of multitiered instruction helps give coherence to this material by beginning with universal practices—such as developing daily schedules that meet all children's needs and designing learning centers that provide flexible learning opportunities and integration of skills—before moving toward systematic-instruction practices that target and remove barriers to a child achieving specific outcomes. Only after this broad perspective on blended practices is firmly in place, do the authors introduce valuable applications in specialized domains or subject areas, such as social and emotional learning, language and literacy, and mathematics. Of special note is the in-depth attention given to supports for young dual language learners; several chapters are devoted to these critical issues.

This edition retains many features that have made *Blended Practices* such an important resource while substantially enhancing those features. Practical materials such as planning forms, checklists, and family interview protocols are available to photocopy or download, and can be adapted to individual contexts. Every chapter is rich with vignettes and case examples of diverse children, teachers, and families; these will help readers engage with the book's content and better understand its applications in daily practice. In some cases the authors have developed parallel vignettes illustrating more- and less-effective ways to implement certain practices. These kinds of illustrations will yield dynamic discussions. Every chapter ends with a set of *Learning Activities* that help readers reflect on and apply strategies described in that chapter. Activities include observing specific practices in a classroom or planning and implementing a new strategy featured in the chapter. Such activities, with their focus on practice, are consistent with research-based recommendations about effective early childhood professional development. Together, these features help to cement that this edition will become an essential resource not only during preservice preparation, but also once teachers are in the field.

Continuing Challenges for the Field

Although this book makes a strong contribution to the creation of a truly unified and professional field of early childhood practice, we must acknowledge that gaps remain in our efforts toward a shared profession. While the field's leadership is moving closer to having a shared vision and common language around inclusion, intensive work is needed to ensure that relevant professional documents reach a wider audience of general early childhood educators. To this end, professional associations and the federal early childhood agencies (U.S. Department of Education and U.S. Department of Health and Human Services) are investing in outreach efforts, such as webinars and guidance documents, to stimulate discussion, interaction, and the expansion of a shared frame of reference.

The presence of blended early childhood teacher education programs whose faculty are drawn from multiple early childhood disciplines provides promise for being exemplars for other programs. However, we have limited research on their effectiveness at the level of student outcomes. The norm continues to be that teachers, and those who teach future teachers, are trained and professionally socialized in separate streams of special education or general early childhood education. Once trained, in spite of unification efforts, they often enter work environments with different regulations and funding streams. Although they increasingly work together and share many beliefs, approaches to education, and core values, they retain distinct professional identities. Despite the work of the National Association for the Education of Young Children (NAEYC), the Division for Early Childhood (DEC), and others to create a more unified approach to the education of all young children and the preparation of those who work with children, these disparities remain, often blocking the pathway to effective blended practices and blended professional preparation.

Another persistent and related challenge is to build the capacity of those faculty in institutions of higher education who are responsible for preparing early childhood teachers for inclusive settings. Our research and that of others documents the "leaky pipeline" that limits the number of qualified, diverse instructors in the early childhood field. Beyond this issue is the lack of effective, ongoing professional development to ensure that early childhood teacher educators have both the content and pedagogical knowledge to fully develop their students' professional competence. Surveys show that early childhood faculty recognize this need, and although some resources exist, robust support for faculty professional development continues to be limited. *Blended Practices* is an example of an excellent resource to use with students, but its use can be greatly enhanced in the hands of fully prepared instructors.

An additional challenge is the absence of systems of support once teachers move from a university setting into the work environment. Though they may wish to implement the evidence-based practices that this book proposes, they may be stymied. The growing field of implementation science reminds us that too often effective implementation is blocked by barriers within and beyond the workplace. The field needs to pay much greater attention to these systems-level issues if practices are to be implemented with the fidelity needed to ensure positive outcomes.

Although it does not offer a simple solution to these challenges, this book refuses to artificially separate the needs of children with disabilities and other special learning and developmental needs from the needs of their typically developing peers. Echoing and expanding on the key themes of the first edition, the authors send readers a convincing message: A systematic, thoughtful, and individualized approach to teaching, drawing from the best thinking in both the early childhood education and early childhood special education fields, is both possible and desirable. We applaud Jennifer Grisham-Brown and Mary Louise Hemmeter for further enhancing a valued resource that contributes so much to our unified vision of professional preparation for today and tomorrow's teachers.

Marilou Hyson, Ph.D.
Consultant,
Early Childhood Development and Education;
Adjunct Professor, University of Massachusetts, Boston

Pamela Winton, Ph.D.
Senior Scientist and Director of Outreach
Frank Porter Graham Child Development Institute
University of North Carolina at Chapel Hill

REFERENCES

Council for Exceptional Children, Division for Early Childhood. (2014). *DEC recommended practices in early intervention/early childhood special education 2014.* Retrieved from http://www.dec-sped.org/recommendedpractices

Department of Health and Human Services Administration for Children and Families. (2016). *Head Start Performance Standards.* Washington, DC. Retrieved from https://eclkc.ohs.acf.hhs.gov/hslc/hs/docs/hspss-final.pdf

Individuals with Disabilities Education Improvement Act (IDEA) of 2004, PL 108-446, 20 U.S.C. §§ 1400 et seq.

U.S. Department of Education. (2015). *Policy statement on inclusion of children with disabilities in early childhood programs.* Retrieved from http://www2.ed.gov/policy/speced/guid/earlylearning/joint-statement-full-text.pdf

Acknowledgments

Much of what we address in this book we learned from teachers, administrators, families, and children with whom we have worked. We wish to recognize some of the many programs that contributed to the development of this book. Specifically, we acknowledge the teachers, children, and families of the Early Childhood Laboratory at the University of Kentucky, Hope for Tomorrow Preschool in Guatemala, Franklin County public school system, Metro Nashville public schools, Williamson County Schools, and the Susan Gray School for Children as well as programs around the country with which we have worked and consulted. We would never have continued our work on this complex topic without their willingness to allow us to work in and with their programs.

We underestimated the many people it takes to make an idea become a book. First and foremost, we wish to thank Johanna Schmitter, Acquisitions Editor, and Melissa Solarz, Associate Editor, from Paul H. Brookes Publishing Co. They provided excellent oversight and incredible patience as we moved from a simple revision to a completely overhauled version of the first edition of this book. We appreciate our contributors, who provided useful insight into applying blended practices to specific topics/populations of children: Julie Harp Rutland, Sarah Hawkins-Lear, Anna A. Hall, Elizabeth McLaren, Ragan H. McLeod, Jessica K. Hardy, Jill F. Grifenhagen, Kathleen Artman-Meeker, and Lillian K. Durán. We are also grateful for the contributions of Kristie Pretti-Frontczak, who coauthored the first edition with us. Although she is now teaching the world about blended practices as a consultant, she found time to coauthor two chapters and provide professional support for the current book. We appreciate her counsel and friendship as we navigated this very long process. We also acknowledge the contributions of those who have supported us, taught with us, provided training with us, kept us grounded, and listened to our ideas along the way. Jennifer wishes to thank her friends and colleagues—Charlotte Manno, Rebecca Crawford, Christy Kaylor, and Kim Nicholas—who provided insight on many aspects of the book, as well as those who kept her grounded and are proud of her efforts—Mom, Milly, Rita, Christy, Debbie, Donna, Melisa, Amy, Carolyn, Kellye, Kathy, and Jannene. Mary Louise wishes to thank the following people for their support and patience, especially when the book took priority over other projects and activities—Jessica Hardy, Ragan H. McLeod, Catherine Corr, James Kretzer, Molly Gilson, Kym Horth, Beverly Hand, Lise Fox, Pat Snyder, Erin Barton, Rob Corso, Tweety Yates, Amy Santos, Micki Ostrosky, Barbara Smith, Phil Strain, Ann Kaiser, Kiersten Kinder, Michelle Wyatt, and Jenn Ledford. Mary Louise would also like to thank all of her colleagues, friends, and family for their ongoing support.

To the teachers, children, and families who teach us

and to our families who have supported us.

Kendall Aroldo Lee Brown
Mi Familia en Guatemala
—JGB

Sandie and Archer Bishop
Graham Hemmeter
In memory of Corinne Brown Hemmeter
—MLH

Setting the Stage for Blended Practices

## CHAPTER 1

Introduction to Blended Practices

Mary Louise Hemmeter and Jennifer Grisham-Brown

Significant movement toward states providing prekindergarten (pre-K) programs for children who are at risk has occurred since the first edition of this book was published in 2005. Combined with federal legislation mandating services for young children with disabilities and other special needs, as well as continued funding for Head Start and Early Head Start, that meant that inclusive preschool programs were becoming more common throughout the country. According to the National Institute for Early Education Research, 42 states and the District of Columbia provided public preschool during the 2014–2015 school year. More than 1.4 million children attended state-funded preschool, with 5% of 3-year-olds and 29% of 4-year-olds enrolled in state-funded preschool (Barnett, 2016). In 2014–2015, 15.9% of 3-year-olds and 41.3% of 4-year-olds served under the Individuals with Disabilities Education Improvement Act (IDEA) of 2004 (PL 108-446) received special education and related services in inclusive early childhood settings.

Additional federal initiatives have significantly increased funding for ensuring the quality of early childhood programs. President Obama signed the American Recovery and Reinvestment Act of 2009 (PL 111-5) into law, which had significant investments specifically for early care and education, including allocating funds to IDEA and serving infants, toddlers, and preschoolers with special needs. Funds were provided in the summer of 2011 for a competitive grant program called the Early Learning Challenge, which was part of the Race to the Top Initiative. The goal of this program was to support states to increase the number of children from low-income families or otherwise disadvantaged children who attend high-quality early childhood programs, implement a system of high-quality early childhood programs and services, and ensure that assessment use is in accordance with the National Research Council's recommendations specific to early childhood. Under the auspices of the Early Learning Challenge grant competition, more than $1 billion has been granted to projects in 20 states since 2011.

The Preschool Development Grants competition, which is administered by the U.S. Department of Education and the U.S. Department of Health and Human Services, was created to help states build (development grants) or expand (expansion grants) high-quality preschool programs in high-need communities. Expansion grants can be used in concert with Race to the Top/Early Learning Challenge grants. Five states were awarded development grants, and 13 states were awarded expansion grants in 2014 (year 1 of the grant), for a total of $226,419,228. These awards will allow more than 18,000 additional children to attend high-quality preschool programs. For example, Tennessee was awarded a $17.5 million expansion grant to create additional preschool seats for children in Shelby County (Memphis) and Metropolitan Nashville Public Schools.

Early childhood Race to the Top funding as well as preschool expansion grants have focused on expanding access and quality to early childhood programs. In addition, state and federal governments are implementing systematic efforts to ensure that early childhood education (ECE) programs demonstrate accountability for positive outcomes for young children. One example of this is the requirement that programs funded under IDEA for children ages birth to 5 years report children's progress toward three outcomes considered essential to children becoming active and successful participants in the settings in which they spend time—positive social-emotional skills, acquisition and use of knowledge and skills, and use of appropriate behaviors to meet their needs. Head Start has implemented a system for ensuring quality that requires grantees that are not meeting quality standards be reconsidered for future funding. Because of the emphasis on accountability and ensuring quality, preschool programs are increasingly being required to document that all children are making progress based on early care and education standards developed either by state governments or by federal programs.

The most recent federal initiative was launched with the publication of a policy statement by the U.S. Department of Health and Human Services and the U.S. Department of Education—the Policy Statement on the Inclusion of Children with Disabilities in Early Childhood Programs (2015). The purpose of the statement was to

> set a vision and provide recommendations to states, local educational agencies (LEAs), schools, and public and private early childhood programs, from the U.S. Department of Health and Human Services and the U.S. Department of Education, for increasing the inclusion of infants, toddlers, and preschool children with disabilities in high-quality early childhood programs (p. 1; 2015).

Furthermore, the policy statement acknowledges that all young children with disabilities should not only have access to high-quality inclusive settings, but they should also be provided with the individualized supports they need to meet high expectations. The policy statement specifically calls for the use of embedded instruction, scaffolding, and tiered models of instruction.

Great interest in how to deliver effective instruction to all children (including those with disabilities) has grown because many of the quality initiatives described previously have a focus on providing services in inclusive settings, including community-based programs, and improving social and preacademic outcomes of the children who attend these programs. The placement of children with disabilities in these programs does not ensure that they will reach high standards. The Council for Exceptional Children's Division for Early Childhood (DEC) and the National Association for the Education of Young Children (NAEYC) published a joint position statement in 2009 in which they identified three defining features of inclusion—access, participation, and supports. Children with disabilities must be included in a preschool program and given effective instruction so they can reach high standards (Barton & Smith, 2015; DEC, 2014; Odom, Buysse, & Soukakou, 2011; Schwartz, Sandall, Odom, Horn, & Beckman, 2002; Strain & Bovey, 2011). The purpose of this book is to integrate knowledge about effective practices for teaching children with and without disabilities into a comprehensive approach that ensures that all children in inclusive settings meet high standards.

CHANGES IN THE SECOND EDITION

In addition to state and federal policy and funding advances related to ECE, a significant amount of research has been published (DEC, 2014) since we wrote the first edition of this book. Although the overall curriculum framework of blended practices has not changed, we know more about how to plan for and implement instruction for children with a variety of learning needs in early childhood settings. These advances have influenced national policy statements and the development of current recommendation practices. NAEYC published a new statement on developmentally appropriate practices (DAP) in 2009 (Copple & Bredekamp, 2009). In addition, DEC updated their recommended practices in 2014. Furthermore, the two organizations published a paper in collaboration with the National Head Start Association on frameworks for implementing a response to intervention (RTI) approach in early childhood programs. These advances in research and subsequent development of recommended practices influenced how we approached the second edition of this book.

Three major changes have been made in this edition. First, because of the essential role that assessment plays in blended practices, it was difficult to fully address assessment and instruction in the same text and do them both well. We made a decision to write a separate text on assessment that aligns with the blended practices instructional approach, titled *Assessing Young Children in Inclusive Settings: The Blended Practices Approach* (Grisham-Brown & Pretti-Frontczak, 2011), which contains a majority of the information on assessment that was in the first edition of this book. Second, there has been a great deal of work done in the area of multitiered systems of support (MTSS) for both behavior and academics (Buysse & Peisner-Feinberg, 2010; Greenwood et al., 2011; Hemmeter, Fox, & Snyder, 2013; Snyder, Hemmeter, McLean, Sandall, & McLaughlin, 2013). This work has influenced our thinking about how to deliver instruction to all children in an inclusive setting. Furthermore, it has led us to think about how to integrate approaches to both instruction and behavioral support. We have organized the chapters in this edition using a tiered approach to instruction to address these issues. Finally, we have added chapters to this edition that address instructional issues related to outcomes in different subject areas. We specifically added chapters on teaching language, literacy, social-emotional skills, and math. These chapters have been added to address the current focus on ensuring that children are making progress in key preacademic domains, including social-emotional development.

TARGET AUDIENCES AND POSSIBLE USES FOR THIS BOOK

This book is designed for use in undergraduate and graduate teacher education programs in ECE and early childhood special education (ECSE), including those that simultaneously train teachers in both disciplines. It bridges the gap between ECE and ECSE by providing students with an integrated approach for working with all young children. Students graduating from an ECE or ECSE program are likely to be teaching children with and without disabilities and will need information on how to integrate effective practices for all young children. In addition, the trend toward blended licensure makes this text an appealing addition to programs preparing personnel to work with children in inclusive settings. In addition, early childhood practitioners will find this book useful in their work with young children. Specifically, the information in this text will be useful to teachers as they attempt to address the wide range of needs of children with and without disabilities in their classrooms. Administrators and training and technical assistance providers will find the information helpful as they provide support to teachers around inclusive practices.

Although much of the information in this book will be relevant to the entire early childhood age range (birth to age 8), the needs of infants and toddlers are very different from those of preschoolers and children in early elementary grades. It would be difficult to address all of those needs in a single text, so this book focuses on children ages 2–5 and on programs that primarily serve children in center-based settings. The information, however, is relevant to a variety of settings, including child care, Head Start, and public school pre-K and kindergarten programs.

DEFINITION OF KEY TERMS

One of the complicated tasks associated with blending ideas and practices is ensuring that the terminology used is understandable and acceptable to relevant audiences. Several key terms that are used throughout this book were carefully selected based on consideration of the different audiences and users. These terms are briefly described next, along with an explanation for why they were selected.

Blended practices: The fields of ECE and ECSE have traditionally approached education of young children from two different perspectives. ECE grew out of research on child development and has focused primarily on creating supportive environments that facilitate and enhance children's development. ECSE was strongly influenced by the field of special education and focuses primarily on individualized approaches to education that meet the unique needs of each child with a disability. A more unified or blended approach is needed as inclusive programs for young children with and without disabilities have emerged. This book evolved from the need to blend practices that are recommended for all children. Teachers need to understand practices that address the needs of all children, including those with disabilities, because of the increasing trend toward inclusive early childhood programs and the challenges to achieving meaningful inclusion. The term *blended practices* is used to refer to the integration of practices that can be used to address the needs of all children in inclusive settings. This is not to suggest that teachers will do the same thing for all children. This book describes how effective practices for addressing the needs of individual children can be integrated so that all children can be meaningfully included in and benefit from the activities and routines of a classroom.

Inclusive programs: The goal of this book is to describe practices that can be used to address the needs of young children with and without disabilities in inclusive settings. Inclusive settings are those settings that are designed to address the needs of children who are typically developing, children who are at risk, and children with disabilities, including child care programs, public school pre-K and kindergarten programs, Head Start programs, and other center-based programs.

Teacher: A variety of terms, including *early childhood educator, interventionist, direct service provider, child care provider,* and *practitioner,* are used to describe the adults who work with young children. Teaching is one common role of adults, regardless of the setting in which the adults work or the type of children with whom the adults work. One has to develop positive and trusting relationships with children, attend to the individual needs of children, and support children in a way that promotes their individual development to be an effective teacher. These are the very things that all adults do when working with young children. Therefore, the term *teacher* will be used throughout this volume to refer to the adults who work with children, regardless of the setting or context in which they work.

HISTORICAL TRENDS

Early childhood inclusion has been greatly influenced by both research and legislation related to programs for young children who are typically developing, are at risk, or have disabilities. As the next section discusses, the roots of early childhood inclusion can be traced to the 1960s and the War on Poverty and were further strengthened by several key pieces of legislation.

Movement Toward Inclusive Programs

The history of inclusive preschool programs can be traced to a number of programs that began in the 1960s and 1970s. Head Start, which was signed into law in 1965, has been one of the most influential programs. Head Start was designed to be a comprehensive program for children and families living in poverty. In the early 1970s, as a result of the Economic Opportunity Act of 1964 (PL 88-452), Head Start mandated that 10% of its slots would be reserved for children with disabilities. This was the first real commitment at the national level to preschool programs for children with and without disabilities. Concurrently, the Handicapped Children's Early Education Program was funded by the U.S. Department of Education in 1968. This program funded the development and replication of model programs for young children with disabilities for more than 25 years. These model programs served as a context for much of the research on effective practices for young children with disabilities in inclusive settings.

The Education for All Handicapped Children Act (EHA) of 1975 (PL 94-142) provided incentives for states to serve preschool-age children with disabilities. EHA also included a provision that children with disabilities should receive a free appropriate public education (FAPE) in the least restrictive environment (LRE). *LRE* is defined as providing services to children with disabilities in settings that are as close as possible to the typical education environment and that meet the needs of the individual student. The Education of the Handicapped Act Amendments of 1986 (PL 99-457), which amended EHA, created a mandate for states to serve children with disabilities ages 3–5 years and maintained the LRE provision. Subsequent amendments strengthened the LRE provision and changed the name to the Individuals with Disabilities Education Act (IDEA) (PL 101-476 and PL 105-17), which was then changed to the Individuals with Disabilities Education Improvement Act of 2004. The Americans with Disabilities Act (ADA) of 1990 (PL 101-336) was another significant piece of legislation. The ADA had a direct impact on inclusion in child care centers in that it mandated that centers could not exclude children with disabilities unless a child's presence would pose a direct threat to the health or safety of others or would require a fundamental alteration of the program. It also required the programs to make reasonable accommodations to both the facilities and their practices for children with disabilities.

National Association for the Education of Young Children/ Council for Exceptional Children's Division for Early Childhood

Two major professional associations have been instrumental in identifying and disseminating information on effective practices for young children with and without disabilities. The NAEYC is the largest professional association of early childhood educators and others focused on improving the quality of programs for children from birth through age 8. The Council for Exceptional Children's DEC is for individuals who work with or on behalf of children with special needs from birth through age 8 and their families. The DEC is dedicated to promoting policies and practices that support families and enhance the optimal development of children.

The NAEYC's first set of guidelines on DAP described a framework for creating early childhood environments that address the developmental needs of young children (Bredekamp, 1987). Although not explicitly excluding children with disabilities, the guidelines were not specific about how practices might need to be adapted or modified to meet the unique needs of children with disabilities. Early childhood special educators argued that although the DAP guidelines were necessary, they were not sufficient for programs that included young children with disabilities (Carta, Schwartz, Atwater, & McConnell, 1991). A positive outcome of these guidelines was the beginning of a dialogue between early childhood educators and early childhood special educators about how to best meet the needs of all young children in inclusive early childhood environments. As a result, the revised guidelines sought to address the needs of all young children, including those with disabilities, in a more comprehensive way (Bredekamp & Copple, 1997;

Copple & Bredekamp, 2009). As programs began to use the principles to guide their curriculum development and implementation, it became clear that the field needed more specific guidance about addressing the specialized needs of children with disabilities. The DEC developed a set of recommended practices for early intervention/ECSE based on an extensive review of the research in early childhood, ECSE, speech-language therapy, occupational therapy, physical therapy, and other related disciplines (Odom & McLean, 1996). These practices were revised and expanded in 2000 (Sandall, McLean, & Smith, 2000), 2005 (Sandall, Hemmeter, Smith, & McLean, 2005), and again in 2014 (DEC, 2014). The revised practices are meant to build on the NAEYC DAP guidelines and are designed to describe specific strategies that can be used to provide individualized supports and services to young children with special needs and their families. The DEC recommended practices assume that all early childhood environments should be developmentally appropriate, and the practices provide guidance for how developmentally appropriate environments can be adapted and/or modified to ensure that children with disabilities are meaningfully included.

As mentioned earlier in this chapter, the DEC and the NAEYC have published a number of position statements and papers related to inclusive practices (DEC, NAEYC, & NHSA, 2013; DEC/NAEYC, 2009). The commitment to blended practices for addressing the needs of all young children in inclusive settings is clearly evident in these statements and demonstrates the work of these two organizations to deliver a common message. This work has led to a common understanding that a high-quality environment is the necessary foundation for inclusive programs, but individualized supports and strategies are needed to meet the unique needs of young children with disabilities (Bailey, McWilliam, Buysse, & Wesley, 1998; Buysse & Peisner-Feinberg, 2010; Horn, Thompson, Palmer, Jenson, & Turbiville, 2004; Odom et al., 2011; Wolery & Bredekamp, 1994). Developmentally appropriate learning environments provide a range of naturally occurring activities and routines that can be used as contexts for providing individualized instruction to children who have special learning needs (Horn, Lieber, Sandall, Schwartz, & Wolery, 2002; Pretti-Frontczak & Bricker, 2004). Although there traditionally has been a focus on individualized instruction primarily for children with disabilities, this text is based on the idea that all children need access to instruction that is individualized based on each child's unique needs, learning style, interests, and background in order for all children to be successful and reach high standards.

Blending Teacher Preparation

Focusing on how teachers are prepared to work with young children in inclusive settings is an important outgrowth of the discussion about DAP. The vast majority of higher education personnel preparation programs prepared early childhood educators and early childhood special educators in separate programs at the same time that the field was emphasizing inclusive programs and blended practices. In the early 1990s, the field began to focus on the importance of training early childhood educators to work with all children, which required higher education faculty to consider the philosophical differences between the fields of ECE and ECSE relative not only to the content of the training program but also to their own teaching practices and beliefs. In a seminal article, Miller (1992) questioned how teacher educators could advocate for inclusion at the service delivery level and maintain separate teacher education programs at the same time. A significant change in teacher education programs has occurred since the early 1990s. Many programs across the country now blend their ECE and ECSE training programs (Chang, Early, & Winton, 2005), and evidence shows that faculty are integrating more topics within personnel preparation programs (Bruder & Dunst, 2005). Furthermore, efforts have been made to more closely align personnel standards across ECE and ECSE (Chandler et al., 2012) and professional associations' personnel standards with state certification standards (Stayton, Smith, Dietrich, & Bruder, 2012).

In blended teacher education programs, faculty across disciplines coteach courses, practicum requirements are completed in inclusive settings, and content is integrated into interdisciplinary coursework and practica. There is, however, a range of approaches to blended teacher education—in some programs, students from different departments complete coursework across departments, and in other programs, the content is blended across disciplines and students from multiple disciplines complete a program together. Data are limited on the outcomes of different types of personnel preparation programs. In fact, some have argued that the content related to special education is minimized by blending teacher education programs (across ECE and ECSE), resulting in teachers with limited expertise working with young children with the most significant disabilities. The purpose of this book is to help teachers understand how practices for children with disabilities can be blended with practices that are important for all children. Furthermore, we have highlighted the range of practices that will be needed to effectively address the needs of all children, including those with the most significant disabilities.

GUIDING THEMES

The preparation of this book was guided by six general themes about quality programs for young children—inclusion, multitiered approaches to instruction, families, diversity, outcomes, and collaboration and teaming. These themes are eloquently addressed in ethical statements, position statements, and recommended practice documents developed by the DEC and the NAEYC. These issues cut across the entire book. Talking about these issues here and referring to them throughout the book conveys their importance in providing quality services to young children in inclusive settings. Although these themes have empirical support, they are also fundamental tenets of the field about quality programs for young children.

Inclusion

This book is based on the field's commitment to inclusive programs for children with and without disabilities. A wealth of research supports inclusion in terms of outcomes for children with and without disabilities as well as broader effects on families and communities (e.g., Barton & Smith, 2015; Guralnick, 2001; Odom, 2002; Odom et al., 2011). As mentioned previously, federal, state, and local policies also reflect a commitment to ensuring that children with disabilities have access to inclusive settings. In addition to efficacy data and policy, there is a fundamental commitment in the field of ECE and ECSE to inclusive programs, which is reflected in policy statements developed by national early childhood organizations.

Multitiered Systems of Support

This book reflects the work on multitiered systems of support (MTSS), which is a data-driven approach for supporting the academic and behavioral outcomes of all children. An MTSS approach uses ongoing screening and assessment to determine the individual needs of all children and provides the level of support and instruction that children need based on that assessment information.

Families

Given the importance of families, both in the lives of young children and their role in working with professionals to design, implement, and evaluate their children's programs, information about families is included across chapters as well as in Chapter 8, which is focused on teaming. Recommended practices in ECE and ECSE have long advocated for families to be actively included in early childhood programs (e.g., Copple & Bredekamp, 2009; DEC, 2014; Sandall et al., 2005).

Family involvement seems especially important for young children because it is in the context of interactions with their families and other significant caregivers that children develop the social-emotional competencies that are critical for their ongoing success in school and life. The family provides a base of support over time that helps children navigate transitions and life events. The early childhood years are an important time in terms of supporting families as they learn about their children's education and social systems. This book focuses on how to involve families in early childhood programs so that the involvement promotes parents' confidence and competence in supporting their children's development and success. In much the same way that it is important to individualize for children, it is important to individualize family involvement based on the unique needs, values, beliefs, and desires of each family.

Diversity

The focus of this book is on strategies teachers can use to meet the diverse needs of all children in inclusive settings. The population of children being served in center-based programs is not only growing in number but also becoming increasingly diverse in ability levels and cultural, linguistic, and socioeconomic backgrounds. Four key principles related to meeting the diverse needs of children and families provide a foundation for implementing the practices discussed throughout this book. First, promoting diversity in inclusive programs requires support and commitment from all levels, including teaching staff, administration, and families. Second, personnel preparation programs should promote and support professionals as they engage in an ongoing process to develop cross-cultural competence. It is not something teachers can learn by reading a book or taking a class. Third, it is important for teachers and other professionals to honor the diverse beliefs, lifestyles, languages, and values of children and families while at the same time providing children and families with the knowledge and supports they need to be successful in a variety of environments and contexts. Finally, it will be important for teachers to identify, use, and evaluate resources and strategies that are culturally, developmentally, and linguistically appropriate for all children, families, and professionals to effectively address the needs of all children in inclusive settings. These guiding principles are entirely consistent with position statements from national professional associations as well as recommended practices in the field. As previously indicated, these principles are relevant to all of the practices described in the book. Although highlighted here, the principles will be addressed in both content and examples throughout this text.

Outcomes

Documenting that programs are resulting in positive outcomes for children and families is an important issue in education. Outcomes include social-emotional outcomes such as problem solving, ability to communicate emotions, persistence with tasks, and ability to develop relationships with peers, as well as preacademic skills such as knowledge about books and print, early indicators of phonological awareness, and knowledge and understanding of numbers. Although measuring outcomes is most prevalent in K–12 education, many states are including preschool children in accountability systems. All states now have a set of early learning guidelines. There has been a great deal of controversy in the field about including young children in accountability systems. This controversy reflects concerns about the appropriateness of and difficulty in assessing young children. Although many in the field of early childhood are reluctant to move in this direction, it is important to be proactive both in terms of identifying outcomes and assessing children's progress on those outcomes. The important piece of this is ensuring that the outcomes, the teaching approaches for addressing the outcomes, and the processes that will be used to assess children's progress toward the outcomes are all developmentally appropriate. These issues will be central to the information presented in this book.

Collaboration and Teaming

Collaboration is essential to effectively address the diverse needs of young children in inclusive settings and their families. Meeting the diverse needs of children with and without disabilities will require a variety of services and supports that range in form and intensity depending on the needs of the children. The diverse and complex range of services that likely are needed will require both coordination and collaboration among professionals and with families. Although this book focuses primarily on strategies teachers and staff use on a daily basis in classrooms, teaming with professionals from other disciplines and with families will be critical in terms of identifying children's needs, developing individualized plans, and providing and evaluating services and interventions. Collaboration among professionals and families increases the likelihood that services will be coordinated and integrated. Finally, the relationship among classroom staff, visitors, and volunteers is a critical aspect of collaboration.

ORGANIZATION OF THIS BOOK

Given the increasing emphasis on child outcomes and the complexity of addressing the needs of children with a wide range of abilities, the authors of this book are advocating the use of a curriculum framework (described in detail in Chapter 2) that links assessment and instruction and provides guidance about how to differentiate instruction in blended classrooms. The curriculum framework is composed of four elements, including assessment, scope and sequence, activities and instruction, and progress monitoring (Grisham-Brown, Hemmeter, & Pretti-Frontczak, 2005). As previously mentioned, information about assessment and progress monitoring are detailed in Grisham-Brown and Pretti-Frontczak (2011). This text will focus on the scope and sequence and activities and instruction elements of the curriculum framework. The book is divided into three main sections, which are described next.

Section I: Setting the Stage for Blended Practices

This section includes this introductory chapter and three additional chapters. Chapter 2 provides an overview of the curriculum framework, which offers a structure for the remaining chapters. The curriculum framework is composed of four elements—assessment, scope and sequence, activities and intervention strategies, and progress monitoring. In addition, this chapter addresses the blending or unification of various theories or perspectives when working in programs for children with and without disabilities and provides examples of different curricular approaches in which blended practices can be implemented. Finally, this chapter provides an introduction to multitiered approaches to instruction. Chapter 3 provides an overview of the types of child outcomes that may be addressed at each tier of instruction. Chapter 4 provides more information on multitiered models of instruction with a focus on practices that cut across tiers and guidelines for implementing multitiered models of instruction. The chapter includes a discussion of practices that are foundational to implementing tiered models.

Section II: Tiered Instruction

Chapters 5–7 provide more detailed information about each tier of instruction. The types and characteristics of instruction that are implemented at each tier are described in these chapters. Each of the chapters includes information on how to implement instruction at each tier as well as information about how to plan for that instruction and practical examples of what instruction might look like within that tier.

Section III: Special Considerations in the Application of Blended Practices

Chapter 8 focuses on teaming with professionals from a range of disciplines and families. This chapter addresses the importance of collaborative partnerships when implementing blended practices. Finally, Chapters 9–12 discuss blending practices to promote outcomes from specific preacademic domains, including social-emotional, language, literacy, and math. These chapters include information about specific outcomes related to the domain as well as teaching strategies and approaches that have been specifically used to address outcomes from each domain.

REFERENCES

American Recovery and Reinvestment Act of 2009, PL 111-5, 123 U.S.C. § 115.

Americans with Disabilities Act (ADA) of 1990, PL 101-336, 42 U.S.C. §§ 12101 *et seq.*

Bailey, D.B., McWilliam, R.A., Buysse, V., & Wesley, P.W. (1998). Inclusion in the context of competing values in early childhood education. *Early Childhood Research Quarterly, 13,* 27–48.

Barnett, W.S., Friedman-Krauss, A.H., Gomez, R.E., Horowitz, M., Weisenfeld, G.G., & Squires, J.H. (2016). *The state of preschool 2015: State preschool yearbook.* New Brunswick, NJ: National Institute for Early Education Research.

Barton, E.E., & Smith, B.J. (2015). *The preschool inclusion toolbox.* Baltimore, MD: Paul H. Brookes Publishing Co.

Bredekamp, S. (Ed.). (1987). *Developmentally appropriate practice in early childhood programs serving children from birth through age 8.* Washington, DC: National Association for the Education of Young Children.

Bredekamp, S., & Copple, C. (Eds.). (1997). *Developmentally appropriate practice in early childhood programs* (Rev. ed.). Washington, DC: National Association for the Education of Young Children.

Bruder, M.B., & Dunst, C.J. (2005). Personnel preparation in recommended early intervention practices: Degree of emphasis across disciplines. *Topics in Early Childhood Special Education, 25,* 25–33.

Buysse, V., & Peisner-Feinberg, E. (2010). Recognition and response: Response to intervention for pre-K. *Young Exceptional Children, 13*(4), 2–13.

Carta, J.J., Schwartz, I., Atwater, J., & McConnell, S. (1991). Developmentally appropriate practice: Appraising its usefulness for young children with disabilities. *Topics in Early Childhood Special Education, 11,* 1–20.

Chandler, L.K., Cochran, D.C., Christensen, K.A., Dinnebeil, L.A., Gallagher, P.A., Lifter, K.,...Spino, M. (2012). The alignment of CEC/DEC and NAEYC personnel preparation standards. *Topics in Early Childhood Special Education, 32*(1), 52–63. doi:10.1177/0271121412437047

Chang, F., Early, D., & Winton, P. (2005). Early childhood teacher preparation in special education at 2- and 4-year institutions of higher education. *Journal of Early Intervention, 27,* 110–124.

Copple, C., & Bredekamp, S. (Eds.). (2009). *Developmentally appropriate practice in early childhood programs serving children from birth through age 8* (3rd ed.). Washington, DC: National Association for the Education of Young Children.

Division for Early Childhood. (2014). *DEC recommended practices in early intervention/early childhood special education 2014.* Retrieved from http://www.dec-sped.org/recommendedpractices

Division for Early Childhood & National Association for the Education of Young Children (DEC/NAEYC). (2009). *Early childhood inclusion: A joint position statement of the Division for Early Childhood (DEC) and the National Association for the Education of Young Children (NAEYC).* Chapel Hill, NC: University of North Carolina, FPG Child Development Institute.

Division for Early Childhood, National Association for the Education of Young Children, & National Head Start Association. (2013). *Frameworks for response to intervention in early childhood: Description and implications.* Los Angeles, CA: Author.

Economic Opportunity Act of 1964, PL 88-452, 42 U.S.C. §§ 2701 *et seq.*

Education for All Handicapped Children Act of 1975, PL 94-142, 20 U.S.C. §§ 1400 *et seq.*

Education of the Handicapped Act Amendments of 1986, PL 99-457, 20 U.S.C. §§ 1400 *et seq.*

Greenwood, C.R., Bradfield, T., Kaminski, R., Linas, M.W., Carta, J.J., & Nylander, D. (2011). The response to intervention (RTI) approach in early childhood. *Focus on Exceptional Children, 43*(9), 1–22.

Grisham-Brown, J.L., Hemmeter, M.L., & Pretti-Frontczak, K. (2005). *Blended practices for teaching young children in inclusive settings.* Baltimore, MD: Paul H. Brookes Publishing Co.

Grisham-Brown, J., & Pretti-Frontczak, K. (Eds.). (2011). *Assessing young children in inclusive settings: The blended practices approach.* Baltimore, MD: Paul H. Brookes Publishing Co.

Guralnick, M.J. (Ed.). (2001). *Early childhood inclusion: Focus on change.* Baltimore, MD: Paul H. Brookes Publishing Co.

Hemmeter, M.L., Fox, L., & Snyder, P. (2013). A tiered model for promoting social-emotional competence and addressing challenging behavior. In V. Buysse & E.S. Peisner-Feinberg (Eds.), *Handbook of response to intervention in early childhood* (pp. 85–101). Baltimore, MD: Paul H. Brookes Publishing Co.

Horn, E., Lieber, J., Sandall, S., Schwartz, I., & Wolery, R. (2002). Classroom models of individualized instruction. In S.L. Odom (Ed.), *Widening the circle: Including children with disabilities in preschool programs* (pp. 46–60). New York, NY: Teachers College Press.

Horn, E., Thompson, B., Palmer, S., Jenson, R., & Turbiville, V. (2004). Inclusive education at different ages: Preschool. In C. Kennedy & E. Horn (Eds.), *Including students with severe disabilities* (pp. 207–221). Boston, MA: Allyn & Bacon.

Individuals with Disabilities Education Act Amendments (IDEA) of 1997, PL 105-17, 20 U.S.C. §§ 1400 *et seq.*

Individuals with Disabilities Education Act (IDEA) of 1990, PL 101-476, 20 U.S.C. §§ 1400 *et seq.*

Individuals with Disabilities Education Improvement Act (IDEA) of 2004, PL 108-446, 20 U.S.C. §§ 1400 *et seq.*

Miller, P.S. (1992). Segregated programs of teacher education in early childhood: Immoral and inefficient practice. *Topics in Early Childhood Special Education, 11*, 39–52.

Odom, S.L. (2002). *Widening the circle: Including children with disabilities in preschool programs.* New York, NY: Teachers College Press.

Odom, S.L., Buysse, V., & Soukakou, E. (2011). Inclusion for young children with disabilities: A quarter century of research perspectives. *Journal of Early Intervention, 33*, 344–356.

Odom, S., & McLean, M. (1996). *Early intervention/early childhood special education: Recommended practices.* Austin, TX: PRO-ED.

Pretti-Frontczak, K., & Bricker, D. (2004). *An activity-based approach to early intervention* (3rd ed.). Baltimore, MD: Paul H. Brookes Publishing Co.

Sandall, S., Hemmeter, M.L., Smith, B.J., & McLean, M. (2005). *DEC recommended practices: A comprehensive guide.* Longmont, CO: Sopris West Educational Services.

Sandall, S., McLean, M.E., & Smith, B.J. (2000). *DEC recommended practices in early intervention/early childhood special education.* Longmont, CO: Sopris West Educational Services.

Schwartz, I., Sandall, S., Odom, S., Horn, E., & Beckman, P. (2002). I know it when I see it: In search of a common definition of inclusion. In S.L. Odom (Ed.), *Widening the circle: Including children with disabilities in preschool programs* (pp. 10–24). New York, NY: Teachers College Press.

Snyder, P., Hemmeter, M.L., McLean, M.E., Sandall, S.R., & McLaughlin, T. (2013). Embedded instruction to support early learning in response to intervention frameworks. In V. Buysse & E.S. Peisner-Feinberg (Eds.), *Handbook of response to intervention in early childhood* (pp. 283–298). Baltimore, MD: Paul H. Brookes Publishing Co.

Stayton, V.C., Smith, B.J., Dietrich, S.L., & Bruder, M.B. (2012). Comparison of state certification and professional association standards in early childhood special education. *Topics in Early Childhood Special Education, 32*, 24–37.

Strain, P.S., & Bovey, E.H. (2011). Randomized, controlled trial of the LEAP model of early intervention for young children with autism spectrum disorders. *Topics in Early Childhood Special Education, 31*, 133–154.

U.S. Department of Health and Human Services and U.S. Department of Education. (2015). *Policy statement on inclusion of children with disabilities in early childhood programs.* Retrieved from http://www2.ed.gov/policy/speced/guid/earlylearning/joint-statement-full-text.pdf

Wolery, M., & Bredekamp, S. (1994). Developmentally appropriate practice and young children with disabilities: Contextual issues in the discussion. *Journal of Early Intervention, 18*, 331–341.

## CHAPTER 2

Curriculum Framework as a Model of Blended Practices

Jennifer Grisham-Brown and Mary Louise Hemmeter

Ms. Nicholas is the program director for the Growing Together Child Devel-opment Center, a blended community-based program that collaborates with the local public school prekindergarten (pre-K) program and Head Start to deliver full-day early care and education to young children birth to 6 years of age. Ms. Nicholas is responsible for supporting teachers to implement a curriculum that addresses the needs of all children, including those who are typically developing, come from low-income homes, and are develop-mentally delayed. Ms. Nicholas has tried packaged curricula that provide teachers with specific activities associated with weekly themes. Although the teachers like the amount of detail and variety of activities, Ms. Nicholas feels that such a model does not reflect current recommended practices and that this sort of curriculum often does not address the varying needs and inter-ests of the children in her program. For example, one "theme of the week" revolved around frogs. Children were matching frogs with lily pads of the same color in one activity. Ms. Nicholas was troubled because the activity seemed to only focus on (and direct the child's learning toward) a single math skill without considering recommended practices for planning for young children in blended classrooms. First, the activity did not allow for the integration of skills from other areas such as literacy or science. Second, the activity didn't seem to work for children who already knew how to match or for those who still needed to learn earlier skills before learning match-ing. Finally, other materials might have been more interesting for teaching matching. Ms. Nicholas increasingly notices that activities such as the frog/ lily pad activity are not working for many children in the classrooms in her program. With these observations fresh in her mind, Ms. Nicholas began considering what she needed to do to ensure that the curriculum at Growing Together directly addresses the learning needs of individual children.

State pre-K programs (e.g., Arkansas, Missouri, North Carolina) are increas-ingly required to select an approved curriculum that may not address the diverse learning needs of children in blended classrooms. The authors use the term *curriculum framework* in this book to represent the idea that a cur-riculum is not a single resource or feature but rather a set of concepts or a structure for classifying and organizing the many elements and processes involved when creating learning ecologies for young children. The pur-pose of this chapter is to introduce a curriculum framework comprising four related elements that can support instructional planning in blended classrooms. This chapter also describes the theories and perspectives that influence curriculum frameworks and three approaches to teaching young children in inclusive settings. The advantages and challenges of each of these approaches are covered. This chapter then provides a review of the advantages and challenges of using two commercially available resources that contain all four elements of a curriculum framework. The chapter concludes with a review of characteristics of a high-quality curriculum framework.

WHAT IS A CURRICULUM FRAMEWORK?

The curriculum framework described in this book is designed to 1) link assessment to instructional practices, 2) serve as a foundation for curriculum design in blended early childhood education (ECE) programs, and 3) provide a process for decision making for teachers who teach diverse groups of children (see Figure 2.1).

A curriculum framework is composed of four elements—assessment, scope and sequence, activities and intervention strategies, and progress monitoring. The umbrella was chosen as a visual depiction of the curriculum framework for two reasons. First, the panels of the umbrella represent the elements of the curriculum framework. They are inherently linked together, and the umbrella will not stay together if one of the elements is missing. For example, if high-quality assessment is not completed on each child, then teachers will be unable to plan for the needs of all children in their class. If teachers do not monitor children's progress on a regular basis, then they

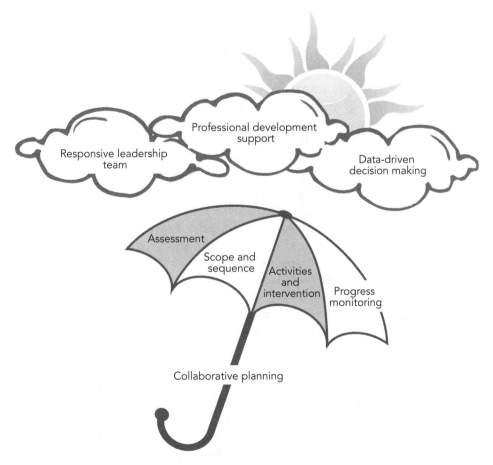

Figure 2.1. Illustration of the curriculum framework. (From Pretti-Frontczak, K. [2015]. *Linking assessment and curriculum [Three part web-based training modules]*. Brooklyn, NY: B2K Solutions, Ltd.)

will not know how to adjust instruction for children to successfully meet their goals. Second, each panel is larger at the bottom than at the top, representing the fact that practices at the bottom are broad and generalized for all children. Practices associated with each element of the curriculum framework become more intense and specialized as each panel narrows. For example, although there are generally accepted instructional practices for all children (e.g., responsive interactions, provision of feedback), there also exists a set of more specialized instructional practices that will be necessary to teach targeted and individual outcomes to specific children.

Description of Elements

An overview of each element of the curriculum framework is provided next, with reference to places in this book where more detailed information is given.

Assessment   Teachers gather assessment data for a variety of purposes, including determining if a child needs special services, monitoring children's progress toward developmental outcomes, and evaluating programs to determine their effectiveness. The purpose of the assessment element of the curriculum framework is to gather information for program planning purposes. Teachers in a blended classroom must gather sufficient programming planning assessment information to plan for groups of children as well as individual children. Program planning assessment should serve as a baseline for all children in the classroom from which later growth can be measured. Therefore, program planning assessment will be conducted near the time that children enter the program (e.g., beginning of school year, when enrolling in program, transition from early intervention to preschool). A curriculum-based assessment (CBA) should be used to conduct program planning assessment because it helps teachers identify specific learning outcomes that can be addressed as part of curriculum planning and development. The assessment and curriculum are unified or linked, which makes it possible for teachers to identify each child's developmental level and then develop curricular activities that address the child's interests, needs, and abilities. Bagnato, Neisworth, and Pretti-Frontczak (2010) indicated that a high-quality CBA should 1) be acceptable to those who use it, 2) be administered using authentic methods and contexts, 3) allow for collaboration among team members, including families, 4) be technically adequate, 5) be sensitive to changes in development over time, 6) be appropriate for children with a variety of needs, and 7) be useful for instruction. Based on the results of the program planning assessment, teachers should have information on 1) the family's concerns and priorities for their child, 2) the child's interests, and 3) the child's strengths and needs in all developmental/content areas. *Assessing Young Children in Inclusive Settings: A Blended Practices Approach* (Grisham-Brown & Pretti-Frontczak, 2011) provides detailed information on program planning assessment, including suggested assessment tools to use as well as specific information on how to conduct authentic assessment.

Scope and Sequence/Sorting The scope and sequence element refers to what we teach children in blended classrooms. *Scope* refers to broad, often-integrated domains and/or content areas (e.g., motor, communication, mathematics, science). *Sequence* refers to the order (e.g., ages, stages, grade levels) in which the content will be taught and learned and is often specified in a developmental hierarchy (from easiest to more difficult) or by grade level. Three primary sources of information provide guidance about what should comprise the scope and sequence in programs for young children—state or agency standards (e.g. early learning standards, Head Start outcomes), developmental areas (e.g., motor, social, communication), and children's individual needs. The scope and sequence element serves as a bridge between the assessment and activities/intervention elements of the curriculum framework in that once assessment data have been collected, teachers must use those data to decide what to teach before they can design activities/interventions in their classroom. Teachers will need to follow the principles of data-driven decision making (Grisham-Brown & Pretti-Frontzak, 2011) to make sound decisions about what to teach. In other words, once assessment data are gathered, documented, and summarized, teachers will need to interpret data trends and patterns found in order to determine where to begin instruction with which children. We refer to three outcome levels in the curriculum framework. For all children, teachers focus on teaching common outcomes that are the generally accepted scope and sequence for young children (e.g., colors, counting, letters, writing). The assessment data might show that some children are struggling with concepts that the rest of the class is learning or that their learning may have stalled. Therefore, teachers may need to identify targeted outcome components (e.g., fluency, latency) for some children. Finally, individual children may be missing a foundational skill or prerequisite that is preventing the child from gaining access to, participating in, or making progress toward the common outcomes identified for all children. Therefore, children may need instruction on individualized outcomes (e.g., following directions, attending to an activity, communicating basic needs) that will support their progress toward common outcomes. Chapter 3 describes each type of outcome in greater detail, as well as the circumstances under which teachers may elect to teach each outcome type.

Activities and Instruction Activities and instruction is the third element of the curriculum framework and the focus of this book. Once teachers have determined what to teach all children, some children, and individual children, they need to plan activities and instructional strategies to teach toward each tier or level of instruction. Three instructional tiers are described in the curriculum framework. Tier 1 is universal instruction and refers to strategies that are used to teach all children and include environmental arrangement, materials selection, use of the principles of universal design for learning, and high-quality interactions with children. Specific information about universal instruction can be found in Chapter 5. Tier 2 is focused instruction and is characterized by the use of scaffolding strategies, peer support, and the formation of small groups. Specific information about focused instruction can be found in Chapter 6. Tier 3 is described as systematic instruction and consists of highly structured intentional teaching sequences that are delivered with high frequency across a variety of activities and routines. Specific information about systematic instruction can be found in Chapter 7. Three important factors should be remembered about activities and instruction in blended classrooms. First, the tiers are additive, meaning that they build on one another. For example, if a child needs Tier 2 instruction, then it should be implemented within the context of Tier 1 instruction (i.e., within the context of a high-quality universal curriculum). Second, instruction is intentional at each tier, meaning that teachers are aware of the outcomes they are teaching and have plans for where, when, with what, and how instruction will be provided. Finally, any child in a classroom, regardless of ability, may require instruction at any tier. For example, a child with a disability may require systematic instruction for some skills he or she needs to learn but may learn other skills with universal instruction. Similarly, a child in a blended classroom who does not have diagnosed disabilities may need systematic instruction on a skill that is preventing his or her participation in the general curriculum.

Progress Monitoring   The final element of the curriculum framework focuses on collecting data to determine the effectiveness of the activities and instruction that have been implemented. Progress monitoring assessment focuses on how and when to revise instruction across all tiers of instruction. In the curriculum framework, we propose that the type and amount of data collected should depend on the type of outcomes assessed (e.g., common, targeted, prioritized). When collecting information on common outcomes (i.e., everything a young child should be learning), periodic readministration of a CBA two to three times per year will provide information on children's growth on those outcomes. More frequent data collection may be required when children are receiving instruction on targeted outcomes to determine the effectiveness of instruction. Teachers may use a rubric, checklist, or subscale of a CBA to conduct periodic probes once a week or month to make sure that instruction is working effectively. Finally, a high frequency of data collection may be needed when children have individualized needs that are preventing their access to and participation in the general curriculum. Teachers should use counts, tallies, work samples, or anecdotal notes on a daily basis to ensure that children are making progress and to immediately know if instruction requires revision. *Assessing Young Children in Inclusive Settings: A Blended Practices Approach* (Grisham-Brown & Pretti-Frontczak, 2011) provides detailed information on progress monitoring assessment, including strategies for conducting ongoing data collection as well as specific details on ways to differentiate data collection so that teachers do not feel like they collect data more than they teach.

Foundation of Curriculum Framework

The notion of a curriculum framework is supported by 1) a blending of child development theories, 2) developmentally appropriate practices (DAP), and 3) evidence-based practices for providing services to young children. Each of these supports is described next.

Theoretical Support Teachers serving diverse groups of children in inclusive settings need to ensure they have a common and comprehensive approach to addressing children's needs and should avoid materials, resources, and approaches that limit the types of learning experiences, strategies, and methods for teaching young children. A blending of existing knowledge allows teachers to better understand the complexities of early development and learning (Emde & Robinson, 2000; Miller, 1989). Pretti-Frontczak and Bricker (2004) and Goffin and Wilson (2001) described a number of theories and perspectives that have contributed to the existing knowledge base and approaches to working with young children (e.g., Piaget, Dewey, Bandura, Vygotsky, Skinner). Although it is beyond the scope of this book to describe in detail the various theories and perspectives that have influenced how to work with young children, it is important to review how each conceptualizes the learning processes, the child's role in learning, and the role of environmental factors. For example, the work of Vygotsky has helped teachers understand and attend to the effects of the immediate and historical sociocultural surroundings on children's development, thus helping teachers interpret actions, plan learning opportunities, and evaluate progress with children's broader community and family context in mind. Furthermore, the work of Piaget continues to guide teachers in ensuring that children are actively involved in the learning process and understanding that children need to explore, experience, manipulate, and receive feedback from their actions. Finally, Skinner's work on the theory of behaviorism is still widely used in all educational contexts, including ECE. The importance of consequences in shaping behavior, the formation of antecedent-behavior-consequence events in instruction, and the emphasis on individual children are among Skinner's contributions to education. Thus, recommended practices continue to stress the importance of engaging in play, building on children's interests and motivation, and following children's lead when creating learning opportunities (Pretti-Frontczak & Bricker, 2004; Widerstrom, 2005). Table 2.1 provides a brief summary of the theories and perspectives that continue to influence curriculum frameworks for young children.

Recommended Practice Support The curriculum framework reflects recommended practices identified in ECE education and early childhood special education. Blended ECE practices increasingly are informed

Table 2.1.   Summary of theories and perspectives that influence approaches to teaching young children

Theory/perspective	Description
Cognitive developmental theory (Piaget)	Learning is an active process and is related to children's interaction with the environment.
	Children are active participants in the learning process and their interactions with the environment are how learning and development occur (e.g., new structures are made).
	The environment should consist of materials and information that are not too far beyond children's current level and should include a variety of concrete experiences.
	Teachers should understand that cognitive development is a prerequisite for learning and that it is critical to know each child and engage him or her in developmentally appropriate activities.
Ecological systems theory (Bronfenbrenner)	Children develop at the center of interconnected relationships and environments that influence their development.
	Children learn and behave as a result of the interactions and influences within multiple systems.
	The many environments in which children are involved influence development.
	Teachers should be aware of how the environment influences children's learning and should involve the community within the classroom and children within the community.
Learning theory (Dewey)	Learning is a social process that occurs through daily interactions with the environment and through natural experiences.
	Children learn best by doing and by acting on the world around them.
	The various environments in which children live should be connected and interrelated.
	Teachers should guide children's learning by providing opportunities for experience and experimentation.
Psychosocial theory (Erikson)	Development occurs in stages that occur throughout life and stresses the relationship between the stages and social experiences.
	Children are passive learners, developing individual personality traits and obtaining skills needed to become dynamic members of their society.
	The environment assists the children in obtaining characteristics needed to adapt to and be a successful member of their society.
	Teachers need to understand the various stages of social-emotional development and ensure that expectations and learning opportunities facilitate children's transition from one state to the next.
Social learning theory (Bandura)	Learning occurs through a series of antecedent-response-consequence contingencies—in which events (antecedents) that happen before and after a behavior (response) serve to set the occasion for the behavior and the feedback (consequence) that results—that increase or decrease the likelihood that the behavior will occur again.
	Children gain knowledge from how the environment reinforces, supports, or punishes a particular behavior.
	The environment reinforces or punishes learning, causing learning to be more or less likely to occur again.
	Teachers should model target behaviors and understand the importance of observation to young children's development.

Table 2.1.   *(continued)*

Theory/perspective	Description
Sociocultural/sociohistorical theory (Vygotsky)	Learning occurs through interactions between a child and an individual who has more knowledge.
	Children initially learn to think and acquire knowledge through interactions with other members of their society who are more knowledgeable, but children will eventually learn to have internal dialogues that instruct and assist them in cognitive development.
	During the initial learning process for children, interactions with the environment facilitate learning by directly teaching the children to think and behave.
	Teachers should incorporate social interaction and play across daily activities to promote cognitive and language development.
Behaviorism (Skinner)	Children learn new skills when the skills are strengthened by reinforcement, and inappropriate behavior is weakened by punishment.
	The fundamental elements of instruction are 1) setting the occasion for learning to occur (antecedent), 2) waiting for children to respond (behavior), and 3) providing feedback based on the children's responses.
	Instruction should be individualized for each learner based on the characteristics of the child as well as the context in which the child is learning.

by collaborative thinking between the field's primary professional organizations—the National Association for the Education of Young Children (NAEYC) and Division of Early Childhood (DEC). Three recommended practice resources support the tenets of a curriculum framework that supports all young children in inclusive ECE programs—recommended practice guidelines, the DEC/NAEYC (2009) joint position paper on early childhood inclusion, and the DEC/NAEYC/National Head Start Association (NHSA) (2013) joint paper on response to intervention (RTI).

Recommended Practice Guidelines   Although NAEYC and DEC have separate recommended practice guideline documents, the two are complementary and intended to be used together. The DAP (Copple & Bredekamp, 2009) guidelines are important as a foundation for all programs serving young children, but more specialized practices may need to be embedded into DAP environments to support children with diverse abilities. The DEC (2014) recommended practices were designed to do that by describing evidence-based practices for children who are at risk for or have disabilities, which can be embedded into community-based inclusive settings. The recommended practices are organized into seven strands of practice as displayed in Table 2.2, including assessment, environment, family, instruction, interaction, teaming and collaboration, and transition.

Early Childhood Inclusion   DEC/NAEYC (2009) described three defining features of inclusive programs that are reflected in the curriculum framework—access, participation, and supports. The curriculum framework is designed so that all children will have access to high-quality early

Table 2.2. Division for Early Childhood recommended practices describing evidence-based practices for children with disabilities

Topic	Recommended practices
Assessment	Families are involved in all aspects of the assessment. Teams work together to gather ongoing assessment information to guide instruction. Assessment tools are comprehensive, sensitive, and appropriate to individual needs of child. Authentic activities, settings, and procedures are used throughout the assessment process.
Environment	Services are provided in natural and inclusive environments Teams work together to modify the physical, social, and temporal environment using assistive technology as needed.
Family	Families are involved in decision making. Family-centered practices are implemented to ensure that families are treated with dignity and respect. Family capacity-building practices are employed to strengthen parenting knowledge and enhance self-efficacy. Families and professionals collaborate to identify goals that prompt family competence.
Instruction	Instruction is based on strengths, preferences, and interests of the child and enhances the child's participation in natural and inclusive environments. A variety of instructional methods are used—inclusive embedded instruction, systematic instructional strategies, and peer-mediated interventions. Adaptations are planned for children with disabilities, including those that are dual language learners. Challenging behavior is addressed through the use of functional assessment information.
Interaction	Children's social-emotional development, communication development, play, and problem-solving skills are addressed. Interactions between children are encouraged through guided support.
Teaming and collaboration	Practitioners from multiple disciplines and families work together to plan services, exchange knowledge and information, and gain access to community-based services. Group facilitation strategies are used to enhance team functioning and interpersonal relationships. Identify one team member to serve as a liaison between the family and team members.
Transition	Information is exchanged between sending and receiving programs before, during, and after the transition about how to support the child's transition. Planned strategies are used before, during, and after the transition to support the child and family.

From Sandall, S., Hemmeter, M.L., Smith, B.J., & McLean, M. (2005). *DEC recommended practices: A comprehensive guide.* Longmont, CO: Sopris West Educational Services; adapted by permission.

care and education experiences by creating environments that work with children with varying needs. DEC/NAEYC indicated that participation of all children is possible if teachers implement tiered instruction so that the individual needs of children are met through a variety of instructional techniques. Finally, necessary supports need to be in place, including collaborative partnerships, sound leadership practices, and effective professional development, in order for inclusive programs to meet the needs of young children. These practices are what hold up the curriculum framework (see Figure 2.1).

Framework for Response to Intervention in Early Childhood Education DEC/NAEYC/NHSA (2013) described a framework for conceptualizing RTI in ECE that shares the features of the curriculum framework described in this book (see Figure 2.1). First, three tiers of instruction are described, with Tier 1 representing broad universal outcomes and instructional practices. Tier 2 represents more targeted outcomes and teaching practices, whereas Tier 3 represents highly individualized outcomes and instructional strategies. Like the curriculum framework described here, the RTI framework is intended to function as an iterative process in which teachers engage in data-driven decision making to determine when to make changes in the type of outcome a child needs to learn and/or the instructional tier that is required to teach the outcome. The data-driven decision-making process includes 1) gathering information on children's development, 2) analyzing data to determine patterns and trends in performance, 3) making decisions about what to teach, 4) delivering high-quality instruction, and 5) evaluating the effectiveness of instruction. These steps depict the process that teachers go through when implementing the curriculum framework. Applications of RTI in ECE settings for academic skills (Recognition and Response) and social-emotional development (Pyramid Model) are described next.

Recognition and Response Buysse & Peisner-Feinberg (2010) described Recognition and Response as an RTI model for teaching early academic skills to children ages 3–5 years. The model comprises three components: 1) using a universal screener and progress monitoring strategies to recognize areas in which children may need additional intervention or decide when to change interventions; 2) three tiers of intervention, including a high-quality core curriculum, intentional teaching, and targeted interventions; and 3) a collaborative program-solving approach to making changes to intervention based on data. Buysse, Peisner-Feinberg, and Burchinal (2012) conducted two pilot studies to show the effectiveness of Recognition and Response with preschool-age children. Results showed that teachers implemented Recognition and Response with fidelity and found it feasible to use in the classroom. In addition, results showed that the implementation of Recognition and Response promoted language and literacy skills in 4-year-olds who participated in the study.

Pyramid Model for Promoting Social-Emotional Competence in Young Children Hemmeter, Fox, and Snyder (2013) described a tiered model for promoting social-emotional competence and addressing challenging behavior called the Pyramid Model. The Pyramid Model consists of four tiers. The universal level includes 1) nurturing and responsive relationships and 2) high-quality supportive environments. The secondary prevention level includes strategies for providing instruction on social skills and emotional competencies. Intensive individualized interventions are used in the tertiary level to address challenging behavior by designing individualized behavioral support plans that include prevention strategies, replacement skills, and new responses to problem behavior. Results of a randomized trial study showed that 1) teachers could implement the Pyramid Model with fidelity, 2) teachers in experimental classrooms rated their children with higher social-emotional skills than teachers in control classrooms, and 3) there was a decrease in teacher-reported challenging behavior in experimental classrooms (Hemmeter, Snyder, Fox, & Algina, 2011).

Research Support In addition to recommended practice support for the curriculum framework, research supports various components of the curriculum framework. Although the curriculum framework has not been researched as a unit, features are supported by evidence-based practices in the research literature. Specifically, work in the areas of 1) linking assessment and instruction and 2) embedding learning opportunities is discussed here.

Linked Assessment and Instruction The curriculum framework is a linked system that is composed of four interdependent program processes—assessment, goal development, intervention, and progress monitoring. In addition to promoting collaboration and active family involvement, a linked approach is designed to assist programs in 1) determining children's strengths, needs, interests, and learning styles; 2) developing meaningful goals and outcomes; 3) planning curriculum and instruction that addresses the individualized needs of all children; and 4) monitoring children's performance over time (Johnson, Rahn, & Bricker, 2015). Research has shown that linked assessment and instruction systems positively affect classroom quality and child outcomes. Hallam, Grisham-Brown, Gao, and Brookshire (2007) examined the effects of linking authentic assessment practices with Head Start outcomes on classroom quality. Results of the study showed that the quality of the language and literacy environment in 26 Head Start classrooms was superior to that of a matched sample of classrooms in which assessment and instruction were not linked. Buysse et al. implemented Recognition and Response, which is a "framework for linking formative assessment to tiered instruction" (2012, p. 1), in 76 pre-K classrooms. Results showed that pre-K children who received the intervention made greater gains in vocabulary, receptive language, and expressive language outcomes than a comparison group of children in their classroom.

Embedded Learning Opportunities The curriculum framework is designed to promote embedding children's goals into ongoing daily activities and routines. Research shows that children who are typically developing, at risk, or have disabilities can learn important skills when embedded learning opportunities are available (Grisham-Brown, Pretti-Frontczak, Bachman, Gannon, & Mitchell, 2014; Grisham-Brown, Pretti-Frontczak, Hawkins, & Winchell, 2009; Grisham-Brown, Ridgley, Pretti-Frontczak, Neilson, Litt, & Nielson, 2006). Grisham-Brown et al. (2009) used embedded instruction to teach writing skills to children with varying developmental needs (e.g., copy simple shapes, copy letters in name) in inclusive preschool classrooms. Results showed that all six of the children met criteria for their target skill, and two of the children made progress toward their target skill. The study shows 1) the impact of embedded instruction on children's outcomes in inclusive ECE settings and 2) that children with a variety of development needs can make progress toward important early learning standards when individual outcomes are identified.

EXAMPLES OF THREE CURRICULUM FRAMEWORKS

Although a common definition of *curriculum* does not exist, the term is frequently used in federal language (e.g., IDEA), in the literature base (e.g., NAEYC & National Association of Early Childhood Specialists in State Departments of Education [NAECS/SDE, 2003]), and in commercially available resources (e.g., *Comprehensive Curriculum of Basic Skills* [American Education Publishing, 2011]; *The Carolina Curriculum for Preschoolers with Special Needs, Second Edition* [Johnson-Martin, Attermeier, & Hacker, 2004]; *The Creative Curriculum for Preschool, Fifth Edition* [Heroman et al., 2010]; *Numbers Plus Preschool Mathematics Curriculum* [Epstein, 2009]). The lack of common terminology makes it difficult to discuss whether something is a curriculum framework. Furthermore, it is difficult to find resources that contain all necessary elements because a curriculum framework (as defined in this book) is much more than a single element or component; again, it often takes multiple resources to construct a curriculum framework.

Using our definition of a curriculum framework and the literature base regarding resources used by preschool teachers in terms of curriculum (e.g., Pretti-Frontczak, 2002; Pretti-Frontczak, Kowlaski, & Brown, 2002), three commercially available resources were identified that contain all elements of a curriculum framework and have utility in inclusive preschool programs: *Assessment, Evaluation, and Programming System* (AEPS®; Bricker, 2002), *The Creative Curriculum for Preschool* (Heroman et al., 2010), and The High/Scope educational approach (High/Scope Educational Research Foundation, 2003a). As previously stated, even these three resources will require programs to supplement and augment to ensure a comprehensive curriculum framework that will effectively address the needs of all children. A brief review of AEPS®, *The Creative Curriculum for Preschool*, and HighScope resources is provided to help teachers working in diverse/inclusive ECE settings better understand the advantages and disadvantages/challenges of using various commercially available resources. In addition to these three curriculum framework examples, two other curricular approaches are discussed.

The Assessment, Evaluation, and Programming System

AEPS® (Bricker, 2002) is a linked system with four elements that mirror those of the curriculum framework. The assessment is used to collect comprehensive information on all key areas of development and two content areas, including fine motor, gross motor, adaptive, cognitive, social-communication, social, literacy, and math. By using the assessment data collected, the AEPS® assists teams in the development of goals for teaching individual children and groups of children. Two curricular guides are available to assist teachers in designing instruction based on identified goals. Ideas for activities, instructional strategies, and materials for each AEPS® goal are provided for those who work in center-based settings as well as for those who work with children in home-based programs. Finally, the AEPS® may be used to collect ongoing progressing monitoring data on children's goals using specific areas or strands within areas. For example, if a teacher has identified writing as a goal for some children in his or her classroom, then he or she may use the prewriting strand on the literacy area to monitor progress. Table 2.3 provides a brief summary of the advantages and disadvantages/challenges of using AEPS® in inclusive programs for young children.

The Creative Curriculum for Preschool

The Creative Curriculum for Preschool (Heroman et al., 2010) was developed with an underlying belief that all children have strengths and abilities. *The Creative Curriculum for Preschool* strives to address learning across

Table 2.3. Advantages and disadvantages/challenges of the *Assessment, Evaluation, and Programming System (AEPS®)*

Advantages	Disadvantages/challenges
Promotes a linked systems approach (links assessment, goals, intervention, and evaluation)	Is comprehensive and requires that teachers have a strong understanding of child development and that programs are grounded in developmentally appropriate practices
Emphasizes and provides strategies for active family involvement and transdisciplinary team collaboration	Requires that teachers are able to individualize instruction and work as a member of a team, which can present challenges if training does not include these aspects
Contains validated strategies for working with young children and utilizes authentic activities and materials	
Emphasizes child-directed activities and individualized daily activities to meet the needs of all young children	
Is aligned with Head Start outcomes and state standards	

Source: Bricker (2002).

multiple content areas (e.g., literacy, math) as well as children's social-emotional development. The Creative Curriculum for Preschool also encourages teachers to individualize instruction to meet the needs of children and gain input from families for planning.

The Creative Curriculum for Preschool promotes the use of effective teaching procedures and contains a "valid and reliable assessment tool for use with preschool children" (Abbott-Shim, 2001, p. 15). In particular, children's progress is monitored with a developmental continuum. Three skill levels identify the child's level of proficiency of the skill, allowing teachers to quickly assess how close a child is to achieving a particular goal. *The Creative Curriculum for Preschool* also contains an implementation checklist that serves as a fidelity measure. Table 2.4 provides a brief summary of the advantages and disadvantages/challenges of using *The Creative Curriculum for Preschool* in inclusive programs for young children.

HighScope

HighScope is predicated on the notion that children should be actively involved in daily activities. The approach is composed of 58 key experiences and addresses children's development in areas such as language and literacy, music, seriation, and social relations (Hohmann & Weikart, 1995). The approach also promotes high teacher–child ratios, teamwork among staff, and parents as partners (Branscombe, Castle, Dorsey, Surbeck, &

Table 2.4. Advantages and disadvantages/challenges of *The Creative Curriculum for Preschool*

Advantages	Disadvantages/challenges
Encourages family involvement and forming relationships with each child and family	Has limited teaching suggestions and strategies for making modifications for children with disabilities
Promotes a balance between teacher direction and child initiation and fosters a positive approach to teaching by looking at the child's capabilities rather than his or her weaknesses	Limited empirical support
Addresses all content areas (e.g., social-emotional, physical, language, cognitive, literacy, mathematics, science and technology, the arts, English acquisition)	Is composed of many pieces and concepts, and how the various pieces can be put together to ensure a comprehensive curriculum framework can be confusing
Provides intentional teaching cards that can be used to assist teacher in differentiating instruction	May require extensive training and cost to ensure program personnel are implementing all aspects
Links assessment and curriculum and illustrates how to align with Head Start, Common Core State Standards, and many state standards	Has limited emphasis on a transdisciplinary team approach
Encourages ongoing monitoring and program evaluation	

Source: Heroman et al. (2010).

Taylor, 2003). Involving children in a set of activities organized around a plan–do–review process is a hallmark attribute of the HighScope approach. This involves having children choose activities in which they wish to participate, work in a variety of interest areas set up around the classroom, and review their work at the conclusion of work time, thus promoting critical abilities such as being able to reflect, predict, question, and hypothesize (Epstein, 2003).

HighScope also consists of resources and strategies to help teachers meet the needs of individual children (High/Scope Educational Research Foundation, 2003a), promote positive social interactions and problem-solving skills (Hohmann & Weikart, 1995), assess children's progress over time (High/Scope Educational Research Foundation, 2003b), and evaluate program effectiveness (High/Scope Educational Research Foundation, 2003c). Table 2.5 provides a brief summary of the advantages and disadvantages/challenges of using HighScope in inclusive programs serving young children.

Additional Curriculum Approaches

In addition to the curriculum frameworks previously described, two more approaches to teaching young children, particularly those served in inclusive preschools, are described here—Montessori and Reggio Emilia (e.g., Branscombe et al., 2003). The two approaches were selected for review because 1) they are commonly cited and described in the early childhood

Table 2.5. Advantages and disadvantages/challenges of HighScope

Advantages	Disadvantages/challenges
Encourages family involvement	Is difficult to identify appropriate key experiences for children with significant disabilities
Promotes active involvement by children and seeks to individualize learning for all children	Discourages specific verbal praise, which some children may need to be motivated to learn some tasks
Covers broad areas of development and learning with a wide developmental continuum for each key experience to facilitate planning for children with a range of abilities in an inclusive classroom	Is composed of many pieces and concepts, and how the various pieces can be put together to ensure a comprehensive curriculum framework can be confusing
Arranges key experiences around content areas (e.g., literacy, numeracy, spacial relations) and can be cross-referenced or aligned with state standards	May require extensive training and cost to ensure that program personnel are implementing all aspects
Links assessment and curriculum and encourages ongoing monitoring and program evaluation	
Is widely researched and linked to positive outcomes for young children	

literature, 2) they are grounded in many of the principles of recommended practice described throughout this book, and 3) they are promoted as approaches that can be implemented or followed by those serving children in inclusive preschool programs. Each approach is briefly described, along with the advantages and disadvantages/challenges to following the approach in inclusive preschool programs.

Montessori

Montessori is a philosophy and set of principles for educating children that was designed by Maria Montessori in Italy in the early 1900s. Montessori is based on the idea that children have a powerful urge to explore, and independence should be emphasized in order for children to reach their potential. The child and teacher work in unison within a Montessori approach, but the teacher does not interfere with the child's exploration. Orderliness and organization are emphasized as well as practical life exercises in which children learn to care for animals and plants, help maintain the order within the classroom, and are independent in grooming and feeding (Wentworth, 1999). Children are also given demonstrations for performing specific tasks and are then left to complete them on their own. According to Lillard (1980), a former Montessori teacher, the Montessori approach works well for children with special needs because the materials are designed so that skills from a variety of developmental levels can be taught. Furthermore, the Montessori approach encourages children to move through lessons and material sequences at their own pace. Table 2.6 provides a brief summary of the advantages and disadvantages/challenges of using Montessori in inclusive programs serving young children.

Table 2.6. Advantages and disadvantages/challenges of the Montessori approach

Advantages	Disadvantages/challenges
Celebrates cultural diversity and individual differences	Some children with significant disabilities may not be able to fully participate, initiate and direct their learning, or complete some activities independently (e.g., feeding, going to the bathroom)
Emphasizes independence as appropriate for all children, particularly those with disabilities	De-emphasizes activities that could offer opportunities for children with a wide range of developmental abilities to participate (e.g., in dramatic play)
Builds on child choice and encourages direct experiences and investigation by children	Lacks specific assessment or progress monitoring strategies and places little emphasis on team collaboration and active family involvement
Emphasizes problem solving and other broad processes (e.g., peace, kindness) that all children need to learn	Lacks empirical support, and content has not been aligned with state/agency standards
Provides opportunities for children to initiate and have an active role in their learning	

Reggio Emilia

The Reggio Emilia approach "focuses on helping the children understand perspective taking, building community and aesthetics through questions and challenging their assumptions" (Branscombe et al., 2003, p. 127). A teacher using the Reggio Emilia approach promotes "negotiated learning" (Forman & Fyfe, 1998, p. 240) by supporting the children's learning through in-depth questions that encourage children to process and articulate how they are learning. Negotiated learning has three components: 1) design, 2) discourse, and 3) documentation. *Design* is when a child makes plans using some media regarding a project that he or she will develop. *Discourse* refers to interactions among those in the environment who are cooperatively working on the project. Finally, *documentation* is evidence of the child's work, in some ways similar to a portfolio, such as audio recordings, photographs, field notes, and work samples.

The use of in-depth areas of studies, in which the children have interest, is central to the Reggio Emilia approach (Katz, 1998). Project-based learning, however, is only one part of the approach. Children in Reggio Emilia schools also engage in dramatic play, block play, and one-shot art activities (Katz, 1998). Emphasizing the involvement of all children is another important feature of the Reggio Emilia approach (Palsha, 2001). The approach involves the use of special supports, small-group project work, integrated therapy, and individualization, all of which facilitate the inclusion of children with special needs into the classroom. Table 2.7 provides a brief summary of the advantages and disadvantages/challenges of using the Reggio Emilia approach in inclusive programs serving young children.

Table 2.7.   Advantages and disadvantages/challenges of the Reggio Emilia approach

Advantages	Disadvantages/challenges
Emphasizes that all children can be successful, which supports including children with special needs	Lacks many of the elements of a curriculum framework and would need to be augmented with an ongoing assessment process, aligned with state/agency standards, and supplemented with strategies for intervention
Focuses on meeting the individual needs of children, and the flexibility of the approach to teaching allows children with a variety of learning styles to fully participate	Specific strategies for including children with disabilities, as well as strategies for actively involving families and working as a transdisciplinary team, are vague
Emphasizes teacher reflection and ongoing documentation of children's progress and work	Lacks empirical support

SUMMARY

This chapter defined a curriculum framework as having four elements—assessment, scope and sequence, activities and instruction, and progress monitoring. Theoretical, recommended practice, and research support for the curriculum framework were detailed. Specific examples of commercially available curriculum frameworks, including AEPS®, *The Creative Curriculum for Preschool,* and HighScope were described, as well as the Montessori and Reggio Emilio approaches. The advantages and disadvantages of each of these commonly used curricula/approaches for teaching young children in blended classrooms were identified. The scope and sequence element of the curriculum framework will be described in Chapter 3, with emphasis on three tiers of outcomes—common, targeted, and individualized.

LEARNING ACTIVITES

1. List and describe each of the four elements of a curriculum framework that teachers should consider when developing an effective curriculum for children of diverse abilities. Explain why each of the four elements must be considered and how they each contribute to quality programming for all young children and their families.

2. Select a curriculum resource used with young children. Review the curriculum and address each of the following questions:

   • How does it address each of the four components?

   • To what extent is it developmentally appropriate?

   • How are the needs of children with disabilities met?

   • What are the advantages and disadvantages/challenges of this curriculum?

REFERENCES

Abbott-Shim, M. (2001). *Validity and reliability of the Creative Curriculum for Early Childhood and the developmental continuum for ages 3–5.* Atlanta, GA: Quality Assist.

American Education Publishing. (2011). *Comprehensive curriculum of basic skills.* Greensboro, NC: Carson-Dellosa Publishing.

Bagnato, S.J., Neisworth, J.T., & Pretti-Frontczak, K. (2010). *LINKing authentic assessment and early childhood intervention: Best measures for best practices* (2nd ed.). Baltimore, MD: Paul H. Brookes Publishing Co.

Branscombe, N.A., Castle, K., Dorsey, A.G., Surbeck, E., & Taylor, J.B. (2003). *Early childhood curriculum: A constructivist perspective.* Boston, MA: Houghton Mifflin.

Bricker, D. (Series Ed.). (2002). *Assessment, Evaluation, and Programming System (AEPS®) for Infants and Children* (2nd ed.). Baltimore, MD: Paul H. Brookes Publishing Co.

Buysse, V., & Peisner-Feinberg, E. (2010). Recognition and response: Response to intervention for pre-K. *Young Exceptional Children, 13*(4), 2–13.

Buysse, V., Peisner-Feinberg, E., & Burchinal, M. (2012, March). *Recognition and response: Developing and evaluating a model of RTI for pre-K.* Poster presented at the Society on Research and Educational Effectiveness, Washington, DC.

Copple, C., & Bredekamp, S. (Eds.). (2009). *Developmentally appropriate practice in early childhood programs serving children from birth through age 8* (3rd ed.). Washington, DC: National Association for the Education of Young Children.

Division for Early Childhood. (2014). *DEC recommended practices in early intervention/early childhood special education 2014.* Retrieved from http://www.dec-sped.org/recommendedpractices

Division for Early Childhood & National Association for the Education of Young Children. (2009). *Early childhood inclusion: A joint position statement of the Division for Early Childhood (DEC) and the National Association for the Education of Young Children (NAEYC).* Chapel Hill, NC: University of North Carolina, FPG Child Development Institute.

Division for Early Childhood, National Association for the Education of Young Children, & National Head Start Association. (2013). *Frameworks for response to intervention in early childhood: Description and implications.* Los Angeles, CA: Author.

Emde, R., & Robinson, J. (2000). Guiding principles for a theory of early intervention: A developmental-psychoanalytic perspective. In J. Shonkoff & S. Meisels (Eds.), *Handbook of early childhood intervention* (pp. 160–178). New York, NY: Cambridge University Press.

Epstein, A.S. (2003). How planning and reflection develop young children's thinking skills. *Young Children, 59*(1) 28–36.

Epstein, A.S. (2009). *Numbers Plus preschool mathematics curriculum.* Ypsilanti, MI: High/Scope Press.

Forman, G., & Fyfe, B. (1998). Negotiated learning through design, documentation, and discourse. In C. Edwards, L. Gandini, & G. Forman (Eds.), *The hundred languages of children: The Reggio Emilia approach—Advanced reflections* (2nd ed., pp. 239–260). Greenwich, CT: Ablex.

Goffin, S.G., & Wilson, C. (2001). *Curriculum models and early childhood education: Appraising the relationship* (2nd ed.). Upper Saddle River, NJ: Merrill/Prentice Hall.

Grisham-Brown, J.L., & Pretti-Frontczak, K. (2011). *Assessing young children in inclusive settings: The blended practices approach.* Baltimore, MD: Paul H. Brookes Publishing Co.

Grisham-Brown, J.L., Pretti-Frontczak, K., Bachman, A., Gannon, C., & Mitchell, D. (2014). Delivering individualized instruction during ongoing classroom activities and routines: Three success stories. In K. Pretti-Frontczak, J. Grisham-Brown, & L. Sullivan (Eds.), *Blending practices for all children* (Young Exceptional Children Monograph Series No. 16). Los Angeles, CA: The Division for Early Childhood of the Council for Exceptional Children.

Grisham-Brown, J.L., Pretti-Frontczak, K., Hawkins, S., & Winchell, B. (2009). An examination of how to address early learning standards for all children within blended preschool classrooms. *Topics in Early Childhood Special Education, 29*(3), 131–142.

Grisham-Brown, J.L., Ridgley, R., Pretti-Frontczak, K., Litt, C., & Nielson, A. (2006). Promoting positive learning outcomes for young children in inclusive classrooms: A preliminary study of children's progress toward pre-writing standards. *Journal of Intensive Behavior Intervention, 3*(1), 171–190.

Hallam, R., Grisham-Brown, J., Gao, X., & Brookshire, R. (2007). The effects of outcomes-driven authentic assessment on classroom quality. *Early Childhood Research and Practice, 9*(2), 1–9.

Hemmeter, M.L., Fox, L., & Snyder, P. (2013). A tiered model for promoting social-emotional competence and addressing challenging behavior. In V. Buysse & E.S. Peisner-Feinberg (Eds.), *Handbook of response to intervention in early childhood* (pp. 85–102). Baltimore, MD: Paul H. Brookes Publishing Co.

Hemmeter, M.L., Snyder, P., Fox, L., & Algina, J. (2011). *Efficacy of a classroom wide model for promoting social-emotional development and preventing challenging behavior.* Paper presented at the annual meeting of the American Educational Research Association, New Orleans, LA.

Heroman, C., Dodge, D.T., Berke, K., Bickart, T., Colker, L., Jones, C.,...Dighe, J. (2010). *The Creative Curriculum for Preschool* (5th ed.). Washington, DC: Teaching Strategies.

High/Scope Educational Research Foundation. (2003a). *High/Scope educational approach: A prospectus for pre-kindergarten.* Ypsilanti, MI: High/Scope Press.

High/Scope Educational Research Foundation. (2003b). *High/Scope preschool child observation record* (2nd ed.). Ypsilanti, MI: High/Scope Press.

High/Scope Educational Research Foundation. (2003c). *Preschool program quality assessment instrument.* Ypsilanti, MI: High/Scope Press.

Hohmann, M., & Weikart, D. (1995). *Educating young children: Active learning practices for preschool and childcare programs.* Ypsilanti, MI: High/Scope Press.

Individuals with Disabilities Education Act Amendments (IDEA) of 1997, PL 105-17, 20 U.S.C. §§ 1400 *et seq.*

Johnson, J., Rahn, N.L., & Bricker, D. (2015). *An activity-based approach to early intervention* (4th ed.). Baltimore, MD: Paul H. Brookes Publishing Co.

Johnson-Martin, N.M., Attermeier, S.M., & Hacker, B.J. (2004a). *The Carolina Curriculum for Infants and Toddlers with Special Needs* (CCITSN) (3rd ed.). Baltimore, MD: Paul H. Brookes Publishing Co.

Johnson-Martin, N.M., Hacker, B.J., & Attermeier, S.M. (2004). *The Carolina Curriculum for Preschoolers with Special Needs* (CCPSN) (2nd ed.). Baltimore, MD: Paul H. Brookes Publishing Co.

Katz, L.G. (1998). What can we learn from Reggio Emilia? In C. Edwards, L. Gandini, & G. Forman (Eds.), *The hundred languages of children: The Reggio Emilia approach—Advanced reflections* (2nd ed., pp. 27–48). Greenwich, CT: Ablex.

Lillard, P.P. (1980). *Montessori in the classroom: An early childhood educator's account of how children really learn.* New York, NY: Schocken Books.

Miller, P. (1989). *Theories of developmental psychology.* New York, NY: W.H. Freeman.

National Association for the Education of Young Children & the National Association of Early Childhood Specialists in State Departments of Education. (2003). *Early childhood curriculum, assessment, and program evaluation.* Washington, DC: Author.

Palsha, S. (2001). An outstanding education for all children: Learning from Reggio Emilia's approach to inclusion. In V. Fu, A. Stremmel, & L. Hill (Eds.), *Teaching and learning: Collaborative exploration of the Reggio Emilia approach* (pp. 109–131). Upper Saddle River, NJ: Merrill/Prentice Hall.

Pretti-Frontczak, K. (2002). *Examining the effects of embedding young children's goals and objectives during daily activities.* Unpublished report, Kent State University, Kent, Ohio.

Pretti-Frontczak, K., & Bricker, D. (2004). *An activity-based approach to early intervention* (3rd ed.). Baltimore, MD: Paul H. Brookes Publishing Co.

Pretti-Frontczak, K.L., Kowlaski, K., & Brown, R.D. (2002). Preschool teachers' use of assessments and curricula: A statewide examination. *Exceptional Children, 69*(1), 109–123.

Wentworth, R.A.L. (1999). *Montessori in the new millennium: Practical guidance on the teaching and education of children of all ages, based on a rediscovery of the true principles and vision of Maria Montessori.* Mahwah, NJ: Lawrence Erlbaum Associates.

Widerstrom, A.H. (2005). *Achieving learning goals through play: Teaching young children with special needs* (2nd ed.). Baltimore, MD: Paul H. Brookes Publishing Co.

## CHAPTER 3

Identifying Outcomes for Children in Blended Early Childhood Classrooms

Jennifer Grisham-Brown, Kristie Pretti-Frontczak, and Mary Louise Hemmeter

Ms. Mattie has just completed the Assessment, Evaluation, and Program-
ming System (AEPS®; Bricker, 2002) on each child in her prekindergarten
(pre-K) classroom and has data on every child's development across all areas.
In addition, Ms. Mattie conducted a home visit with each child's family
and has some idea of their concerns and priorities for the upcoming school
year. She has also spent about 5 weeks with the children, and she knows the
activities and materials they prefer and which friends like to play together.
Given all of this assessment information, Ms. Mattie has to use the data to
guide and continue the instruction she delivers. Her program requires that
she follow the early learning standards for her state, which guide her about
what 3- to 5-year-old children need to learn. Some children in Ms. Mattie's
class are struggling with outcomes that are taught on a regular basis (e.g.,
concept of colors, shapes, and numbers). Moreover, Ms. Mattie has three
children in her class with individualized education programs (IEPs) who
have individual goals and two additional children who are not receiving spe-
cial education but seem to be missing foundational skills or are demonstrat-
ing challenging behavior that is interfering with their learning. Ms. Mattie
needs direction about what to teach each child in her classroom, along with
the outcomes for which she is accountable according to her agency and state.

It is critical for teachers to engage in ongoing reflection and data-driven decision making in order for them to determine what outcomes to teach in a blended classroom. To this end, it is important for teachers to be aware of what they are trying to accomplish in a given activity, routine, or interaction. The "what" teaching element of the curriculum framework is referred to as the *scope and sequence*. *Scope* refers to the breadth of what is taught in a pre-K classroom (i.e., content/developmental areas), and *sequence* refers to the order in which outcomes are taught (see Chapter 2). Grisham-Brown and Pretti-Frontczak (2013) described three different types of instructional sequences. First, skills can be taught in a developmental sequence, which is a generally agreed-on order in which children acquire skills, taking into account the fact that the children's culture or the presence of a specific impairment may affect the sequence. Second, research has shown that some skills lay the foundation for children to learn other skills, resulting in teaching in peda-gogical sequences. For example, rhyming is often taught as a foundational skill for learning early literacy skills. Finally, skills may be taught in a logical sequence, meaning that teachers select skills based on what makes the most sense to teach a child at a given point in time. For example, if a child does not have a functional way to express his or her wants and needs, then that skill might be taught before other skills.

Teachers in a blended classroom must identify three types of out-comes in their classroom and plan instruction accordingly. Common outcomes, which are expectations that states, agencies, funding sources, and programs have for all children within a given age group, need to be identified. Second, *targeted outcomes* are defined as skills that require more support in order to help children who are struggling or whose learning and development has stalled. Finally, individualized outcomes are foundational skills or prerequisite behaviors that children need to learn in order to gain access to, participate in, and make progress toward the common outcomes that other children are learning. Individualized outcomes are based on a child's unique needs and are often documented on various individualized plans, including IEPs for children with identified disabilities (Johnson, Rahn, & Bricker, 2015). Yet, children who will need this level of support may not qualify for special education services. The purpose of this chapter is to describe common, targeted, and individualized outcomes, with emphasis on how they are identified. We provide information on instructional strategies that are effective and efficient for teaching each type of outcome in Section II of this book. In addition, we discuss the importance of determining whether outside variables might be affecting children's learning.

COMMON OUTCOMES

Common outcomes for all young children are increasingly likely to be set by national organizations and federal or state policies (see Chapter 2; Schumacher, Irish, & Lombardi, 2003). Common outcomes as described here should not to be considered synonymous with the Common Core State Standards (CCSS: National Governors Association for Best Practices & Council of Chief State School Officers, 2010), but, rather, they are a set of knowledge and skills that serve as the scope and sequence for children in any state or region or those associated with a particular early childhood education (ECE) program (e.g., Head Start). Common outcomes, as we define them, are often categorized by age or grade level and organized around various content areas, including language and literacy, mathematics, science, social-emotional, and social studies (Seefeldt, 2005). Common outcomes may also be categorized by developmental areas (e.g., motor, cognition, communication, social) or subject area (e.g., literacy, math, science) found within a curriculum-based assessment (CBA) or a comprehensive curriculum. As such, common outcomes are designed to organize, prioritize, and frame what all children are to learn at various stages or ages of development or education (e.g., Copple & Bredekamp, 2009; National Research Council, 2001). Common outcomes often represent the values and priorities of primary stakeholders, such as policy makers, educators, and community members, and are designed to inform curriculum design, implementation, and evaluation for children with and without disabilities. In other words, teachers and teams are expected to design activities, implement learning opportunities, and evaluate all children's progress toward the content and skills noted in the common outcomes. Four sources of common outcomes can be found in early childhood literature and are described in the following sections.

Early Learning Standards

Common outcomes have primarily been defined by early learning standards since 2001. A *standard* is defined as a "general statement that represents the information, skills, or both, that students should understand and be able to do" (Bodrova, Leong, Paynter, & Semenov, 2000, p. 33). Furthermore, "standards are not standardized, nor are they a set of curricula. Standards are sets of well-articulated and well-understood student competencies" (Kurtenbach, 2000, p. 1). For example, "recognizes and demonstrates an understanding of environmental print" and "indicates an awareness of letters that cluster as words, words in phrases or sentences by use of spacing, symbols, or marks" are two examples of state-level standards for children in pre-K. These standards (also referred to as *content standards, child* or *learning outcomes, indicators,* and *foundations*) guide programs in terms of what should be addressed/introduced at a given age or grade level.

The prevalence of state standards for young children has dramatically increased since the 1980s. Almost every state has pre-K early learning standards, and half have a process in place to monitor a program's use of the standards (Scott-Little, Lesko, Martella, & Milburn, 2007). Individual states commonly have standards posted on their department's web site. For example, the early learning content standards for Kentucky are found on the Kentucky Governor's Office of Early Childhood web site (see http://kidsnow.ky.gov/Improving-Early-Care/Pages/Tools-and-Resources. aspx). Furthermore, national resources are available to guide states in issues related to early learning standards, such as developing/revising early standards and aligning standards with assessment and curricula (see e.g., http://www.earlylearningguidelines-standards.org).

Head Start Early Learning Outcomes Framework

Familiarity with the Head Start Early Learning Outcomes Framework (HSELOF) (http://eclkc.ohs.acf.hhs.gov/hslc/hs/sr/approach/cdelf/index.html) is essential for teachers serving children in Head Start programs. The HSELOF is designed to serve as a guide to Head Start programs as they engage in ongoing assessment and progress monitoring of children's skills, abilities, knowledge, and behaviors. The framework consists of five central domains (i.e., approaches to learning; social-emotional; language and literacy; cognition; and perception, motor, and physical) that should be addressed for children birth to 5 years of age in Early Head Start and Head Start programs. In addition to the domains, there are subdomains within each domain. For example, the subdomains for social-emotional include relationships with adults, relationships with other children, emotional functioning, and sense of identity and belonging. Goals within each subdomain are broad behaviors and skills and developmental progression that lead toward each goal for each age level. Indicators for pre-K students are also identified; these are specific skills children need to know before entering kindergarten. Head Start programs are required to align their curricula, assessment, and professional development practices with the framework.

Office of Special Education Program Outcomes

Beginning in 2005, the Office of Special Education Programs (OSEP) developed three child outcomes for young children receiving services from Part C (early intervention) and Part B 619 (early childhood special education) of IDEA. The purpose of the outcomes is to assist with measuring progress of young children with disabilities receiving special education services. Programs must measure children's progress on the outcomes when they enter and exit early intervention and pre-K. The outcomes are as follows:

1. Positive social-emotional skills (including social relationships)

2. Acquisition and use of knowledge and skills (including early language/ communication [and early literacy])

3. Use of appropriate behaviors to meet their needs

Common Core State Standards

Since 2009, 43 states and the District of Columbia have adopted the CCSS, which is a set of standards in math and literacy. The CCSS affects young children in that the standards begin in kindergarten. Five areas of math are covered in kindergarten, including counting and cardinality (e.g., counting and comparing numbers of objects), operations and algebraic thinking (e.g., understanding concepts of addition and subtraction), number and operations in base 10 (e.g., gain foundation for place value), measurement and data (e.g., understand measureable attributes), and geometry (e.g., identify shapes). Following are 9 literacy standards that must be addressed in kindergarten.

1. Ask and answer questions about text.

2. Retell familiar stories.

3. Identify characters, setting, and main story events.

4. Ask and answer questions about unknown text in story.

5. Recognize common types of texts.

6. Identify author and illustrator.

7. Describe relationship between illustrations and story.

8. Compare experiences of characters in story.

9. Engage in group reading activities.

IDENTIFYING COMMON OUTCOMES

As previously stated, the challenge of assessing state or agency standards (i.e., common outcomes) is that they are typically written in a broad manner that is not easily measurable. For example, "shows increasing awareness of print in classroom, home, and community settings" is one of the indicators in the HSELOF. This indicator involves the attainment of a variety of skills such as pointing to words, pretending to read words, and recognizing name in print. This is an example of using typical developmental sequences to demonstrate attainment of a broader standard. Teachers need to use CBAs to identify the skills that relate to the attainment of the standard. It also is important that teachers understand the developmental sequences of the skills that lead to the attainment of the standard. Teachers and teams must also be able to assess each child's progress toward standards, regardless of the child's developmental level. Alignment documents among various state and program standards/outcomes and commonly used CBAs are generally available on publishers' web sites. For example, Teaching Strategies has aligned individual state standards, Head Start outcomes, and CCSS with items on the TSGold assessment (http://teachingstrategies.com/search/alignment).

Instructional Considerations

Information about strategies for teaching common outcomes may be found in Chapter 6. It is critical that teams and teachers attend to the interrelatedness of development when designing instruction using early learning standards as the foundation for what young children learn. In other words, given that standards are typically based on content areas (e.g., literacy, math, science, social studies), it is critical that teachers understand how various skills from across developmental domains (e.g., social-emotional, motor, adaptive) and content areas are interrelated and interdependent and avoid focusing just on the behaviors listed in the standards. For example, if a teacher wants a child to complete an art activity alongside other children in a small group using crayons, paints, clippings from magazines, stencils, and felt, then the teacher needs to consider all skills a child needs or requires to be successful in the activity and not only those aligned with state standards. The teacher would need to ensure that the child is able to sit in a child-size chair, manipulate objects, understand basic spatial concepts, share and exchange objects, and follow simple directions. The activity is inherently composed of skills from various domains of development and content areas. A comprehensive and integrated curriculum framework attends to both developmental and content areas considered key to children's overall growth and development. In other words, skills targeted for young children to learn should be framed or connected to developmental areas and content areas. In fact, most skills organized by developmental area can easily be merged or aligned with specific content areas. The challenge for teachers and teams comes when their assessment tool is organized by developmental areas and the outcomes listed in state or agency

Table 3.1. Alignment among content areas, benchmarks for Kentucky's early learning standards, and developmental areas

Content area	Kentucky early learning standards (benchmarks)	Developmental area
Language arts	Book appreciation and knowledge Phonological awareness Alphabet knowledge Print concepts and conventions Early writing	Receptive and expressive language Cognitive Fine motor
Mathematics	Numbers and counting Shapes and spatial relations Comparisons and patterns Measurement	Cognitive
Science	Scientific skills and method	Cognitive Expressive language
Health/mental wellness	Independent behavior Social cooperation Social problem solving	Adaptive Social-emotional
Social studies	History and events Understand surroundings Economic concepts Follow rules within home, school, and community Roles and relationships within family and community Diversity	Cognitive Social-emotional Expressive and receptive communication Adaptive
Physical development	Locomotor skills Nonlocomotor skills Combines motor skills Eye–hand coordination	Gross motor Fine motor

standards are organized solely by content area or are organized by both developmental and content areas. Teachers need to take the time to cross-walk or align their ongoing assessment practices with state or agency standards so that they can see the relationship between skills, whether they are organized developmentally or by content area. Table 3.1 illustrates the alignment among content areas, benchmarks for Kentucky's early learning standards, and developmental areas.

TARGETED OUTCOMES

There are at least two instances when teachers and teams need to consider addressing targeted outcomes for individual or small groups of children. The first instance is when children are struggling to demonstrate a common outcome. Children may struggle for a number of reasons, including having difficulty performing an aspect or component of a larger set of skills, having difficulty with a concurrent or related set of skills, having difficulty with generalizing use of the common outcome, or having difficulty with adapting to changing conditions and situations. The second instance is when learning and development appear to have stalled. Children's development has stalled when there is limited change or improvement over time.

In other words, the child's performance does not continue to reflect higher forms or more complex forms of the common outcome. Any number of variables may hamper or interrupt development and learning, including lack of impulse control, needing unusually long periods of time to process and take action, performance quality, or the inability to demonstrate the common outcome in multiple and varied ways over time. Thus, we define and use the word *struggling* to refer to instances in which an individual or small group of children may be having difficulty with some aspect of learning the common outcome. We define and use the word *stalled* to refer to instances in which a child or small group of children has stopped making progress or where there is an interruption in learning and development associated with a common outcome (Pretti-Frontczak, 2014).

Whether a child or group of children is having difficulty or whether there is a lack of changes in performance over time is something that is determined once a child has received consistent and quality universal instruction. In fact, children will require more support from time to time to address things they struggle with doing or when their performance over time has stalled, regardless of their strengths or identified disability. What becomes essential is gathering, summarizing, and analyzing formative assessment information to help teachers and teams plan and revise instruction (Grisham-Brown & Pretti-Frontczak, 2011).

Formative assessment data also help teachers and teams identify the targeted outcomes that become the focus of instructional efforts. When formative assessment data reveal that a subset of children are struggling to learn or their learning and development has stalled, a teacher or team should identify and intervene on these more targeted outcomes. The following section provides examples of targeted outcomes and describes how to identify them.

Examples of Targeted Outcomes

What should be the focus of instruction when teachers and teams have examined their formative assessment data and concluded that individual or small groups of children need instruction regarding a targeted outcome? What is the targeted outcome that should be taught? This is a critical question to ask and not an easy one to answer. Unfortunately, we change the location of where instruction is delivered (e.g., move instruction to a corner of the room, to the hallway, to a different room in the building), we change the person who delivers the instruction (e.g., turn to a resource teacher or specialist), we change the frequency of instruction (e.g., begin to deliver massed trials), or we change the instructional strategy (e.g., use more adult-directed strategies) when a child struggles or when his or her performance has stalled. Although it is important to consider changing locations, personnel, frequency, and strategies as part of quality universal instruction, we must also change what is being taught when a child has greater and more individualized needs. Examples of what can be taught when a child is struggling or when learning and development has stalled are provided in Table 3.2.

Table 3.2.   Examples of Tier 2 outcomes

Examples of what to teach when child or children are struggling	Examples of what to teach when child or children's learning has stalled
Targeted outcome: Component of a complex skill	Targeted outcome: Latency

Children should be able to demonstrate common outcomes that have multiple components and steps as they grow and learn. When a child or group of children is having difficulty with a certain aspect or component of a complicated set of tasks, these aspects or components can become the targeted outcomes.

Problem solving and associations are two examples of common outcomes that have multiple components.

- *Problem solving* can be defined as "the ability to address a situation by completing one or all of the following steps/components: 1) recognizing the problem, 2) thinking of possible solutions, 3) carrying out solutions, and/or 4) evaluating the outcome" (Pretti-Frontczak, Jackson, Korey-Hirko, Brown, & Smith, 2013, p. 27).
  - Thus, if a child or group of children is struggling, then they may be able to do steps 1, 2, and 3 but require more support to perform the step 4. Step 4 (i.e., the component of evaluating the outcome) becomes the targeted outcome.
- *Demonstrating knowledge and skills surrounding association concepts* is another example of a common outcome that comprises multiple components. This common outcome actually comprises four components (i.e., four different association concepts), including quantity, size, space, and time. In this instance, a child or group of children may need additional support to address a single component of the common outcome by having teachers and teams focus on the targeted outcome of quantity associations.

Children should be able to take action within a reasonable amount of time and with some degree of planning and purpose. When a child or group of children's development and learning have stalled, they may struggle with a long latency period or a lack of a latency period.

- A child demonstrates a significant time lag (i.e., long latency period) from when a directive is given or initiation is determined until he or she takes action. This child may need constant and frequent reminders and encouragement, may be noncompliant, and may have difficulty recovering from high emotional states to more neutral emotional states. Thus, decreasing the latency between the stimulus and the child's response becomes the targeted outcome.
- A child does not demonstrate a time lag (i.e., no latency period) and often engages in impulsive actions or rushes to demonstrate/initiate the required/desired task with no or little time between directive or request and his or her action. This child may also have difficulty with delaying gratification or developing and executing a plan with logical steps. This child may have few inhibitions and struggle with stopping, feeling, and thinking before taking an action. Thus, the targeted outcome revolves around executive functioning skills, such as problem solving or persistence, to help the child better plan and act on his or her feelings.

Targeted outcome: Concurrent skill development	Targeted outcome: Quality of performance

Development in the early years is characterized by its high degree of variability, interrelatedness, and interdependence. In other words, the whole child is developing, and the complexities of learning are affected by many factors, making it hard to determine if a child is just doing something at a different yet acceptable rate of growth, or if he or she is struggling.

For example, children are concurrently or simultaneously learning the common outcomes of one-to-one correspondence, labeling, and comparing and contrasting when learning about associations (i.e., relationships or connections between objects, people, or events).

- When a child or group of children is struggling with concurrent common outcomes, teachers and teams may need to target a single concurrent skill that is related to the desired common outcome. For example, comparing/contrasting may be the targeted outcome when teaching comparing/contrasting concurrently.

Children performing a desired task are often able to demonstrate a concept or skill in such a way that it may hinder the accuracy of the performance. The quality of the children's performance is the concern.

Examples of concerns with quality, which becomes the targeted outcome, include intelligibility (talks too loud, too soft, too fast, too slow), interactions with others (too friendly, too withdrawn), or levels of engagement (too energetic, too passive, too effortful, too effortless, too few, too many).

(continued)

Table 3.2. *(continued)*

Examples of what to teach when child or children are struggling	Examples of what to teach when child or children's learning has stalled
Targeted outcome: Generalized use	Targeted outcome: Increasing complexity of responses

Targeted outcome: Generalized use

A child or group of children may also need targeted outcomes that address their lack of generalization (i.e., lack of use/demonstration of the common outcome) to a variety of materials, people, events, or locations. In other words, a child or group of children may be struggling with demonstrating a common outcome in a variety of locations, with a variety of people, or with a variety of materials. How to use skills in other locations, with other people, or with a variety of materials becomes the targeted outcome.

Targeted outcome: Increasing complexity of responses

Children begin to combine skills in new and more complex ways as they grow and learn. Furthermore, they are able to do things that are more abstract and not preferred.

For example, there will be times when most of the children in a class continue to learn to count higher quantities of objects and use increasingly complex terms regarding quantity (e.g., equivalent, amount, aggregate, sum, set). Yet, individual or small groups of children may continue to only count up to 10 objects and only use basic quantity terms such as *more, some,* and *few.*

Targeted outcome: Adjusting and adapting

All children may have difficulty with adjusting or adapting to changing conditions or situations at one time or another; however, when this difficulty keeps a child from making progress, teachers and teams may need to provide more focused support to help the child.

Examples of a child or group of children struggling with adapting or adjusting include

- Difficulty applying sufficient force to grasp or manipulate objects such as pencils, paintbrushes, hammers, and spoons
- Difficulty knowing how strong of a grasp is needed to open a variety of objects, including bottles, doors, cans, and containers
- Difficulty following rules or expectations at school that differ from home or community settings (e.g., child care center)
- Difficulty adjusting to social norms and routines that differ between home and school or different days of the week
- Difficulty directing attention in order to count objects, sort objects, participate in a group activity, or follow directions

Helping the child or group of children adapt and adjust to changing conditions and situations becomes the targeted outcome.

When a child tends to use an earlier or easier skill, such as pointing to a desired object in response to questions instead of giving a verbal response, which would be more appropriate for his or her age, is another example of stalled progress.

When a child or group of children's development and learning have stalled, it can mean they have stopped moving from single to multiple means of expression, moving from simple to complex demonstrations of knowledge and skills, moving from concrete to abstract thinking and doing, and moving from what is familiar and preferred. How to move toward the harder, complicated, more abstract, or even less preferred version of the skill becomes the targeted outcome.

From Pretti-Frontczak, K. (2014). *Addressing targeted outcomes as part of a multi-tiered system of support.* Brooklyn, NY: B2K Solutions, Ltd.; from Pretti-Frontczak, K., & Winchell, B. (2014). *Manual for assessing patterns in early childhood Development.* Brooklyn, NY: B2K Solutions, Ltd.

Identifying Targeted Outcomes

Teachers and teams should identify patterns as they gather, summarize, and analyze formative assessment information (Grisham-Brown & Pretti-Frontczak, 2011; Tomlinson, 2014). *Patterns* are defined as recurring events, meaning those that repeat in a predictable manner, and include the following scenarios—a child applies too much force every time he or she holds or manipulates an object, a child requires multiple reminders to comply every time he or she is asked to stop one activity and start another, and adults are aware that a child will likely grab or rush to an object he or she wants.

Identifying patterns (through analysis of formative assessment data) helps determine the targeted outcome.

Looking for patterns is like playing the board game Clue, in which players aim to predict who committed the crime, the location where the crime was committed, and the weapon that was used. For example, a player may predict that Miss Scarlett committed the crime in the library with the candlestick, based on the evidence collected during the game. Similarly, teachers and teams are using the evidence (i.e., formative assessment data) to find recurring events or events that repeat in a predictable manner when they are looking for patterns in children's behaviors. For example, teachers and teams using the common outcome of participation would analyze formative assessment data they gathered and summarized to determine if a child (or group of children) is able to participate in large groups, in small groups, or during one-to-one activities. Furthermore, teachers and teams might determine if a child or group of children is able to participate in a variety of activities including those that are routine, child directed, or planned. Finally, teachers and teams would determine if children are able to participate with verbal reminders, full support, or visual cues. In essence, teachers and teams are trying to determine which behaviors and events are recurring or predictable, meaning they will occur at the same time, under the same conditions, and in the same way. Such information will help determine why a child is struggling or why his or her performance has stalled. Examples of patterns include but are not limited to patterns of unexpected performance, need for assistance, and interfering behaviors (see Table 3.3).

All too often, however, teachers and teams only look for problems or deviations from what is expected when they identify patterns. A more powerful and informative pattern to begin with is related to a child's strengths. Patterns of strengths are indicators that the child's development is on target and concerns or more intensive interventions are not warranted. Thus, teachers and teams should start with the pattern of strength by looking at attributes such as whether the child or group of children

- Is independent (defined differently for each child) and can work on their own to complete tasks, get needs met, and participate in daily routines

- Demonstrates flexibility in terms of starting and stopping actions, what they play with, what they eat, whom they interact with, and when they are redirected

- Is adaptable to the situation or circumstances (i.e., they can adapt to increasing challenges or demands, changes in the environment from what they expected, and differences in caregiving expectations)

- Consistently demonstrates a set of skills

- Demonstrates generative skills that they can use under changing conditions and demands over time (e.g., they are able to change the size of their grip, amount of force, and action made when opening a variety of doors and containers)

Table 3.3.　Patterns and examples

Pattern	Definition	Brief explanation/examples
Pattern of unexpected performance	Represents instances in which the child demonstrates a skill that seems higher or harder than what is expected for his or her age or is missing a skill that is easier or should have emerged earlier in development. This pattern is sometimes referred to as having *splinter skills*.	Development and learning during the early years tends to follow predictable sequences. Developmental milestones is one type of sequence with which teachers and teams are familiar. Pedagogical is another type of sequence for which research and experience tells us the order that most children will learn a particular set of skills. A pattern of unexpected performance is observed when children do not follow expected developmental or pedagogical sequences. Children who are sequential language learners may exhibit a pattern of unexpected performance. For example, they may appear to have more advanced language because they have memorized key phrases, but they appear to have a delay at the same time because of the number of words they use. Children with disabilities often will demonstrate patterns of unexpected performance in which they have what many refer to as *splinter skills*. For example, they may be able to perform skills expected of their age in some developmental areas (or may even be advanced in certain areas), but they may be missing foundational or earlier skills in other areas of development because of their disability.
Pattern of assistance	Represents instances in which objects from the environment or people have to complete part or all of the task/response for the child	Assistance alone does not warrant concern because assistance might be expected based on what is known about developmental expectations. Furthermore, assistance is not merely presenting a prompt, cue, or reminder. *Assistance* here refers to an adult or peer having to complete part or most of the common outcome for the child. Although some level of assistance is commonly required for all children who are learning a new skill, the amount of assistance should decrease over time. Assistance can emerge as a concern when children need assistance beyond what is expected of a novice learner, beyond the children's age or present level of ability or developmental readiness, beyond cultural differences, or beyond a lack of prior exposure. For example, a child who is 4 years old needs reminders of how to follow a familiar social routine, or a child who is 5 years old needs help to manipulate objects.

(continued)

Table 3.3.   (*continued*)

Pattern	Definition	Brief explanation/examples
Pattern of interfering behavior	Represents instances in which a child demonstrates something other than the desired or expected concept or skill	By identifying patterns of interfering behaviors, teams can focus on supports and strategies that will help the child demonstrate more constructive responses, such as being helpful, playing with friends, sharing, taking the perspective of others, and being adaptable to changing events.

By identifying patterns of interfering behaviors, teams can focus on supports and strategies that will help the child demonstrate more constructive responses, such as being helpful, playing with friends, sharing, taking the perspective of others, and being adaptable to changing events.

Not all interfering behaviors are aggressive or purposeful; however, many times they are (e.g., hitting, biting, throwing). At times, behaviors can interfere given that the child (by choice or otherwise) is unable to maintain or establish attention, walks away from interactions or tasks, or even outright refuses to participate.

Examples of interfering behaviors may include
- Aggression (e.g., biting, kicking, screaming, hitting)
- Destruction (e.g., throwing, slamming, ripping, tearing)
- Repetition
- Distraction (e.g., picking skin, showing interest in another activity or person)
- Self-injurious (e.g., head banging, self-biting)
- Arguing (e.g., outbursts, yelling)
- Refusal/protest (e.g., pushing materials away)
- Ignoring
- Withdrawal
- Disengagement, complacency
- Lack of responsiveness and initiation

From Pretti-Frontczak, K., & Winchell, B. (2014). *Manual for assessing patterns in early childhood development.* Brooklyn, NY: B2K Solutions, Ltd.

INDIVIDUALIZED OUTCOMES

Grisham-Brown and Pretti-Frontczak stated that individualized outcomes are "foundational skills and/or prerequisite skills that are tied to a common expectation or standard" that are "designed to ensure full access, participation, and progress toward common outcomes" (2013, pp. 229, 230). Although individualized family service plan outcomes and IEP goals and objectives are priority outcomes for children with disabilities, other children in blended classrooms may need instruction on foundational and prerequisite skills. For example, a child with challenging behavior may need more individualized instruction on a social skill that is preventing his or her access to classroom activities and routines.

It is important that teachers develop measurable and observable statements (often called *goals* and *objectives*) when addressing individualized outcomes in order for systematic instructional strategies to be designed, implemented, and evaluated. The following section describes 1) how to select individualized outcomes based on assessment information, 2) steps for prioritizing outcomes, and 3) suggestions for writing statements that will guide instruction and enhance learning.

Selecting Individualized Outcomes

A number of quality indicators have emerged across the literature related to selecting individualized outcomes, including measurability, functionality, generality, and addressability (McWilliam, Jung, & Pretti-Frontczak, 2004; Pretti-Frontczak & Bricker, 2001). McWilliam (2009) suggested that individualized outcomes should include those that promote a child's participation in daily routines and is necessary or useful at home, in school, and in the community. Measurability is not only a recommended practice but is also federally mandated when developing children's IEP goals and objectives. Measurability ensures that a criterion is used to determine the success of the intervention and document changes in a child's performance (i.e., a criterion level of performance is noted for each behavior). Furthermore, the behavior must be observable in order to be measurable. Observable behaviors are those that can be seen or heard and which multiple people can agree have occurred (i.e., the behavior is an action that has a beginning and end). For example, "child responds with verbal or motor action to group direction provided by an adult" and "child greets peers by vocalizing, verbalizing, hugging, patting, touching, or smiling" are examples of measurable and observable target behaviors, whereas "child participates during group activities" and "child improves interactions with peers" are not.

Although identifying and writing measurable and observable behaviors is important, it is equally important to attend to whether the behaviors 1) are critical for children's participation in daily routines, 2) can be used in a variety of settings and conditions, and 3) are stated in a way that all team members can understand. Table 3.4 provides definitions and examples of four quality indicators. Teachers should consider the quality indicators as they strive to select meaningful behaviors (skills and processes) for children to acquire and use across their daily routines.

Prioritizing Individualized Outcomes

Given the number and types of skills and processes children learn during the early years, it is often difficult for teachers and teams to determine which to address at any given time. Teachers and teams need rules that help them prioritize individualized outcomes based on a child's needs, strengths, and interests. Without procedures for prioritizing, teachers and teams may become overwhelmed and feel that all skills and processes are of equal importance and require equal instructional time and progress monitoring efforts. Teachers can adopt the following set of practices to avoid these challenges:

• Engage in comprehensive assessment practices to ensure prioritized outcomes are developmentally appropriate for an individual child.

Table 3.4. Definitions and examples of each of the four quality indicators

Quality indicator	Definition	Examples
Measurability	Measurable behaviors contain a criterion or level of acceptable performance. The target behavior should also be observable, meaning it can be seen or heard and multiple people can agree it has occurred (i.e., the behavior is an action that has a beginning and end).	Walks 15 feet without assistance Prints first name correctly Zips coat independently Pours liquids without spilling Gives toy to peer without reminders
Functionality	Functional behaviors are those children need in most or all situations to 1) ensure access to activities and events, 2) promote independence, and 3) increase interactions with others and the environment. Without functional behaviors, someone else will likely have to perform tasks for the child (e.g., carry the child, feed the child).	Moves around the environment independently Communicates wants, needs, and ideas Initiates toileting routine Feeds self
Generality	Generative behaviors are those that represent generic processes or groups of related behaviors (e.g., problem solving, maneuvering, manipulating, preparing, participating) rather than specific or discrete skills (e.g., states two classroom rules, walks on a balance beam for four steps, stacks three blocks, gets puzzle and brings to table, follows directions at circle time). Generative behaviors are also ones that children can use across settings, people, materials, and events and that assist children in adapting to changes in the physical environment and expectations.	Manipulates various toys (e.g., puppets, books, blocks, hammers, musical instruments), objects (e.g., spoons, juice pouches, pencils), and materials (e.g., buttons, zippers, strings) with both hands. Manipulation of toys, objects, and materials is needed across daily activities (e.g., dressing, toileting, feeding) and can be used when interacting with a variety of people (e.g., family members, friends, teachers).
Addressability	Addressability ensures that targeted behaviors can be taught across daily activities and can be taught or easily elicited by various team members (i.e., the target behaviors are written with little or no professional jargon).	Plays using one object to represent another object (e.g., uses a stick as a pencil, uses a crayon as a bottle, uses a block as a telephone). Alternates between speaker and listener roles (e.g., pauses after making a comment or asking a question and looks toward communicative partner) when talking with familiar adults (e.g., parents, teachers, therapists) and peers during daily activities.

From Pretti-Frontczak, K. (2014). *Addressing targeted outcomes as part of a multi-tiered system of support.* Brooklyn, NY: B2K Solutions, Ltd.

- Obtain information regarding team members' concerns to ensure that prioritized outcomes are needed across settings and contexts.

- Understand the difference between common outcomes for all children, targeted outcomes for children who are struggling or whose development has stalled, and those that require systematic instruction for individual children.

- Select individualized outcomes that address multiple areas of need. For example, teaching a child to manipulate objects promotes play development, promotes independence with feeding and dressing, and is critical for early writing development and therefore addresses multiple areas of need.

Writing Individualized Outcomes Using an Antecedent-Behavior-Consequence Formula

Teachers and teams working in inclusive settings are increasingly expected to write individualized plans for all children, not only those with disabilities. For example, Head Start teachers have to identify individualized outcomes and write individualized plans for all children in their program (Head Start Bureau, 2003). Furthermore, some state and agency standards designed for all children may be written in broad terms and may not provide the level of information or detail necessary to guide instruction. For example, a Kentucky early learning benchmark reads, "shows interest and understanding of basic concepts and conventions or print," (Kentucky Governor's Office of Early Childhood, 2002) and a HSELOF (2015) indicator reads, "demonstrates flexibility, imagination, and inventiveness in approaching tasks and activities." Broad statements such as these may leave teachers wondering what specifically to teach and how to monitor children's progress toward such concepts.

A straightforward formula has been suggested when developing individualized outcomes (e.g., Alberto & Troutman, 2012; Johnson et al., 2015; Kizlik, 2003). The formula for writing effective individualized outcomes includes three components. First, the antecedents under which the individualized outcome will occur and can be observed or the occurrence or event that happens before the behavior should be noted. Second, a measurable behavior (i.e., one that is defined, has a beginning and an end, and is an action or verb and becomes the individualized outcome) is determined. Third, a performance criterion that includes how well the child is to perform the individualized outcome, how often the child is to repeatedly perform the behavior at criterion (e.g., for 2 consecutive days), and how often progress will be assessed (e.g., weekly) is specified. Grisham-Brown and Hemmeter (1998) also suggested adding specific activities in which the individualized outcome can be taught. Table 3.5 provides examples of individualized outcomes written using the ABC formula. Table 3.6 provides a summary of resources that teachers and teams can use to help them develop and write individualized outcomes for children, particularly IEPs for children with disabilities. Using the ABC formula helps to ensure that instructional efforts are clear and all team members understand expected child performance.

IMPORTANT OUTCOME SELECTION CONSIDERATIONS

There are three important considerations for teachers and teams to make as they engage in data-driven decision making around who needs to learn what and the most effective and efficient instructional practice that

Table 3.5.   Examples of target behaviors written using an antecedent-behavior-criterion formula

Antecedent/condition	Behavior	Criterion
During daily activities (e.g., small group, center time, snack time, outdoor play) . . .	→ Sam will manipulate a variety of objects, toys, and materials . . .	→ that require use of both hands at the same time, while performing different movements. Sam will manipulate three different objects, toys, and materials one time a day for 2 consecutive weeks.
During daily transitions . . .	→ Sam will go from one activity to the next . . .	→ without crying, hitting others, or throwing materials two times per week for 3 consecutive weeks.
During daily activities (e.g., small group, center time, snack time, outdoor play) and when asked, "What do you want?" . . .	→ Sam will express her wants and needs using two- or three-word verbal utterances . . .	→ at least once during three different activities within a 1-week period.

should be applied. Fidelity is the first consideration and is discussed in detail in Chapter 7. It is hard to assume that a change in what children are being taught is needed without assurances that instruction is delivered as intended. Rather, fidelity data may support changes to how an instructional strategy is used; how often, when, and where it is delivered; and how it is delivered versus changes to what is being taught. The second consideration

Table 3.6.   Resources for developing target behaviors for young children

Allen, E., & Cowdery, G.E. (2015). *The exceptional child: Inclusion in early childhood classrooms* (8th ed.). Stamford, CT: Cengage Learning.

Bateman, B.D., & Linden, M. (2012). *Better IEPs: How to develop legally correct and educationally useful programs* (5th ed.). Longmont, CO: Sopris West Educational Services.

Deiner, P.L. (2013). *Inclusive early childhood education: Development, resources, and practice* (6th ed.). Belmont, CA: Wadsworth.

Grisham-Brown, J., Pretti-Frontczak, K., Hawkins, R., & Winchell, B. (2009). Addressing early learning standards for all children within blended preschool classrooms. *Topics in Early Childhood Special Education, 29,* 131–142.

Horn, E., Lieber, J., Li, S., Sandall, S., & Schwartz, I. (2000). Supporting young children's IEP goals in inclusive settings through embedded learning opportunities. *Topics in Early Childhood Special Education, 20,* 208–223.

Jung, L.A. (2007). Writing SMART objectives that fit the ROUTINE. *Teaching Exceptional Children, 39*(4), 54–58.

Lignugaris-Kraft, B., Marchand-Martella, N.E., & Martella, R.C. (2001). Writing better goals and short-term objectives or benchmarks. *Teaching Exceptional Children, 34*(1), 52–58.

Pretti-Frontczak, K., & Bricker, D. (2000). Enhancing the quality of individualized education plan (IEP) goals and objectives. *Journal of Early Intervention, 23,* 92–105.

is grounded in the understanding that early development is highly inter-related and interdependent. Take, for example, the ability to count objects. When children are able to count objects in correct order, they need a variety of interrelated skills, including recall, comprehension, memory, symbolism, sequencing, labeling, and one-to-one correspondence. Children will appear to be struggling or their performance will appear stalled at times because of difficulties with one or more related behaviors versus the common outcome. Making sure that universal instruction is being delivered toward all related skills is needed in these instances.

Finally, four variables may influence how outcomes are selected because they may affect a child's progress but not necessitate teaching different outcomes (see Table 3.7). Specifically, teachers and teams should consider how a child's age, cultural differences, teacher characteristics, and child characteristics may affect when a child needs continued learning opportunities related to an outcome and not additional instruction on a different outcome.

Table 3.7.   Variables that influence outcome selection

Variable	Description
Age	For the most part, children acquire new skills with the passage of time, and they become more able as they get older. Furthermore, there is immense variability in the early years as to when children are expected or tend to acquire various skills. Thus, before teachers and teams become too concerned, they should familiarize themselves with the typical developmental sequences and time lines under which children acquire various skills and provide allowances for children to progress at different rates and in different sequences.
Cultural differences	Children live within families, and families live within larger communities, each of which consist of differing beliefs, values, and traditions. There are times when a child's performance may differ from what is expected in one culture but may be on track given another culture's beliefs and practices. Teachers and teams should be sensitive to cultural differences and how that might affect both what and how children are learning.
Teacher characteristics	Teacher characteristics such as style, temperament, and preferences may influence a teacher's reaction to situations and interpretation of the data. For example, if a teacher's own style is to talk often and be very expressive, then he or she may see a child who tends to be nonverbal as having a delay or attributing a negative attribute (e.g., concluding the child is withdrawn). It will be important for teachers to reflect on how their own views, characteristics, and values are affecting decisions about the children in their class.
Child characteristics	Similar to the idea that children develop and learn at different rates and in different ways, each individual child has his or her own set of prefer-ences and temperaments, which further affects how and when various skills may be demonstrated. Teachers and teams need to, as best they can, determine which things might be just part of a child's makeup (e.g., being shy, taking more time to process, wanting things a par-ticular way) and when something warrants instructional consideration. These child characteristics should be considered when thinking about what to teach and how to teach.

From Pretti-Frontczak, K. (2014). *Addressing targeted outcomes as part of a multi-tiered system of support.* Brooklyn, NY: B2K Solutions, Ltd.

SUMMARY

This chapter described what learners in blended classrooms need to be taught. Common outcomes are established by local, state, and national learning standards and need to be taught to all learners. Targeted outcomes should be identified and taught when children's development is stalled or they are struggling in a particular area. Finally, individualized outcomes should be selected for children when they are missing a foundational skill that prevents them from gaining access to, participating in, and making progress toward common outcomes. Children in blended classrooms may likely need to learn all three types of outcomes. The challenge for teachers in blended programs is deciding when to teach what skills to which child. The curriculum maps in many ECE programs are pacing guides that suggest teaching all children skills in a specific sequence. Although such tools may simplify planning, they do not account for the individual needs of children in blended classrooms. The framework described in this chapter for identifying what to teach children is strongly recommended in lieu of predetermined skill sequences. Chapters 5, 6, and 7 describe universal, focused, and systematic instruction. Each type of instruction lends itself to instruction of common (universal), targeted (focused), and individualized (systematic) outcomes.

LEARNING ACTIVITIES

1. What are the differences among common outcomes for all children, targeted outcomes for some children, and individualized outcomes for particular children?

2. Contact the state department responsible for overseeing programs for preschool-age children to request a copy of your state's pre-K standards. Explain how the standards are being addressed in the program in which you are working. If you are not working in a program, then contact a local program and interview a staff member about how his or her program is addressing the standards.

3. Select a classroom activity that is typically engaging to the children in your classroom. Identify how the following could be addressed by the activity. How does the activity allow for children with different ability levels to participate? Provide concrete examples. How does the activity consider the different cultural, physical, and social-emotional experiences and environments of the children in your classroom? How does the activity allow for children to be challenged just above their development? What changes might you make in the activity to address these issues?

4. Review a child's individualized plan (preferably an IEP). To what extent are the goals and objectives measurable and observable? Are they functional, generative, and able to be addressed by all team members?

REFERENCES

Alberto, P.A., & Troutman, A.C. (2012). *Applied behavior analysis for teachers* (9th ed.). Boston, MA: Pearson Education.

Allen, E., & Cowdery, G.E. (2015). *The exceptional child: Inclusion in early childhood classrooms* (8th ed.). Stamford, CT: Cengage Learning.

Bateman, B.D., & Linden, M. (2012). *Better IEPs: How to develop legally correct and educationally useful programs* (5th ed.). Longmont, CO: Sopris West Educational Services.

Bodrova, E., Leong, D.J., Paynter, D.E., & Semenov, D. (2000). *A framework for early literacy instruction: Aligning standards to developmental accomplishments and student behaviors: Pre-K through kindergarten* (Rev. ed.). Retrieved June 1, 2004, from http://www.mcrel.org/PDF/Literacy/4006CM_EL_Framework.pdf

Bricker, D. (Series ed.). (2002). *Assessment, Evaluation, and Programming System (AEPS®) for Infants and Children* (2nd ed.). Baltimore, MD: Paul H. Brookes Publishing Co.

Copple, S., & Bredekamp, S. (Eds.). (2009). *Developmentally appropriate practice in early childhood programs serving children from birth through age 8* (3rd ed.). Washington, DC: National Association for the Education of Young Children.

Deiner, P.L. (2013). *Inclusive early childhood education: Development, resources, and practice* (6th ed.). Belmont, CA: Wadsworth.

Grisham-Brown, J., & Hemmeter, M.L. (1998). Writing IEP goals and objectives: Reflecting an activity-based approach to instruction for young children with disabilities. *Young Exceptional Children, 1*(3), 2–10.

Grisham-Brown, J., & Pretti-Frontczak, K. (2011). *Assessing young children using blended practices.* Baltimore, MD: Paul H. Brookes Publishing Co.

Grisham-Brown, J., & Pretti-Frontczak, K. (2013). A curriculum framework for supporting young children served in blended programs. In V. Buysse & E.S Peisner-Feinberg (Eds.), *Handbook of response to intervention in early childhood* (pp. 223–235). Baltimore, MD: Paul H. Brookes Publishing Co.

Grisham-Brown, J., Pretti-Frontczak, K., Hawkins, R., & Winchell, B. (2009). Addressing early learning standards for all children within blended preschool classrooms. *Topics in Early Childhood Special Education, 29,* 131–142.

Head Start Bureau. (2003). *The Head Start leader's guide to positive child outcomes: Strategies to support positive child outcomes.* Washington, DC: Author.

Head Start Bureau. (2016) *Head Start Early Learning Outcomes Framework.* Retrieved from http://eclkc.ohs.acf.hhs.gov/hslc/hs/sr/approach/cdelf/index.html

Horn, E., Lieber, J., Li, S., Sandall, S., & Schwartz, I. (2000). Supporting young children's IEP goals in inclusive settings through embedded learning opportunities. *Topics in Early Childhood Special Education, 20,* 208–223.

Johnson, J., Rahn, N.L., & Bricker, D. (2015). *An activity-based approach to early intervention* (4th ed.). Baltimore, MD: Paul H. Brookes Publishing Co.

Jung, L.A. (2007). Writing SMART objectives that fit the ROUTINE. *Teaching Exceptional Children, 39*(4), 54–58.

Kentucky Governor's Office of Early Childhood (2016). *Kentucky early learning standards.* Retrieved from http://kidsnow.ky.gov/Improving-Early-Care/Pages/Tools-and-Resources.aspx

Kizlik, B. (2003). *Examples of behavioral verbs and student activities.* Retrieved from http://www.adprima.com/examples.htm

Kurtenbach, K. (2000). Standards-based reform: The power of external change agents [Electronic version]. *Connections, A Journal of Public Education Advocacy, 7*(1), 1, 4–5.

Lignugaris-Kraft, B., Marchand-Martella, N.E., & Martella, R.C. (2001). Writing better goals and short-term objectives or benchmarks. *Teaching Exceptional Children, 34*(1), 52–58.

McWilliam, R.A. (2009). *Goal Functionality Scale III.* Chattanooga, TN: TEIDS-Plus Study, Siskin Children's Institute.

McWilliam, R., Jung, L., & Pretti-Frontczak, K. (2004, February). *Measuring the quality of intervention plans.* Poster presented at the biannual Conference on Research Innovations in Early Intervention, San Diego, CA.

National Governors Association Center for Best Practices & Council of Chief State School Officers. (2010). *Common Core State Standards.* Washington, DC: Authors.

National Research Council. (2001). *Eager to learn: Educating our preschoolers.* Washington, DC: National Academies Press.

Pretti-Frontczak, K. (2014). *Addressing targeted outcomes as part of a multi-tiered system of support.* Brooklyn, NY: B2K Solutions.

Pretti-Frontczak, K., & Bricker, D. (2000). Enhancing the quality of individualized education plan (IEP) goals and objectives. *Journal of Early Intervention, 23,* 92–105.

Pretti-Frontczak, K., & Bricker, D. (2001). Use of the embedding strategy during daily activities by early childhood education and early childhood special education teachers. *Infant-Toddler Intervention: Transdisciplinary Journal, 11*(2), 111–128.

Pretti-Frontczak, K., Jackson, S., Korey-Hirko, S., Brown, T., & Smith, M. (2013). *Big ideas for early learning: Glossary.* Brooklyn, NY: B2K Solutions.

Pretti-Frontczak, K., & Winchell, B. (2014). *Manual for assessing patterns in early childhood development.* Brooklyn, NY: B2K Solutions.

Schumacher, R., Irish, K., & Lombardi, J. (2003). Meeting great expectations: Integrating early education program standards in child care. *Center for Law and Social Policy, 3,* 1–7.

Scott-Little, C., Lesko, J., Martella, J., & Milburn, P. (2007). Early learning standards: Results from a national survey to document trends in state-level policies and practices. *Early Childhood Research and Practices, 9*(1).

Seefeldt, C. (2005). *How to work with standards in an early childhood classroom.* New York, NY: Teachers College Press.

Tomlinson, C.A. (2014). The bridge between today's lesson and tomorrow's. *Educational Leadership, 71*(6), 10–14.

## CHAPTER 4

Recommended Instructional Practices

Jennifer Grisham-Brown and Mary Louise Hemmeter

Dr. Baker teaches undergraduate early childhood education (ECE) students at a community college in a midwestern city. The state where the community college is located has recently received a sizeable federal grant to work toward blending publicly funded school-based prekindergarten (pre-K) programs for children with disabilities with Head Start and child care programs. As a result, Dr. Baker and her colleagues are trying to create a teacher education program that will prepare their students for the contexts in which they will eventually work. They recognize the complexity of training teachers to work in highly diverse early childhood settings. Yet, they want their students to understand that there are recommended practices that must be in place, regardless of where their students may eventually work.

Although the focus of this book is on differentiating instruction for children with varying abilities, there are key practices that are relevant to all tiers of instruction. This chapter provides an overview of recommended instructional practices that should be addressed, regardless of the tier of instruction that is being provided. In addition, the chapter defines the types of support that teachers may provide to any child who needs assistance in their classroom. Finally, an introduction to three tiers of instruction is provided, along with information for selecting instructional strategies.

PRACTICES THAT ARE FOUNDATIONAL TO HIGH-QUALITY INSTRUCTION TIERS

Chapters 5, 6, and 7 of this book will focus on three tiers of instruction for supporting young children with diverse learning needs in blended classrooms. Four practices should always be present in a blended classroom, regardless of the tier of instruction, to ensure that the needs of all children are met, including differentiating instructional strategies, determining each child's zone of proximal development, and embedding learning opportunities across daily activities and routines.

Differentiation

Differentiating instruction is necessary in a blended classroom to meet the needs of a diverse groups of learners. Instruction can be differentiated by 1) group size, 2) who provides the instruction, and 3) the intensity of instruction. Instruction can occur in a large-group activity, small-group activity, or one-to-one instructional situation and can be provided by the classroom staff or specialists from a variety of disciplines (e.g., teacher of the visually impaired, occupational therapy) (Jackson, Harjusola-Webb, Pretti-Frontczak, Grisham-Brown, & Romani, 2009). The intensity of instruction increases as children's need for instructional support increases. It is important to remember that all children need differentiated instruction, not only those with special learning needs. For example, a child who is on target in all developmental areas may need more intensive instruction to promote more advanced learning in a particular area of development. Children with intensive learning needs in some areas of development may not need intensive instruction in all areas of development. For example, a child with autism spectrum disorder who needs systematic instruction to learn prosocial and communication skills may learn fine motor, gross motor, and cognitive skills in the same manner as his or her typically developing peers through access to hands-on materials and engagement in developmentally appropriate activities.

Zone of Proximal Development

A common assumption that teachers make when providing instruction is that the same level of support is right for all children. For example, teachers often expect that all children will respond appropriately to a verbal direction such as, "Pick the center you want to play in first today." In fact, some children may not have the cognitive skills to respond to that verbal direction. When a child does not respond, teachers may mistakenly assume the child is not following directions. Teachers must have detailed information about each child's developmental level, including his or her zone of proximal development (Vygotsky, 1978), to provide support that meets the individual needs of all children. The zone of proximal development is the actual developmental level of a child as determined by his or her ability to perform a task independently or to complete the task with some guidance from an adult or more competent peer (Cook, Klein, Tessier, & Daley, 2011; Gestwicki, 2014). The key to effectively teaching young children is to know when to give enough support so that children are not frustrated, yet not too much support so that they are not challenged. Consider the following examples. If a child is trying to put together a puzzle, then the teacher must observe the child's problem-solving skills as he or she attempts many problem-solving schemes. If the child becomes apparently frustrated (e.g., breathing deeply, slamming/pushing the pieces into the puzzle, walking away from the task), then the teacher should provide additional support. Yet, if the child continues to try to figure out where each piece goes without showing signs of frustration, the teacher should not provide unnecessary support, thereby interrupting the learning process. Being aware of the length of time it takes for a child to process information is the key to knowing when to provide support. Teachers often do not allow children enough processing time before providing subsequent information/assistance or expecting compliance. This happens under at least two circumstances. First, a child might be attempting to solve a task such as building a block tower. The teacher may jump in and give assistance instead of allowing the child time to figure out how to complete the task. Second, teachers often question children about their play or a particular situation without allowing them adequate time to respond. For example, a teacher might ask, "What do you think will happen next?" during storytime. The teacher may provide the answer or call on another child to provide the answer before the child has time to process the question and respond. It is also possible to wait too long to provide the level of assistance a child needs, thereby frustrating a child who may need additional support to solve a problem or answer a question. For example, if a child needs assistance putting on his or her coat, the teacher should avoid letting the situation get to the point that the child is crying or otherwise showing signs of frustration because he or she cannot fasten his or her coat. After allowing the child to try to fasten his or her coat independently, the teacher should provide support before the child shows signs of being overly anxious or frustrated. Teachers should also have an understanding of each child's processing abilities or the modalities the child primarily uses to process information. For example, some children process information better auditorily, whereas others process information better visually. These differences have implications for the type of support a child will need (e.g., verbal versus visual cues).

Creating and Providing Embedded Learning Opportunities

Embedded learning opportunities refers to the implementation of instruction within developmentally appropriate environments and activities. The rationale for using ELOs within blended classrooms is, by design, the blending of theoretical positions traditionally rooted in ECE and early childhood special education. Embedded learning opportunities are compatible with the principles of this book; the authors of this book believe all children should be educated in authentic, developmentally appropriate environments and activities within those environments. Embedded learning opportunities are "a process of addressing children's functional and generative goals during daily activities in a manner that expands, modifies, or is integral to the activity or event in a meaningful way" (Pretti-Frontczak, Grisham-Brown, Hawkins, & Jackson, 2013, p. 213). Embedded learning opportunities offer a means for attending to common, targeted, or individualized outcomes of children without preventing them from engaging in interesting, developmentally appropriate learning experiences. There are three parts of to an embedded learning opportunity—antecedent, behavior, and consequences.

Antecedent   The antecedent is any event that sets the occasion for a behavior to occur. The antecedent includes where, when, with what, and how teachers/peers set the occasion for the instruction. *Where* refers to the location of instruction and can include places inside and outside of the classroom, such as the playground or a specific center in the room. *When* refers to the time of day that instruction will occur and can include transitions, teacher-planned activities, or routine activities. *With what* refers to the materials that will be used for instruction and includes items such as books, manipulatives, and musical instruments. Finally, the antecedent includes "how" the environment is set up or a teacher/peer cues the child to demonstrate the expected response. If a teacher is trying to get children in his or her class to ask for assistance, then he or she might put preferred toys in a container that is difficult for children to open; thereby creating a situation for children to ask for help. Teachers/peers can give direct cues to get the child to respond, including, "How many friends are at school today?" "What do you want?" "Tell your friend that you want to play."

Response Once an occasion has been set for a child to respond, the teacher must give the child time to respond. The child can demonstrate three types of responses. First, he or she might respond as expected by the teacher (i.e., correct response). In order to know what is correct, teachers need to write the outcomes for their lessons so that they are measurable and observable behaviors (see Chapter 3). Second, the child might perform the expected behavior incorrectly. For example, a teacher asks the child to count five objects and the child says, "1, 2, 3, 7, 9." Finally, he or she might not respond at all. Ensuring that you give the child sufficient time to respond is the key to determining if the child is, in fact, not responding. Additional support should be provided if the child does not respond in the expected amount of time or if he or she responds incorrectly.

Consequences The consequence, which is what follows the child's response, is the third element of an embedded learning opportunity. As with other aspects of instruction, teachers need to plan for how they will respond once the child performs or attempts to perform a target skill. Given that a child may respond in one of three ways, different consequences are used, depending on the child's response. If the child performs the skills correctly, then the teacher or environment provides reinforcement to strengthen the likelihood that the child will perform the response again. If the child performs the skill incorrectly, or does not respond, then teachers should provide additional support or prompts so the child can respond correctly.

Reinforcement Reinforcement is when children receive positive feedback after they correctly demonstrate a behavior. Four issues must be considered when selecting and providing reinforcement to young children. First, teachers should consider that children should be intrinsically motivated to learn, rather than extrinsically motivated (Johnson, Rahn, & Bricker, 2015). This means that children perform certain skills because of the satisfaction that comes from doing them (intrinsic motivation), not because of some expected outside reward (extrinsic motivation) (Kohn, 1999). For example, friends Joshua and Ethan spend long stretches of time building elaborate block structures during free play. When new blocks are introduced, they eagerly try to figure out how to use the blocks to enhance their structure. They have begun to draw building plans and use them as models for their structures. These two 4-year-olds are motivated to continue with this task day after day not because their teacher is praising them but because their curiosity motivates them to continue to try new block configurations. External reinforcement may be needed on occasions, however, in inclusive pre-Ks, particularly with children who have challenging behavior. For example, if

Mabel has a target behavior to remain with the group during circle time for longer periods of time, then the teacher might give her a sticker when she remains with the group.

Second, children are more likely to be intrinsically motivated to learn if consequences are natural and logical. Natural consequences occur when adults provide no specific feedback and the environment or situation provides the feedback (Cook et al., 2011). For example, the natural consequence of Kendall going outside on a snowy day with his jacket unfastened is that he will likely get cold. When natural consequences are used, teachers may make connections for children between their behavior and the consequence (Gestwicki, 2014). Ms. Sarah might need to say to Kendall, "You got cold today on the playground because you didn't fasten your jacket." A logical consequence is "feedback that is immediate and directly integral to the response; it helps the child discern the relationship between the response and the subsequent feedback" (Pretti-Frontczak et al., 2013, p. 211). For example, if Lucas appropriately asks for something to drink, he will get a cup of something to drink and his thirst will be quenched—a logical consequence. Logical consequences are used in situations in which natural consequences may be harmful or unavailable (Cook et al., 2011). For example, if Kendall was unable to put on his coat at all, then Ms. Sarah would not allow him to suffer the natural consequences of going outside in subzero conditions without a coat.

Third, recommended practices suggest that it is important to provide specific or explicit feedback when giving verbal reinforcement (Copple & Bredekamp, 2009; DEC, 2014). Specific or explicit feedback implies that the teacher is focusing on the relationship between what a child does and the outcome of the behavior. Research has shown the effects of specific verbal praise on children's engagement in classroom instruction (Fullerton, Conroy, & Correa, 2009). For example, instead of telling a child he or she did a good job putting away toys following center time, the teacher should say, "Scarlett, thank you for putting the toys back on the shelf where they belong. Now, we will be able to find our favorite toys when we start to play tomorrow."

Finally, unrelated feedback or consequences should be provided subtly, with a plan in place for making the feedback more natural and logical (Howard, Williams, Port, & Lepper, 2001). In fact, Sulzer-Azaroff (1992) argued that natural or logical consequences may not be available in some situations. She provided examples related to learning to read and doing complicated math. Pre-K teachers in the past did not have to think about how to respond to teaching academic skills such as these. In the present standards-based climate of pre-K, however, teachers may have to use more contrived consequences to teach children specific content. According to Sulzer-Azaroff, "Teachers intuitively supplement with social reinforcers when essential to overcome insufficient natural reinforcement" (p. 82). In general, children should be provided with positive, descriptive verbal feedback when they are learning new skills. For example, Ms. Sarah may say to Gabriel when he correctly identifies the letter G, "Gabriel, you are on your way to writing your very own letter to your grandfather!"

Prompts   If a child does not respond or if a child does not respond as expected, teachers need to provide additional support so that the child can perform the expected response. A prompt is anything that increases the likelihood of a child demonstrating an expected behavior. Noonan and McCormick (2014) described natural prompts and instructional prompts. Natural prompts are those that result from some type of environmental condition that occurs over time, resulting in a child behaving in a certain way. For example, if a child is thirsty, thirst prompts the child to ask for something to drink. An instructional prompt is some type of teacher support that is added to a situation so the child can successfully perform the expected behavior. Seven types of prompts are described next.

Verbal Prompts   Verbal prompts are probably the most common way that teachers support learning. Teachers can provide verbal support in many ways. First, teachers can provide indirect verbal cues that give children partial information about what they need to do (Noonan & McCormick, 2014). A question is sometimes used to give indirect verbal support and help children organize their thoughts. For example, if a child is trying to work an ambulance puzzle, then the teacher might say, "Which piece looks like it might go with the siren?" The teacher is not telling the child which piece to put in next but is providing a verbal hint regarding which one goes next. Teachers can also give children direct verbal prompts, telling them exactly what to do to perform a task. For example, when a child is washing his or her hands and appears not to know what to do after putting his or her hands under the water, the teacher may say, "Rub your hands together so they will get clean." That verbal support tells the child exactly what to do to accomplish the task. Care should be given to provide verbal support at a level that is consistent with the child's receptive language abilities and, more specifically, slightly in advance of his or her current abilities. Although all children can benefit from verbal support, some may need more simplified information based on their receptive language and cognitive development. The teacher might simplify the statement by saying, "Rub your hands" for children who are developmentally younger and those with developmental delays.

Gestures   Children may need additional information, paired with verbal support, to complete a task or solve a problem. Teachers can use gestures by pointing to relevant parts of the task while giving verbal support. In the hand-washing example just mentioned, the teacher may point to the child's hands while telling the child to rub his or her hands together. Children may need this visual prompt (paired with a verbal prompt) to assist them in interpreting the verbal information the teacher is giving. Gestures are often used to guide young children through transitions. As teachers say, "Pick up the toys and put them on the shelf," they simultaneously point to the toys and the shelf to provide additional support for the children to complete the task. The decision to use verbal support in conjunction with the gesture may depend on the child or the situation. For example, teachers may only gesture when they are trying to direct a child to do something and not draw attention to him or her.

Modeling Modeling is another common strategy to support young children's learning. Modeling is also the backbone of Vygotsky's (1962) sociocultural theory and is a suggested strategy for teaching appropriate social behavior to young children with disabilities in inclusive preschool classes (Berk & Winsler, 1995). Teachers use both verbal and physical models by showing children how to complete a task or part of a task. Let's say that the teacher wants to teach Cohen one-to-one correspondence by having him distribute napkins, straws, and cups to children at his snack table. If this is the first time Cohen has been asked to do this task, the teacher may begin by modeling how to complete the task by first giving each child a napkin. Cohen then has the opportunity to complete the task by distributing straws and cups. Sometimes children have difficulty with only one part of a task, so the teacher may model only that part. For example, if Mikki is having difficulty zipping her coat, the teacher might model how to do it and then unzip the coat so Mikki has an opportunity to do it on her own. In this situation, the teacher also might model what to do by zipping his or her own coat.

Tactile Prompts   Two types of tactile prompts are described in the literature. A tactile prompt can mean touching a child somewhere on his or her body to signal for him or her to do something. For example, a teacher might touch a child on his or her shoulder for him or her to sit down during circle time. In addition, teachers may use objects as tactile prompts for giving information to a child about an activity. For example, a teacher might have a child touch a spoon as a reminder that mealtime is approaching. Although using objects is primarily associated with teaching children who are visually impaired (Chen, Friedman, & Calvello, 1990), using objects as tactile prompts may also be useful for children with low receptive language skills who need additional information in order to follow directions.

Spatial Prompts Noonan and McCormick described spatial prompts as "placing a stimulus in a location that increases the likelihood of a correct response" (2014, p. 121). Examples of spatial prompts in a classroom might include placing books on a child's circle spot or putting a spoon in a child's bowl to remind him or her to eat with it instead of his or her fingers.

Physical Prompts   There are times that all children need a more intense level of support to complete a task or solve a problem. In giving physical support, the teacher provides some type of physical assistance to a child (e.g., hand-over-hand assistance, holding the child's hand up the stairs, holding part of the materials a child is manipulating). As with all types of supports, differing levels of physical support can be provided. For example, if Sophie is first learning to use scissors, the teacher may put his or her hands on top of Sophie's hand to show her how the scissors work (full physical assistance). This support can be reduced over time so that Sophie receives less physical assistance from the teacher as she learns to use the scissors independently, thereby providing partial physical assistance. The teacher may change the intensity or pressure of the physical support so that the child is manipulating the scissors more by herself. In addition, the teacher may change where the physical support is provided. Instead of placing his or her hands directly on top of Sophie's hands, the teacher may move them more toward her wrists, allowing Sophie more independence. Whether changing the intensity or placement of the physical support, the teacher who gradually changes the physical support can still be ready to provide more support as the child needs it. It is critical that the teacher use only the highest level of physical prompt needed so that the child does not become too dependent on adult support. In some situations, a child might need physical support for some parts of a task and not for others. For example, if Emma needs assistance eating with a spoon, the teacher may need to provide physical assistance only when Emma is scooping the food onto the spoon. Emma may not need the support while bringing the spoon to her mouth and lowering the spoon; therefore, none should be provided. It should be noted that some children have tactile defensiveness and will have difficulty tolerating physical support. These children sometimes accept physical support better if hand-under-hand guidance is provided, in which the teacher guides children by having them put their hand on top of the teacher's hand.

Visual/Pictorial Prompts Pictorial prompts can be used to represent key components of a task through two-dimensional drawings or pictures. Teachers use them in early childhood programs to remind children of the steps of a task or activity that they do on a regular basis, such as brushing teeth or washing hands. Similarly, pictorial prompts can be used in the classroom to give children information about how to use materials within an activity (e.g., paints at paint easel), where to put materials (e.g., pictures on shelves), and promote appropriate social skills (e.g., rules with pictures for "helping hands" and "walking feet"). Pictorial prompts can also be helpful in assisting children in understanding the passage of time and the sequence of activities. Teachers may develop a pictorial representation of each activity in the daily routine (e.g., circle time, snack time, outdoor play) and sequence the pictures according to the daily schedule. Pictorial schedules can assist children who have difficulty with transitions by showing them the sequence of classroom activities and routines.

There are several advantages to using pictorial prompts to support a child's learning. First, pictorial prompts are supports that we use throughout life. For example, pictorial road signs give us information about what rules to follow while driving. In addition, pictorial cues can be used without the teacher being present. If the teacher is using pictorial prompts to show children how to use watercolors (e.g., put the brush in paint, paint, rinse the brush), then he or she can leave the art center and the children can continue to have assistance without the teacher being present. Given that there will be children at varying developmental levels, it is important that teachers maximize their resources so that all children are supported at an appropriate level. The use of pictorial prompts can assist with this. Finally, learning to make meaning of a symbolic form such as a picture is an important prerequisite to reading (Whitmore & Goodman, 1995). Teachers who use this type of support in their classrooms are promoting early literacy development. Teachers also can write words next to each picture so children are exposed to print.

Considerations   As previously mentioned, embedded learning opportunities are the preferred method of providing instruction to children in blended classrooms. Some children may need instruction that is more didactic in format, however, meaning that children are removed from ongoing classroom routines and activities for brief periods of time to receive some of their instruction. Examples of when this type of instruction might be needed are if a child is highly distractible, if a child is working on a specific skill that requires great focus, or if a child needs more opportunities to practice than might naturally occur in the ongoing classroom activities and routines. For example, the American Speech-Language-Hearing Association (2007) recommended that children who have apraxia receive short therapy sessions in a therapy room when learning verbal language. The practice of using embedded learning opportunities as the primary way of providing instruction in blended classrooms does not preclude didactic instruction for children who need it for short periods of time to teach some skills. It is important to note that we are not suggesting that all instruction be delivered in a didactic format for these children. Rather, teachers may combine didactic instruction and embedded learning opportunities, which supports the generalization of what is learned in didactic contexts.

Visual representations of learning opportunities related to targeted behaviors or standards can be created in order to plan embedded learning opportunities. These visual representations are referred to as *embedding schedules* (Johnson et al., 2015; see Figure 4.1). Across the top are the target behaviors that will be addressed for the child. Down the side are the activities that occur throughout the school day. The corresponding blocks (i.e., intersecting boxes) list examples of specific behaviors a child can demonstrate/practice within a designated activity.

In summary, the elements of embedded learning opportunities serve as the teaching sequence of all instructional strategies. First, a situation has to be created for a child or group of children to demonstrate an expected outcome. Second, the child or group of children will do something that may or may not be an expected outcome. Finally, based on what the

Classroom Embedding Schedule

Child's name: Kendall   Date: 4/28/16

Teacher's name: Ms. Ricard

Schedule of activities	Kendall's target behaviors		
	Write letters	**Manipulate objects**	**Retell stories**
Breakfast	Sign in at breakfast table.	Open milk carton and cereal container.	Discuss what he did the evening before at home.
Small group	Write letters in sensory materials (e.g., Gak). Sign name on artwork.	Button oversized shirt prior to messy activities.	Ask him to retell what he did at the end of the small-group activity.
Greeting circle	Sign up for a job for the day.	Help teacher put cassette tape in tape player.	Share important happenings in his life.
Centers/work time	Write out grocery list in dramatic play. Write letters at writing center or on computer.	Fasten dress-up clothes in dramatic play.	Act out and retell a story with puppets or flannel board figures.
Outdoor play	Write letters with sidewalk chalk.	Button/snap/zip coat before going out to play.	Discuss important happenings in his life on walk to playground.

Figure 4.1. Embedding schedule.

child or group of children does, the teacher provides feedback that supports or strengthens learning.

ADAPTATIONS AND MODIFICATIONS TO SUPPORT PARTICIPATION

In addition to providing prompts and cues to support children's learning, adaptations and modifications may be used across instructional tiers. The following section addresses four specific ways teachers can ensure full access and participation in classroom activities: 1) encourage peer support, 2) manipulate environmental variables, 3) adapt materials, and 4) utilize advances in technology. Sandall and Schwartz (2008) provided an even more comprehensive list of what they term *curriculum modifications* (see Table 4.1).

Table 4.1. Types of curriculum modifications

Modification type	Definition	Strategies
Environmental support	Altering the physical, social, and temporal environment to promote participation, engagement, and learning	Change the physical environment. Change the social environment. Change the temporal environment.
Materials adaptation	Modifying materials so that the child can participate as independently as possible	Have materials or equipment in the optimal position (e.g., height). Stabilize materials. Modify the response. Make the materials larger or brighter.
Simplification of the activity	Simplifying a complicated task by breaking it into smaller parts or reducing the number of steps	Break it down. Change or reduce the number of steps. Finish with success.
Use of child preferences	Identifying and integrating a child's preferences if he or she is not taking advantage of the available opportunities	Hold a favorite toy. Use a favorite activity. Use a favorite person.
Special equipment	Using special or adaptive devices that allow a child to participate or increase his or her level of participation	Use special equipment to increase access. Use special equipment to increase participation.
Adult support	Intervening to support the child's participation and learning	Model. Join the child's play. Use praise and encouragement.
Peer support	Utilizing peers to help children learn important objectives	Model. Have helpers. Use praise and encouragement.
Invisible support	Purposefully arranging naturally occurring events within one activity	Sequence turns. Sequence activities within a curriculum area.

From Sandall, S.R., & Schwartz, I.S. (with Joseph, G.E., Chou, H.-Y., Horn, E.M., Leiber, J., Odom, S.L., & Wolery, R.). (2002). *Building blocks for teaching preschoolers with special needs* (p. 46). Baltimore, MD: Paul H. Brookes Publishing Co.; adapted by permission.

Encourage Peer Support

Teachers often embrace the notion that young children can support one another's learning. This is central to Vygotsky's (1962) theory and a primary rationale for inclusive educational practices for children with and without disabilities (DEC, 2014; Sandall, Hemmeter, Smith, & McLean, 2005; Sandall, McLean, & Smith, 2000). We know, however, that peers often need assistance to actually support one another. Sometimes the structure of an activity can provide the opportunity for peers to learn from one another. Cooperative learning is a strategy in which all children work toward a common goal (Berk, 2005). Classroom activities are specifically designed so that children must work together to complete a project. This creates opportunities for more competent children to support children who may have difficulty with certain components of the task. It also enables each child's strengths to emerge because all skills will be needed in order to achieve desired outcomes.

Modeling is an important component in providing peer support. Too often, children who have developmental delays are viewed as the "babies" in the classroom. Young children view them as someone to do things to instead of someone to do things with. Successful peer support requires that instructional staff model appropriate interactions, including 1) giving a child the least amount of assistance he or she needs to be successful, 2) allowing the child to be as independent as possible, and 3) ensuring that the child is an active participant in all classroom activities and routines. Peers can learn to appropriately support one another in the presence of this type of modeling, along with verbal encouragement from the adults in the class.

Manipulate Environmental Variables

At times, teachers will need to modify aspects of the physical environment to support all children. Although some environmental supports might be obvious (e.g., adequate space for a child with a wheelchair to move around the room, braille choice boards for children with visual impairments), other environmental supports are less obvious but can often serve as an additional teacher if designed and used appropriately. This might include using individualized visual cues (e.g., visual schedule, visual choice board) for children who have difficulty following verbal directions, arranging the circle area to reduce distractions for children with attention issues, and providing visual role necklaces to help children play in the dramatic play center.

Adapt Materials

There are three types of materials that can be adapted to support learning of young children with special needs. First, teachers can adapt existing classroom materials so children with a variety of learning needs can use them. In addition, teachers can add simple, inexpensive materials to the environment to improve learning opportunities for children. For example, a teacher might develop a picture schedule of daily activities with objects relating to each activity in the day for a child who has a visual or cognitive impairment. Classroom supplies can easily be altered so that children with fine motor problems can use them. Hand grips can be placed over paintbrushes or markers so that they are easier to grasp. Paper can be taped or otherwise secured to the table for a child who has difficulty holding the paper down while drawing or painting. White paper can be placed on a contrasting black placemat for a child with a visual impairment to better see materials for an art activity. A piece of foam with tape can be placed on a computer mouse so that a child who cannot click a regular mouse can use a drawing software program to make a picture.

Second, teachers can purchase a wide variety of materials that are specially designed for children with special learning needs. First, there are a variety of types of equipment that can support a child's mobility. Some young children may use wheelchairs for mobility, whereas others may be learning to walk using a reverse walker. There are also many materials that help children develop self-feeding skills. Specially designed spoons that curve inward, scoop bowls with suction cups on the bottom, and nonslip placemats are helpful in supporting a child's independence in feeding. There are also materials to promote fine motor development, such as slant boards so children can secure paper in an upright fashion instead of horizontally. In addition, the American Printing House for the Blind develops numerous materials for children who are blind or have low vision. One such item is a light box; materials can be placed on the box so children can better see what they are doing while playing with manipulatives or art materials.

There is also specially designed equipment for children with disabilities to use on the playground. Elevated sand tables can be purchased so that a wheelchair can be placed underneath them. Adapted swings that provide trunk support also are available. In general, some children need adaptive seating or positioning equipment to participate in ongoing activities. Figure 4.2 shows a child sitting in an adaptive chair that provides him support during circle time. Many other pieces of equipment can be purchased, such as prone or supine standers for standing and corner chairs for sitting that provide children with adequate trunk support so they can better use their hands for many activities. Many of these devices, however, are very expensive. Care should be given to select materials that are likely to be used and that will not prevent positive interactions among children. For example, some seating equipment places children above or below table level, which makes it awkward for children to work together. Similarly, some equipment is extremely bulky and takes up large amounts of space in the classroom. Many communities have lending libraries from which adaptive materials can be borrowed. Trying out an expensive piece of equipment before purchasing it is always advised. In the event that this is not possible, careful team planning should occur to make sure that the appropriate piece of equipment is purchased and that it will, in fact, serve to support the child's learning.

Figure 4.2. Using adaptive equipment to promote children's engagement in ongoing activities and routines.

Utilize Advances in Technology

Technology can enhance the inclusion of young children with significant disabilities in early childhood programs. In general, technology can serve three purposes to support the learning of young children. First, it can assist children with motor impairments to gain access to the environment and materials and give them control over some aspect of their lives (Flaghouse Forum, 2011). It is essential that children have these opportunities because they learn by interacting with their environment. Adaptive switches can be used by children who have sensorimotor impairments so they can have those opportunities. Adaptive switches are microswitches that are very sensitive to touch and can be attached to battery-operated toys and electrical devices so that a child can have access to his or her environment. For example, a child can use an adaptive switch to move a battery-powered truck around the block area if he or she cannot do so with his or her hands. In addition, a child might be able to operate a tablet, such as an iPad, during a game of Freeze in opening circle. Adaptive switches can be used to create many learning opportunities for children who cannot otherwise interact with their environment.

Second, augmentative and alternative communication (AAC) systems can assist young children who have speech-language delays. Because pre-K-age children are still rapidly developing, it is often unwise to purchase the most expensive AAC system for a young child until the team is certain the child will need it in the long term. A team of professionals who specialize in working with children who have communication difficulties must make this decision. The most important function of an AAC device is that it enables a child to get his or her message across without getting frustrated. For example, if a child is having juice at the snack table and runs out, then he or she should have some way of asking for more. Similarly, if a child is playing in the block area and grows bored with the activity, then the child should have a way of letting others know that he or she would like to change activities. In the absence of having a way to express these important messages, a child might use his or her behavior to do so (e.g., throw a cup across the table, scatter blocks on the floor and disrupt others' play). The use of tablets, such as iPads, is becoming increasingly more common as an AAC device. iPads can be programmed based on the individual communication needs of each child.

Finally, many early childhood programs now have computers in the classroom to support the learning of basic concepts and to promote literacy. There are a variety of ways to ensure that children can use a computer. Some are relatively simple to use, whereas others are quite sophisticated and expensive. Some examples include 1) a touch screen so that the child can operate the computer through the computer monitor, 2) expanded keyboards that enable a child to respond to pictures or letters on large, over-sized keys, and 3) adaptive switches with switch interfaces so a child can activate computer programs with the single touch of a switch. An adult should facilitate computer instruction for all children and especially for children with special learning needs.

INSTRUCTIONAL TIERS

Instructional tiers refer to the different levels of support that occur in a blended classroom and are selected based on the needs of each child. Three instructional tiers represent different levels of intensity, frequency, and precision in their implementation (see Chapter 2). The tiers associated with the curriculum framework (i.e., universal, focused, and systematic instruction) will be described in detail in Chapters 5–7. Generally speaking, universal instruction is Tier 1 instruction, focused instruction is Tier 2 instruction, and systematic instruction is Tier 3 instruction. Universal instruction is the basis on which all other instruction is built and is appropriate for all children. In fact, some suggest that if high-quality universal instruction is implemented, then other types instruction will rarely be needed (Horn & Banerjee, 2009). Universal instruction includes high-quality interactions among teachers and children, a high-quality social and physical environment, and the implementation of the principles of universal design for learning. Focused instruction is designed to address the needs of some children in a program and includes the use of scaffolding strategies, small-group instruction, and peer-mediated strategies. Finally, systematic instruction is designed to support the individualized learning needs of children. Systematic instruction is intensive in nature and involves a set of highly pre-scribed procedures that will support children in learning priority skills.

The similarities and differences between the three types of instructional tiers as well as information about how to choose which tier of instruction to use are described in the following section.

Similarities

The three instructional tiers are similar in that prompts are used across all tiers, complete teaching sequences are necessary, instruction is intentional at all tiers, and data-driven decision making should occur across tiers. These similarities are described here.

Use of Prompts   Each of the prompts previously described are used in all three tiers. The frequency, precision, and extent to which prompts are individualized varies across tiers. Prompts in Tier 1 are used across the day for all children. For example, while asking children to stand from sitting in a circle time activity, the teacher may gesture for children to stand. Prompts in Tier 2 are used to provide additional support for small groups of children or an individual child. For example, if a small group of children are working on writing their name, then the teacher may model how to make each letter. Finally, prompts in Tier 3 are used in precise and systematic ways in accordance with specific instructional procedures. For example, if teaching a child to wash his or her hands, then the teacher may use a verbal prompt followed by a model and a physical prompt for each step of the task the child cannot perform.

Complete Teaching Sequence   Regardless of the type of instructional strategy, teachers need to deliver complete teaching sequences in order for children to receive necessary feedback on the respected response. As previously described, a complete teaching sequence includes an antecedent-behavior-consequence event. Teachers often do not complete the teaching sequence, which results in the child not getting practice on how to perform the skill. Consider the following scenario.

> *Ms. Savannah is trying to teach Ben to follow one-step directions. She asks Ben to put his artwork in his cubby during cleanup time. When he doesn't immediately get up from the art table and move toward his cubby, Ms. Savannah says more loudly, "Put your artwork in your cubby!" Again, Ben doesn't respond right away, so Ms. Savannah screams "Ben, put your artwork in your cubby now!" When Ben doesn't immediately respond, Ms. Savannah grabs the paper and puts it in Ben's cubby.*

Ms. Savannah uses a naturally occurring routine (i.e., cleanup time) as the context for working on an important outcome for Ben. She delivers the task request, yet she never completes the teaching sequence. Instead of waiting for Ben to respond, she continues to provide the same task request without providing any additional support. Finally, she ends up performing the task for Ben. In this book, we refer to this type of exchange as *not closing the teaching loop.* Ben does not have the opportunity to practice the skill because

Ms. Savannah does not provide the necessary support for Ben to follow the direction. Delivering complete teaching sequences is important for all tiers of instruction.

Intentionality   Teachers should be intentional about how they deliver instruction, regardless of the tier. It may have been sufficient in the past to say that "children learn through play" with no regard for what the children are learning as they play. With the accountability now evident in most early childhood programs (see Chapter 1), it has become necessary for teachers to be clear about how the activities they plan, materials they choose, grouping patterns they organize, and teaching strategies they implement affect children's outcomes. Epstein said that intentional teaching is "planful, thoughtful, and purposeful" and that teachers "use their knowledge, judgment, and expertise to organize learning experiences for children" and "act with specific outcomes and goals in mind for all domains of children's development and learning" (2014, p. 1). Although the outcomes will change and the instructional strategies will change in a tiered instructional model, teachers still have a responsibility for being clear about what they are teaching at each instructional tier.

Data-Driven Decision Making   Teachers need to gather, document, summarize, analyze, and interpret assessment information to inform instructional decisions across all tiers of instruction (Grisham-Brown & Pretti-Frontczak, 2011). Grisham-Brown and Pretti-Frontczak (2013) discussed three important reasons for engaging in data-driven decision making when implementing tiered instruction. First, data can help teachers know when children might need more intensive instruction. Second, data can help teachers modify instruction as it occurs. For example, if data show that a child is making many errors by impulsively responding before prompting is provided, the teacher might modify instruction to provide instructional prompts more quickly, eliminating the child's errors. Finally, data show teachers when children acquire identified outcomes so that new outcomes may be selected.

Differences

Figure 4.3 assists teachers in understanding the differences among universal, focused, and systematic instruction. First, moving from universal to systematic instruction implies that the teacher's (or other adults in the classroom) role changes as instruction changes. Bredekamp and Rosegrant (1992, 1995) first suggested that teacher behaviors should be conceptualized along a continuum and that those behaviors change from nondirective to *directive instruction*, defined as the amount and type of support that is provided to children. Not only do teachers provide more and different types of support moving up the instructional tiers, but they also do so with more precision and consistency. In fact, precision and consistency are necessary in order for targeted and systematic instruction to be successful in achieving positive outcomes for children (Odom, 2009; Odom et al., 2010). Third, teachers

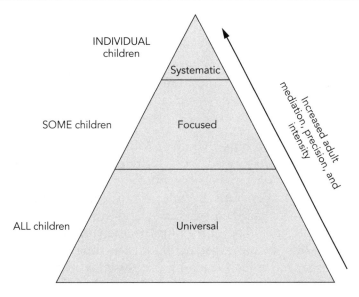

Figure 4.3. Tiered instruction.

provide instruction with greater intensity or frequency as they move up the tiers of instruction. As previously mentioned, the use of embedded learning opportunities is recommended, regardless of the tier of instruction. Although embedded learning opportunities occur with some regularity during universal instruction, they need to occur regularly, consistently, and with precision when systematic instruction is employed. Consider the following scenario, which highlights the difference between universal and systematic instruction.

All of the children in Miss Delmy's class need to learn to count. Therefore, Miss Delmy embeds learning opportunities for all children to count throughout the day. The children count the steps leading toward the playground. They count the number of friends present at school each day, and they count the number of crackers on their plate at snack. These naturally occurring embedded learning opportunities result in the majority of the children in the class learning to count. Counting is meaningless for Willi, however, who cannot follow simple directions or understand the concept of counting. Therefore, Miss Delmy provides additional opportunities for Willi to learn to follow one-step directions. She asks him to walk up the steps of the slide ladder and to put crackers on his plate at snack. After providing the one-step direction, Miss Delmy waits for 3 seconds for Willi to respond. If he responds correctly, then she uses descriptive verbal praise to reinforce him. If he does not respond in 3 seconds, then Miss Delmy provides partial physical prompts so that he can perform the action associated with the one-step direction. Miss Delmy creates 10 opportunities a day for Willi to follow one-step directions and consistently follows the systematic instruction plan she developed for teaching him this important skill.

Considerations for Selecting Instructional Tiers

Three issues should be considered when implementing tiered instruction: 1) understanding the relationship between the tier of instruction selected and the outcome taught, 2) the importance of selecting strategies that have an evidence base for the outcome being taught, and 3) the cumulative nature of tiered instruction.

Relationship to Outcome   Chapter 3 discussed three different types of outcomes—common, targeted, and individualized. Generally speaking, the instructional tiers match the outcome. In other words, universal instruction should generally be selected to teach common outcomes, focused instruction for targeted outcomes, and systematic instruction for individualized outcomes. The curriculum framework, however, does not preclude the use of systematic instruction for teaching common outcomes. For example, enhanced milieu teaching (i.e., systematic instruction) might be used to support ongoing interactions among all children in the classroom (i.e., common outcome). The match between outcome and instructional tier, however, is recommended for decision-making purposes. The idea of matching outcome and instruction has long been recommended as an approach for making decisions about instruction. Wolery and Wilbers (1994) indicated that highly individualized or specific outcomes (i.e., individualized outcomes) are better matched with instructional strategies that require a great deal of adult mediation. Yet, instructional strategies requiring less adult mediation are better matched with more general outcomes (i.e., common outcomes).

Evidence Base   Identifying strategies that result in children learning skills in specific areas of development or content areas is a second consideration for selecting instructional strategies. More specifically, teachers need to consider strategies that have an evidence base for teaching skills that are both effective and efficient. Strategies are effective when children learn important outcomes when they are used. Strategies are efficient when children learn skills quickly and with few errors. The evidence base for instructional strategies associated with each tier is described in Chapters 6–8.

Cumulative Nature of Tiered Instruction   Strategies at Tier 1 serve as the foundation for all other instructional tiers in any tiered model (e.g., Pyramid Model, Building Blocks). If a child needs Tier 2 support, that support is added to what the child is receiving in a high-quality universal curriculum. Similarly, if a child needs Tier 3 instruction, he or she continues receiving instruction in a high-quality universal curriculum as well as focused instruction, as needed. It is also important to remember that children are not tiers. For example, it is possible for a child to need Tier 3 instruction in one area (e.g., social-emotional) and have the capacity to learn skills in other areas with universal instruction.

SUMMARY

This chapter described the practices that are foundational to high-quality instruction, including differentiating instruction, being aware of the child's zone of proximal development, making data-driven decisions about intentional instruction, and embedding learning opportunities. Tiered instruction was introduced, with the similarities and differences between Tier 1 (universal), Tier 2 (focused), and Tier 3 (systematic) instruction discussed.

Each instructional tier is described in detail in Chapters 5–7. We will use the Intentional Instructional Sequence (IIS) decision-making process described by Pretti-Frontczak and Grisham-Brown (2012) to show the relationship between the instructional tiers. The process includes five components of planning that are essential for designing instruction for all children: 1) what to teach, 2) when to teach, 3) where to teach, 4) with what to teach, and 5) how to teach. *What* to teach refers to common, targeted, and individualized outcomes that we teach children (see Chapter 3). *When* to teach refers to the time of day instruction will occur and can include planned activities such as reading children a book and doing music/movement activities associated with the book. Instruction can also occur during routine activities such as mealtime, washing hands, or arrival/departure. After determining when to provide instruction, teachers must decide *where* to teach. Possible classroom locations might include interest centers, the playground, or the cafeteria. *With what* to provide instruction refers to those materials that are necessary to elicit identified outcomes and can include art materials, blocks, gadgets and tools, loose parts, and sensory materials. Finally, teachers must make decisions about *how* to teach children. As previously mentioned, instructional practices generally lend themselves to teaching specific outcome types. Figure 4.4 is a planning form that shows all five elements of an IIS for universal, focused, and systematic instruction (a reproducible form can be found in Appendix 4A). Examples of how to complete the planning form for each tier are provided in Chapters 5–7.

Intentional Instructional Sequence Planning Form

Outcome	When	Where	With what	How to teach		Progress monitoring
Common outcome(s)				Instructional strategy (universal)	Feedback	
Targeted outcome(s)				Instructional strategy (focused)	Feedback	
Individualized outcome(s)				Antecedent Instructional strategy (systematic)	Behavior (individualized outcome) / Consequences	

Figure 4.4. Intentional Instructional Sequence Planning Form. (From Pretti-Frontczak, K., & Grisham-Brown, J. [2012]. *Manual for designing and delivering intentional instruction.* Brooklyn, NY: B2K Solutions; adapted by permission.)

LEARNING ACTIVITIES

1. Schedule a visit to an inclusive pre-K classroom. Ask the teacher to share some of the children's target skills with you. As you observe, determine when, where, and how the teacher embeds the target skills into the curriculum of the class. Keep an observational log of what a child's target skill is, how the child was given learning opportunities to practice the skill, and what the outcome was (i.e., Did the child engage in the activity? How long was the child engaged in the activity?).

2. Why is planning for instruction a crucial part of creating a context in which all children can have multiple learning opportunities?

3. Observe a blended classroom for 2 hours. List all of the prompts that are used to support the children in the classroom. Next to the type, give an example of the prompt that you saw or heard. In addition, list any adaptations or modifications that you saw. Consider the following modifications and adaptations: environmental supports, utilizing peer support, adapting materials, and utilizing advances in technology.

REFERENCES

American Speech-Language-Hearing Association. (2007). *Scope of practice in speech-language pathology* [Scope of practice]. Available from http://www.asha.org/policy

Berk, L.E. (2005). *Child development* (7th ed.). Needham, MA: Allyn & Bacon.

Berk, L.E., & Winsler, A. (1995). *Scaffolding children's learning: Vygotsky and early childhood education*. Washington, DC: National Association for the Education of Young Children.

Bredekamp, S., & Rosegrant, T. (1992). *Reaching potentials: Appropriate curriculum and assessment for young children* (Vol. 1). Washington, DC: National Association for the Education of Young Children.

Bredekamp, S., & Rosegrant, T. (1995). *Reaching potentials: Transforming early childhood curriculum and assessment* (Vol. 2). Washington, DC: National Association for the Education of Young Children.

Chen, D., Friedman, C.T., & Calvello, G. (1990). *Learning together: A parent guide to socially based routines for visually impaired infants*. Louisville, KY: American Printing House for the Blind.

Cook, R.E., Klein, M.D., Tessier, A., & Daley, S.E. (2011). *Adapting early childhood curricula for children in inclusive settings* (8th ed.). Upper Saddle River, NJ: Pearson Education.

Copple, C., & Bredekamp, S. (Eds.). (2009). *Developmentally appropriate practices in early childhood programs servicing children birth to age 8*. Washington, DC: National Association for the Education of Young Children.

Division for Early Childhood. (2014). *DEC recommended practices in early intervention/early childhood special education 2014*. Retrieved from http://www.dec-sped.org/recommendedpractices

Epstein, A.S. (2014). *The intentional teaching: Choosing the best strategies for young children's learning*. Washington, DC: National Association for the Education of Young Children.

Flaghouse Forum. (2011, July). Ability switches: The nuts and the bolts. *Exceptional Parent, 41*(7), 30–31.

Fullerton, E.K., Conroy, M.A., & Correa, V.I. (2009). Early childhood teachers' use of specific praise statements with young children at risk for behavioral disorders. *Behavioral Disorders, 34*(3), 118–135.

Gestwicki, C. (2014). *Developmentally appropriate practice: Curriculum and development in early education* (5th ed.). Albany, NY: Delmar.

Grisham-Brown, J., & Pretti-Frontczak, K. (2011). *Assessing young children in inclusive settings: The blended practices approach*. Baltimore, MD: Paul H. Brookes Publishing Co.

Grisham-Brown, J., & Pretti-Frontczak, K. (2013). A curriculum framework for supporting young children served in blended programs. In V. Buysse, E.S. Peisner-Feinberg, & H.P. Ginsburg (Eds.), *Handbook of response to intervention in early childhood*. Baltimore: Paul H. Brookes Publishing Co.

Horn, E., & Banerjee, R. (2009). Understanding curriculum modifications and embedded learning opportunities in the context of supporting all children's success. *Language, Speech, and Hearing Services in Schools, 40,* 406–415.

Howard, V.F., Williams, B.F., Port, P.D., & Lepper, C. (2001). *Very young children with special needs: A formative approach to the 21st century* (2nd ed.). Upper Saddle River, NJ: Pearson Education.

Jackson, S., Harjusola-Webb, S., Pretti-Frontczak, K., Grisham-Brown, J., & Romani, J.M. (2009). Response to intervention: Implications for early childhood professionals. *Language, Speech, and Hearing Services in Schools, 40,* 1–11.

Johnson, J., Rahn, N.L., & Bricker, D. (2015). *An activity-based approach to early intervention* (4th ed.). Baltimore, MD: Paul H. Brookes Publishing Co.

Kohn, A. (1999). *Punishment by rewards: The trouble with gold stars, incentive plans, A's, praise, and other bribes*. Boston, MA: Houghton Mifflin.

Noonan, M.J., & McCormick, L. (2014). *Teaching young children with disabilities in natural environments* (2nd ed.). Baltimore, MD: Paul H. Brookes Publishing Co.

Odom, S.L. (2009). Evidence-based practice, implementation science, and outcomes for children. *Topics in Early Childhood Special Education, 29*(1), 53–61.

Odom, S.L., Fleming, K., Diamond, K., Lieber, J., Hanson, M., Butera, G.,...Marquis, J. (2010). Examining different forms of implementation and in early childhood curriculum research. *Early Childhood Research Quarterly, 25,* 314–328.

Pretti-Frontczak, K., & Grisham-Brown, J. (2012). *Manual for designing and delivering intentional instruction*. Brooklyn, NY: B2K Solutions.

Pretti-Frontczak, K., Grisham-Brown, J., Hawkins, S.R., & Jackson, S. (2013). An activity-based approach to intervention:

Meeting the diverse needs of young children with special needs. In J. Yuen, K. Lyen, K. Poon, L. Hin, & M. Pathnapuram (Eds.), *Rainbow dreams: A holistic approach to helping children with special needs* (3rd ed., pp. 209–223). Singapore: Rainbow Centre.

Sandall, S., Hemmeter, M.L., Smith, B.J., & McLean, M. (2005). *DEC recommended practices: A comprehensive guide.* Longmont, CO: Sopris West Educational Services.

Sandall, S.R., & Schwartz, I.S. (2008). *Building blocks for teaching preschoolers with special needs* (2nd ed.). Baltimore, MD: Paul H. Brookes Publishing Co.

Sulzer-Azaroff, B. (1992). Is back to nature always best? *Journal of Applied Behavior Analysis, 25,* 81–82.

Vygotsky, L.S. (1962). *Thought and language.* Cambridge, MA: The MIT Press.

Vygotsky, L.S. (1978). *Mind in society: The development of higher psychological processes.* Cambridge, MA: Harvard University Press.

Whitmore, K.F., & Goodman, Y.M. (1995). Transforming curriculum in language and literacy. In S. Bredekamp & T. Rosegrant (Eds.), *Reaching potentials: Appropriate curriculum and assessment for young children* (Vol 1., pp. 145–166). Washington, DC: National Association for the Education of Young Children.

Wolery, M., & Wilbers, J.S. (1994). Introduction to the inclusion of young children with special needs in early childhood programs. In M. Wolery & J.S. Wilbers (Eds.), *Including children with special needs in early childhood programs* (pp. 1–22). Washington, DC: National Association for the Education of Young Children.

APPENDIX 4A

Intentional Instructional Sequence Planning Form

Outcome	When	Where	With what	How to teach		Progress monitoring
				Instructional strategy (universal)	Feedback	
Common outcome(s)						

Outcome	When	Where	With what	How to teach		Progress monitoring
				Instructional strategy (focused)	Feedback	
Targeted outcome(s)						

89

APPENDIX 4A   **Intentional Instructional Sequence Planning Form** *(continued)*

Outcome	When	Where	With what	How to teach			Progress monitoring
				Antecedent Instructional strategy (systematic)	Behavior (individualized outcome)	Consequences	
Individualized outcome(s)							

Tiered Instruction

## CHAPTER 5

Universal Instructional Practices

Mary Louise Hemmeter and Jennifer Grisham-Brown

Ms. Wu's inclusive prekindergarten classroom is located in an elementary school. She has 16 children in her classroom. Twelve of the children are at risk, and four have identified disabilities. Two of the children who are at risk are also English language learners. The classroom curriculum is linked to the state's early learning standards. On one particular day, the children are working on an ongoing project about form and function. This unit has been planned around early learning standards related to science, math, language, social-emotional, and literacy. Four children, including one with autism, are building toys from recyclable objects. Two are creating a ball and scoop game with old milk jugs, and two are using water bottles to make pins for bowling. Another group is outside testing balls of different sizes and materials (e.g., Styrofoam, rubber, crumpled paper) to determine which ones work best for playing with the ball and scoop and for knocking down their bowling pins. Two children are talking about a chair that broke in the classroom and are thinking of ways they might fix the crack in it using different kinds of tape or glue. The rest of the children are planning a game day when they will invite the children from another class to come over and play with all of the toys they've made. Mr. Lambert (the classroom assistant), Kiersten and Alex (parent volunteers), and Chelsea (the student teacher) are each engaged with one of the groups of children. Mr. Lambert is outside with the children who are working with balls of different materials. Indigo assists Buck, a young boy in a wheelchair who is trying to knock down the bowling pins with a rubber ball, and Kiersten is helping Cameron understand the process by showing him a set of pictures that help explain what they are doing. Inside, Chelsea is in the hall asking the children to suggest materials they will need to design their display that will go up in the hall to tell people about game day and show teachers, families, and others what they have been working on. Alex is working with the group of children in the classroom while Ms. Wu is circulating around observing the children, collecting data on child outcomes, and assisting children and adults as needed.

In this scenario, all children are engaged, teachers and parent volunteers are busy interacting with children, and the overall climate of the classroom is positive. It is no accident that this classroom is running so smoothly and that children with disabilities are participating alongside their peers in meaningful ways; rather, it is the result of careful planning on the part of the teacher and other classroom staff. The teachers have used the children's interests and needs to plan activities that are engaging and appropriately challenging for all children. This chapter describes universal practices for creating a classroom where all children are meaningfully included in activities and routines alongside their peers.

Universal practices are implemented for a number of reasons. First, these practices are designed to ensure that all children have access to a general education curriculum. These practices provide a developmentally appropriate, engaging environment in which more focused and systematic support can be provided for individual children who have varying levels of need. Second, universal practices are designed to support common outcomes (see Chapter 3). Universal practices are generally designed to address state early learning guidelines or some other set of standards that are used to guide early childhood education (ECE) settings. Ms. Wu uses her state's early learning guidelines in planning classroom activities. Third, universal practices are used to provide exposure to important content and learning opportunities for all children throughout the day. Universal practices are happening all of the time. Universal practices might be not be obvious in some cases (e.g., environmental arrangement); however, they are intentionally planned and designed.

It will be necessary to plan for and provide individualized supports based on each child's unique needs and abilities to ensure that all children can fully participate in the classroom. Universal design for learning (UDL) is a way to promote access and participation (Campbell & Milbourne, 2014; Center for Applied Special Technology [CAST], 2006; Conn-Powers, Cross, Traub, & Hutter-Pishgahi, 2006; Horn & Banerjee, 2009). UDL involves designing classroom environments to address a range of abilities and needs by incorporating flexible goals, opportunities to respond, and ways to be engaged, as well as a variety of materials, methods, and strategies (Conn-Powers et al., 2006). Early childhood teachers have traditionally focused on making modifications or adaptations to environments that have been designed primarily for typically developing children. UDL is a more efficient way of designing environments to support all children (Horn & Banerjee, 2009). The classroom described in the opening vignette has been designed based on UDL principles. This chapter uses the principles of UDL to describe how to create a classroom environment that is both appropriate for all young children and provides a context for more targeted and individualized instruction to occur. This chapter will focus on the UDL principles related to the physical and social environment as well as those that guide the organization of learning opportunities. We will describe three general categories of universal practices: 1) organizing the learning environment, 2) setting up the social environment and delivering instruction, and 3) creating strategies for developing and planning the content of instruction.

ORGANIZING THE LEARNING ENVIRONMENT

This section describes strategies for designing the physical and temporal aspects of the environment so that all children have opportunities to be full participants in classroom activities and routines. This section specifically addresses creating the daily schedule, including routines, activities, and transitions; designing the learning environment; and developing and promoting classroom expectations.

Designing a Schedule to Meet the Needs of All Children

The classroom schedule is an essential component of effective early childhood environments. A well-designed and well-implemented schedule promotes children's engagement, teaches children to be independent, helps them anticipate transitions, and prevents challenging behaviors (Hemmeter, Ostrosky, & Corso, 2012; Lawry, Danko, & Strain, 1999; Strain & Hemmeter, 1997). *Engagement* refers to "the time children spend interacting in a developmentally and contextually appropriate manner" (McWilliam & Bailey, 1995, p. 123). Engagement can include playing with toys, working with materials, interacting with peers, observing what others are doing related to the activity, or attending to someone who is talking or teaching. A number of issues should be considered when designing classroom schedules, including the number of children in the class, the age of the children, the number of adults available during different times of the day (i.e., staffing patterns), the length of the school day, and the best learning times for the children (i.e., when they are most alert and attentive). The following sections provide guidelines for developing and implementing schedules to ensure that all children are engaged in meaningful learning experiences.

Balance the Type and Structure of Activities   It is important to balance the type of activities along a number of different dimensions when designing a schedule. First, schedules should have a balance of child- and teacher-directed activities. Both types of activities serve important purposes, and the goal in designing a schedule is to maximize the time children spend engaged in activities and reduce the transition time spent between activities. Teachers should also consider children's attention spans and plan the balance of teacher-directed and child-chosen activities accordingly. For example, if children are not yet able to play independently and rely on adult guidance and interactions to sustain their interests, then free play or free choice should be scheduled at a time when the most adults are present. Second, schedules should have a balance in terms of the children's activity levels. In designing a schedule, it is important to ensure not only that children have opportunities to be active each day but also that these opportunities are scheduled at times of the day when children are likely to need a break from the structure of other activities. For example, if children spend much of the morning in opening circle, centers, and structured work time, then an opportunity for gross motor play, outdoor play, or free play with opportunities for higher activity levels should be scheduled before children are asked to participate again in a more structured activity such as teacher-directed small-group or buddy reading.

Attend to the Length of Activities   The age and attention spans of the children and how these relate to the duration of activities should be a key consideration in planning a classroom schedule. It will be important to minimize the length of some activities, particularly large-group activities in which all children are participating at the same time, especially at the beginning of the year (Lawry et al., 1999). The length will depend on the age of the child and the extent to which the activity is engaging and allows for high levels of child participation. Typically, the younger the children, the shorter the activity, with the caution that children of all ages need enough time to become engaged and fully participate and that teachers should change activities when children appear to be bored or uninterested. Furthermore, large-group activities should be scheduled at a time when an extra adult is available to support children who can't sit at circle as long as the rest of the group. Some activities, such as center time, may last significantly longer given that children are often encouraged to move from center to center as they wish and direct how they participate and interact with various materials, peers, and adults. This does not, however, mean that center time activities should not be structured or planned. It is important to remember that low levels of engagement are likely to result if activities are not well planned, regardless of whether an activity is child- or teacher-directed, whereas careful planning increases children's interests, involvement, and the number and type of learning opportunities that can be presented. Activities in which teachers are available to support children's engagement and provide ample choices and materials are appropriately challenging and interesting to all children should take up a significant portion of the classroom schedule (Copple & Bredekamp, 2009; Pretti-Frontczak & Bricker, 2004).

Implement the Schedule Consistently   The schedule must be implemented consistently for children to learn it. When schedules change from day to day, children do not learn the routine and are less likely to learn to anticipate what happens next. For example, if on Mondays and Tuesdays the children go outside after center time, on Wednesdays they go to music after center time, and on Thursdays and Fridays it varies, then they may be confused as to what they do next. This confusion can lead to challenging behavior. Children can learn what happens next and can anticipate what they should do to get ready when a schedule is implemented consistently. It is also easier to prepare children for changes in the schedule when it is implemented consistently.

> The children in Ms. Janey's class go outside every day after circle time. Today, however, a special friend is coming to visit after circle time. A chef from a local restaurant is coming to show the children how to make pasta. Ms. Janey knows that she must prepare the children for this change so they won't be disappointed that they don't get to go outside. Ms. Janey explains the change several days ahead of the chef's visit by reviewing the daily schedule, showing the children a picture of the chef, and asking them to tell her what they will do different that day. She puts a stop sign on top of the center icon on Phillip's individual picture schedule and talks to him about what the stop sign means that day. On the day that the chef is coming, Phillip comes to opening group with his picture schedule and shows the other children when in the schedule the chef is coming. Another child says, "Yeah, that means that today after circle we line up at the door so we can go to the kitchen." The children in Ms. Janey's class understand the change and are prepared for what that means.

Minimize and Plan for Transitions   Transitions between activities can be especially problematic. Too many transitions, transitions without adequate and appropriate warnings, and transitions that require children to wait with nothing to do can lead to challenging behavior. Three strategies can be used to minimize the problems associated with transitions and increase the likelihood that children will make the transition independently and that time spent in transition will be minimized (Hemmeter, Ostrosky, Artman, & Kinder, 2008). First, minimize the number of transitions in which all children have to make the transition at the same time. This can be done by 1) allowing children to go to the bathroom as they need to rather than going as a whole group, 2) including activities such as snack as a choice during centers rather than as a separate activity that requires all children to make the transition at the same time, and 3) allowing children to move between activities independently (e.g., individual children can move between activities as they finish rather than having to wait for the whole group to finish). Second, when all children have to make a transition at the same time, the teacher should be prepared with an engaging activity for those children who make the transition quickly and are waiting for the other children (e.g., have children sing a song, do a quick finger play, have books available to read while waiting). In addition, the teacher could pair children up as buddies to help each other make the transition. Finally, prepare children for transitions by giving them a warning. Warnings can be given in a variety of ways, including verbal signals, music, or blinking of lights. Some children, however, might need more individualized warnings such as a tap on the shoulder, a pictorial cue, or a peer buddy to help them through the transition.

Use Routines and Transitions as Opportunities for Teaching   Even in classrooms in which transitions are minimized, children will likely spend a significant amount of time either in transition or in routine activities such as eating, cleaning up, going to the bathroom, and washing hands. Adults can use these times as opportunities for teaching. Not only can self-help skills (e.g., washing hands, brushing teeth) be taught during transitions and routines, but these activities also provide an opportunity to teach skills from other content areas (e.g., literacy, math, language, communication). For example, children can be taught to make choices (e.g., kind of soap, color of cup), request materials (e.g., paper towels, food, drink), help a friend (e.g., help a friend get the paper towels to dry his or her hands, hold the door open for a friend who uses a wheelchair, show a friend how to hang his or her coat in his or her cubby), solve a problem (e.g., "Oh, no, there are not enough napkins. What can we do?"), or sort objects (e.g., sort dishes by clean versus dirty). This is also a good time to embed instruction on children's individualized education program goals and objectives. For example, if Collin is working on using two-word utterances, then the teacher can embed language intervention strategies to promote the use of two-word utterances that are relevant to the transition.

Teach the Schedule and Expectations   A key to successful schedules is the extent to which children are taught the schedule and the expectations for their behavior during each activity and transition (Campbell & Milbourne, 2014; Hemmeter et al., 2012; Lawry et al., 1999). Children should be taught the schedule and the routines within the schedule to promote independence and help children understand routines. The children are not likely to know the schedule during the first week of school and may need a lot of support to get from one activity to another. They learn the routine and the expectations over time. Many children can learn the schedule, routines, and expectations in a relatively short period of time if the schedule is consistently implemented and if the teacher is proactive in teaching the schedule and expectations. This can be done by reviewing the schedule each morning or using visual prompts or cues that help each child understand (Kimball, Kinney, Taylor, & Stromer, 2003). Visuals might include pictures of the activities, a picture schedule, or materials that represent the activity (e.g., a crayon to represent the art center, a block to represent the block center, a microscope to represent the science center). The children can assist with the development of the visual schedule by taking photographs or selecting pictures that will help them remember the activity. Figure 5.1 is an example of a visual display of the class schedule. The teacher must also

Figure 5.1.   Visual schedule.

address expectations for children during the various activities. Teaching about the schedule and the expectations should involve teacher explanation, visual reminders, opportunities for children to discuss the schedule and expectations, and feedback to the children. Although some children will learn the daily routines with minimal assistance, some children will need more intentional teaching to learn the routine, including using visuals, providing a child with an individual picture schedule, providing a peer buddy to help the children participate in the daily routine, and delivering systematic instruction. Figure 5.2 provides examples of visuals that might be used to provide more support to children who need it.

Figure 5.2. Examples of visuals for individual children. (continued)

Figure 5.2. *(continued)*

Designing Learning Centers and Selecting Materials

Early childhood environments often are structured around learning centers. Learning centers provide natural opportunities for promoting children's independence, choice making, acquisition of new skills, and social interactions. They also provide a context in which skills across content and developmental areas (e.g., math, science, language, literacy, social-emotional) can be integrated. Furthermore, teachers can embed learning opportunities across a range of ability levels within any given learning center. Learning centers can be used to incorporate a variety of child preferences in terms of activities and materials. Learning centers must be systematically designed and planned in order to be effective, however (like all other aspects of the learning environment). Several issues should be considered when designing learning centers in order to maximize the effectiveness of the centers in terms of promoting children's engagement and acquisition and generalization of skills.

Integration of Skills   One of the primary benefits of learning centers is that they can be used to promote children's growth and development across content areas. For example, children can integrate their knowledge about science and literacy in the same activity while also working on fine motor skills and learning to interact with other children. It is important to have materials that promote skills across areas within each learning center in order for this integration to happen. For example, in a dramatic play area that is designed to be a restaurant, there might be materials that promote science-related skills (e.g., measuring, quantifying), writing skills (e.g., taking orders, writing down a recipe), reading (e.g., reading a menu or a magazine while waiting for a table), and social skills (e.g., taking someone's order, eating a meal with a friend). Although a classroom might have a reading and writing center, there can also be reading and writing materials in other centers that relate specifically to those centers. For example, there might be books about roads or buildings in the block area, books about experiments in the science center, and writing materials in the listening center.

Consider Children's Interests and Abilities When Designing Learning Centers   Three issues should be considered when designing learning centers. First, learning centers provide an ideal way to ensure that children's individual interests are addressed. Materials that are highly engaging to an individual child can be included in learning centers along with materials that are engaging to the majority of the children. For example, Noah is a young boy who loves trains and has difficulty engaging with other materials. Trains might be added where appropriate in order to promote his engagement in a variety of centers. Trains could be added to the block center (e.g., build a track for the train), science center (e.g., measure the size of the trains, compare how fast different trains go), or to the dramatic play center that is currently a toy store. Learning centers also provide a context for ensuring that issues of diversity are addressed throughout the classroom. For example, books can be selected that reflect different ethnic groups, child characteristics, and family compositions; dramatic play materials can be included that represent different professions; and activities can be selected that represent different ability levels. Second, in combination with teacher support, children's differing ability levels can be addressed through the presence of different types of materials (e.g., simple puzzles versus puzzles with interlocking pieces, markers that have modified grips alongside markers with typical grips). Finally, teachers should carefully select materials that can be used to teach specific skills to increase opportunities for teaching new skills in the context of learning centers. For example, if children are learning about rhyming words, materials that relate to rhyming can be incorporated into the learning centers, including books about rhyming, posters of rhyming words that relate to the learning center, materials that have rhyming names, and rhyming games.

Ensure that All Learning Centers Are Engaging   Children often want to use the same center at the same time in many preschool classrooms. Although this can be addressed through limiting the number of children in a learning center, a more proactive approach would be to increase the interest level of other centers, which can be accomplished in a number of ways. First, rotate materials in and out of centers. The center itself may not change, but new toys or materials can be added to attract interest. For example, the discovery center might always have some materials for experiments, but the specific experiment may change as the children learn the concepts associated with the experiment or as they lose interest in the experiment. This also is important in terms of addressing the progressing skill levels of children. Letting children help decide what goes on in a center is a second way to ensure interest in all centers. The teacher can review a center and its purpose during a large- or small-group activity and ask the children to think about new things that could go in that center. Finally, some centers may need to change entirely over the course of the year. For example, the dramatic play area might have a grocery store theme at the beginning of the year but might change based on children's interests and current events in the children's lives. It might become a post office, a pizza restaurant, or a campground.

Teach Children About the Centers and Expectations   A key ingredient in terms of the effectiveness of learning centers is the extent to which the children are taught about the content of the centers and the behavior expectations during times they are engaged in learning centers. Children can be taught about the learning centers and expectations in the context of group time and while actually engaged in learning centers. Pictures of centers, materials from centers, or a tour of centers can be used to teach children about what is in the centers and the kinds of things they can do at each center. During small group, the teacher could lead a discussion and some role-play around the roles for the new dramatic play area. All children will need to be taught the expectations for their behavior during center time, including making choices, how many children can be in a center at a given time, how the classroom expectations apply to centers, whether materials should be kept in the center in which they are located, how to clean up at the end of center time, and how to play with others. Although group instruction related to these expectations might work for some children, others will need more individualized teaching and supports to meaningfully engage in centers. For example, a child with autism might need a set of pictures of the centers to help him or her decide what center to go to first. Another child might need a teacher or peer to help him or her learn what to do in a specific center. The key to effective center time will be that children are given the level of support they need to engage in the centers in a meaningful way.

SETTING UP THE SOCIAL ENVIRONMENT AND DELIVERING INSTRUCTION

This section describes strategies for setting up the social environment and delivering instruction, including how teachers build relationships with children, create a classroom community, design learning activities, and deliver instruction. Because this chapter focuses on universal practices, the instructional procedures and strategies described in this section are designed to promote the engagement and learning of all children toward common outcomes.

Building Relationships

Adult–child interactions and relationships are powerful tools for working with young children. Establishing a close, nurturing relationship with each individual child in their care is one of the single most important things teachers can do (Hyson, 2004, 2008). These relationships set the stage for children's success by providing a secure foundation for emotional development (Dombro, Jablon, & Stetson, 2011; Hyson, 2004; Shonkoff & Phillips, 2000). Relationships provide a context for the child to learn about his or her feelings and the feelings of others and to develop self-confidence and self-esteem. Children learn about the effect of their behaviors on others and begin to understand that their behavior gives them some control over their environment. These relationships are an important foundation for the teaching and learning processes. Children are willing to take chances and learn new things in the context of supportive relationships. Many strategies can be used to build relationships with children, including having one-to-one authentic conversations with the child, talking to the child about his or her family, giving the child real choices, being on the child's level, acknowledging the child's efforts, being responsive to the child, and laughing with the child. Many of the teaching strategies that are discussed later in this chapter are also useful in building relationships.

Although the importance of relationships may seem obvious, it is often difficult to establish supportive relationships with every child either because of individual child characteristics or because of the sheer demands of running a classroom of active, eager young children. A child who needs these relationships the most is often the least likely to have access to them. For example, children with the most challenging behaviors would benefit greatly from ongoing, positive interactions with adults and peers, but their behaviors often interfere with the interactions that lead to these types of relationships. Teachers may respond to a child with persistently challenging behavior only when he or she is engaging in challenging behavior, and other children may avoid the child because they are afraid of the child or his or her behaviors. Adults may not pay attention to the child when he or she is engaged in appropriate behavior because they want to avoid further challenging behavior. Thus, this child has very few opportunities to learn from positive interactions. Relationship building may be more difficult with children who are nonverbal, have autism, or are more introverted. Teachers will need to be intentional about ensuring that they have meaningful relationships with all children in their classroom.

In addition to teacher–child relationships, relationships with families and relationships with colleagues are foundational to the provision of high-quality inclusive programs. These relationships will be critical to effective teaming around planning and implementing instruction. Adult–adult relationships are covered in detail in Chapter 8.

Creating a Sense of Community

It is important at the universal level to create a community of children in which everyone feels like he or she belongs. This goes beyond the development of the physical environment. Adult–child relationships previously described are an important component of creating a sense of community. Strategies that support community building within ECE classrooms include planning activities for children to work together, posting children's work and pictures of children's families in the classroom, having expectations that promote community (e.g., be a team player, be helpful), having celebrations for individual children and the whole class, teaching social problem solving, and identifying authentic and meaningful jobs (e.g., watering the plants) that children can do that help the classroom. In addition, the teacher's behavior toward children, colleagues, and families will also contribute to the sense of community. For example, how classroom staff work together provides a model for how children should work together. How teachers talk to families demonstrates to children that the teacher cares about their family. These strategies create a more positive context for learning.

Designing Classroom Activities

Teaching can and should occur throughout the day and across activities and environments in order to promote the use of skills in the contexts in which they are needed. Teachers must carefully plan activities and experiences to maximize the naturally occurring opportunities for instruction. The characteristics of different activities and experiences that should be considered when planning instruction include types of activity and composition of groups.

Types of Activities   Three types of activities occur across a typical preschool classroom schedule: 1) child-directed activities, 2) teacher-directed or planned activities, and 3) routine activities (Johnson, Rahn, & Bricker, 2015). Child-directed activities are those in which children can make choices about what they do, whom they play with, how long they do activities, and what kinds of materials they use. These activities typically include centers, free play, and outdoor play. Child-directed activities provide numerous learning opportunities related to individual children's targeted behaviors. These activities provide a context for teachers to promote general outcomes such as task persistence, social skills, and independence for all children as well as more targeted outcomes for individual children. Teachers should carefully plan how the learning environment is arranged and the materials that are available in order to maximize learning opportunities during child-directed activities. If a teacher decides that he or she is going to embed learning opportunities related to problem solving during center time for three specific children, then materials must be provided that are of interest to those children and that are appropriately challenging so that the children need to use problem-solving skills. For example, if Tatianna, Keyshaun, and Mary are all interested in constructing a model of a playground (because they are studying playgrounds), then the teacher could provide a variety of activities such as measuring playground equipment, reading books about designing structures, and providing opportunities to generate ideas about what they should investigate about playgrounds.

Teacher-directed activities can focus on an individual child or small or large groups of children. Optimally, these activities should focus on the interests of the children and should provide multiple opportunities for all children to participate. Teacher-directed activities provide opportunities for children to practice skills such as following directions, attending to tasks, and taking turns. They also provide opportunities for peer modeling, which can be used as a strategy for teaching more individually targeted behaviors. For example, during circle time, the teacher might introduce new materials that are being added to the block center. The teacher could ask a more competent peer to demonstrate what he or she might do with the new materials as a model for a child who is working on functional play skills.

In many preschool classrooms, children spend a considerable amount of time in routine activities such as eating meals, making transitions, toileting, washing hands, and cleaning up. The time spent in these routine activities should be used to maximize and promote both individualized target behaviors and broader outcomes for all children. Routine activities can be used to teach a variety of skills, including adaptive skills (e.g., dressing, toileting, cleaning up), social skills (e.g., finding a friend and helping him or her clean up toys), and language skills (e.g., asking a child what he or she did during center time that day). Routine activities also provide opportunities to teach children about taking care of the environment, taking care of physical needs, and following directions.

Group Composition The composition of groups should also be considered when planning the learning environment. Instruction can and should occur in the context of large groups, small groups, and one-to-one interactions. Each of these arrangements provides a context for different kinds of instruction and outcomes.

Large-group activities include circle time, storytime, morning meeting, and other activities that involve the whole class or a large group of children engaged in the same activity at the same time. Large-group activities can be used to set the tone for the day, create a sense of community, discuss issues that affect the whole class, teach important skills about being a part of a group, introduce new classroom activities, and provide an opportunity for the entire classroom to be together. They also can be among the most problematic times of the day for many teachers. Large-group activities are often hard to conduct given the many different abilities, interests, and needs of children. Table 5.1 provides a summary of guidelines that may be useful in planning large-group activities.

Table 5.1.   Guidelines for planning and implementing large-group activities

Planning the activities

Be clear about the purpose and goals of the activities (e.g., songs, stories, friend of the day, lessons) planned during group time to ensure that each activity is meaningful.

Teach the expectations of group time and use visuals. Review the expectations on a regular basis and provide feedback to children engaging in the expectations.

Consider the length of group time.

Assign adults to provide feedback and support to children who have a difficult time during large-group activities. Make a plan for fading support over time to ensure children don't become dependent on the support.

Implementing the activities

Provide opportunities for all children to be actively involved in a way that is meaningful to them. Provide different ways for responding and participating based on individual children's needs. For example, some children are more engaged in songs if there are props for them to manipulate or visuals to go along with the lyrics.

Embed choices (e.g., choosing what song to sing, where to sit, or what book to read), especially for children who have a difficult time at group.

Assign jobs to children during the activity, especially to those children who have a difficult time with large-group activities.

Monitor children's behavior and give them positive, descriptive feedback on their participation and behavior.

Make modifications in the activity if multiple children are having a difficult time attending.

Establish a large-group routine, but vary activities within the routine so they are not the same from day to day. Allow children to make choices about some activities within the routine.

Review the plans for the day (i.e., class schedule), but be creative and talk about the plans in different ways to maintain children's engagement over time.

Evaluating the activities

Monitor children's engagement and participation over time to ensure the activities are engaging. If needed, make changes to the activities to enhance participation and engagement.

The success of large-group activities depends on careful planning as well as responsiveness on the part of the teacher. The activity must have a clear purpose, and the teacher will have to think about what variations and supports will be needed to ensure that all children are actively involved. A variety of different options for actively involving children exist, but any option should be individualized for the children in the group. A study comparing different strategies children could use to respond during large group found that providing children with their own response board (e.g., a board with several different response cards representing the weather choices) so that they could each respond to different questions was most effective compared with other strategies (Godfrey, Grisham-Brown, Schuster, & Hemmeter, 2003). Children's attending was greater and there were fewer challenging behaviors when these cards were used (Godfrey et al., 2003). This strategy can be individualized in terms of the type of response board each child has (e.g., some might have pictures, some might have words, some might have symbols). Large-group activities can and should be used for more specific instructional and community building purposes. Well-planned large-group activities can be instrumental in creating a sense of community in the classroom. They can be used for discussing and role playing class rules/expectations and social skills, planning field trips, developing ideas for projects, and making decisions that have an impact on the whole classroom (e.g., identifying materials to add to the dramatic play center, identifying ideas for projects, deciding what to do for Family Night).

Small-group activities provide a context for presenting new information to children, promoting cooperative work among students, and using peers as models. Small-group activities are unique in that they allow for individualized teaching as well as peer modeling and interaction. Children have more opportunities to respond and be actively involved with the teacher and other children in small-group activities than they typically have during a large-group activity. Think back to the scenario at the beginning of this chapter. Alex, a parent volunteer, was working with a small group of children. The level of support he was providing to those children would have been difficult in a large-group context. Small-group activities are discussed in more detail in Chapter 6 as they relate to promoting targeted outcomes.

One-to-one teacher–child interactions and activities provide ideal contexts for building relationships with children as well as focusing on individualized outcomes for children. Teacher–child interactions are important for all children and can be used to support children who have a difficult time attending in group situations, need extra practice on specific skills, or need one-to-one attention from an adult. One-to-one interactions also can be used as instructional contexts for specific skills and are described in more detail in Chapter 7 as a context for addressing individualized outcomes. It is important to consider how to integrate small-group, large-group, and one-to-one interactions, however, when designing a classroom schedule.

Planning Instructional Activities for All Children

Careful planning is the key to successful instructional activities, whether they are large group, small group, or one to one and whether they are child directed, teacher directed, or routine. Three essential features of UDL should be considered to ensure that all children are meaningfully engaged in classroom activities (CAST, 2004; Division for Early Childhood [DEC], 2014; Hitchcock, Meyer, Rose, & Jackson, 2002; Orkwis, 1999; Orkwis & McLane, 1998):

1. *Multiple means of representation:* This principle ensures that questions, expectations, and learning opportunities are designed using various formats and at different levels, addressing a range of abilities and needs.

2. *Multiple means of engagement:* This principle ensures that different levels of support are provided for promoting children's attention, curiosity, and engagement and addressing a range of interests, preferences, ideas, and learning styles. Engagement is facilitated by providing various levels of support.

3. *Multiple means of expression:* This principle ensures that children have opportunities to respond in individualized ways, using a range of resources, toys, and materials to demonstrate what they know and to express their ideas, feelings, and needs.

The goal is for all children to participate in classroom activities and routines in a way that is meaningful to them and consistent with the ongoing flow of the activity or routine (Horn, Thompson, Palmer, Jenson, & Turbiville, 2004).

Teaching strategies at the universal level are designed to promote children's engagement in the activities and people in the child's environment, provide children with content-specific information (e.g., language modeling), and provide a positive and supportive context for learning. Although it is beyond the scope of this chapter to describe all of the possible universal strategies that could be used, we focus on some key strategies that are effective with young children.

Instructional Support Practices The Classroom Assessment and Scoring System (CLASS®; Pianta, La Paro, & Hamre, 2008) includes thre dimensions that measure teachers' instructional support for children: 1) concept development, 2) quality of feedback, and 3) language modeling. These three dimensions are related to children's success in literacy and general knowledge (Mashburn et al., 2008). Teacher–child interactions and environmental arrangement provide the context in which instructional support practices can be implemented. Although it is beyond the scope of this chapter to describe the instructional support dimensions in detail, we provide a brief overview of each.

Concept development refers to the use of strategies and discussions that promote children's cognitive and higher level thinking skills (Pianta et al., 2008). This involves asking questions or having discussions that require children to analyze situations, predict what will happen, consider alternatives, problem-solve, and reflect. For example, the teacher would ask "why" or "how" questions such as 1) *"Why do you think Miguel ran away?"* 2) *"What do you think will happen if the vet leaves the gate open?"* 3) *"How can you tell which one is bigger?"* These questions are intentionally designed to engage children in deeper investigations. Concept development also involves helping children generate their own ideas, create their own products, and develop their own plans. This might involve helping children brainstorm class plans and activities. Concept development strategies are effective when the discussions, activities, and questions are linked to each other, build on previous experience and learning, and reflect the lives of each of the children.

The quality of feedback teachers provide to children is a second dimension of instructional support (Pianta et al., 2008). High-quality feedback results in children's learning and engagement. This includes providing the amount of support each child needs to be successful. The teacher's response to a child is an opportunity to help the child figure out the answer or facilitate his or her deeper level of understanding. Feedback might also be provided in a way that gives a child more information about the issue being discussed (expansions), encourages the child to persist at a difficult activity, or recognizes his or her solution to a problem.

Finally, instructional support includes the use of language modeling strategies (Pianta et al., 2008), which include conversations, open-ended questions, repetition and extensions, self- and parallel talk, and the use of language to promote new vocabulary. These strategies build on the responsive interaction strategies described by a number of researchers (Girolametto, 1988; Kaiser & Roberts, 2013). Responsive interaction strategies are designed to promote social interactions and engagement between children and their peers or caregivers. When using responsive interaction strategies, adults or peers follow the child's lead, comment on what the child is doing, respond to the child's communicative attempts, and provide language models. Specific responsive interaction strategies include following the child's lead, contingent responsiveness, language modeling, matched turns, and expansions. Responsive interaction strategies are designed to result in more balanced turns and longer interactions. Teachers can support the development of more complex language in the context of these interactions through modeling and prompting.

Behavior Support Strategies   Children are often more cooperative, more engaged, and more likely to engage in appropriate social behaviors when they have opportunities to make decisions or choices about what they do, how they do it, and with whom they interact. Choice making gives children more control over their environment, rather than always having to do what others tell them to do. Although it is not possible or preferable to allow children to make choices all the time, it is helpful to identify those times when children can make meaningful choices. For example, children may be given choices about what center they go to, whom they play with, what they do in the center, and what materials they use. Children can be given choices during snack time regarding what color plate they use, whom they sit by, and what they have to drink (e.g., milk or water). Jai might be given a choice between a number of quiet activities she can do on her cot while other children are napping. Choices can also be used to help make decisions for the whole classroom. For example, the teacher might give children a choice of going on a walk or going to the playground. It might be that some children can go on a walk with one teacher while other children can play on the playground with a different teacher. The teacher could also support the children to make a group choice and graph the number of children who want to go on a walk versus the number of children who want to play on the playground. Numerous opportunities exist throughout a classroom day to allow children to make choices. Providing opportunities for choice may have to be individualized for some children. Some children might need a visual of the choices (e.g., a visual of two different songs and the child points to his or her choice). Some children might be able to choose from multiple options, whereas some children might be learning to make a choice between only two options.

Positive descriptive feedback or *descriptive praise* refers to "adults or peers providing children with feedback that describes, using positive terms, the behavior expectation observed, and it can involve providing information about the effect of the behavior on the environment" (Hemmeter, Snyder, Kinder, & Artman, 2011, p. 97). Descriptive praise (e.g., "You were a super friend today when you helped Kellen clean up her toys") delivered correctly avoids some of the pitfalls associated with more general praise (e.g., "Good job"). Descriptive praise is a key component of positive behavior interventions and supports and is part of many multicomponent behavioral support interventions (e.g., Hemmeter, Ostrosky, & Fox, 2006; Slider, Noell, & Williams, 2006). It has been associated with on-task behavior and engagement (Stormont, 2002; Sutherland, Wehby, & Copeland, 2000) and decreases children's challenging behavior (Fullerton, Conroy, & Correa, 2009; Stormont, Smith, & Lewis, 2007). Some examples of descriptive praise are, "I can tell you are ready because you are sitting on your name and your eyes are looking at me," "Jeff looked so proud when he finished his picture all by himself," and "Mimi and Dex worked together to make a picture for Ms. Ragan. She will be so happy." Descriptive praise should describe behaviors and the effects of behaviors on the environment (e.g., "I know you really wanted to go to another center but you stayed and helped Mia finish the puzzle") and should not focus on characteristics of the child (e.g., "You are so patient").

Differential reinforcement is the use of positive feedback for those behaviors that are desirable (e.g., sitting quietly while another child is talking at group time) and may involve ignoring behaviors that are undesirable. This strategy helps the teacher focus on what children are doing appropriately rather than focusing on children who are engaging in inappropriate behaviors. Furthermore, it provides a description of the appropriate behavior (e.g., "Lila is being respectful because she is listening to her friend") that can serve as a model for all children. It is important to avoid using differential reinforcement to shame other children into being good. In other words, avoid praising a child who is engaging in the appropriate behavior while looking upset at a child who is not engaging in that behavior. Differential reinforcement should be used in ECE classrooms as a positive strategy for helping children understand expected behaviors.

Identifying and teaching classroom rules and behavioral expectations is another important universal strategy. Teaching behavioral expectations is a positive approach to behavior support and serves to provide a context for the classroom that is positive and focused on helping children know what to do and what is expected of them. Behavioral expectations can be broad (e.g., be safe, be respectful, be a team player) or they can be stated as rules (e.g., use listening ears, calm touches, inside voices). When using broadly stated expectations (e.g., be safe), the teacher can provide examples of what it means to be safe (e.g., put your toys up, only one child on the slide at a time). Classroom rules and expectations also serve to maximize consistency across adults in the classroom. Teachers, assistants, and other classroom personnel can be consistent in the way they support children's behavior in the classroom. In addition, classroom expectations can be shared with families and provide a context for discussing differences in expectations and behavior across settings. Systematically teaching rules and expectations is a critical step in using classroom rules and expectations. Children can help make posters by selecting the pictures or icons that will help them remember the rules and expectations when they look at the posters. Puppets, DVDs, role-playing, modeling, and class discussion can be used during large- and small-group activities. Teachers can acknowledge and describe the children's behavior throughout the day as children demonstrate behavioral expectations. When a child breaks a rule, teachers can talk with the child about the rule and the consequences. Examples and nonexamples of children following the expectations can then be discussed during large and small groups on subsequent days. It is likely to take an extended period of time for children to really learn and understand the expectations.

DESIGNING AND ORGANIZING THE CONTENT OF LEARNING EXPERIENCES

This section focuses on how to design and organize the content of learning experiences by addressing the following topics: 1) using conceptual organizers as a means of framing the context of instruction, 2) using curriculum webs for planning the content of instruction, and 3) implementing some general principles related to designing authentic learning activities.

Using Conceptual Organizers

Conceptual organizers "are the 'meaning-centered' approaches that are designed to enhance comprehension and depth of understanding or curriculum content" (Bredekamp & Rosegrant, 1992, p. 67). Conceptual organizers are meant to serve as a framework for teachers to integrate content around meaningful and interesting ideas or concepts. Conceptual organizers can include thematic units and projects.

Thematic units are used to organize activities around a broad topic or concept (Helm & Katz, 2001). For example, a teacher may develop a thematic unit on recycling and plan activities and provide materials related to that topic, such as going on a field trip to a recycling center, looking for things that can be recycled, or reading stories about recycling (see Kingore & Higbee, 1988, and York, 1998, for examples of thematically based resources). Although thematic units may occur over short periods of time (e.g., 1 week), they may extend into several weeks or for the entire school year, depending on the children's interest (Branscombe, Castle, Dorsey, Surbeck, & Taylor, 2003). Topics, objectives, and activities for the children are decided on or predesignated, and resources are typically brought in by the teacher when organizing and planning themes (Gestwicki, 1999; Helm & Katz, 2001).

Projects are "sustained, in-depth activities initiated by children or children and teachers together for the purpose of studying a topic in depth to increase understanding and appreciation" (Branscombe et al., 2003, p. 168). The length of a project is determined by the progression of the project. Teachers organize the project based on what children do not know, and children learn by being involved in the investigation (Helm & Katz, 2001). Numerous benefits to the project approach are cited in the literature (Branscombe et al., 2003; Bredekamp & Copple, 1997; Katz & Chard, 2000), including

- Allowing opportunities for children to problem-solve, generate ideas, reflect, estimate, hypothesize, and make predictions

- Providing numerous ways for children to learn through art, writing, storytelling, and dramatic play

- Facilitating cooperation among children

Important considerations should be taken into account when this aspect of curriculum planning begins, regardless of the type of conceptual organizer used. First, it is essential that teachers have input from children when determining topics (Copple & Bredekamp, 2009). Gestwicki (1999) suggested recording children during play to determine their interests. Teachers should consistently base activities and events on children's current interests and individual needs rather than rely on curriculum plans that are developed and reused year after year. For example, teachers may repeatedly study "all about me" in September, "pumpkins" in October, "winter" in December, "spring" in April, and so forth. Using this sort of stagnant approach may make it difficult to ensure that children are motivated and interested in planned activities. This is not to say that teachers cannot use themes to organize their ideas. Themes can be a useful and appropriate way to organize curricula within inclusive programs if they are done properly. The problem lies in planning curricula without consideration of children's interests and needs.

Ensuring that the nature of what is being studied is relevant to the children in the classroom or linked to something that is meaningful to the children is equally important to successful curriculum planning (Copple & Bredekamp, 2009). The following vignette illustrates how daily events can be shaped into learning opportunities that are developmentally appropriate and relevant.

> *It is springtime, and the children in Ms. Barros's class have been spending a great deal of time outdoors. Several of the children have discovered all kinds of creatures while digging under a shade tree. These insects have been a source of interest to nearly all of the children in the class. A large group gathers under the tree each day to explore what is under the earth. One rainy day at circle time, Ms. Barros decides to lead a discussion about the creatures on the playground. She asks the children what they have learned about the bugs. Then she asks them what they would like to know. That question prompts numerous responses (What do they eat? Why do they live underground? How many legs do they have?). Ms. Barros begins planning a unit/theme around bugs using these and other questions. While planning activities (e.g., reading books about bugs, searching for bugs in the discovery table, doing an experiment about what bugs eat), she decides that this is an excellent topic for the children to study. First, most of the children are interested in and have firsthand experience with bugs. In addition, the topic lends itself to the development of activities that are rich with opportunities for children to practice many different skills.*

In addition to selecting a conceptual organizer that builds on children's interests and allows for activities that are relevant to their daily lives, it is essential that conceptual organizers be chosen that allow teachers to address all areas of learning and development. Although teachers must attend to state and program standards, they must also ensure that the standards encompass all critical areas of learning and development, including social-emotional, language and literacy, math, science, and physical health. Furthermore, teachers must ensure that individual children's needs are met in the context of daily activities. Conceptual organizers should guide teachers in creating opportunities for teaching broad outcomes as well as individually targeted behaviors from across content and developmental areas. Once aware of these, teachers can design activities and experiences that address those needs. If several children in the class are having difficulty communicating their wants and needs, then it is critical to plan activities that create opportunities for them to learn those skills. For example, a teacher can promote communication skills while children are serving food at mealtimes by giving small amounts and encouraging them to request or ask for more, modeling conversation among children, and asking probing questions in an effort to expand communication. Similarly, teachers want to design activities that address broad learning processes. Open-ended projects or experiments create opportunities for children to make predictions, solve problems, persist at a task, and interact with other children. For example, if the teacher develops an experiment about what bugs eat, then he or she might 1) have children work together to list ideas of what bugs might eat, 2) let children make predictions about what bugs will eat, and 3) have children say why they think bugs eat some food items and not others.

Using Curriculum Webs for Curriculum Planning

It is important that planning efforts are flexible and open ended to allow for change and incorporation of new ideas and interests (e.g., Gestwicki, 1999). A curriculum web is one strategy that promotes this type of curriculum planning (Gestwicki, 1999). Curriculum webs can be used in a variety of ways, including 1) determining what children might learn about a particular topic, 2) identifying questions children might ask about a topic, 3) listing activities that might create opportunities for the children to learn about the topic, or 4) identifying content that might be embedded into the topic (Helm & Katz, 2001).

Figure 5.3 provides an example of a web-planning format. Teachers get input from children and identify a central theme or project to use as the conceptual organizer. "Fall" is the theme in Figure 5.3. The eight content blocks that surround the theme highlight the common outcomes that will be addressed for all young children. Common outcomes are often dictated by state or agency standards. As previously described, conceptual organizers offer the opportunity to teach across content areas (e.g., literacy, math, science) and developmental areas (e.g., communication, social, motor). All standards and areas of development do not need to be addressed by a single theme or project, but selected themes/projects should provide multiple opportunities for the group of children to be exposed to all relevant outcomes across the school year. After identifying the common outcomes for all children and noting those that will be the focus during a particular theme/project, teachers identify a variety of activities that will allow them to address the identified outcomes/standards. Teachers should also identify embedded learning opportunities within each activity and then monitor children's targeted and individualized outcomes as well. The eleven activity balloons in Figure 5.3 provide examples of activities related to the theme, behaviors that can be targeted through embedded learning opportunities for specific children, and methods of data collection that can be used to monitor children's progress. For example, embedded learning opportunities related to "uses words, phrases, and sentences to inform" and "walks independently" can be created in the Leaf Hide-and-Seek activity. Furthermore, teachers can note how a child's progress will be monitored (e.g., collecting a language sample, making jottings). The planning process illustrated in

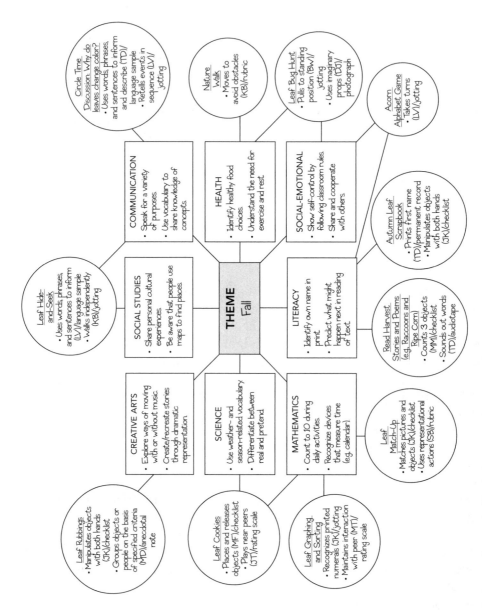

Figure 5.3. A web-planning format. (Initials represent children whose individually targeted skills can be embedded in a particular activity, followed by the method of data collection that can be used to measure progress [e.g., checklist, jottings].)

Figure 5.3 allows the learning needs of all children to dictate the development of activities instead of the other way around (i.e., develop activities and then hope that children will learn something from them) and to ensure that embedded learning opportunities are provided across activities. Teachers (as well as other team members including families) have a stronger idea about what to teach (groups of children and individual children) and where to teach (i.e., the activities or contexts for providing instruction) once they have completed a curriculum web.

Designing Authentic Learning Activities

In addition to addressing the needs of children, activities should be authentic. Branscombe et al. stated that children should be engaged in "tasks that they have a genuine need to accomplish" (2003, p. 33). Branscombe et al. noted that "authentic tasks" utilize realistic materials, occur within daily routines, and are generated from projects or studies of specific topics. In other words, the tasks should result in meaningful outcomes for a child. Authentic tasks also result in the need to use skills and processes from a variety of content areas. Following is an example of an authentic activity in Ms. Barros's class.

> *Ms. Barros and a group of five children decided to make cookies for an upcoming parent meeting. Ms. Barros displayed a recipe with words and symbols for the amount of the various ingredients that went in the recipe. Children took turns reading the recipe and then completing the step. Each child had his or her own materials (e.g., rolling pin, cookie cutters of various shapes and sizes), as well as an opportunity to knead the dough. While the children rolled their dough and made their cookies, Ms. Barros asked the children to describe the texture of the dough and provide their predictions about what made the texture sticky and what would make it not sticky, and she encouraged social-communication when children wanted to borrow one another's cookie cutters. At the end of the activity, Ms. Barros asked the children to sequence the steps they followed while making cookies.*

Contrast this activity with the following.

> *Trays with materials that are intended to capture the children's attention are sitting on two small tables. A set of large beads and a string on each tray is on one table. In addition, there is a picture model for how to sequence the beads (e.g., red, green, yellow, blue). A round bin separated with six dividers is on the other table. A number, along with dots that correspond with the number (e.g., 2 = 2 dots), is at the bottom of each section. A set of counting bears is on the tray. Children are encouraged to put the number of bears in the section that matches the numeral or dots. Some children do these activities semi-independently, with occasional verbal support from one of the classroom teachers. Although children frequently visit the table, most simply do the task and quickly move on.*

These are examples of scenarios frequently observed in preschool class-rooms. It should be clear which is more authentic, however, when considering issues of authenticity. The children in Ms. Barros's classroom are working toward a real-life goal (e.g., assisting with providing snacks for an upcoming parent meeting) while making cookies. This activity offers numerous opportunities for children to learn a variety of skills across content areas (e.g., math, literacy, civics, communication). Furthermore, although the counting bear activity leads to an outcome (albeit, prescribed by the teacher), it is not one that would be considered authentic, nor does it create opportunities for integration of skills across content areas. The children are really just working on sequencing with the stringing beads task or numeracy in the bear sorting task.

Universal Instruction in Action

An Intentional Instructional Sequence (IIS) decision-making process (Pretti-Frontczak & Grisham-Brown, 2012) can be used to ensure that instruction is delivered as planned (see Chapter 4). The IIS is a process and should augment the curriculum web suggested in this chapter for lesson planning. The IIS process includes five steps essential for designing instruction for all children, regardless of the type of outcome or instructional strategy: 1) what to teach, 2) when to teach, 3) where to teach, 4) with what to teach, and 5) how to teach. Figure 5.4 contains an IIS described for universal instruction.

SUMMARY

This chapter focused on universal strategies that are used to ensure that all children have access to the general education curriculum and that all children are making progress toward common outcomes. This chapter provided important information on scheduling, designing learning centers, planning learning activities, selecting materials, implementing effective large and small groups, and planning experiences that ensure that all children are engaged and learning. The practices described in this chapter provide a context in which Tier 2 and Tier 3 practices can be implemented.

Intentional Instructional Sequence Planning Form

Outcome	When	Where	With what	Instructional strategy (universal)	How to teach — Feedback	Progress monitoring
Common outcome(s)						
KECS.LA.2.1 Engages in active listening in a variety of situations	Center Time	Library	Copies of the book *Polar Bear, Polar Bear, What Do You Hear?* by Bill Martin, Jr., and Eric Carle	Read story to children, asking the following questions: • What is the title of the book? • What animals are in the story? • What color is the _____ (fill in animal name)?	Give specific verbal praise when children answer a question correctly (e.g., "Yes, the yellow lion comes next").	Use a checklist in which each child's name is listed and give the frequency with which the child correctly sequenced the animals in retelling the story.
KECS.LA.3.1 Listens to and/ or responds to reading materials with interest and enjoyment			Hand-size felted objects of each animal in the story	Ask a series of questions about what the polar bear and friends hear: • Say, "Which animal sound does the polar bear hear first?" • Say, "What does it sound like to have a lion roaring in your ear?" • Say, "What does the lion then hear?"	Give hints if the children are having difficulty determining which animal comes next (e.g., "What animal is long and can curl itself?"). Supply the answer if children get the wrong answer, and have them repeat the correct answer.	Self-assessment— have children go through the story to determine if the order of the animals is correct according to the story.
KECS.LA.3.6 Tells and retells a story (KECS: Kentucky Early Childhood Standards)			Flannel board			

Figure 5.4. Intentional Instruction Sequence Planning Form for universal instruction. (From Pretti-Frontczak, K., & Grisham-Brown, J. [2012]. *Manual for designing and delivering intentional instruction.* Brooklyn, NY: B2K Solutions, Ltd.; adapted by permission).

LEARNING ACTIVITIES

1. Audio or video-record several preschool children over several days. Listen to the recordings and determine if there are common themes discussed among the children. Develop a curriculum web for your classroom based on the children's conversations.

2. List each learning center within an inclusive classroom. From the curriculum web you designed in Question 1, describe how outcomes noted in each balloon from your web will be embedded within the classroom routine.

3. Develop a classroom schedule addressing the issues provided in the chapter regarding designing a schedule to meet the needs of all young children. Compare your schedule with a fellow student's schedule. How are they alike? How are they different?

4. Observe a classroom for the entire time the children are present. Answer the following questions:

   • How many transitions occur during the day?

   • How much time is spent in transitions?

   • How are learning opportunities embedded into transition times?

   • To what extent do children complete transitions independently? What types of supports or prompts are provided to help children during transitions?

5. Observe a preschool classroom, paying close attention to the learning centers. Take detailed notes about each center (e.g., materials found within the centers, skills that are being addressed, engagement, interest level of the children). Interview the classroom teacher to find out how he or she developed the centers in terms of the type of center and materials in the center as well as how he or she increases the likelihood that children will be engaged.

REFERENCES

Branscombe, N.A., Castle, K., Dorsey, A.G., Surbeck, E., & Taylor, J.B. (2003). *Early childhood curriculum: A constructivist perspective.* Boston, MA: Houghton Mifflin.

Bredekamp, S., & Copple, C. (Eds.). (1997). *Developmentally appropriate practice in early childhood programs* (Rev. ed.). Washington, DC: National Association for the Education of Young Children.

Bredekamp, S., & Rosegrant, (1992). *Reaching potentials: Transforming early childhood curriculum and assessment* (Vol. 1). Washington, DC: National Association for the Education of Young Children.

Campbell, P., & Milbourne, S.A. (2014). Together is better: Environmental teaching practices to support all children's learning. *Young Exceptional Children Monograph Series, 16,* 21–38.

Center for Applied Special Technology. (2004, March 12). *Universal design for learning.* Retrieved from http://www.udlcenter.org/aboutudl/udlguidelines_theorypractice

Center for Applied Special Technology. (2006). *Teaching every student.* Retrieved from http://www.cast.org/our-work/publications/2014/universal-design-learning-theory-practice-udl-meyer.html#.V_udtpMrKi4

Conn-Powers, M., Cross, A.F., Traub, E., & Hutter-Pishgahi, L. (2006, September). The universal design of early education: Moving forward for all children. *Beyond the Journal: Young Children on the Web,* 1–9.

Copple, C., & Bredekamp, S. (Eds.). (2009). *Developmentally appropriate practice in early childhood programs serving children from birth through age 8* (3rd ed.). Washington, DC: National Association for the Education of Young Children.

Division for Early Childhood. (2014). *DEC recommended practices in early intervention/early childhood special education 2014.* Retrieved from http://www.dec-sped.org/recommendedpractices

Dombro, A.L., Jablon, J.R., & Stetson, C. (2011). Powerful interactions. *Young Children, 66*(1), 12–16.

Fullerton, E.K., Conroy, M.A., & Correa, V. (2009). An investigation of early childhood teachers' use of specific praise during transition activities with young children at high risk for emotional/behavioral disorders. *Behavioral Disorders, 34,* 118–135.

Gestwicki, C. (1999). *Developmentally appropriate practice: Curriculum development in early education* (2nd ed.). Albany, NY: Delmar.

Girolametto, L.E. (1988). Improving the social-conversational skills of developmentally delayed children: An intervention study. *Journal of Speech and Hearing Disorders, 53,* 156–167.

Godfrey, S.A., Grisham-Brown, J.L., Schuster, J.W, & Hemmeter, M.L. (2003). The effects of three active responding techniques on student participation and social behavior with preschool children with special needs. *Education and Treatment of Children, 26,* 255–272.

Helm, J.H., & Katz, L. (2001). *Young investigators: The project approach in the early years.* New York, NY: Teachers College Press.

Hemmeter, M.L., Ostrosky, M., Artman, K., & Kinder, K. (2008). Moving right along: Planning transitions to prevent challenging behavior. *Young Children, 63*(3), 18–25.

Hemmeter, M.L., Ostrosky, M., & Corso, R. (2012). Preventing and addressing challenging behavior: Common questions and practical solutions. *Young Exceptional Children, 15,* 31–44.

Hemmeter, M.L., Ostrosky, M., & Fox, L. (2006). Social and emotional foundations for early learning: A conceptual model for intervention. *School Psychology Review, 35,* 583–601.

Hemmeter, M.L., Snyder, P., Kinder, K., & Artman, K. (2011). Impact of performance feedback delivered via electronic mail on preschool teachers' use of descriptive praise. *Early Childhood Research Quarterly, 26,* 96–109.

Hitchcock, C., Meyer, A., Rose, D., & Jackson, R. (2002). *Technical brief: Access, participation, and progress in the general curriculum.* Retrieved from http://aem.cast.org/about/publications/2002/ncac-curriculum-access-participation-progress.html#.V_54GJMrKi4

Horn, E., & Banerjee, R. (2009). Understanding curriculum modifications and embedded learning opportunities in the context of supporting all children's success. *Language, Speech, and Hearing in Schools, 40,* 406–415.

Horn, E.M., Thompson, B., Palmer, S.B., Jenson, R., & Turbiville, V. (2004). Preschool. In C.H. Kennedy & E.M. Horn (Eds.), *Including students with severe disabilities* (pp. 207–221). Boston, MA: Pearson Education.

Hyson, M. (2004). *The emotional development of young children: Building an emotion-centered curriculum.* New York, NY: Teachers College Press.

Hyson, M. (2008). *Enthusiastic and engaged learners: Approaches to learning in the early childhood classroom.* New York, NY: Teachers College Press.

Johnson, J., Rahn, N.L., & Bricker, D. (2015). *An activity-based approach to early intervention* (4th ed.). Baltimore, MD: Paul H. Brookes Publishing Co.

Kaiser, A.P., & Roberts, M.Y. (2013). Parent-implemented enhanced milieu teaching with preschool children with intellectual disabilities. *Journal of Speech, Language, and Hearing Research, 56,* 295–309.

Katz, L., & Chard, S. (2000). *Engaging children's minds: The project approach* (2nd ed.). Stamford, CT: Ablex.

Kimball, J.W., Kinney, E.M., Taylor, B.A., & Stromer, R. (2003). Lights, camera, action! Using engaging computer-cued activity schedules. *Teaching Exceptional Children, 36,* 40–45.

Kingore, B.W., & Higbee, G.M. (1988). *We Care: A preschool curriculum for children ages 2–5.* Parsippany, NJ: Good Year Books.

Lawry, J., Danko, C., & Strain, P. (1999). Examining the role of the classroom environment in the prevention of problem behaviors. *Young Exceptional Children Monograph Series, 1,* 49–61.

Martin, B., Jr., & Carle, E. (1997). *Polar bear, polar bear, what do you hear?* New York, NY: Holt and Company.

Mashburn, A.J., Pianta, R.C., Hamre, B.K., Downer, J.T., Barbarin, O.A., Bryant, D., . . .Howes, C. (2008). Measures of classroom quality in prekindergarten and children's development of academic, language, and social skills. *Child Development, 79,* 732–749.

McWilliam, R.A., & Bailey, D.B. (1995). Effects of classroom social structure and disability on engagement. *Topics in Early Childhood Special Education, 15,* 123–147.

Orkwis, R. (1999). *Curriculum access and universal design for learning.* Reston, VA: ERIC Clearing House on Disabilities and Gifted Education. (ERIC Document Reproduction Service No. ED437767)

Orkwis, R., & McLane, K. (1998). *A curriculum every student can use: Design principles for student access.* Reston, VA: ERIC Clearing House on Disabilities and Gifted Education. (ERIC Document Reproduction Service No. ED423654)

Pianta, R.C., La Paro, K., & Hamre, B.K. (2008). *Classroom Assessment Scoring System* (CLASS®). Baltimore, MD: Paul H. Brookes Publishing Co.

Pretti-Frontczak, K., & Bricker, D. (2004). *An activity-based approach to early intervention* (3rd ed.). Baltimore, MD: Paul H. Brookes Publishing Co.

Pretti-Frontczak, K., & Grisham-Brown, J. (2012). *Manual for designing and delivering intentional instruction.* Brooklyn, NY: B2K Solutions.

Shonkoff, J.P., & Phillips, D.A. (2000). *From neurons to neighborhoods: The science of early childhood development.* Washington, DC: National Academies Press.

Slider, N.J., Noell, G.H., & Williams, K.L. (2006). Providing practicing teachers classroom management professional development in a brief self-study format. *Journal of Behavioral Education, 15,* 215–228.

Stormont, M. (2002). Externalizing behavior problems in young children: Contributing factors and early intervention. *Psychology in the Schools, 39,* 127–138.

Stormont, M., Smith, S., & Lewis, T. (2007). Teacher implementation of precorrections and praise statements in Head Start classroom as a component of program-wide system of positive behaviour support. *Journal of Behavior Education, 6,* 280–290.

Strain, P., & Hemmeter, M.L. (1997). Keys to being successful when confronted with challenging behaviors. *Young Exceptional Children Monograph Series, 1,* 17–27.

Sutherland, K.S., Wehby, J.H., & Copeland, S.R. (2000). Effect of varying rates of behavior-specific praise on the on-task behavior of students with EBD. *Journal of Emotional and Behavioral Disorders, 8,* 2–8, 26.

York, S. (1998). *Big as Life: The everyday inclusive curriculum* (Vols. 1 & 2). St. Paul, MN: Redleaf Press.

## CHAPTER 6

Focused Instructional Strategies

Kristie Pretti-Frontczak, Jennifer Grisham-Brown, and Mary Louise Hemmeter

Ms. Christy teaches in a blended prekindergarten (pre-K)/Head Start class-room at an early childhood education center in a primarily low-income school district. Her school administration has done an excellent job provid-ing professional development on the state's early learning standards and Head Start Early Learning Outcomes Framework. The school district also participates in the state's quality rating system, so they have emphasized the importance of having a high-quality environment and positive interactions between children and adults in the classroom. Yet, when completing the curriculum-based assessment on all children in her classroom during the first month of school, Ms. Christy notices that three children in her class are really struggling with some important skills that are preventing them from participating fully in some of the classroom routines. She believes that she needs to design focused instructional opportunities for these three children to learn the missing skills so they can be more successful in her class.

When a subset of children is struggling or their development and learn-ing has stalled, teachers and teams will need to use formative assessment information to identify targeted outcomes that require instructional effort that differs from what was described in Chapter 5 or that is described in Chapter 7. For example, if a child is struggling with a component of a larger, more complex skill, then the universal strategies discussed in Chapter 5 may not be the most effective or efficient way to support the child's learn-ing. Similarly, if development for three or four children has stalled only in terms of the quality of their performance, then teachers and teams may not need the systematic strategies discussed in Chapter 7. Access to a set of strategies that can address short-term needs and build on the emerging skills of young children is needed. This chapter defines the characteristics of focused instruction, outlines several considerations for implementation, and provides several examples of how to deliver focused instruction in a blended classroom.

FOCUSED INSTRUCTION

A key message in this book is that the same instructional strategy can be used to meet a variety of needs and outcomes; however, teachers and teams need to consistently adjust the frequency, intensity, and degree of precision with which they systematically plan, deliver, and evaluate instruction. In addition, and perhaps above all, teachers and teams need to know when a particular strategy is a good match for an identified outcome. This means that teachers and teams need to select, deliver, and monitor the child's response to instruction to ensure that a match was made between desired outcomes and instructional effort. Although a bit daunting, it will be neces-sary to engage in a planning process that is highly dynamic and flexible to ensure the successful learning of all children.

Teachers and teams will use formative assessment in the case of tar-geted outcomes (see Chapter 3) to guide decision making and will gain

Table 6.1. Preview of focused instructional strategies

Instructional strategy	Example
Embedded learning opportunities	Greater number of learning opportunities are created, delivered, and monitored across the daily routine and a greater number of correct models are provided.
Environmental adaptations	Alterations are made to the setting or situation/activity to provide additional support.
Intentional small-group activities	Intentional formation of small groups of three to five children that allows for more flexibility in pace, level of difficulty of tasks, and relevance/timeliness of feedback given
Peer modeling	Peers mediate additional learning opportunities by modeling and giving feedback on targeted outcomes.
Scaffolding	Purposeful tailoring, more individualized process given child's readiness and needs, and carefully planned contingencies

access to the full continuum of supports, prompts, and cues to deliver instruction and provide systematic feedback. Table 6.1 includes a preview of the focused instructional strategies that are defined and illustrated in this chapter. The strategies in Table 6.1 may look similar to the universal strategies discussed in Chapter 5; however, they differ in several critical ways, each of which is described later in this chapter.

Characteristics of Focused Instruction

One characteristic of a focused strategy is that it is paired with a targeted outcome (i.e., an outcome associated with a child or small group of children who are struggling or whose development and learning has stalled). A second characteristic of a focused strategy is that it is used on a short-term or temporary basis to support or jump-start development and learning. Unlike universal strategies, focused strategies may be used each day for a few weeks or a month but not as a consistent part of the universal instructional efforts. A third characteristic of a focused strategy is that it is geared for an individual child or a small group of children (i.e., a subset of the children served). Unlike universal strategies, focused strategies are not consistently used for all children but for select children based on formative assessment information. Finally, focused strategies do not require as much precision or personalization.

Teachers and teams will notice a few other attributes when they deliver focused instruction, including 1) how often the instruction is delivered, 2) the degree of intentionality required, and 3) the level of precision or fidelity that is required to obtain desired results. A mathematical or exact formula to guide decision making when considering the frequency of instruction does not exist. In fact, many continue to ask and wonder, "How many learning trials?" "How much instruction?" "How many dosages will be most effective?" Although there is no empirical answer to these questions, teachers and teams can follow guidelines to ensure that more opportunities are provided when addressing targeted outcomes. First, teachers and teams should determine how many times opportunities can be realistically created throughout the day, given other demands, staffing patterns, and even the child's attendance. Second, teachers and teams should determine how logical and meaningful the multiple opportunities are for the child. Solely creating didactic, massed, or even illogical opportunities just for the sake of creating more instructional trials is a trap into which teachers can easily fall. Third, teachers and teams should determine if they are able to obtain and sustain a child's attention and interest across the multiple and varied opportunities they have identified. Teachers and teams may want to create an embedding schedule (see Chapter 4) to identify the multiple and varied learning opportunities that can be delivered. Finally, working with other adults (e.g., child care providers, family members) and coaching them on how to deliver instruction during the activities and routines when they are with the child is one way to increase the frequency of instruction.

Intentionality is a second attribute to consider, which may seem odd given that all instruction should be intentional; however, we are thinking of intentionality as the paring between the outcome and the selected strategy. Thus, intentionality has to do with knowing what to teach as well as how to teach and translates into knowing what targeted outcome is being addressed and which focused strategies can be implemented as a matched pair. In addition, intentionality also presumes that teachers and teams know why a particular strategy would be considered effective and efficient. Consider the targeted outcome addressing a concern around latency in which a child needs support because he or she lacks impulse control (i.e., the child acts too quickly and does not wait or take sufficient time to plan or decide on the best course of action when he or she wants something, needs to solve a problem, or follows steps in a sequence). Effective focused strategies include setting challenges for the child to systematically achieve—singing songs that repeat and add on or build or telling group stories in which one child begins and the next child picks up where the previous child left off. Although these may seem like universal strategies, a teacher and team would use them knowing that they are effective and efficient ways to intentionally teach aspects of latency (a targeted outcome) in order to address a child or group of children who are struggling or when development and learning has stalled around the amount of wait time needed to plan and sequence actions.

The precision or degree of fidelity needed to achieve desired results is a final attribute to consider when selecting and implementing focused instruction. There is not an empirical or mathematical formula that says one has to implement a particular strategy with 90% precision or fidelity (see Chapter 4). Teachers and teams need to embody a mixture of careful planning and the need to be flexible and make moment-to-moment decisions when considering precision or fidelity in the delivery of focused instruction. Although the need for planning and developing various types of written plans (e.g., lesson plans, activity plans) is promoted as a critical ingredient for quality instruction throughout this book, we recognize that as children's needs begin to vary, so does the level to which we need to be fluid in knowing when to teach, where to teach, what to teach with, and how to vary levels of support or consequences. The next section discusses how to deliver this type of dynamic and flexible, yet focused, instruction as it applies to a variety of targeted outcomes.

Support for Implementing Focused Instruction

Although focused instruction takes more effort to deliver than universal instruction, it is necessary to address targeted outcomes so all children can demonstrate progress toward common outcomes. Five focused strategies, along with the evidence base for each, are described in the following sections. The strategies illustrate the characteristics of focused instruction: 1) addressing targeted outcomes, 2) serving a temporary or short-term need, and 3) being used for a clearly defined subset of the children served.

Embedding Learning Opportunities Embedded learning opportunities are a means of delivering focused instruction for targeted outcomes. Delivering embedded learning opportunities can be temporarily incorporated into the daily routine for subsets of children who are struggling or when development and learning has stalled for some children.

Delivering embedded learning opportunities has a strong evidence base and has been the focus of several studies concerning young children with and without disabilities. Researchers have repeatedly found that embedding learning opportunities leads to improved child performance with a variety of social skills (Craig-Unkefer & Kaiser, 2002; Kurt & Tekin-Iftar, 2008; Macy & Bricker, 2007; McBride & Schwartz, 2003) as well as with a variety of academic skills (Daugherty, Grisham-Brown, & Hemmeter, 2001; Grisham-Brown, Ridgley, Pretti-Frontczak, Litt, & Nielson, 2006; Grisham-Brown, Pretti-Frontczak, Hawkins, & Winchell, 2009; Horn, Lieber, Li, Sandall, & Schwartz, 2000; Wolery, Anthony, Caldwell, Snyder, & Morgante, 2002). See Pretti-Frontczak, Barr, Macy, and Carter (2003) as well as Barton, Bishop, and Snyder (2014) for more comprehensive reviews of embedded learning opportunities. Several key ingredients have emerged across the research base in order for embedded learning opportunities to be effective. Box 6.1 includes a list of the key ingredients for successful embedded learning opportunities.

A means of systematically delivering embedded learning opportunities to address targeted outcomes is needed. Using embedding schedules can assist in the delivery of embedded learning opportunities and, in the case of focused instruction, embedded learning opportunities for targeted outcomes (see Chapter 4). Teachers and teams need to complete the following

---

Box 6.1.   Key ingredients for successful embedded learning opportunities

- Match exists among children's attention, the targeted outcome, and adult/ peer action

- Motivating so that children are interested, engaged, and ready to interact and it doesn't interrupt the child's activity

- Meaningful adult/peer actions that are integral to the situation and lead to useful responses by children

- Moment-to-moment changes are made to planned embedded learning opportunities and teachable moments are capitalized on

---

steps to create or adapt an existing embedding schedule and generate additional learning opportunities to address targeted outcomes:

1. Identify a child or subset of the children who are struggling to demonstrate a common outcome, or identify a subset of children for whom learning and development appears to have stalled. Identifying children stems from analyzing and interpreting ongoing assessment information.

2. Examine daily routines and activities to determine when embedded learning opportunities are being delivered to all children regarding common outcomes. These instances serve as the starting point for delivering embedded learning opportunities related to targeted outcomes.

3. Identify additional times within the daily schedule to deliver embedded learning opportunities to jump-start development and learning for a subset of the children. Keep in mind, however, the key ingredients for delivering successful embedded learning opportunities highlighted in Box 6.1.

Once teachers and teams have a clear sense of whom to teach, what to teach, and when to teach, they are ready to create or adapt an embedding schedule. Figure 6.1 provides an example of an embedding schedule for a subset of children, specifically Rachel, Zoe, and Alyssa. The targeted outcome for the subset of children was identified through ongoing assessment, and both the common outcome of classification and the targeted outcome of increasing complexity are operationally defined in the embedding schedule. Figure 6.1 also includes examples of how the focused instruction can be delivered across the daily schedule.

Environmental Adaptations   Environmental adaptations is the next focused instructional strategy. If a teacher or team has ever answered the question, "What can I/we do to make it possible for children to be more

Embedding schedule for Rachel, Zoe, and Alyssa	
Common outcome *Classification* defined as • Groups (joins) and sorts (separates) objects and pictures of objects • Groups and sorts by concrete (e.g., color, shape, size, sound, texture) and abstract (e.g., ideas, function, class name, pattern, temperature, quantity, quality, spatial relations, ownership) properties	**Targeted outcome** Uses multiple and more complex classification skills: • Groups and sorts pictures of familiar objects by concrete properties. *Note:* increase in complexity by grouping and sorting pictures, not just objects. • Groups and sorts objects by concrete properties and at least one abstract property. *Note:* increase in complexity by starting to group and sort by abstract properties.
When to teach (daily routine)	**How to teach (focused instruction)**
Arrival	Provide a visual schedule check-in system for 1) who is at home and 2) who is at school. Children receive a photograph card with a picture of themselves, their first name, or a symbol that represents them. Children then move the card from the "home" column to the "school" column when they arrive. This visual support can be printed or incorporated into a smart board. Adults use self-talk to describe the two categories and the change in categories (e.g., "I can see from our chart that two of our friends are still at home and 12 are here at school").
Library	Play "Story Sort." Collect small objects and pictures from a recently shared read-aloud story. For example, select pictures and objects from *Three Billy Goats Gruff* such as different-size billy goats, a troll, a bridge, and a grassy hill, as well as nonstory elements such as a toothbrush, snake, car, and tall building. Label two small buckets with "in the story" and "not in the story." • Adults use self-talk to model sorting objects into the buckets. Say, "I am going to play a game. First, I remember the characters in the story we read this morning, *Three Billy Goats Gruff*. When I think of the story, I first think of the title of the story and that helps me remember that there were billy goats in the story. When I look at my sorting objects, I see a picture of a big billy goat. That was in the story, so I am going to pick him up and put him in the bucket that is labelled 'in the story.'" • Adults use self-talk to model nonexamples. Say, "Hmmm, I don't think a toothbrush was in this story. I am going to put the toothbrush in the bucket labeled 'not in the story.' I see these words crossed out inside a big red circle, which helps me pick the right bucket. I am going to put the toothbrush in this bucket because I don't think it was in the story, and I will check the illustrations in the book to make sure I am right."
Morning circle	Play "What's My Rule?" when grouping and sorting pictures and objects by a common properties (e.g., shape, texture, function). Ask why the pictures and objects go together. Ask the children to find other objects that belong. Ask children to guess your grouping or sorting rule.

(continued)

Figure 6.1. Embedding schedule for subset of children. (From Pretti-Frontczak, K. [2014]. *Addressing targeted outcomes as part of a multi-tiered system of support.* Brooklyn, NY: B2K Solutions; adapted by permission.)

Figure 6.1.   *(continued)*

Outdoor classroom	Play "Texture Scavenger Hunt and Re-sort." Introduce texture vocabulary words (e.g., *shiny, dull, smooth, rough, hard, soft*) by having children touch and explore textured objects. As children gather natural materials, ask open-ended questions about the textures they are noticing (e.g., "What texture words could you use to tell someone about that rock? What is the difference between the pine cone and the seashell? How do some of the materials feel the same?"). Set up hula-hoops for texture sorts (which can be abstract) outside, and prompt children to categorize the textures. Follow up with a re-sort by using colors or shapes of the objects.
Snack	Brainstorm the snack schedule with children to create a menu that includes one liquid and one solid for each day. For example, say, "We are going to plan for a liquid and a solid for snack. A liquid can be poured. Milk is a liquid. We could have milk as our liquid." Play "Thumbs Up" for each example and nonexample during a snack time conversation. Create a visual (Venn diagram) for children to sort the empty containers (e.g., milk, crackers, soup, yogurt).
Free play/centers (loose parts)	Encourage free sorts (e.g., provide a variety of materials with similar and different attributes and observe how children arrange, group, or sort), and interview children to understand their categories and rules for sorting and grouping. Model changing the category from color to shape or from size to color (e.g., "I first made color groups by putting all the black buttons together, but then I noticed that some black buttons are circles and some are squares, so I changed to shape groups and added the other colored shape buttons").
Closing circle and transition to home	Play "Category, Category." Say labels of pictures and objects and prompt children to respond with a "yes" or "no" as they leave circle and begin to make the transition to home. For example, under the category of pets, list and have children say "yes," or "no" if the word label aligns to the category (e.g., dog, cat, rabbit, fish, carrot, horse, hamster, bicycle).

engaged and independent?" then they have used the strategy of environmental adaptations (Campbell & Melbourne, 2014; Melbourne & Campbell, 2007). When people hear the word *adaptations,* they may think about children with identified disabilities or related terms such as *accommodations* or *assistive technology.* An environmental adaptation as used here means to alter the setting or situation to provide temporary support to a child or subset of children. Environmental adaptations include alterations to the location where instruction is delivered and the materials that are used; who is present during the activity; as well as the ways in which things are organized, displayed, and sequenced. Box 6.2 includes several examples of environmental adaptations.

Box 6.2. Examples of environmental adaptations

- Providing self-correcting materials

- Incorporating technology-based and assistive materials/devices

- Providing longer response time

- Using adaptive equipment

- Using visual schedules/reminders

- Shortening the length of an activity

- Giving some children fidget toys to hold

- Taping paper to a table for stability

- Using pictures and verbal directions

Environmental adaptations are a focused instructional effort because they adhere to the three characteristics of matching a targeted outcome, being temporary, and being for a subset of children. We examine how a pre-K teacher designed and implemented focused instruction during a "Making a Mr. Potato Head Using a Pumpkin" activity to further illustrate how environmental adaptations can be used.

The Mr. Potato Head activity was conducted during the morning's free play in which Ms. Brooke had identified associations (i.e., how things are related in terms of quantity, size, and spatial and temporal concepts) as the common outcome she was teaching all of the children. The activity was available to the children all week, and Ms. Brooke noticed toward the end of the week that some of the children were struggling with a component of associations (i.e., spatial relations). She could see from the patterns and trends in the week's assessment data that Clark and Christopher were struggling to use spatial terms (e.g., in, on, above, next to*), and they were having trouble with spatial concepts, such as following directions in which they had to put objects in a particular space or identify where objects were in relation to other objects. Ms. Brooke altered the environment by pairing pictures of completed Mr. Potato Heads with spatial words. For example, she put the spatial term* on *by the hat in the picture where it was "on" Mr. Potato Head, and she put the term* next to *by one of the eyes in the picture to illustrate it was "next to the other eye." She also used self-correcting materials by drilling different-size holes in the pumpkin that would only fit certain body parts so the boys would correctly put the mustache above the lip or the nose between the eyes. She made these environmental adaptations specifically for Clark and Christopher and kept them in place for another 2 weeks until she started to see progress in their knowledge and use of spatial relations.*

The type of evidence to support the use of environmental adaptations ranges from promising to probable. In other words, there is promising evidence to support environmental adaptations, such as using fidget toys. This means that the evidence mainly comes from professional wisdom, which can include anecdotes of practitioners who have tried the strategy and witnessed its effectiveness and by extrapolating from the evidence base for other populations of children such as older students (Aupperlee, 2009; Voytecki, 2005). Other environmental adaptations (e.g., using visual schedules and supports) have a stronger evidence base, which may include sufficient theoretical underpinnings and some empirical research with different populations in different settings (Cramer, Hirano, Tentori, Yeganyan, & Hayes, 2011; Ennis-Cole, 2012; Johnston, Nelson, Evans, & Palazolo, 2003; Schneider & Goldstein, 2010; Waters, Lerman, & Hovanetz, 2009).

Intentional Small-Group Activities Forming intentional small groups is another focused strategy. In such instances, teachers and teams are able to present new information to children, promote cooperative play among children, make use of peer models, capitalize on observational learning events, and allow children multiple opportunities to practice and generalize skills they have learned in other settings (Ledford, Lane, Elam, & Wolery, 2012; Ledford & Wolery, 2013). In fact, the number of advantages of intentional small-group activities makes them one of the most effective tools in a teacher's or team's arsenal. Table 6.2 provides a summary of the advantages of intentional small-group activities along with the research to support their use.

Harnessing the power of intentional small-group activities, however, requires careful planning and consideration by teachers and teams. First, they must be clear about the purpose of the small group, which is easily done, just as long as they have taken the steps needed to identify a targeted outcome for which child or which small group of children. Second, they need to understand that this type of small-group activity differs from center time activities in which small numbers of children may be playing with or near one another. Third, teachers and teams need to engage in systematic planning to determine the size of the group, the composition of the group, and when to form and embed the small group into the daily schedule. Once these aspects are determined, teachers and teams can think about the activity itself and materials that may be needed. Box 6.3 provides an example of using intentional small-group activities as focused instruction.

Although intentional small-group activities can provide excellent opportunities for emphasizing and supporting children on a variety of targeted outcomes, teachers and teams need to avoid two common pitfalls. First, avoid dividing the class of 24 in half and considering it a small group; intentional small groups are ideally composed of three to five children. Second, avoid randomly placing children into small groups (e.g., by the color of their shirt) or as a way to manage challenging behaviors (e.g., separating two children who often argue and have difficulty sharing).

Table 6.2. Advantages and research support regarding intentional small-group activities

Advantage	Research support
Children can learn behaviors being taught to other children	Ledford, J.R., Lane, J.D., Elam, K.L., & Wolery, M. (2012). Using response-prompting procedures during small-group direction instruction: Outcomes and procedural variations. *American Journal on Intellectual and Developmental Disabilities, 117*(5), 413–434. Ledford, J.R., & Wolery, M. (2013). Peer modeling of academic and social behaviors during small-group direct instruction. *Exceptional Children, 79*(4), 439–458.
Provide additional opportunities to develop friendships and learn critical social skills (e.g., sharing)	Brown, W.H., Odom, S.L., McConnell, S.R., & Rathel, J.M. (2008). Peer interaction interventions for preschool children with developmental difficulties. In W.H. Brown, S.L. Odom, & S.R. McConnell (Eds.), *Social competence of young children: Risk, disability, and intervention* (2nd ed., pp. 141–163). Baltimore, MD: Paul H. Brookes Publishing Co. Frea, W., Craig-Unkefer, L., Odom, S.L., & Johnson, D. (1999). Differential effects of structured social integration and group friendship activities for promoting social interaction with peers. *Journal of Early Intervention, 22*(3), 230–242. Sperry, L., Neitzel, J., & Engelhardt-Wells, K. (2010). Peer-mediated instruction and intervention strategies for student with autism spectrum disorders. *Preventing School Failure, 54*(4), 256–264.
More efficient use of instructional time in delivering individualized instruction without having to rely on one-to-one activities	Harris, K.I., Pretti-Frontczak, K., & Brown, T. (2009). Peer-mediated intervention: An effective, inclusive strategy for all young children. *Young Children, 64*, 43–49.
Children, particularly those with disabilities, are afforded more opportunities to spend time with peers versus adults	Guralnick, M.J. (2010). Early intervention approaches to enhance the peer-related social competence of young children with developmental delays: A historical perspective. *Infants and Young Children, 23*(2), 73–83. Hollingsworth, H.L., & Buysse, V. (2009). Establishing friendships in early childhood inclusive setting: What roles do parents and teachers play? *Journal of Early Intervention, 31*(4), 287–307.
Expectations can be tailored to the needs of the children, and the complexity of what they should attend to can be reduced	Horn, E., & Banerjee, R. (2009). Understanding curriculum modifications and embedded learning opportunities in the context of supporting all children's success. *Language, Speech, and Hearing Services in Schools, 40*, 406–415. van de Pol, J., Volman, M., & Beishuizen, J. (2010). Scaffolding in teacher–student interaction: A decade of research. *Educational Psychology Review, 22*(3), 271–296.
Teachers and teams can be clearer and more accurate in terms of how to reinforce different child responses	Stanton-Chapman, T.L., & Snell, M.E. (2011). Promoting turn-taking skills in preschool children with disabilities: The effects of a peer-based social communication intervention. *Early Childhood Research Quarterly, 26*, 303–319. doi:10.1016/j.ecresq.2010.11.002

Peer Modeling　Using peers to mediate learning opportunities is a fourth focused instructional strategy. The research on learning from peers is well documented (Brown, Odom, McConnell, & Rathel, 2008; Guralnick, 2010; Ledford & Wolery, 2015; Meyer & Ostrosky, 2014; Robertson, Green, Alper, Schloss, & Kohler, 2003). Peer-mediated interventions, in particular, have been shown to be effective in supporting the development of social skills in young children with disabilities (English, Goldstein, Shafer, & Kaczmarek, 1997; Hughett, Kohler, & Raschke, 2013; Kohler, Greteman,

---

Box 6.3.   Example of a small-group activity

Based on formative assessment information, Ms. Mayra recognized that several children needed additional support in order to follow directions, which is a skill that emerges concurrently with comprehension, auditory discrimination, and working memory and allows children to demonstrate compliance and participate in daily routines. Having identified following directions as a targeted outcome for three children, Ms. Mayra knew what to teach and whom to teach and was ready to determine whether and which other children to include and when to form the intentional small-group activity. Ms. Mayra decided to create a small group of four children, the three who needed focused instruction on following directions and one other child who consistently showed that he or she was able to follow directions, even multiple-step directions. Ms. Mayra also decided to plan a cooking activity that could be facilitated during center time because it lent itself to providing multiple opportunities to follow directions, ranging from simple to complex, in order to support the differing cognitive levels of the children in the group. Finally, Ms. Mayra included the more competent peer to serve as a model and help support children as the activity progressed.

Raschke, & Highnam, 2007). For example, children without disabilities are taught to initiate play with a child who has social skills delays. Specific behaviors such as offering a toy or asking a child to play a game are taught to children through role-play situations with adults.

Peer modeling differs from broad-based observational learning opportunities (i.e., universal) and highly prescriptive peer-mediated intervention strategies (i.e., individualized). Peer modeling as a focused instructional strategy can be delivered by a peer with or without an iden-tified disability, can be used to support social skills as well as other skills in which a subset of children is struggling, and can increase the number of learning opportunities on a temporary basis. Thus, simply put, *peer modeling* is defined as a competent peer showing/doing and reinforcing the desired targeted outcome for another child. To that end, however, there are a number of things teachers and teams should do to make effec-tive use of peer models, as well as a number of cautions. Table 6.3 pro-vides a summary of what to do (and why) when using peer modeling as a focused instructional strategy.

As depicted in the following scenario, successful peer modeling requires that teachers and teams help peer models 1) give the least amount of assistance the other child/children needs to be successful, 2) allow the child/children to be as independent as possible, and 3) ensure that the child/children are active participants in all classroom activities and routines.

Table 6.3. Summary of what to do and why when using peer modeling as a focused instructional strategy

What to do	Why important
Provide all children an opportunity to be the peer model.	Any child can serve as a peer model, even those with identified disabilities. The important aspect of this strategy is identifying competent peers who can help others perform the targeted outcome. Children who have developmental delays are too often viewed as the "babies" in the classroom. Young children view them as someone to do things to instead of someone to do things with.
Match peer models with subsets of children based on shared interests.	Children who have shared interests are more likely to engage in sustained play and interactions.
Use multiple combinations of peer models.	Using only one child to serve as a peer may result in concerns with fatigue, reliance on only one peer, and the need to provide the receiving child with opportunities to engage with multiple children.
Provide training, support, and positive/descriptive feedback to peer models.	Ensures fidelity and keeps motivational levels high

The teaching team in Ms. Tracy's blended Head Start classroom discovered that Kaliah, who had recently become more independent with using her hands to manipulate and activate objects, wasn't consistently using the skill across the daily routine. Instead, Kaliah tended to watch others stack blocks versus creating her own structure, ask for help to peel and prepare foods, and use one hand as she engaged in writing and drawing activities. The targeted outcome for Kaliah was to generalize the use of one hand to hold or steady an object and use the other hand to manipulate or to use both hands to manipulate. To help Kaliah use and generalize the targeted outcome, the teaching team created a list of all the ways the skill could be demonstrated across the daily schedule (e.g., stacking, pouring, cutting, tearing, snapping, stringing). They took pictures of children who could demonstrate the targeted outcome while engaging in Kaliah's favorite activities or playing with her favorite materials. Finally, the team identified two peers from the classroom who enjoyed similar activities as Kaliah and were competent in manipulating a wide variety of objects with both hands. The teaching team held a brief meeting each morning with the two peer models. The team picked a peer model for the day during the morning meeting (i.e., peers were rotated daily to reduce fatigue), and he or she was shown four cards—one that represented the peer modeling or prompting for Kaliah, one illustrating a peer waiting for Kaliah to respond, one illustrating how peers could help Kaliah manipulate objects using both hands, and one showing how to praise Kaliah when she manipulated objects (e.g., giving her a high five). The cards were generally used to remind the peers how they could encourage Kaliah to do what the child was doing in the picture or what they were doing during a particular activity.

Scaffolding   *Scaffolding* is a fifth focused instructional strategy and is often defined as "targeted assistance (hinting) provided to students to help them grasp a concept that they are right on the cusp of learning. Originating from the work of psychologist Lev Vygotsky to ensure the most positive progression for each student, instruction should be targeted in the zone between what the student can do independently and what he or she can do with a bit of scaffolding or assistance" (Northwest Evaluation Association, 2013, p. 23). Scaffolding can be thought of as a means of guiding and supporting others as or when needed. Scaffolding embodies the characteristics of focused instruction the best out of all of the strategies discussed in this chapter in terms of being used at a small-group level and is temporary by design.

As a focused instructional strategy, scaffolding includes the purposeful tailoring of the amount and type of support given to a subset of children as well as carefully planned contingencies. Chapter 4 provided descriptions and the evidence base of different types of supports and prompts that can be used, from clues and hints to physical assistance, and Chapter 7 describes systematic ways to select and deliver supports and prompts. This chapter, Chapter 6, illustrates how teachers and teams can mediate children's learning when they make moment-to-moment decisions about how much support to give children (Bredekamp & Rosegrant, 1992, 1995). Figure 6.2 shows how teachers and teams decide whether a child needs support, what type of assistance is needed, and at what point the child does need support. In other words, moment-to-moment decisions are made in terms of how much support to give (e.g., a nod of encouragement versus taking the child by the hand and directing him or her), when to add more support (e.g., a visual symbol), and how long to delay before prompting again.

Focused Instruction in Action

An Intentional Instructional Sequence (IIS) decision-making process (Pretti-Frontczak & Grisham-Brown, 2012) can be used to ensure that instruction is delivered as planned (see Chapter 4). The IIS is a process and should augment other forms of lesson planning. The IIS process includes five essential steps for designing instruction for all children, regardless of the type of outcome or instructional strategy, including 1) what to teach, 2) when to teach, 3) where to teach, 4) what to teach with, and 5) how to teach. Furthermore, the IIS process is additive, in the sense that focused instruction (and eventually systematic instruction) is delivered in addition to universal instruction. Figure 6.2 contains the IIS described for universal instruction in Chapter 4 and then builds on it by adding focused instruction for a targeted outcome during the same activity, in the same location, and with the same materials.

Intentional Instructional Sequence Planning Form

Outcome	When	Where	With what	How to teach		Progress monitoring
				Instructional strategy (universal)	Feedback	
Common outcome(s)						
KECS.LA.2.1 Engages in active listening in a variety of situations	Center time	Library	Copies of the book *Polar Bear, Polar Bear, What Do You Hear?* by Bill Martin, Jr., and Eric Carle	Read story to children, asking the following questions: • What is the title of the book? • What animals are in the story? • What color is the _____ (fill in animal name)?	Give specific verbal praise when children answer a question correctly (e.g., "Yes, the yellow lion comes next").	Use a checklist in which each child's name is listed and give the frequency with which the child correctly sequenced the animals in retelling the story.
KECS.LA.3.1 Listens to and/ or responds to reading materials with interest and enjoyment			Hand-size felted objects of each animal in story	Ask a series of questions about what the polar bear and friends hear: • Say, "Which animal sound does the polar bear hear first?" • Say, "What does it sound like to have a lion roaring in your ear?" • Say, "What does the lion then hear?"	Give hints if the children are having difficulty determining which animal comes next (e.g., "What animal is long and can curl itself?").	
KECS.LA.3.6 Tells and retells a story (KECS: Kentucky Early Childhood Standards)			Flannel board		Supply the answer if children get the wrong answer, and have them repeat the correct answer.	Self-assessment— have children go through story to determine if the order of the animals is correct according to the story.

(continued)

Figure 6.2. Intentional Instructional Sequence Planning Form for universal and targeted instruction. (From Pretti-Frontczak, K., & Grisham-Brown, J. [2012]. *Manual for designing and delivering intentional instruction.* Brooklyn, NY: B2K Solutions, Ltd.; adapted by permission).

Figure 6.2. (continued)

Outcome	When	Where	With what	How to teach		Progress monitoring
				Instructional strategy (focused)	Feedback	
Targeted outcome(s)						
Follows directions within the allotted time (i.e., between 5 and 10 seconds)	Center time	Library	Copies of the book *Polar Bear, Polar Bear, What Do You Hear?* by Bill Martin, Jr., and Eric Carle

Hand-size felt objects of each animal in story

Flannel board | Give multiple directions using verbal and visual support at the start of the activity, during the activity, and making the transition to the next activity.

Encourage three to four children to work together (two who struggle and two who do not) to follow your directions by placing hand-size animals in the order they appeared in the story, by size, and by color.

Revisit the visual schedule toward the end of the activity to remind children of what is coming next and the actions they'll be expected to take (e.g., put materials away, line up, go to another area in the room).

Provide physical support for children as needed (e.g., guiding to and from the library, putting materials away, placing objects on flannel board). | After 5–10 seconds of giving the direction, if the child or group of children follows the direction, then affirm, provide descriptive praise, or provide natural consequences.

When child or children do not respond within the allotted time, give the direction again. The restatement should use the word *need* (e.g., "You *need* to put the toy on the shelf." "You *need* to line up"). | Use a count and tally system to record the number of times the child or children followed directions within the allotted time. |

Figure 6.2. *(continued)*

Outcome	When	Where	With what	How to teach			Progress monitoring
				Antecedent Instructional strategy (systematic)	Behavior (individualized outcome)	Consequences	
Individualized outcome(s)							

SUMMARY

The purpose of Chapter 6 was to define the characteristics of focused instruction, outline several considerations for implementing focused strategies, and provide several examples of how to deliver focused instruction within a blended classroom. Focused instruction is necessary when a subset of children are struggling or their development and learning has stalled. Five focused instructional strategies were discussed, including embedded learning opportunities, environmental adaptations, intentional small-group activities, peer modeling, and scaffolding. Systematic instructional strategies are discussed in the next chapter.

LEARNING ACTIVITIES

1. Design a small-group activity to use in a preschool classroom. After designing the activity, refer to page 132 that describes high-quality small-group activities. Explain which guidelines you followed and which you did not. How would you revise the activity plan to ensure that all children can participate and are engaged?

2. Create an activity matrix for a subset of children your classroom. Indicate the common and targeted outcomes. Also, indicate activities during the day that address the targeted outcomes and note the focused instructional strategies you would use. Refer to Figure 6.2.

3. Describe a child in your classroom or a hypothetical child and select a targeted language or communication outcome that could be addressed using peer modeling. How would you decide which peers to use? How would you train the peers? In what activities could you plan to use peer modeling?

REFERENCES

Aupperlee, A. (2009, August 5). *Teachers use movement to keep fidgeting students alert in classroom.* Retrieved from http://www.tlc space.com/wp-content/uploads/2012/11/teachers-use-movement-to-keep-fidgeting-students-alert-in-classroom.pdf

Barton, E.E., Bishop, C.C., & Snyder, P. (2014). *Quality instruction through complete learning trials: Blending intentional teaching with embedded instruction.* Los Angeles, CA: Division for Early Childhood of the Council for Exceptional Children.

Bredekamp, S., & Rosegrant, T. (1992). *Reaching potential: Appropriate curriculum and assessments for young children* (Vol. 1). Washington, DC: National Association for the Education of Young Children.

Bredekamp, S., & Rosegrant, T. (1995). *Reaching potential: Transforming early childhood curriculum and assessment* (Vol. 2). Washington, DC: National Association for the Education of Young Children.

Brown, W.H., Odom, S.L., McConnell, S.R., & Rathel, J.M. (2008). Peer interaction interventions for preschool children with developmental difficulties. In W.H. Brown, S.L. Odom, & S.R. McConnell (Eds.), *Social competence of young children: Risk, disability, and intervention* (2nd ed., pp. 141–163). Baltimore, MD: Paul H. Brookes Publishing Co.

Campbell, P.H., & Melbourne, S.A. (2014). Together is better: Environmental teaching practices to support all children's learning. In K. Pretti-Frontczak, J. Grisham-Brown, & L. Sullivan (Eds.), *Blending practices for all children* (Young Exceptional Children Monograph Series No. 16, pp. 21–38). Los Angeles, CA: Division for Early Childhood of the Council for Exceptional Children.

Craig-Unkefer, L.A., & Kaiser, A. (2002). Improving the social communication skills of at-risk preschool children in a play context. *Topics in Early Childhood Special Education, 22,* 3–13.

Cramer, M., Hirano, S.H., Tentori, M., Yeganyan, M.T., & Hayes, G.R. (2011, May). *Classroom-based assistive technology: Collective use of interactive visual schedules by students with autism.* Proceedings of the 2011 Annual Conference on Human Factors in Computing Systems, New York, NY.

Daugherty, S., Grisham-Brown, J., & Hemmeter, M. (2001). The effects of embedded skill instruction on the acquisition of target and nontarget skills in preschoolers with developmental delays. *Topics in Early Childhood Special Education, 21,* 213–221.

English, K., Goldstein, H., Shafer, K., & Kaczmarek, L. (1997). Promoting interactions among preschoolers with and without disabilities: Effects of a buddy skills-training program. *Exceptional Children, 63,* 229–243.

Ennis-Cole, D. (2012, October). *Promising applications of technology and software preferences of children with autism spectrum disorders.* Paper presented at the 35th Annual Proceedings at the Annual Convention of the Association for Educational Communications and Technology, Louisville, KY.

Frea, W., Craig-Unkefer, L., Odom, S.L., & Johnson, D. (1999). Differential effects of structured social integration and group friendship activities for promoting social interaction with peers. *Journal of Early Intervention, 22*(3), 230–242.

Grisham-Brown, J., Pretti-Frontczak, K., Hawkins, S.R., & Winchell, B.N. (2009). Addressing early learning standards for all children within blended preschool classrooms. *Topics in Early Childhood Special Education, 29*(3), 131–138.

Grisham-Brown, J., Ridgley, R., Pretti-Frontczak, K., Litt, C., & Nielson, A. (2006). Promoting positive learning outcomes for young children in inclusive classrooms: A preliminary study of children's progress toward pre-writing standards. *Journal of Early and Intensive Behavior Intervention, 3*(1), 171–190.

Guralnick, M.J. (2010). Early intervention approaches to enhance the peer-related social competence of young children with developmental delays: A historical perspective. *Infants and Young Children, 23,*(2), 73–83.

Harris, K.I., Pretti-Frontczak, K., & Brown, T. (2009). Peer-mediated intervention: An effective, inclusive strategy for all young children. *Young Children, 64,* 43–49.

Hollingsworth, H.L., & Buysse, V. (2009). Establishing friendships in early childhood inclusive setting: What roles do parents and teachers play? *Journal of Early Intervention, 31*(4), 287–307.

Horn, E., & Banerjee, R. (2009). Understanding curriculum modifications and embedded learning opportunities in the context of supporting all children's success. *Language, Speech, and Hearing Services in Schools, 40,* 406–415.

Horn, E., Lieber, J., Li, S., Sandall, S., & Schwartz, I. (2000). Supporting young children's IEP goals in inclusive settings through embedded learning opportunities. *Topics in Early Childhood Special Education, 20*(4), 208–223.

Hughett, K., Kohler, F.W., & Raschke, D. (2013). The effects of a buddy skills package on preschool children's social interactions and play. *Topics in Early Childhood Special Education, 32*(4), 246–254. doi:10.1177/0271121411424927

Johnston, S., Nelson, C., Evans, J., & Palazolo, K. (2003). The use of visual supports in teaching young children with autism spectrum disorder to initiate interactions. *Augmentative and Alternative Communication, 19*(2), 86–103.

Kohler, F.W., Greteman, C., Raschke, D., & Highnam, C. (2007). Using a buddy skills package to increase the social interactions between a preschooler with autism and her peers. *Topics in Early Childhood Special Education, 27*(3), 155–163.

Kurt, O., & Tekin-Iftar, E. (2008). A comparison of constant time delay and simultaneous prompting within embedded instruction on teaching leisure skills to children with autism. *Topics in Early Childhood Special Education, 28*(1), 53–64.

Ledford, J.R., Lane, J.D., Elam, K.L., & Wolery, M. (2012). Using response-prompting procedures during small-group direction instruction: Outcomes and procedural variations. *American Journal on Intellectual and Developmental Disabilities, 117*(5), 413–434.

Ledford, J.R., & Wolery, M. (2013). Peer modeling of academic and social behaviors during small-group direct instruction. *Exceptional Children, 79*(4), 439–458.

Ledford, J.R., & Wolery, M. (2015). Observational learning of academic and social behavior during small group-direct instruction. *Exceptional Children, 81*(3), 272–291.

Macy, M.G., & Bricker, D. (2007). Embedding individualized social goals into routine activities in inclusive early childhood classrooms. *Early Child Development and Care, 177*(2), 107–120.

McBride, B.J., & Schwartz, I.S. (2003). Effects of teaching early interventionists to use discrete trials during ongoing classroom activities. *Topics in Early Childhood Special Education, 23*(1), 5–17.

Martin, B., Jr., & Carle, E. (1997). *Polar bear, polar bear, what do you hear?* New York, NY: Holt and Company.

Melbourne, S.A., & Campbell, P.H. (2007). *CARA's kit: Creating adaptations for routines and activities.* Washington, DC: National Association for the Education of Young Children.

Meyer, L.E., & Ostrosky, M.M. (2014). An examination of research on the friendships of young children with disabilities. *Topics in Early Childhood Special Education, 34*(3), 186–196.

Northwest Evaluation Association. (2013). *Teacher-detailed user guide for the Children's Progress Academic Assessment.* Retrieved from http://www.irvingisd.net/cms/lib010/TX01917973/Centricity/Domain/1401/CPAA_Detailed_Teacher_User_Guide.pdf

Pretti-Frontczak, K. (2014). *Addressing targeted outcomes as part of a multi-tiered system of support.* Brooklyn, NY: B2K Solutions.

Pretti-Frontczak, K., Barr, D.M., Macy, M., & Carter, A.M. (2003). An annotated bibliography of research and resources related to activity-based intervention, embedded learning opportunities, and routines-based instruction. *Topics in Early Childhood Special Education, 23*(1), 29–39.

Pretti-Frontczak, K., & Grisham-Brown, J. (2012). *Manual for designing and delivering intentional instruction.* Brooklyn, NY: B2K Solutions.

Robertson, J., Green, K., Alper, S., Schloss, P.J., & Kohler, F. (2003). Using a peer-mediated intervention to facilitate children's participation in inclusive childcare activities. *Education and Treatment of Children, 26*(2), 182–197.

Schneider, N., & Goldstein, H. (2010). Using social stories and visual schedules to improve socially appropriate behaviors in children with autism. *Journal of Positive Behavior, 12*(3), 149–160.

Sperry, L., Neitzel, J., & Engelhardt-Wells, K. (2010). Peer-mediated instruction and intervention strategies for student with autism spectrum disorders. *Preventing School Failure, 54*(4), 256–264. doi:10.1080/10459881003800529

Stanton-Chapman, T.L., & Snell, M.E. (2011). Promoting turn-taking skills in preschool children with disabilities: The effects of a peer-based social communication intervention. *Early Childhood Research Quarterly, 26,* 303–319. doi:10.1016/j.ecresq.2010.11.002

van de Pol, J., Volman, M., & Beishuizen, J. (2010). Scaffolding in teacher–student interaction: A decade of research. *Educational Psychology Review, 22*(3), 271–296.

Voytecki, K.S. (2005). *The effects of hand fidgets on the on-task behaviors of a middle school student with disabilities in an inclusive academic setting.* Retrieved from http://etd.fcla.edu/SF/SFE0001142/Voytecki-Karen-dissertation.pdf

Waters, M.B., Lerman, D.C., & Hovanetz, A.N. (2009). Separate and combined effects of visual schedules and extinction plus differential reinforcement on problem behavior occasioned by transitions. *Journal of Applied Behavior Analysis, 42*(2), 309–313.

Wolery, M., Anthony, L., Caldwell, N.K., Snyder, E.D., & Morgante, J.D. (2002). ELOs in inclusive EC settings: 32 embedding and distributing constant time delay in circle time and transitions. *Topics in Early Childhood Special Education, 22*, 14–25.

## CHAPTER 7

Systematic
Instructional Practices

Jennifer Grisham-Brown and Mary Louise Hemmeter

Mr. Kenneth has an extremely diverse group of children this year in his Head Start classroom. Although all of the children in his classroom are from low-income families, three of the children have developmental delays, and six of the 18 children are dual language learners. Mr. Kenneth feels confident in his ability to design universal instruction that addresses the Head Start outcomes. He also has learned to analyze the assessment data he collects to design intentional small groups for children who are struggling with components of the outcomes. Mr. Kenneth is at a loss, however, for what to do with children in his classroom who are missing basic skills to help them participate in many classroom activities. Regardless of how often he works with these children, they just aren't getting it. He has taken a course on working with children with special needs and has learned about making adaptations and creating more learning opportunities. The problem is that those ideas are not working. Plus, some of the children who are having these problems don't have diagnosed developmental disabilities. Mr. Kenneth is growing increasingly frustrated by his inability to support these children.

The situation in which Mr. Kenneth finds himself is not uncommon for teachers in blended classrooms. Sometimes, teachers in blended classrooms do not feel like they have enough strategies in their toolkit to address the needs of all the children in their classroom. Even teachers who can gather and use assessment information to make instructional decisions often do not know how to support children with more intensive learning needs. This chapter describes *systematic teaching strategies,* which we define as a set of practices that are generally used to teach Tier 3 outcomes, although they may be used for other types of outcomes in specific situations. Systematic teaching strategies are highly structured practices that are delivered with precision and intensity and are individualized for children based on their learning needs and characteristics. The purpose of using systematic instructional strategies is described. Next, two types of systematic instructional strategies are discussed. The chapter also includes a set of generic instructional strategy intervention plans that appear in Appendix 7A.

PURPOSES OF SYSTEMATIC INSTRUCTIONAL STRATEGIES AT TIER 3

Each instructional tier generally addresses a corresponding set of outcomes (see Chapter 4). Therefore, systematic instructional strategies are generally used to support the acquisition of Tier 3 outcomes (see Chapter 3). Tier 3 strategies are specifically designed to remove barriers to learning, increase social skills, and address prerequisite skills. It is important to note that the reasons for using systematic instruction have to do with what children need to learn and are not based on whether children have developmental delays. Teachers need to be aware of the strategies described in this chapter because they are powerful interventions for addressing any of the learning needs described here.

Barriers to Learning

A barrier preventing a child from learning outcomes like other children is one reason that a child might need Tier 3 instruction. A child who speaks a different language than the primary language spoken in the classroom represents one learning barrier. The child may need to learn simple English vocabulary in order for him or her to gain access to information in the classroom. Systematic instruction to teach vocabulary is needed because not knowing the primary language spoken in the classroom is preventing the child from gaining access to the general curriculum.

A child who has a challenging behavior that prevents him or her from focusing on instruction represents another barrier to learning. If a child is demonstrating challenging behavior because he or she does not have the necessary communication skills to express him- or herself, then systematic instruction could be used to teach the child more appropriate communication strategies. Learning content that is part of the general curriculum may not be possible if the child is engaged in challenging behavior. Experts on dealing with challenging behavior agree that challenging behavior serves a purpose for a child, and a replacement skill must be taught (Noonan & McCormick, 2014). A functional behavioral assessment (FBA) is used to determine the purpose the challenging behavior is serving for the child (Noonan & McCormick, 2014). For example, results of an FBA may show that a nonverbal child expresses frustration by throwing or tearing up materials whenever he or she cannot accomplish a task. Systematic instruction should be used to teach the child to ask for help in order to replace the challenging behavior.

Foundation/Prerequisite Skills

A second reason that Tier 3 instruction might be needed is when a child is missing a foundational or prerequisite skill. Foundational skills are developmental milestones that a child has not learned well beyond the age at which he or she should demonstrate the skill. For example, a 4-year-old child should be able to use three- or four-word sentences to express his or her wants and needs. If the child is using gestures and word approximations at that age, then teaching the child more complex symbolic forms of communication might require systematic instruction. Similarly, prerequisite skills are those skills that a child needs to learn in order to develop more complex skills. For example, if a 4-year-old child cannot manipulate objects using one hand to perform one task and the other hand to perform a second task (i.e., bilateral coordination), teachers will want to use systematic instruction to teach the fine motor skill. If the child has no bilateral coordination, it will be impossible for him or her to learn more sophisticated fine motor skills such as writing.

SYSTEMATIC TEACHING STRATEGIES

It is beyond the scope of this book to discuss every systematic teaching strategy available to teachers in blended classrooms. Instead, this chapter focuses on systematic teaching strategies that have been widely used with young children or may be implemented with fidelity by teachers and other personnel in early childhood education environments. Two broad categories of systematic teaching strategies are specifically discussed: 1) enhanced milieu teaching and 2) response prompting procedures. Specific strategies are identified for each category, along with examples of skills that can be taught with the strategies.

Enhanced Milieu Teaching

Enhanced milieu teaching involves an adult purposefully and intentionally manipulating the child's environment (i.e., milieu) to promote the development and use of language skills (Hart & Rogers-Warren, 1978). Prompting strategies, in combination with environmental arrangement and responsive intervention techniques, are known as enhanced milieu teaching (Hancock & Kaiser, 2002; Hemmeter & Kaiser, 1994; Kaiser, Hancock, & Nietfeld, 2000). Table 7.1 describes each of the environmental arrangement strategies and provides an example of how to use them in the classroom. Both are integral parts for using the four milieu teaching prompting strategies described in this section. The milieu teaching strategies have generally been used to teach communication and social skills. Table 7.2 provides information on the specific communication skills that may be taught with each of the milieu teaching strategies. Research on the milieu teaching strategies shows that families can reliably implement the strategies within the context of home routines (Hemmeter & Kaiser, 1994; Mobayed, Collins, Strangis, Schuster,

Table 7.1. Environmental arrangement strategies

Name	Description	Example
Access	Child is engaged in a preferred activity or with a preferred material, and the teacher limits access to the activity, giving the child an opportunity to communicate.	The teacher is pushing the child on a swing on the playground. He or she stops, creating an opportunity for the child to ask the teacher to start again (e.g., "More swing, please").
Unexpected event	Child is engaged in a familiar activity or routine, and the teacher does something different than what is expected, giving the child an opportunity to comment on the correct way the activity is to be conducted.	The teacher is in the math center counting objects as he or she puts them on a scale. He or she counts 1, 3, 4, 7, 2, allowing the child to correct the teacher by counting 1 to 5 in order.
Insufficient material	Child is involved in an activity with familiar materials, and the teacher leaves out a material that is needed in order to complete the activity, creating an opportunity for the child to request the missing material.	The teacher removes the crayons, markers, and pencils from the writing center, thereby creating an opportunity for the child to request a writing utensil.

Table 7.2.   Skills taught with enhanced milieu teaching

Procedures	Skills
Modeling	Turn-taking Verbal imitation Basic vocabulary
Mand-model	New forms of communication (e.g., child is gesturing to express wants/needs, and the target is to teach single-word signs such as MORE or EAT)
Naturalistic time delay	Initiate communication, as opposed to responding to others' initiations
Incidental teaching	Expansions of current communication forms (e.g., child currently says "eat" to ask for a bite of food, and you want to teach the child to say "eat banana" (or another food)

& Hemmeter, 2000), and classroom teachers have been trained to implement elements of enhanced milieu teaching with fidelity (Harjusola-Webb & Robbins, 2012; Mudd & Wolery, 1987).

Teachers implementing milieu teaching procedures must know exactly what they want to teach the child (e.g., labeling objects). In addition, the teacher has to decide when to approach the child to create a teaching opportunity, which is based on what the child is involved with that presents the opportunity for the expected response. Care must be given when using the milieu strategies to make sure that the teacher enters the play area and begins the interaction by establishing joint attention based on the child's interest. If the teacher arbitrarily walks into the play area and asks something out of the blue that is unrelated to the child's focus, such as what the child is wearing, then the child will likely ignore the teacher and continue playing.

Modeling   Teachers implementing the modeling procedure use a verbal or visual model to teach new communication skills to a child. A verbal model is used if using speech to communicate is the goal for the child. A visual model would be used if using sign language or pictures to communicate is the goal for the child. The modeling procedure is used to elicit communication responses from a child who may not have the vocabulary, imitation, or turn-taking skills necessary to communicate (Collins, 2012; Noonan & McCormick, 2014). For example, if a child shows interest in a baby doll in the classroom, then the teacher says "doll" in an attempt to teach the child to verbally label the object. In this example, the model procedure would be used with a child who does not know the label for the object (i.e., baby doll).

Mand-Model   The mand-model procedure is used to promote new forms of communication across activities and routines with children who do not initiate communication with others (Collins, 2012; Noonan & McCormick, 2014). Mand-model is implemented when the child uses the target skill in restricted situations or has become dependent on the use of a model prior to exhibiting the skill. The child is prompted to first answer a question related to the target skill before being given the model. For example, while the child is playing in the dramatic play area, the teacher may decide that there will be opportunities to teach the child to label objects. The teacher in this scenario would approach the child and ask a question (i.e., a mand) that is related to what the child is doing: "Oh, you have on a very nice outfit for working at the office. What are those things on your legs?" The teacher then gives the child time to respond by saying, "They're pants" (i.e., a model). If the child correctly says the name of the object, then the teacher provides verbal feedback and waits for another opportunity to have the child label objects. If the child does not say the object label within a designated period of time, then the teacher says, "Those are pants" (i.e., models the response) and gives the child an opportunity to imitate the model. After the child models the correct response, the teacher provides verbal feedback and allows the child to continue in play.

Naturalistic Time Delay   Naturalistic time delay has primarily been used to teach children to make requests (Noonan & McCormick, 2014). It is simply defined as increasing the time between asking the child what he or she wants and giving the child assistance to make the expected request. It is typically used with children who primarily use nonverbal ways of communicating (e.g., grunting, banging on a table, reaching for something) and need to be taught a more formal way of communicating or with children who have become dependent on prompts. The procedure begins with the teacher withholding something that the child wants. For example, a child at the snack table might want more applesauce in his or her bowl. Presently, the child will respond to the teacher's question about what he or she wants but will not request the bowl independently. The teacher does nothing when this occurs but looks at the child as if to say, "I'm not sure what you want." At the same time, the teacher waits a predetermined length of time so that the child has an opportunity to request. If the child uses the target request, the teacher then gives him or her more applesauce. If the child says nothing, the teacher provides either a mand or a model of what the child should say. For example, after waiting 5 seconds, the teacher could either provide a mand (e.g., tell me what you want) or a model (e.g., say "more"). From that point, the teacher follows the steps of the model or mand-model procedure.

Incidental Teaching   The purpose of incidental teaching is to expand a child's language attempts. It assumes that the child has some form of communication that needs to be expanded or changed (e.g., the child uses gestures to communicate but is learning to use single words). Incidental teaching involves the use of the previous three procedures following a child's request. In other words, when a child makes a request, the teacher uses one of the other three procedures to prompt the child to use a more complex skill. For example, if a child reaches for a toy that is out of reach (and is working on using single words to make a request), the teacher could say, "Tell me what you want" and follow the steps of the mand-model procedure. After giving the mand (i.e., "tell me what you want"), the teacher waits for the child to provide the response in a form that is appropriate for that child (i.e., a single word). As previously discussed, the length of time the teacher waits will depend on how long it reasonably takes the individual child to process the response. The teacher must be careful not to wait too long to provide assistance, which may frustrate the child, who is anxious to receive the desired toy. If the child has processing or motor planning difficulties, however, the teacher should not provide assistance too quickly without giving the child a chance to respond. If the child uses the form of communication that the teacher expects, then the teacher provides the child with immediate access to the toy. If the child does not use the target response, the teacher gives the child a model for the expected response (e.g., "say 'toy'"). The teacher then waits again to allow the child time to imitate the response. The child gains access to the toy when he or she imitates the response.

Evidence Base   Modeling has been used to teach a number of communication skills, including vocalizing, saying single words, gesturing, and saying multiword sentences (Woods, Kashinath, & Goldstein, 2004) and play actions and expansions (Frey & Kaiser, 2011). Teachers have used modeling to teach infants, toddlers (Woods et al., 2004), and preschoolers (Frey & Kaiser, 2011; Hancock & Kaiser, 2002) with language delays, general developmental delays, and autism. The mand-model procedure has been used to teach requesting to infants and toddlers with language delays (Mobayed et al., 2000).

Research often examines the use of two or more milieu teaching procedures. Hemmeter and Kaiser (1994) taught families of young children with disabilities to use all four prompting strategies, which resulted in increases in children's target language skills. For example, Hancock and Kaiser (2002) used modeling, the mand-model procedure, time delay, and incidental teaching to teach preschoolers with autism two- and three-word utterances. Similarly, Harjusola-Webb and Robbins (2012) taught teachers and teaching assistants to use modeling and time delay, along with other strategies (e.g., giving choices), to teach expressive communication skills to preschoolers with autism. Christensen-Sandfort and Whinnery (2013) found the milieu teaching strategies effective in increasing communication for preschoolers with autism. Yoder and Stone (2006) compared the effects of enhanced milieu teaching and the Picture Exchange Communication System (PECS) and found enhanced milieu teaching more effective than PECS in teaching joint attention and turn-taking to young children with autism.

Response Prompting Procedures

Response prompting procedures are a set of procedures that are intended to reduce the number of errors that children make while learning new skills. Prompts are used to reduce errors and are faded so that the child eventually performs the skill under normal circumstances. For example, Emma's teacher might use physical prompting to teach her to put on her jacket, but the physical prompting is eventually faded and Emma puts her coat on when asked to do so at recess and dismissal. Because response prompting strategies stem from behavioral learning theory, Table 7.3 provides definitions that may be useful in understanding the descriptions of the procedures. In this section, six procedures are described. All were chosen because they 1) have been used to teach individualized outcomes to young children, 2) can be implemented with fidelity by classroom teachers or parents, and 3) have been implemented within the context of natural activities and routines.

Graduated Guidance   The graduated guidance procedure has primarily been used to teach skills for which physical assistance is needed, such as independent feeding, walking, or avoiding dangerous situations (Collins, 2012). The graduated guidance procedure only uses a physical prompt to provide support to a child. Prompts are provided on a moment-to-moment basis as needed. For example, if teaching a child to eat with a spoon, the teacher would provide physical assistance on steps with which the child struggles and would "back off" when the child does not need assistance. Denny et al. (2001) trained a mother of a 2½-year-old child with cri-du-chat syndrome to use graduated guidance. The procedure was used to teach independent eating and ball rolling in the child's home. Results showed that the child learned to feed himself independently and maintained and generalized the skill. The child's performance on ball rolling was more variable, but the child did make progress on the skill and was able to generalize his performance level to another adult without intervention.

System of Least Prompts   The system of least prompts procedure is often used to teach chained tasks such as brushing teeth, but it can be used to teach discrete skills such as labeling objects. A minimum of three prompts must be identified and ordered from the least to most intrusive (e.g., verbal, model, physical). For example, if teaching a child to put on his or her coat at dismissal, the child is first given the opportunity to perform the

Table 7.3.   Terminology associated with response prompting procedures

Term	Definition/example
Discrete skills	Single skills that are measurable and observable (e.g., saying "hi" to a friend)
Chained task	Tasks made of multiple discrete skills (e.g., washing hands)
Controlling prompt	Prompt that ensures a child can perform a skill (e.g., hand-over-hand physical prompting may ensure that a child washes his or her hands)
Prompt hierarchy	Ordering prompts by a level of assistance, which might be the least amount of assistance needed to the most amount of assistance or vice versa (e.g., verbal prompt, model prompt, physical prompt)

skill independently before increasing assistance is provided. After the child is provided the opportunity to perform the skill independently, the teacher waits a predetermined length of time (e.g., 3 seconds) before providing the first prompt level. Additional assistance is provided as needed, with wait time inserted between each prompt level. The system of least prompts has been used to teach a variety of skills, including adaptive skills (Grisham-Brown, Schuster, Hemmeter, & Collins, 2000) and putting objects in a container (Grisham-Brown et al., 2000). The procedure also has been used to teach preschoolers with a variety of disabilities (Grisham-Brown et al., 2000).

Most to Least Prompts   The most to least prompts procedure is also used to teach chained or discrete skills, but it is used primarily with children who need more assistance when they are first learning a skill and are more likely to make errors if given an opportunity to perform the task independently (Collins, 2012). As with the system of least prompts, a minimum of three prompt levels must be selected; however, they are ordered from the most intrusive to the least intrusive. For example, if a teacher wants to teach a child to wash his or her hands, then the teacher would start by providing physical prompting for all steps of the task. If the child tolerates the physical prompting, then the teacher might use a model prompt to show the child the steps of washing hands. Once the child can wash his or her hands using a model, the teacher could use a verbal prompt for each step of the task. If the child can complete all steps with a verbal prompt, then he or she is given an opportunity to perform the task independently. The teacher reverts back to a more intrusive prompt when the child cannot perform the skill with the current prompt level. For example, if the child does not follow the verbal prompt, then the teacher would provide the model. The most to least prompting procedure has been used to teach signing UP and MORE (Grisham-Brown et al., 2000). The procedure has also been used to teach preschoolers (Grisham-Brown et al., 2000) as well as children with a variety of abilities, including learners with multiple disabilities (e.g., Grisham-Brown et al., 2000).

Time Delay   The time delay procedures that are described in the response prompting literature differ from naturalistic time delay (previously described) in two ways. First, naturalistic time delay is always used within the context of ongoing activities and routines, whereas time delay is often used in small group, teacher-directed lessons. Second, some form of nonverbal cue is used in naturalistic time delay to set the occasion for the child to respond, whereas time delay always uses a verbal task direction prior to waiting for the child to respond. The time delay procedure has been used to teach a variety of discrete and chained skills. In fact, most teachers have likely used some form of a time delay procedure without even realizing it. Teachers using time delay provide a task direction and then wait for a predetermined period of time before providing a controlling prompt. The first time the teacher presents the task, he or she immediately provides the controlling prompt. For example, if Ms. Kanisha wants Sam to pick up his toys, she gives the task request ("Pick up your toys, Sam") and immediately provides physical support for Sam to pick up his toys. This is called a zero-second delay interval because there is no time between when Ms. Kanisha asked Sam to pick up his toys and when she provided the prompt. Thereafter, Ms. Kanisha inserts a predetermined delay interval between giving the task direction and providing physical support. There are two types of time delay that differ according to how the delay interval is determined—constant time delay and progressive time delay.

Constant Time Delay Teachers using constant time delay select a length of time to wait between giving the task direction and providing the controlling prompt, and that amount of time remains the same throughout instruction. For example, Ms. Kanisha may decide to wait 3 seconds before helping Sam pick up his toys. She will consistently count to three before providing the controlling prompt. Constant time delay has been used to teach counting (Daugherty, Grisham-Brown, & Hemmeter, 2001), choice making (Clark & McDonnell, 2008), turning on an adaptive switch (Grisham-Brown et al., 2000), sight word reading (Alig-Cybriwsky, Wolery, & Gast, 1990; Appelman, Vail, & Leiberman-Betz, 2014), prewriting skills (e.g., copying shapes, writing letters in name) (Grisham-Brown, Pretti-Frontczak, Hawkins, & Winchell, 2009), preacademic skills (e.g., identifying shapes, basic concepts) (Aldemir & Gursel, 2014), and recreation skills (Kurt & Tekin-Iftar, 2008). The procedure has been used to teach preschoolers (Aldemir & Gursel, 2014; Clark & McDonnell, 2008; Daughterty et al., 2001; Grisham-Brown et al., 2000), kindergarteners (Appelman et al., 2014; Clark & McDonnell, 2008), and primary-age children (Kurt & Tekin-Iftar, 2008). Children with a variety of a variety of abilities, including cortical visual impairment (Clark & McDonnell, 2008), developmental delays (Aldemir & Gursel, 2014; Alig-Cybriwsky et al., 1990; Daugherty et al., 2001), orthopedic disabilities/cerebral palsy (Grisham-Brown et al., 2000), autism (Grisham-Brown et al., 2000; Kurt & Tekin-Iftar, 2008), mild learning disabilities (Appelman et al., 2014), and typical development (Alig-Cybriwsky et al., 1990; Grisham-Brown et al., 2009), have benefited from the procedure.

Progressive Time Delay Teachers using progressive time delay slowly increase the length of time to wait between giving the task direction and providing the controlling prompt. The length of time starts with 1 second and steadily increases each day by 1 second until the maximum delay interval is reached (e.g., 5 seconds). For example, after the zero-second delay session, Ms. Kanisha may decide to wait 1 second before helping Sam pick up his toys, followed by 2 seconds, and so forth. The idea behind slowly increasing the delay interval is that many young children are impulsive and will make errors in learning before assistance is provided. Ledford and Wolery (2013) used progressive time delay to teach naming words and colors to preschoolers with Down syndrome and autism and to those with typical development.

Additional Issues

The procedures described in this chapter have primarily been used with young children with developmental disabilities or with those who are at risk for disabilities. Emerging evidence shows, however, that systematic teaching strategies are effective for teaching children with and without disabilities in blended classrooms. In a series of case studies, Grisham-Brown, Pretti-Frontczak, Bachman, Gannon, and Mitchell (2014) taught a kindergartner who was an English language learner to name letters in the alphabet using constant time delay, a Head Start student to eat with utensils using a peer-mediated strategy, and a child receiving early intervention in child care to sign MORE using the mand-model procedure. Using systematic teaching strategies in blended classrooms will require consideration about who will implement the strategies, the degree of fidelity with which the strategies have to be implemented, and the context for providing instruction.

Implementers   Teachers and research assistants with special education experience have often been the implementers of research conducted on systematic instruction strategies. Sufficient evidence, however, shows that parents, paraprofessionals, and peers can implement any of these procedures with fidelity as long as they have support. For example, Mobayed et al. (2000) taught parents of young children with disabilities to implement the mand-model procedure to teach their children language skills during daily activities. The parents received training and instructive feedback and implemented the procedure with fidelity, and the children learned their target skills. Grisham-Brown et al. (2000) taught paraprofessionals to use various response prompting procedures (e.g., time delay, most to least prompting) to teach functional skills to preschoolers with multiple disabilities. The paraprofessionals received training and weekly feedback and reliably implemented the procedures, and three of four children made progress over baseline performance in the study. Finally, Jones and Schwartz (2004) taught siblings and peers to use a time delay procedure to teach basic concepts (e.g., actions, professions, opposites) to children with autism. Results showed that the siblings and peers successfully implemented the procedures, and the children with autism learned their target skills. Given the demands of teaching in a blended classroom, involving others in delivering systematic teaching strategies is recommended and quite possible, based on research.

Implementation Fidelity   The importance of implementing instruction with fidelity must be mentioned. Fidelity means that teachers implement the steps of the procedure with as much precision as possible. Consider a recipe for your favorite cake. If you do not follow the steps correctly or leave out a step, the cake may sink in the middle, taste like salt, or burn. The same idea holds true for instruction. If a teacher inaccurately implements a strategy, the child may not learn the intended outcome. Implementation science suggests that children are more likely to learn if teachers are taught to do something with fidelity and they implement with fidelity (Odom, 2009).

The level of fidelity at which a teacher must implement instruction in order for children to learn is still unknown. Two studies suggest that 100% procedural fidelity may not be necessary, and there may be key pieces of instruction that are more important than others. Odom et al. (2010) evaluated teachers' implementation fidelity of a language and literacy curriculum for preschoolers who were at risk. The researchers examined both structural (i.e., how often, number of lessons) and process (i.e., following steps of lessons) fidelity that affected children's outcomes. Interestingly enough, the level of implementation was between 60% and 80%, suggesting that teachers who make implementation mistakes may still affect children's outcomes. Grisham-Brown, Ruble, Wong, and McGrew (in preparation) examined common elements of instruction to determine if there were specific key features of instruction that must be in place in order for learners with autism to acquire important communication, social, and academic skills. They examined teachers' implementation of a variety of teaching strategies with young children with autism, ages 3–8 years, and looked at teaching behaviors that should occur across any procedure (e.g., getting the child's attention, waiting for the child to respond, providing reinforcement). These behaviors were highly correlated with children's acquisition of individualized education program goals. Results from this research suggest that teachers who may not be able to learn the nuances of each specific systematic teaching strategy might still be effective if they implement key elements of any of the strategies.

Context   Systematic teaching strategies have been implemented in a variety of different contexts. Early research on using response prompting procedures with preschoolers was conducted in a didactic format, meaning that children were removed from ongoing classroom activities and routines and many instructional trials were delivered in successive order (e.g., Alig-Cybrisky et al., 1990). Although children acquired and, to some extent, maintained and generalized skills in that format, more recent research suggests that young children with disabilities also can be taught when systematic teaching strategies are embedded into ongoing classroom activities and routines (e.g., Daugherty et al., 2001; Grisham-Brown et al., 2009; Grisham-Brown, Ridgley, Pretti-Frontczak, Litt, & Nielson, 2006). Providing all instruction in a didactic format or all instruction in the context of the classroom may not be the solution for some children. Children with certain disabilities (e.g., autism) may need instruction in both contexts. Schwartz, Sandall, McBride, and Boulware (2004) developed a successful model for children with autism in which instruction was provided in both contexts. The children in their model program attended a half-day inclusive preschool program in which instruction was embedded into ongoing classroom activities. The children spent the remainder of their day in extended instructional time in which they received instruction in a more didactic format. Although the goal should be to provide instruction within the context of ongoing classroom activities and routines as much as possible, there will be times when didactic instruction may be needed. Combined instructional approaches should be considered in these situations.

Systematic Instruction in Action

Intervention plans that specify the steps of specific systematic teaching strategies are included in Appendix 7A. These intervention plans include three elements. First, the antecedent sets the occasion for the child to respond and includes how to set up the environment, how to establish joint attention with the child, how to deliver the task direction, and how long to wait for the child to respond. Second, the correct and incorrect responses expected of the child are provided. The correct response should include measureable observable behaviors that constitute a correct response. The incorrect response includes behaviors the child should not perform, including not responding at all. Finally, the consequence for each type of response (i.e., correct and incorrect response) is detailed. For the correct response, a plan should include how the environment or the teacher will provide feedback that reinforces the child for providing the correct response. For the incorrect response, teachers detail the prompts they need to provide until the child finally demonstrates the correct response. In some cases, the child might immediately respond correctly after the first prompt is provided, in which case the teacher provides reinforcement. At other times, the child might need additional, more intrusive prompts before demonstrating the correct response. Supporting the child until the correct response is demonstrated is the key to successfully implementing the intervention plan. The intervention plans in Appendix 7A are written generically so that teachers can individualize them for each child. The intent of providing them is to support teachers in implementing the evidence-based practices provided in the chapter with some level of fidelity.

Systematic Instruction and Intentional Instructional Sequence

An Intentional Instructional Sequence (IIS) decision-making process (Pretti-Frontczak & Grisham-Brown, 2012) can be used to ensure that instruction is delivered as planned. The IIS is a process and should augment other forms of lesson planning. The IIS process includes five steps essential for designing instruction for all children, regardless of the type of outcome or instructional strategy: 1) what to teach, 2) when to teach, 3) where to teach, 4) with what to teach, and 5) how to teach. Furthermore, the IIS process is additive—systematic instruction is delivered in addition to the universal instruction and focused instruction. Figure 7.1 contains the IIS described for universal instruction at the end of Chapter 5 and focused instruction at the end of Chapter 6. It builds by adding systematic instruction for an individualized outcome during the same activity, in the same location, and with the same materials. In the sample, the child's individualized outcome is saying single words, and the systematic strategy is the mand-model procedure.

Intentional Instructional Sequence Planning Form

Outcome	When	Where	With what	Instructional strategy (universal)	Feedback	Progress monitoring
Common outcome(s)						
KECS.LA.2.1 Engages in active listening in a variety of situations KECS.LA.3.1 Listens to and/or responds to reading materials with interest and enjoyment KECS.LA.3.6 Tells and retells a story (KECS: Kentucky Early Childhood Standards)	Center time	Library	Copies of the book *Polar Bear, Polar Bear, What Do You Hear?* by Bill Martin, Jr., and Eric Carle Hand-size felted objects of each animal in the story Flannel board	Read story to children, asking the following questions: • What is the title of the book? • What animals are in the story? • What color is the _____ (fill in animal name)? Ask a series of questions about what the polar bear and friends hear: • Say, "Which animal sound does the polar bear hear first?" • Say, "What does it sound like to have a lion roaring in your ear?" • Say, "What does the lion then hear?"	Give specific verbal praise when children answer a question correctly (e.g., "Yes, the yellow lion comes next"). Give hints if the children are having difficulty determining which animal comes next (e.g., "What animal is long and can curl itself?"). Supply the answer if children get the wrong answer, and have them repeat the correct answer.	Use a checklist in which each child's name is listed and give the frequency with which the child correctly sequenced the animals in retelling the story. Self-assessment—have children go through story to determine if the order of the animals is correct according to the story.

Figure 7.1. Intentional Instructional Sequence Planning Form for universal, focused, and systematic instruction. (From Pretti-Frontczak, K., & Grisham-Brown, J. [2012] *Manual for designing and delivering intentional instruction.* Brooklyn, NY: B2K Solutions, Ltd.; adapted with permission.)

Figure 7.1. (continued)

Outcome	When	Where	With what	How to teach		Progress monitoring
				Instructional strategy (focused)	Feedback	
Targeted outcome(s)						
Follows directions within the allotted time (i.e., between 5–10 seconds)	Center time	Library	Copies of the book *Polar Bear, Polar Bear, What Do You Hear?* by Bill Martin, Jr., and Eric Carle Hand-size felted objects of each animal in the story Flannel board	Give multiple directions using verbal and visual support at the start of the activity, during the activity, and making the transition to the next activity. Encourage three to four children to work together (two who struggle and two who do not) to follow your directions by placing hand-size animals in the order they appeared in the story, by size, and by color. Revisit the visual schedule toward the end of the activity to remind children of what is coming next and the actions they'll be expected to take (e.g., put materials away, line up, go to another area in the room). Provide physical support for children as needed (e.g., guiding to and from the library, putting materials away, placing objects on flannel board).	After 5–10 seconds of giving the direction, if the child or group of children follows the direction, then affirm, provide descriptive praise, or provide natural consequences. When child or children do not respond within the allotted time, give the direction again. The restatement should use the word *need* (e.g., "You *need* to put the toy on the shelf." "You *need* to line up").	Use a count and tally system to record the number of times the child or children followed directions within the allotted time.

Figure 7.1. *(continued)*

Outcome	When	Where	With what	How to teach			Progress monitoring
				Antecedent Instructional strategy (systematic)	Behavior (individualized outcome)	Consequences	
Individualized outcome(s)							
Child says single words (e.g., labels colors of objects, labels body parts of animals)	Center time	Library	Copies of the book *Polar Bear, Polar Bear, What Do You Hear?* by Bill Martin, Jr., and Eric Carle Hand-size felted objects of each animal in the story Flannel board	Adult and child look at and attend to the pictures in the book. Adult delivers a mand (e.g., verbal direction, verbal request, ask a question) that prompts the child to say a single word: • "Say, 'blue'" • "Tell me, 'nose'" • "Which color is the lion?" • "What is this (while pointing to an animal's tail)?" Adult waits 3 seconds for the child to respond.	Child responds correctly by saying the prompted single word within the 3-second response time. Child does not respond within the 3 seconds. Child makes an attempt to say the single word but is unintelligible (e.g., substitutes the first consonant sound in the word, omits the first consonant sound).	Affirm and expand. Provide another mand and wait 3 seconds. Provide model of correct response. Provide descriptive praise or natural consequence when the child says the prompted word. Provide corrective model of the desired word and wait 3 seconds. Provide descriptive praise or natural consequence when the child says the prompted word.	Use a count and tally system to record the number of times the child correctly demonstrates the individualized outcomes (i.e., the number of times he or she says single words), the number of times the child provides an incorrect or unintelligible response, and when the child provides no response.

SUMMARY

The purpose of Chapter 7 was to define the purposes of systematic instruction, identify specific systematic instruction strategies, and discuss their use in blended classrooms. Systematic instruction is necessary when children experience barriers to learning or when they are missing foundational or prerequisite skills that are preventing their access to, participation in, and ability to make progress toward the general curriculum. Systematic instructional strategies discussed included enhanced milieu teaching and response prompting procedures.

LEARNING ACTIVITIES

1. Consider an activity in your classroom or observe an activity in a preschool classroom. Consider what individualized instructional strategies are being used and why. Decide whether the strategy being used is effective for the individualized outcome and discuss possible alternatives (e.g., other response prompting procedures or enhanced milieu teaching strategies).

2. Choose an individualized outcome for a specific or hypothetical child. Decide which individualized instructional strategy to use. Create a fidelity checklist and data sheet to ensure all members of the team can implement the instruction and track progress. Decide how best to train members of the team to implement and track this outcome.

3. Expand on the IIS you created in Chapter 6. Add the individualized outcomes. Remember to frame the How to Teach section in the antecedent-behavior-consequence format.

REFERENCES

Aldemir, O., & Gursel, O. (2014). The effectiveness of the constant time delay procedure in teaching preschool academic skills to children with developmental disabilities in a small group teaching arrangement. *Educational Sciences: Theory and Practice, 14*(2), 733–740.

Alig-Cybriwsky, C., Wolery, M. & Gast, D. (1990). Use of constant time delay procedure in teaching preschoolers in a group format. *Journal of Early Intervention, 14*, 99–116.

Appelman, M., Vail, C.O., & Leiberman-Betz, R.G. (2014). The effects of constant time delay and instructive feedback on the acquisition of English and Spanish sight words. *Journal of Early Intervention, 36*(2), 131–148.

Christensen-Sandfort, R.J., & Whinnery, S.B. (2013). Impact of milieu teaching on communication skills of young children with autism spectrum disorder. *Topics in Early Childhood Special Education, 32*(4), 211–222.

Clark, C., & McDonnell, A. (2008). Teaching choice making to children with visual impairments and multiple disabilities in preschool and kindergarten classrooms. *Journal of Visual Impairment and Blindness, 102*(7), 397–409.

Collins, B.C. (2012). *Systematic instruction for students with moderate and severe disabilities.* Baltimore, MD: Paul H. Brookes Publishing Co.

Daugherty, S., Grisham-Brown, J., & Hemmeter, M. (2001). The effects of embedded skill instruction on the acquisition of target and non-target skills in preschoolers with developmental delays. *Topics in Early Childhood Special Education, 21*, 213–221.

Denny, M., Marchand-Martella, N., Martella, R.C., Reilly, J.R., Reilly, J.F., & Cleanthous, C.C. (2001). Using parent-delivered graduated guidance to teach functional living skills to a child with cri du chat syndrome. *Education and Treatment of Children, 23*(4), 441–454.

Frey, J.R., & Kaiser, A.P. (2011). The use of play expansions to increase the diversity and complexity of object play in young children with disabilities. *Topics in Early Childhood, 31*(2), 99–111.

Grisham-Brown, J., Ruble, L.A., Wong, W.H., McGrew, J. (in preparation). Common elements teaching sequence.

Grisham-Brown, J., Pretti-Frontczak, K., Bachman, A., Gannon, C., & Mitchell, D. (2014). Delivering individualized instruction during ongoing classroom activities and routines: Three success stories. *Young Exceptional Children Monograph 16: Blended Practices for All Children,* 97–110.

Grisham-Brown, J., Pretti-Frontczak, K., Hawkins, S.R., & Winchell, B.N. (2009). Addressing early learning standards for all children within blended preschool classrooms. *Topics in Early Childhood Special Education, 29*(3), 131–138.

Grisham-Brown, J., Ridgley, R., Pretti-Frontczak, K., Litt, C., & Nielson, A. (2006). Promoting positive learning outcomes for young children in inclusive classrooms: A preliminary study of children's progress toward pre-writing standards. *Journal of Early and Intensive Behavior Intervention, 3*(1), 171–190.

Grisham-Brown, J., Schuster, J.W., Hemmeter, M.L., & Collins, B.C. (2000). Using an embedding strategy to teach preschoolers with significant disabilities. *Journal of Behavioral Education, 10*(2/3), 139–162.

Hancock, T.B., & Kaiser, A.P. (2002). The effects of trainer-implemented enhanced milieu teaching on the social communication of children with autism. *Topics in Early Childhood Special Education, 22*(1), 39–54.

Harjusola-Webb, S., & Robbins, S. (2012). The effects of teacher-implemented naturalistic intervention on the communication of preschoolers with Autism. *Topics in Early Childhood Special Education, 32*(2), 99–110.

Hart, B., & Rogers-Warren, A.K. (1978). A milieu approach to teaching language. In R.L. Schiefelbusch (Ed.), *Language intervention strategies* (pp. 193–235). Baltimore, MD: University Park Press.

Hemmeter, M.L., & Kaiser, A.P. (1994). Enhanced milieu teaching: Effects of parent-implemented language intervention. *Journal of Early Intervention, 18*(3), 269–289.

Jones, C.D., & Schwartz, I.S. (2004). Siblings, peers, and adults: Differential effects of models for children with autism. *Topics in Early Childhood Special Education, 24*(40), 187–198.

Kaiser, A.P., Hancock, T.B., & Nietfeld, J.P. (2000). The effects of parent-implemented enhanced milieu teaching on the communication of children with Autism. *Early Education and Development, 11*(4), 423–446.

Kurt, O., & Tekin-Iftar, E. (2008). A comparison of constant time delay and simultaneous prompting within embedded instruction on teaching leisure skills to children with autism. *Topics in Early Childhood Special Education, 28*(1), 53–64.

Ledford, J., & Wolery, M. (2013). Peer modeling of academic and social behaviors during small group direct instruction. *Exceptional Children, 79*(4), 439–458.

Martin, B., Jr., & Carle, E. (1997). *Polar bear, polar bear, what do you hear?* New York, NY: Holt and Company.

Mobayed, K.L., Collins, B.C., Strangis, D.E., Schuster, J.W., & Hemmeter, M.L. (2000). Teaching parents to employ mand model procedures to teach their children requesting. *Journal of Early Intervention, 23*(2), 165–179.

Mudd, J.M., & Wolery, M. (1987). Training head start teachers to use incidental teaching. *Journal of the Division of Early Childhood, 11*(2), 124–133.

Noonan, M.J., & McCormick, L. (2014). *Teaching young children with disabilities in natural environments* (2nd ed.). Baltimore, MD: Paul H. Brookes Publishing Co.

Odom, S.L. (2009). Evidence-based practice, implementation science, and outcomes for children. *Topics in Early Childhood Special Education, 29*(1), 53–61.

Odom, S.L., Fleming, K., Diamond, K., Lieber, J., Hanson, M., Butera, G., … Marquis, J. (2010). Examining different forms of implementation and in early childhood curriculum research. *Early Childhood Research Quarterly, 25,* 314–328.

Pretti-Frontczak, K., & Grisham-Brown, J. (2012). *Manual for designing and delivering intentional instruction.* Brooklyn, NY: B2K Solutions.

Schwartz, I.S., Sandall, S.R., McBride, B.J., & Boulware, G.L. (2004). Project DATA (developmentally appropriate treatment for autism): An inclusive school-based approach to educating young children with autism. *Topics in Early Childhood Special Education, 24*(3), 156–168.

Woods, J., Kashinath, S., & Goldstein, H. (2004). Effects of embedding caregiver-implemented teaching strategies in daily routines on children's communication outcomes. *Journal of Early Intervention, 26*(3), 175–193.

Yoder, P., & Stone, W. (2006). Randomized comparison of two communication interventions for preschoolers with autism spectrum disorders. *Journal of Consulting and Clinical Psychology, 74*(3), 426–435.

Sample Intervention Plans

Model Intervention Plan

Child's name: _____

Target skill: _____

Antecedent	Behavior	Consequence
Initiate instruction in situation in which child needs to communicate Establish joint attention Deliver verbal (or sign) model Wait for child to respond	(Correct response) ⟶ Child communicates need using expected form of communication	Provide access to what child requests
	(Incorrect response) ⟶ Child does not communicate using expected form of communication or Child does not respond following wait time	Provide access to what child requests and Repeat verbal or visual model

Mand-Model Intervention Plan

Child's name: _____

Target skill: _____

Antecedent	Behavior	Consequence
Initiate instruction in situation in which child needs to communicate Establish joint attention Deliver verbal (or sign) mand Wait for child to respond	(Correct response) ⟶ Child communicates need using expected form of communication	Provide access to what child requests
	(Incorrect response) ⟶ Child does not communicate using expected form of communication or Child does not respond following wait time	Provide verbal or visual model Wait for child to respond If child responds correctly, provide positive verbal feedback and access to activity or material and If child responds incorrectly, provide access to the material or activity while repeating the correct response

(page 1 of 5)

Naturalistic Time Delay Intervention Plan

Child's name: _____

Target skill: _____

Antecedent	Behavior	Consequence
Initiate instruction in situation in which child needs to communicate Establish joint attention Deliver a naturalistic time delay using an expectant look Wait for child to respond	(Correct response) ⟶ Child communicates need using expected form of communication	Provide access to what child requests
	(Incorrect response) ⟶ Child does not communicate using expected form of communication or Child does not respond following wait time	Provide a verbal mand Wait for child to respond If child responds correctly, provide access to what child requests and positive verbal feedback If child responds incorrectly, provide verbal or visual model Wait for child to respond If child responds correctly, provide access to what child requests and positive verbal feedback If child responds incorrectly, repeat the correct response while providing access to the desired activity or material

Incidental Teaching Intervention Plan

Child's name: _____

Target skill: _____

Antecedent	Behavior	Consequence
Initiate instruction in situation in which child needs to communicate Establish joint attention Wait for child to respond	(Correct response) ⟶ Child communicates need using new or expanded form of communication	Provide access to what child requests
	(Incorrect response) ⟶ Child uses current form of communication or Child does not respond following wait time	Model the new or expanded form of communication Wait for child to respond If child responds correctly, provide access to what child requests and positive verbal feedback Model the new or expanded form of communication Wait for child to respond If child responds correctly, provide access to what child requests and positive verbal feedback If child responds incorrectly, repeat the correct response while providing access to the desired activity or material

(page 2 of 5)

Incidental Teaching Intervention Plan

Child's name: _____

Target skill: _____

Antecedent	Behavior	Consequence
Initiate instruction following a child request Establish joint attention Deliver a naturalistic time delay using an expectant look, a mand, or a model, depending on how much support child needs Wait for child to respond	(Correct response) Child communicates need using expected form of communication ⟶	Provide access to what child requests and positive descriptive feedback
	(Incorrect response) Child does not communicate using expected form of communication or Child does not respond following wait time ⟶	Provide a more intensive prompt Wait for child to respond If child responds correctly, provide access to what child requests and positive verbal feedback If child responds incorrectly, provide verbal or visual model Wait for child to respond If child responds correctly, provide access to what child requests and positive verbal feedback If child responds incorrectly, repeat the correct response while providing access to the desired activity or material

Graduated Guidance Intervention Plan

Child's name: _____

Target skill: _____

Antecedent	Behavior	Consequence
Establish joint attention Provide task direction Wait for child to respond	(Correct response) Child demonstrates behavior according to definition of correct behavior before controlling prompt is provided ⟶	Provide reinforcement
	(Incorrect response) Child demonstrates incorrect behavior according to definition of correct behavior before the controlling prompt or Child does not respond following delay interval ⟶	Provide physical assistance Wait for child to respond If child still responds incorrectly or does not respond, then provide more intrusive physical assistance until child successfully demonstrates the correct behavior

(page 3 of 5)

System of Least Prompts Intervention Plan

Child's name: _____

Target skill: _____

Antecedent	Behavior	Consequence
Establish joint attention Provide task direction Wait for child to respond	(Correct response) ⟶ Child independently demonstrates behavior according to definition of correct behavior	Provide reinforcement
	(Incorrect response) ⟶ Child demonstrates incorrect behavior according to definition of correct behavior or Child does not respond following delay interval	Provide least intrusive prompt level Wait for child to respond If child still responds incorrectly or does not respond, then provide more intrusive prompt Wait for child to respond If child still responds incorrectly or does not respond, then provide controlling prompt

Most to Least Prompts Intervention Plan

Child's name: _____

Target skill: _____

Antecedent	Behavior	Consequence
Establish joint attention Provide task direction 1. Immediately provide controlling prompt until criterion is met with controlling prompt 2. Immediately provide less intrusive prompt until criterion is met with that prompt level 3. Wait for child to respond independently	(Correct response) ⟶ Child independently demonstrates behavior according to definition of correct behavior	Provide reinforcement
	(Incorrect response) ⟶ Child demonstrates incorrect behavior according to definition of correct behavior or Child does not respond following delay interval	Provide controlling prompt

(page 4 of 5)

Constant Time Delay Intervention Plan

Child's name: _____

Target skill: _____

Antecedent	Behavior	Consequence
Establish joint attention Provide task direction Wait for child to respond • Zero seconds for first session • Constant maximum delay for remaining sessions	(Correct response) Child demonstrates behavior according to definition of correct behavior before controlling prompt is provided ⟶	Provide reinforcement
	(Incorrect response) Child demonstrates incorrect behavior according to definition of correct behavior before the controlling prompt or Child does not respond following maximum delay interval ⟶	Provide controlling prompt Wait for child to respond Provide reinforcement if child responds correctly
	Child demonstrates incorrect behavior according to definition of correct behavior after the controlling prompt ⟶	Provide controlling prompt again Wait for child to respond Provide reinforcement if child responds correctly Provide controlling prompt

Progressive Time Delay Intervention Plan

Child's name: _____

Target skill: _____

Antecedent	Behavior	Consequence
Establish joint attention Provide task direction Wait for child to respond • Zero seconds for first session • Increasing delay interval until maximum delay is reached for remaining sessions	(Correct response) Child demonstrates behavior according to definition of correct behavior before controlling prompt is provided ⟶	Provide reinforcement
	(Incorrect response) Child demonstrates incorrect behavior according to definition of correct behavior before the controlling prompt or Child does not respond following delay interval ⟶	Provide controlling prompt Wait for child to respond Provide reinforcement if child responds correctly
	Child demonstrates incorrect behavior according to definition of correct behavior after the controlling prompt ⟶	Provide controlling prompt again Wait for child to respond Provide reinforcement if child responds correctly Provide controlling prompt

(page 5 of 5)

Special Considerations in the Application of Blended Practices

## CHAPTER 8

The Team Process of Planning, Implementing, and Revising Instruction

Julie Harp Rutland, Sarah Hawkins-Lear, Jennifer Grisham-Brown, and Mary Louise Hemmeter

Ms. Abby has just met a new child and family that will be joining her blended preschool class. Her program is operated by the local public school system and includes children with developmental delays, children who qualify for Head Start, and children whose families have elected for their children to have preschool experience. Lili is her new child, is 4 years old, and has significant disabilities. It was important to Lili's parents that she receive the best care during her first 3 years; therefore, they kept her at home with her grandmother due to her significant needs. As her parents look ahead to Lili entering kindergarten, they feel she would benefit from an inclusive preschool classroom experience with other children with and without disabilities. Lili's mother has concerns about her ability to interact with other children, which is based on limited experiences with other children her age. The family knows how to interact with Lili at home and knows how she responds. Lili's mother is concerned that teachers and children at the preschool will not know how to interact with her like they do at home. Lili's transdisciplinary assessment shows that she has developmental delays in the areas of communication, social-emotional, cognition, and fine motor. Ms. Abby now understands that she will have to rely on the parent's knowledge of Lili and the expertise of therapists as she considers how to best support Lili in her first school experience. Ms. Abby is left wondering how she can accomplish this task, despite having access to those resources. Where does she begin?

Ms. Abby, like many other teachers, is challenged to meet the needs of a child such as Lili, along with an entire class of individual and unique children and families. In addition to planning for children and families, it is important for teachers to understand the services and supports available to them. Prekindergarten (pre-K) classrooms are increasingly similar to Ms. Abby's in that they blend program resources from a variety of sources (e.g., Head Start, publicly funded preschools/pre-K, child care settings). Duplication of services, supports, and resources may create inconsistency and inefficiency as a result of blending funding resources. For example, a child may qualify for both Head Start and publicly funded preschool/pre-K in their state. The child in this scenario would automatically be assigned a family service provider through Head Start and would also qualify for family resource services through the public school system. Although the child and family would benefit from such services, consideration must be given to duplication of services such as referrals to resources. Another overlap may occur in home visiting practices. Head Start and publicly funded preschools/pre-K practice home visiting, so this family would have an extraordinary amount of home visits scheduled throughout the year.

Teachers in such programs must also adhere to the regulations of both programs, which may lead to multiple assessment tools for the child and classroom. Head Start may use one assessment tool to evaluate the classroom environment, whereas the publicly funded preschool/pre-K may use a different assessment tool. This creates duplication in classroom assessment for the teacher of a blended classroom. Furthermore, each of the programs has program review periods. For example, if Head Start has a review every third year and the publicly funded preschool/pre-K has a review every fifth year, then there will come a year in which both programs are under review. As you can imagine, this can be overwhelming for many teachers.

Ms. Abby and teachers in similar situations must rely on collaborative partnerships with all involved because of the complexity of working in a blended classroom with resources and supports from a variety of agencies. Collaborative relationships are the underpinning of the curriculum framework and tie effective teaming strategies to collaborative partnerships (see Figure 8.1). Collaborative partnerships support children, families, teachers, and related services personnel.

This chapter provides an overview of teaming and the various individuals involved. The chapter specifically identifies members of the team (e.g., families, related services personnel, paraprofessionals, co-teachers, itinerant teachers) and how each can be involved in the process of gathering assessment information, selecting goals, planning activities and instruction, and collecting progress monitoring data. In addition, characteristics of successful teaming and challenges to teaming are described.

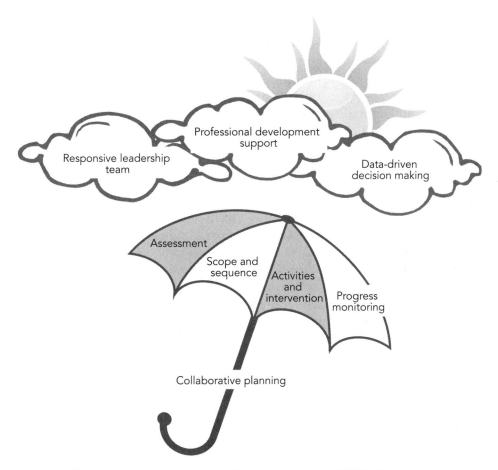

Figure 8.1. Illustration of the curriculum framework. (From Pretti-Frontczak, K. [2015]. Linking assessment and curriculum [Three part web-based training modules]. Brooklyn, NY: B2K Solutions, Ltd.)

CHARACTERISTICS OF SUCCESSFUL TEAMING

The term *team* in early childhood education (ECE) suggests a group of professionals and family members that understand the importance of working together to address the needs of young children. Individually, each team member has a unique expertise, with individual values, beliefs, and experiences that shape perspectives. Members of the team, however, must recognize that they need one another to accomplish their goals. These teams may develop close working relationships over time that serve to further support the child's development (Cloninger, 2004). Successful teaming can only be achieved, however, when all members have an understanding of their roles as they work collaboratively to share information and work toward agreed-on outcomes.

Teacher education programs tend to focus on teaching and working with the children in the classroom, but what about the adults in the classroom? Prospective teachers need to 1) be aware of the importance of partnerships with other colleagues and families and 2) understand how to create positive working relationships with other adults in order to increase the likelihood of successful inclusive practices (McCormick, Noonan, Ogata, & Heck, 2001).

Bell (2004) highlighted specific characteristics that team members should demonstrate in order to effectively work together. Individuals must be agreeable for successful teaming. This does not mean that a team member automatically agrees with all suggestions, but he or she demonstrates flexibility and mutual respect for all team members. It is inevitable that team members will have conflict, as is discussed later in this chapter, but disagreement may occur respectfully.

Being reliable, being on time for meetings and classroom visits, and being prepared for each interaction are additional characteristics of a successful team member. Simply stated, team members must be conscientious. Most all of us have been involved in a group or team in which one or more of the members were not punctual or prepared. This type of behavior hinders the success of the team. Therefore, team members should prepare in advance, arrive on time, and be organized.

Team members must be competent in their area of expertise, understanding the most up-to-date and research-based practices. Each member brings his or her own expertise, and the team depends on that knowledge. Each member has specific expertise in which he or she is responsible, regardless of the number of team members.

Finally, it is helpful to be socialized in the organization, or have an understanding of the processes and systems within. There is much to learn when working with a team in an ECE setting—school procedures and processes, teachers, families, and teaming practices and routines. Although team functioning will develop and change over periods of time, it is important that incoming members are supported as they get acclimated to the new environment (Bell, 2004).

TRANSDISCIPLINARY TEAMING

In addition to understanding the individual characteristics that contribute to successful teaming, it is also important to understand the roles and expectations of each member based on the teaming model or approach of the team. Several different teaming models may be used to deliver early childhood services, with each differing in regard to the level of family participation, team communication, assessment process, and intervention methods. The transdisciplinary model is a team of professionals that work collaboratively and share responsibilities (Cloninger, 2004). Families are full, active, and participating members of the transdisciplinary team, with team communications that are a continuous transfer of information, knowledge, and skills. Transdisciplinary teams conduct assessments together and develop plans based on family priorities, needs, and resources. One person is the primary service provider for the child and family in a transdisciplinary team, and the other team members provide support by sharing information about strategies and information specific to their expertise. All team members are responsible for sharing their knowledge with the primary service provider, and the primary service provider is responsible for implementing the plan with the child and family. This sharing of expertise is called *role release* and is a distinguishing characteristic of the transdisciplinary model. Having one team member consistently interact with the child and family and act as the primary provider with all team members who are collaborating to work toward the child's goals will decrease the likelihood of overlaps and gaps in services because there can be many members on any one particular team.

FAMILIES AS TEAM MEMBERS

Most early childhood teacher preparation programs emphasize the decades of research supporting the importance of family involvement (Fields-Smith & Neuharth-Pritchett, 2009; Zins, Weissberg, Wang, & Walberg, 2004) with an understanding that children are viewed within the context of the family and community (Bronfenbrenner, 1979; Copple & Bredekamp, 2009; Hanson & Lynch, 2013). Both the National Association for the Education of Young Children (NAEYC) and the Division for Early Childhood (DEC) of the Council for Exceptional Children (CEC) advocate the importance of involving families in early childhood programs. Specifically, NAEYC guidelines recommend that families be involved in three ways: 1) as decision makers, 2) as providers and receivers of information, and 3) as participants in the daily activities within the program (Copple & Bredekamp, 2009). The DEC (2014) recommended practices emphasize family–professional partnerships and involvement in all aspects of the child's program, which includes assessment, intervention, and evaluation. The process of planning, implementing, and evaluating a quality curriculum framework depends on the partnerships that programs have with families. It is necessary, however, to understand the diverse nature of modern-day families to ensure that all members of the team are involved.

Family Differences

Children live within the context of families who represent a range of diversity and needs. Many children have parents who come from other countries, speak their native language in the home, and practice customs and traditions of those various cultures. The majority of children do not come from what was once considered a traditional family model, with a mother and father living in the home. Teachers may have children in single-parent families; children being raised by grandparents, stepparent families, and gay/lesbian parents; and children being raised in foster homes. Children may live in more than one home or have multiple family models. With the diverse nature of families in mind, we must consider the family in a broad sense, including all of the individuals that make up each unique family. Therefore, practices for teaming with families need to be individualized, and a number of variables such as communication barriers, family structure, work schedules, and prior school experiences must be considered. The next section describes how families may be involved as team members in assessment, outcome development, planning activities and instruction, and progress monitoring.

Roles and Responsibilities

It has been said that the parent is the child's first teacher and that a family knows their child best. Family members would be an asset to each individual team considering that the basic premise of teaming is that all members have unique expertise in which they share knowledge. Although teachers espouse beliefs regarding the value of including families as members of the team, families are all too often involved only as recipients of information. For example, it is common practice to tell parents what their children are going to learn, to tell them about the school's policies, and to tell them about the curriculum.

It is important for families to receive information about their children's educational program, but families may assume additional roles and responsibilities. Families can provide a wealth of information that can be useful in designing, implementing, and evaluating the preschool curriculum as it applies to their child, but families are often unsure of their role and just how they can contribute to the team.

Assessment   It is clear to see how families can provide a wealth of valuable information that may or may not be observed in a typical classroom. Families have the opportunity to observe behaviors and skills across a variety of settings and across a period of time, which are valuable for determining eligibility and level of development. Teachers need broad information about the family, including cultural values, primary language used by the family, length of acculturation in this country, and specific cultural practices that may have an impact on the child's education (Losardo & Notari-Syverson, 2011). Much of the information can only be provided by the family of the child. Furthermore, families can provide assessment information regarding child development, behaviors, and preferences. Families may elect to share this information through informal interactions such as telephone calls or e-mails. Many preschool programs, however, offer more formal interactions such as home visits or conferences. Many tools can be used to get information from families: the Family Report of the Assessment, Evaluation, and Programming System for Infants and Children (AEPS®; Bricker, 2002); Choosing Outcomes and Accommodations for Children (COACH): A Guide to Educational Planning for Students with Disabilities (Giangreco, Cloninger, & Iverson, 2011); Developmental Observation Checklist System (DOCS): A Systems Approach to Assessing Very Young Children (Hresko, Miguel, Sherbenou, & Burton, 1994); and Reach for the Stars: Planning for the Future (Haynes & Grisham-Brown, 2013).

Families may help determine which specific tool or approach is best for their child. Once a tool is selected, families may rate behaviors, respond to questions or interviews, and help determine if the information collected is representative of their child's actual abilities. In addition to providing an accurate and reliable assessment of the child (Bedore, Peña, Joyner, & Macken, 2011; Feldman et al., 2012; Johnson, Wolke, & Marlow, 2008; Vangalder, 1997), family involvement in this process increases awareness of their child's development, thus enhancing their contributions to the planning process (Bauer & Shea, 2003; Grisham-Brown & Pretti-Frontczak, 2011). Table 8.1 lists these tools as well as the information that parents provide in each.

Table 8.1. Sample tools for gathering information from families

Tool	Assessment information provided by families from their perspective
Assessment, Evaluation, and Programming System for Infants and Children (AEPS®; Bricker, 2002)	Home routines Community routines Child interests and preferences Priorities for learning Child's developmental status
Choosing Outcomes and Accommodations for Children (COACH): A Guide to Educational Planning for Students with Disabilities (Giangreco, Cloninger, & Iverson, 2011)	Child's developmental status Key relationships in child's life Priorities for learning Possible teaching strategies Child's interests and preferences
Reach for the Stars: Planning for the Future (Haynes & Grisham-Brown, 2013)	Child's developmental status Child's interests and preferences Possible teaching strategies Family's desire for child's future

Outcomes Scope and Sequence   Recommended practice suggests that outcomes be derived from the priorities and concerns of families (DEC, 2014). An understanding of the family's priorities and goals enables teachers to plan and implement for the unique needs of the child and family (Bauer & Shea, 2003; Guralnick, 2001). Therefore, it is important for teachers to understand what families want their children to learn. Families must provide this information in order for teachers to have an understanding of what is important to families. The family's role in the development of outcomes and the steps necessary to reach this goal is to reflect on and share these needs. The family's ideas for outcomes will allow the other team members to understand how outcomes affect the child and family. Families need to reflect on their needs and consider how these are connected with outcomes. Lili's family had concerns about communication and peer interaction. Not only did her assessment confirm their concerns, but it also identified delays in the areas of cognition and fine motor. The following are examples of goals specifically developed for Lili:

- Independently request objects and materials

- Take turns while participating in an activity

- Verbally identify shapes

- Grasp utensils using whole hand and grasp

Asking questions about the outcomes and objectives is another role for families. Families must understand that it is their role to help develop outcomes and have an understanding of the scope and sequence of the objectives. It is important to create an environment in which questions are welcome because families may not have an understanding of professional terminology and intervention practices. The outcome will be important to the family when they understand its significance, and the outcome must be functional in order for it to be important to the family. Functional outcomes are more likely to be practiced across a variety of settings. Most important, we need to remember that families are the ones who must live with the outcomes that have been developed.

Activities and Instruction   We previously discussed developing outcomes and their impact on families, but developing activities and instruction is just as important. Family members can provide suggestions and ideas about developing activities and instruction and what will work across a variety of settings.

Families at School   Families can have a role as an educator in the home and preschool classroom. DiNatale (2002) provided specific suggestions for how families can assist with instruction within each learning center. Parents can help children write their names at the art center, explore math concepts in the block center, point out differences in weight between empty and full containers in the science center, and talk about changes in plants and other living things during outdoor play. They can assist the teacher in delivering instruction by working with small groups of children or even leading the children in a story. DiNatale pointed out that a primary benefit of parent involvement is that it "results in children receiving more individual attention" (p. 90).

Families at Home Preschool teachers are faced with myriad family situations to which they must be responsive when involving families. For example, if the child's primary culture does not advocate teaching preschool children to be independent in self-care routines, this would be important to know in programs in which such independence is encouraged. In addition to developing activities and instruction, teachers must also consider how the family's routines and habits will lend opportunities for extending activities and instruction to the home. Specifically, families need to share information about routines that occur at home and school, such as the child's bathroom routines or putting the child down to sleep, as well as some routines that may be unique to home. The routines-based interview (RBI) is one method for collecting information regarding family routines (McWilliam, 1992, 2005). The RBI is a process used to help families identify needs that can be addressed through outcome and activity development. This semistructured interview can be conducted by the teacher and creates an opportunity for families to think through their typical daily routines by sharing what works well and what does not work well. The changes families would like to see in their typical routines lead to functional outcomes (McWilliam, 2010).

Once the RBI has been conducted, an activity matrix can be developed to provide ideas for activities that are both related to outcomes and can occur within the typical routines of the family. An activity matrix includes routines, skills related to outcomes, and suggestions on how to embed those skills within the routine. Think back to Lili in the case story. How can her family address the outcomes developed by her team? One way to accomplish this is by using an activity matrix. Figure 8.2 is an activity matrix for Lili's family. A blank version of this activity matrix is available in Appendix 8A.

Progress Monitoring Families have an important role in collecting data and making sure that observed behaviors are maintained. Families may have suggestions for additional activities or revision of activities once they implement the activities that are developed to address the outcomes for their child. Families can provide useful insights into how they guide and support their child in his or her development. For example, it is useful for the teacher to know the types of encouragement, limits, and consequences used by parents to guide the child's behavior so the teacher can better understand the behaviors and reactions in the classroom (McWilliam, Casey, & Sims, 2009). Although teacher and family approaches may be different, this information can sometimes provide an explanation regarding why some strategies are working or not working. Similarly, teachers may need to know

Activity Matrix

Routine/ activity	Skills related to the outcomes			
	Requesting objects and materials	Taking turns	Identifying shapes	Grasping utensils
Meals and snacks	Place mealtime items (e.g., condiments, drinking cup, utensils, napkins) just out of reach so that she will request them when needed.	Pass a basket or plate of mealtime items to take turns selecting or serving.	Shape of plate, napkin, foods (triangle pizza slices, round cookie)	Provide her with utensils to feed herself and to help prepare the meal (e.g., wooden spoons for mixing, plastic knives, cut-up bananas).
Travel in car	Keep a tub of toys/ activities in the car and let her choose what she would like to have on each trip.	Play "I Spy" in the car as you travel from place to place, taking turns with passengers in the car.	Point out road signs and the many objects you see on the road. Identify the shape of each object.	Provide glow sticks for night travel that will give her practice holding utensils similar in size.
Play	When playing with playdough, giver her options to select the color and utensils. You can also do this with books, game pieces, and blocks.	Take turns rolling a ball, saying, "My turn, your turn." This can also be done using blocks while building a tower or blowing bubbles.	Use playdough and different-shaped cookie cutters to make shapes with hands or draw shapes in the dough. Talk about the shapes as they are made.	Provide utensils (e.g., rolling pin, scissors, plastic knife) to use with playdough.
Personal care	As she is getting dressed for the day, for bedtime, or for going outside, be sure to place some objects (e.g., shoes, favorite sweater, hair accessories, umbrella) just out of reach so that she will make a request.	Take turns brushing hair, saying, "Now it is Daddy's turn to brush your hair."	Point out the shapes of items in the bathroom (e.g., square wash cloth, square soap, round sponge, round sink) during bath time. Use soap to draw shapes on the shower wall.	Brushing teeth and brushing hair will give her opportunities to practice, even if you need to help afterward to see that the job is accomplished.

Figure 8.2.   Sample activity matrix for Lili.

the approach parents take in teaching new skills to their child. Families who are direct in their approach to teaching a child something new may have difficulty understanding how their child can learn though play. Teachers have to understand a child's interests in order to provide effective early care and education. Families can help teachers understand their child's preferences. It is important for teachers to gather this information on an ongoing basis because preferences frequently change when children are young. Teachers may provide families with suggestions and methods for recording behaviors, which will provide a wealth of data. Figure 8.3 is an example of a Family Data Collection Sheet that may have supported Lili's family when collecting data on requesting items. A blank version of the Family Data Collection Sheet appears in Appendix 8B.

Although family involvement is important in all aspects of a young child's education, it is equally important to recognize and respect that the extent to which families are involved may differ from family to family (McCann, Bull, & Winzenberg, 2012). The family's level of involvement depends on many factors, including the extent to which they believe their involvement makes a difference in their child's education, the school's openness to family involvement, and other commitments. Active family involvement must ultimately be balanced with respect for their needs as individuals and family units.

Family Data Collection Sheet

Child's name: Lili

Target skill: Requesting objects and materials

Date	Routine/activity	Child response	Observer
8/4	Picking toys for travel	She selected two items (bracelet, car) by naming each one.	Mom
8/4	Getting ready for bed	Lili said, "yellow jammies" when I asked her to pick her pajamas and "blankie" when she noticed it was not in her bed (we put it on a shelf).	Dad

Figure 8.3.   Family Data Collection Sheet.

RELATED SERVICES PERSONNEL AS TEAM MEMBERS

Active family involvement does not mean absolving professionals of their responsibilities. It is still the responsibility of teachers and related services personnel to help families choose a reasonable course of action for achieving targeted behaviors. Team members will help families accomplish this by suggesting and providing appropriate strategies for individualized goals (Bauer & Shea, 2003; Guralnick, 2001). Families are the most familiar with their child, but they are not always familiar with appropriate interventions or developmentally appropriate practices. It is the job of the teachers and related services personnel to share their expertise, help guide families, and facilitate teamwork when working together.

Team Members

Related services personnel are individuals from various disciplines who focus on appropriate interventions that address the child's target outcomes. These individuals assist the teacher and family members with specific supports to reach target outcomes. Children may have a variety of related services personnel on their team. The following section describes the possible team members.

Assistive Technology Specialist   The assistive technology (AT) specialist helps the child with the challenges of everyday life. He or she may focus on the child's communication or ability to overcome functional limitations. The AT specialist may provide the child with a low- or high-tech device to overcome barriers to inclusion.

Audiologist   The audiologist focuses on the hearing ability of the child and identifies hearing impairment or loss. There are various degrees of hearing loss a child may have, and this may result in specific supports provided. An audiologist may prescribe and fit for hearing aids and devices based on those needs.

Teacher of the Deaf/Hard of Hearing   The teacher of the deaf or hard of hearing assists the team in designing communication systems for learners with these impairments. They might also assist with the management of listening aids in the classrooms such as hearing aids, FM devices, and cochlear implants.

Dietitian   A dietitian is a member of the team when a child has health-related issues that affect learning. The dietitian focuses on the child's diet. In addition to caloric intake, he or she may address the child's specific dietary restrictions.

Occupational Therapist   The occupational therapist focuses on the child's participation in everyday tasks, including improving fine motor skills, adaptive skills, and feeding and sensory problems.

Orientation and Mobility Specialist   The orientation and mobility specialist works with children who have visual impairments. This specialist helps the child learn how to navigate in his or her home, school, and community.

Physical Therapist   The physical therapist assists children with physical disabilities, including improving gross motor skills such as walking, posture, standing, and muscle strength.

School Nurse   The school nurse focuses on the school health needs of children, including administering medication, performing medical procedures such as suctioning, and providing the teaching staff with guidelines for medical emergencies.

School Psychologist   The school psychologist performs and interprets assessments on children with regard to eligibility for special education services. They also provide consultation with the school staff and families.

Speech-Language Pathologist   The speech-language pathologist (SLP) focuses on the child's participation in communicative conversations. He or she may address articulation and language delays and feeding issues and may assist the child with augmentative and alternative communication.

Social Worker   The social worker provides the family with resources they may need within the community. The social worker also can act as a liaison between the school and the family.

Teacher of the Visually Impaired   The teacher of the visually impaired focuses on the visual ability of the child. There are various degrees of vision loss a child may have that will determine the types of support the vision specialist will prescribe.

All of the related services personnel described provide expert advice on the development of outcomes for the individual child. Once outcomes are decided on, they can work as a team to determine interventions that the family and teacher can use in school, at home, or in community settings (e.g., church, local park, restaurant). Members of the team rely on one another for expertise, shared knowledge, and responsibilities such as assessment, intervention planning, and progress monitoring.

Roles and Responsibilities

It may be confusing as to who plays which role when working with children who have disabilities. If a child has a team of five or more specialists, then it becomes a matter of who is going to provide what service, where the service will take place, and how the service is delivered. Following are strategies to help related services personnel-work together to provide efficient and effective practices.

Assessment   Transdisciplinary assessment involves families, teachers, and a team of related services personnel. It assesses children during natural and functional activities, thereby allowing team members to observe multiple skills within their specific domain. To begin this type of assessment, the child's team determines specific skills to assess, which may be a part of a curriculum-based assessment (CBA). Examples of commonly used CBAs are AEPS® (Bricker, 2002), Teaching Strategies GOLD, and The High/Scope Preschool Child Observation Record (High/Scope Press, 2003). Assessment activities are developed for the child after the team chooses the CBA and specific skills to observe. Assessment activities are based on the child's preferences and needs and information gained from the parent interview section of any of the previous assessments. It is important to know the child's preferences when developing activities so he or she will be motivated to participate in the assessment. For example, if a child is observed playing in the dramatic play center a lot, the team may decide to implement an activity within this center. After the activities are chosen, the team develops an activity protocol to use that addresses specific skills. For example, the team members can assess the following skills during dramatic play: conversational turn-taking; articulation; following two- and three-step directions while pretend cooking; fastening snaps, buttons, zippers on baby doll clothing or dress-up clothes; and the child sitting in a chair or moving around within the center. In addition, the teacher could address cognitive skills such as identifying the colors of cups or counting the number of cups while preparing the class snack.

Outcomes Scope and Sequence   The team develops outcomes for the child after the assessment is complete. First, the team summarizes the information collected during the evaluation and assessment process. The information will be better understood and more meaningful when provided in a way that addresses the priorities of the family within their everyday lives. Next, the team addresses concerns they may have and works with the parents to develop outcomes. It is important for the team to keep in mind that the outcomes should be functional for the child and should be naturally embedded within activities and routines across a variety of environments when possible and appropriate. Finally, the outcomes must be specific and measurable so that everyone on the team understands the goal and can measure progress.

Activities and Instruction   Activities and instruction are developed for the child after the outcomes are established. The activities are going to be preferential to the child and occur within the natural environment. Related services personnel and the classroom teachers implement activities while embedding the child's individual outcomes. Related services personnel typically work with children and teachers one to two times per week for about 30 minutes. Additional instruction needs to take place across the week in order for children to acquire and generalize outcomes. There must be a role release between the teacher and related services personnel in order for this to occur. Role release takes place when the related services personnel trains the teacher on a specific intervention and releases his or her role to the teacher (Cloninger, 2004). For example, a child may be working on the /b/ sound; therefore, the SLP will train the teacher on an intervention to use to facilitate the production of the /b/ sound. As this occurs, the SLP releases his or her role to the teacher. The teacher can now continue to work on the /b/ sound across daily activities and routines. If the child is receiving multiple therapies, then each therapist can train the teacher on specific interventions and release his or her role.

Activities can be implemented within large groups, small groups, and during one-to-one instruction while addressing specific outcomes. For example, if a child's outcome is to count to 10, then the skill can be addressed during 1) a large-group activity while the class is counting how many friends are present for the day, 2) a small-group activity such as counting the number of blocks in a tower in the block center, or 3) one-to-one instruction while reading a book and asking the child to count the number of pages in the book or count the number of insects on a page.

Lili's team conducted a transdisciplinary assessment and determined that Lili had weaknesses in the areas of communication, social-emotional, cognition, and fine motor; specifically, skills related to requesting objects and materials, turn-taking, identifying shapes, and using utensils. Ms. Abby learned through the parent interview that Lili enjoyed playing with playdough. Therefore, Ms. Abby designed an activity with playdough that addresses the family and team's concerns for Lili. First, she collects the materials, which are a variety of utensils, including rolling pins, cookie cutters, and scissors, and playdough. The next step is for Ms. Abby to embed the outcomes as she implements the activity. Let's take a minute to think about some ways she can address each outcome using the playdough activity:

- *Communication: Sabotage the environment by placing the materials needed for playdough activities just out of reach so that Lili will have to request the items in order to play.*
- *Social-emotional: Use playdough (which we know is a preferred activity for Lili) as a center activity. By providing a limited number of each material (e.g., one rolling pin, one pair of scissors, one plastic knife, one pizza cutter), Lili will be prompted by a teacher to take turns with peers as they use the materials.*
- *Cognition: While Lili is playing with the playdough in the center area, the teacher will ask her to identify the shapes associated with the cookie cutters and playdough.*
- *Fine motor: Ms. Abby will observe Lili's ability to manipulate each object while she is playing with the utensils.*

As a special educator, Ms. Abby feels that she can effectively address Lili's outcomes during the playdough activities; however, she needs support in the development of other activities. Ms. Abby observes Lili's therapists working with her as they model other activities, and she has them train her on the specific interventions. For example, the occupational therapist repositions Lili's grasp on the fork at lunchtime and demonstrates the grasp to Ms. Abby. The occupational therapist is releasing his or her role as he or she is training Ms. Abby and sharing specific knowledge and skills. When therapists role release their intervention strategies, teachers can address those outcomes across the day and week without having to wait for the child's specific therapy time. Ms. Abby models her newly learned skills for the therapists to ensure that she is implementing them correctly before she begins the activity and instruction on her own. These activities do not have to be limited to one child, multiple children may participate while working on individual outcomes.

Progress Monitoring   It is necessary to determine how the team is going to monitor progress after the activities and instruction are planned. Readministering the CBA with the children either mid-year or at the end of the year is the first way progress can be monitored. The teacher can determine how much progress has or has not been made toward outcomes compared with data from the beginning of the school year. Having the primary provider conduct the assessment is the second way progress can be monitored. In other words, he or she may readminister part of the CBA. Finally, the team may collect data on the child's individualized instructional objectives. For example, the teacher may work with Lili on shape identification throughout the week and collect daily progress data.

Paraprofessionals, Co-teachers, and Itinerant Teachers as Team Members

More and more, the traditional classroom is being replaced with a team of adults collaborating to meet the needs of young children. Some of the most collaborative team members are those working side by side in the classroom. Two or more adults in a classroom can share perspectives on the daily occurrences of not only the whole group but also individual children. Shared responsibilities such as curriculum development, assessment, implementation of activities, communication, and creation strategies for working with individual children can provide opportunities to develop and strengthen collaborative teaming. Children in such classrooms have daily opportunities to observe how people work together to resolve problems, communicate effectively, and develop a sense of connectedness.

Paraprofessionals   Paraprofessionals (teaching assistants, educational assistants, or aides) in some schools work side by side with the teacher in the class. The number of paraprofessionals increased by nearly 50% in the 1990s in response to requests from families, shortages of fully qualified professionals, and heightened outcomes in the classroom (French,

2003). More than half a million paraprofessionals are employed in public schools (Likins, 2003). They assist teachers and therapists as they work with children who have disabilities to support participation in inclusive settings. Paraprofessionals are a valuable resource to classrooms; however, they may not have formal qualifications to be solely responsible for completing some of the tasks required in a blended classroom.

Co-teachers   Co-teaching is another model for sharing teaching responsibilities. Co-teaching occurs in blended classrooms in which an early childhood educator shares responsibilities with an early childhood special educator, and they function in a collaborative team with equal responsibility, sharing the physical classroom as well as planning and assessing. This means that members of the team who have differing roles take on specific tasks and do so as equals rather than following the direction of a specified leader. Table 8.2 describes several different co-teaching arrangements—one teaching/one helping, parallel teaching, team teaching, station teaching, and alternative teaching (Salend, 2008).

Itinerant Teachers   Itinerant teachers are those who are not physically in the classroom throughout the entire day. Depending on the structure of the program, lead teachers may not specialize in special education, but they have an itinerant special education teacher who develops, models, and sometimes implements the interventions that address the specified learning outcomes developed by the team. For example, Lili does not have an itinerant teacher because Ms. Abby is a special educator. If Ms. Abby was not a special educator, then she may have asked a special educator to support her in the classroom on an itinerant or consulting basis.

Whatever the title, paraprofessionals, co-teachers, and itinerant teachers are all members of the team, interacting with children and families, and must have an understanding of assessments, development of outcomes,

Table 8.2.   Co-teaching variations

Variation	Description
One teach, one help	One teacher, usually the general education teacher, assumes teaching responsibilities, and the special educator provides support to individual children as needed.
Parallel teaching	Teachers teach the same or similar content in different class groups, providing smaller group learning.
Team teaching	Both teachers share teaching responsibilities equally. Requires that the teachers work together to develop a plan to divide tasks. Sometimes called *interactive teaching*.
Station teaching	Learning stations are created in the classroom, and co-teachers provide individual supports as the children participate in each station.
Alternative teaching	One teacher may take a smaller group of children to another location for specialized instruction.

activities and instruction, and progress monitoring. The next section describes the specific roles and responsibilities of all categories of teachers in the classroom.

Roles and Responsibilities

Professionals in classrooms can often be unsure of their roles and responsibilities as team members. At times, there is a mutual understanding of one another's expertise or experience in an area, which can lead to one individual taking the lead in some cases. The expectations may vary depending on your program and team composition; however, the following are some suggested roles and responsibilities when teaming.

Assessment   All teaching professionals have the responsibility of getting to know the children and families in the class. Learning about each child's personality, abilities, and preferences is essential to the development of appropriate outcomes and activities. Assessment may occur through formal methods, such as home visits or surveys, and may or may not include the use of assessment tools. It is important to note that everyone on the team can contribute information about the child's abilities; however, only those that have been trained to use the assessment tools should be responsible for completing the assessment and reporting the results. Paraprofessionals may not be solely responsible for assessment, outcome development, or planning of activities and instruction; however, they are currently performing ongoing assessments and planning or delivering instruction in some instances (Carroll, 2001; Sands, Kozleski, & French, 2000). Every team member in the classroom can observe children as they complete tasks and engage in interactions with others. Such observations provide important information on a child's abilities and needs. Taking notes and pictures, saving work samples, and recording are some ideas for assessing in the classroom. The combined information from team members provides a true picture of the child and his or her developmental level.

Furthermore, it is the responsibility of all the professionals in the classroom to not only collect information for child assessments but also have the ability to share and discuss this information with families and other team members. Professionals in the classroom have a variety of information to share with families, including information on assessment in general, such as what one is assessing, why one is assessing, and when one is assessing. Paraprofessionals and co-teachers have a lot of information to share when considering the experiences a child has in a given day—what the child is exploring, new skills demonstrated, and communication.

Outcomes Scope and Sequence   Team member qualification, training, and experience will determine who is responsible for developing outcomes. Once outcomes are determined, however, each team member should understand the priorities for the child's learning, the child's needs, and how tasks fit into the broad goals and outcomes. This is important because all members of the team need to be prepared to share outcomes with others, including not only what each is doing but also why.

Activities and Instruction   Co-teachers and paraprofessionals may be responsible for instructing the whole class, providing and addressing challenging behavior, modifying activities to meet children's needs, reading aloud to children, and helping children with personal hygiene (Ratcliff, Jones, Russell Vaden, Sheehan, & Hunt, 2011). Although professionals are trained to develop intervention strategies, the evidence shows that paraprofessionals are successful at implementing strategies and interventions (Killoran, Templeman, Peters, & Udell, 2001; Minondo, Meyer, & Xin, 2001). For example, Ms. Abby meets with her paraprofessionals at the beginning of the school year to train them on specific interventions that she uses within the classroom. She also uses video clips of the interventions so her paraprofessionals can refer to them across the school year.

Progress Monitoring   It is the responsibility of every team member to monitor a child's progress once the outcomes have been determined and clearly communicated. This can be done in a variety of ways and depends on the opportunities available to each professional. The important piece in progress monitoring is that each of the team members communicates what they observe and discover so that everyone has access to the information. Team members can accomplish progress monitoring across the classroom in multiple ways. One way is to develop activity matrices for specific children and place them within various learning centers in the classroom. For example, Ms. Abby could take Lili's goals and embed them across the classroom using the matrix. Team members who interact with Lili can refer to her matrix to determine goals that should be addressed and simultaneously collect data. Another example is to have sticky notes across the classroom with specific children's goals written on them. Team members who interact with the children can collect data and record them on the sticky note. When the interaction is complete, the team member can stick the note in the child's folder or where the team member keeps the recorded data. Team members have multiple opportunities to collect data across the day/week because data sheets are readily available. Please note that Ms. Abby will have all clipboards covered with a blank piece of paper for confidentiality.

CHALLENGES TO TEAMING

Although we know that there are multiple benefits to teaming, and we also understand the characteristics of effective teams, there will still be challenges faced in the process. Think back to Miss Nicole's concerns and how this challenged the group. These differences of opinion could have proven to be a much greater problem in a less effective team, but they were able to address the concerns and come to a resolution. Understanding the challenges common to teaming is important to the success of each team.

Team Communication

Communication is one of the greatest challenges to teaming. Several factors must be considered when planning for communication. First, determine which method or methods of communication will work best for each team. Some team members may prefer to communicate through informal means such as a telephone call, e-mail, or notes, whereas others may prefer more formal methods such as home visits, conferences, or regularly scheduled meetings. Whatever the method, successful collaborative teaming relies on communication that works for all team members.

Planning Time

In addition to communication needs, teams must consider the scheduling needs of the entire team. It is important for professionals in the classroom to establish regular planning time together as a team to collaborate and also to receive professional development that supports the entire team. Joint opportunities for professionals in the classroom to attend trainings as a team have resulted in positive feelings among members (Hughes & Valle-Riestra, 2008). It is also important to think about the time required for meetings and whether these may be an issue for families (e.g., busy working families, those who have several children). Many families have work schedules that make attending team meetings during the day very difficult. Providing families with plenty of advanced notice will decrease the likelihood of conflicts in scheduling.

Roles and Responsibilities

Understanding individual roles and responsibilities is another challenge for teams. Clearly, team members assume a wide range of responsibilities; therefore, the first consideration is to ensure that everyone on the team has an understanding of their responsibilities, being mindful of equal distribution. The team functions much more efficiently with no overlapping of tasks when there is an understanding of individual roles. Plan to have opportunities to orient new members of the team to not only the classroom and responsibilities, but also to the expectations of collaboration with all team members, including the family. This can go a long way in making a new member of the team feel welcome. When steps are taken to communicate roles, expectations, and values, other members (e.g., families, related services personnel) will see a cohesive classroom team working to benefit all of the children.

Conflict Resolution

There are times when a conflict is minor and other times when it may prevent us from working toward the team goal. Conflict is inevitable within any group of people interacting over a period of time. Therefore, the challenge is not to avoid conflict but to manage it so it does not affect the team functioning and child outcomes.

A sign of successful teaming is recognizing the expertise in others without feeling diminished by their strengths as well as feeling comfortable admitting that you do not have all the answers. Look at how you can grow from criticism and recognize that everyone on the team is focused on outcomes.

Ms. Abby and Lili have come a long way from Ms. Abby's first thoughts of "where to begin?" Teaming will look different for each child in the class, and teams will continue to evolve and adapt to meet changing needs in the classrooms. Your teaming efforts will be successful when you include all team members, keep in mind the characteristics of effective team members, understand the challenges to teaming, and handle conflict well.

Ms. Abby decided that teaming was the best way to support Lili. Once assessments were completed and specific needs were identified, team members were selected based on their expertise and knowledge. Lili's team included her family, Ms. Abby, and related services personnel in the areas of occupational therapy (Mr. Mason) and speech-language pathology (Miss Nicole). Ms. Abby has a background in special education and felt confident in her knowledge about addressing both cognitive and social-emotional concerns, but she needs support with Lili's occupational therapy and speech-language pathology needs. The entire team was ready to get started shortly after the assessment and set a convenient time for an initial meeting to discuss the priorities and concerns of all team members. Lili's ability to interact with peers was her family's greatest concern. Other members of the team also had concerns, which led to the development of the previously introduced outcomes. The outcomes were determined as a team so that everyone was on the same page; however, determining how to address each of the outcomes did not come without conflict. Miss Nicole's preference was to pull Lili out of the class to work on her communication goals, but this was met with some concerns from Ms. Abby and Lili's family. Pulling Lili out of her peer environment did not seem beneficial because peer interactions is one of her primary concerns, but the team members were careful to respectfully disagree. Miss Nicole was reluctant, but a resolution was found through the development of the home activity matrix and Ms. Abby's playdough classroom activities. The activities demonstrated how all members of the team could work collectively on all of the outcomes and how this could spread across all of her environments if everyone had the appropriate skills. Miss Nicole and Mr. Mason trusted both Ms. Abby and Lili's family as they released their roles by sharing knowledge and modeling intervention strategies. Now Lili would have continuity at school, at home, and in the community as she interacted with multiple people in a variety of settings and routines.

The team did have some challenges with scheduling the next meetings and setting up some times to model activities for Lili's grandmother. They had to work around many schedules because of the group's size, but they were committed to finding a day and time that would work for everyone. Mr. Mason was excited to share information with Lili's grandmother that might provide her with opportunities to practice skills at home. Although her grandmother was not very excited about the messy prospect of Lili holding her own fork, brushing her own teeth, and pouring liquids independently, she was very interested in how these opportunities would provide her granddaughter with opportunities to practice using skills. What a team effort!

SUMMARY

Although challenging, meeting the needs of individual children and families can be attained through teaming. However, members of the team must have the knowledge required, along with clear roles and responsibilities in order to function effectively. A teaming approach that includes shared responsibility and collaboration of all team members in planning for, implementing, and revising instruction, leads to heightened outcomes for both children and families. With an understanding of the many challenges that are typical to such teams, the experience will not only be successful, but enjoyable!

LEARNING ACTIVITIES

1. Review Ms. Abby's situation in the vignette on page 174. Write a list of questions she should ask these parents and the child's therapists related to her concerns.

2. Develop a home activity matrix similar to the one in Figure 8.2 for a child to show family members how they can support learning outcomes during home activities and routines such as playing at the park, making a snack, or getting ready for bed.

3. Attend an individualized education program meeting. Observe team members, note if parents were present, and note communication strategies that were used during the meeting. Take notes throughout the meeting. Pay close attention to interactions among team members and the family members present. Were the family members actively involved and, if so, how? Did the family act as active decision makers? Were questions answered in family-friendly language? After the meeting, reflect on how the family was or was not involved in the meeting and how, if at all, you would have done things differently.

4. Observe a preschool classroom and note the interactions among the adults on the team working together throughout the day. Consider who does what and how (i.e., in the classroom or pull-out). Interview the teacher, and ask him or her how he or she decided the roles and responsibilities of each team member, how certain people are trained for the roles, and how he or she communicates with the team about expectations.

REFERENCES

Bauer, A.M., & Shea, T.M. (2003). *Parents and schools: Creating a successful partnership for students with special needs.* Upper Saddle River, NJ: Merrill/Pearson Education.

Bedore, L.M., Peña, E.D., Joyner, D., & Macken, C. (2011). Parent and teacher rating of bilingual language proficiency and language development concerns. *International Journal of Bilingual Education & Bilingualism, 14*(5), 489–511. doi:10.1080/13670050.2010.529102

Bell, S.T. (2004). *Setting the stage for effective teams: A meta-analysis of team design variables and team effectiveness.* Unpublished doctoral dissertation, Texas A & M University, College Station.

Bricker, D. (Series ed.). (2002). *Assessment, Evaluation, and Programming System for Infants and Children (AEPS®)* (2nd ed.). Baltimore, MD: Paul H. Brookes Publishing Co.

Bronfenbrenner, U. (1979). *The ecology of human development.* Cambridge, MA: Harvard University Press.

Carroll, D. (2001). Considering paraeducator training, roles, and responsibilities. *Teaching Exceptional Children, 34*(34), 60–64.

Cloninger, C. (2004). Designing collaborative educational services. In F.P. Orelove, D. Sobsey, & R.K Silberman (Eds.), *Educating children with multiple disabilities: A collaborative approach* (4th ed., pp. 11–13). Baltimore, MD: Paul H. Brookes Publishing Co.

Copple, C., & Bredekamp, S. (Eds.). (2009). *Developmentally appropriate practice in early childhood programs* (3rd ed.). Washington, DC: National Association for the Education of Young Children.

DiNatale, L. (2002). Developing high-quality family involvement programs in early childhood settings. *Young Children, 57*(5), 90–95.

Division for Early Childhood. (2014). *DEC recommended practices in early intervention/early childhood special education 2014.* Retrieved from http://www.dec-sped.org/recommendedpractices

Feldman, M., Ward, R., Savona, D., Regehr, K., Parker, K., Hudson, M.,...Holden, J. (2012). Development and initial validation of a parent report measure of the behavioral development of infants at risk for autism spectrum disorders. *Journal of Autism and Developmental Disorders, 42*(1), 13–22. doi:10.1007/s10803-011-1208-y

Fields-Smith, C., & Neuharth-Pritchett, S. (2009). Families as decision makers: When researchers and advocates work together. *Childhood Education, 85,* 237–242.

French, N.K. (2003). Paraeducators in special education programs. *Focus on Exceptional Children, 36*(2), 1–16.

Giangreco, M.F., Cloninger, C.J., & Iverson, V.S. (2011). *Choosing outcomes and accommodations for children (COACH): A guide to educational planning for students with disabilities* (3rd ed.). Baltimore, MD: Paul H. Brookes Publishing Co.

Grisham-Brown, J., & Pretti-Frontczak, K. (2011). *Assessing young children in inclusive settings: The blended practices approach.* Baltimore, MD: Paul H. Brookes Publishing Co.

Guralnick, M.J. (2001). A developmental systems model for early intervention. *Infants and Young Children, 14*(2), 1–18.

Hanson, M.J., & Lynch, E.W. (2013). *Understanding families: Approaches to diversity, disabilities, and risk* (2nd ed.). Baltimore, MD: Paul H. Brookes Publishing Co.

Haynes, D., & Grisham-Brown, J. (2013). *Reach for the stars: Planning for the future* (2nd ed.). Louisville, KY: American Printing House for the Blind.

Heroman, C., Burts, D.C., Berke, K., & Bickart, T.S. (2010). *Teaching Strategies GOLD® objectives for development & learning: Birth through kindergarten.* Bethesda, MD: Teaching Strategies, LLC.

High/Scope Press. (2003). *The High/Scope preschool child observation record* (2nd ed.). Belmont, CA: Wadsworth Publishing.

Hresko, W.P., Miguel, S.A., Sherbenou, R.J., & Burton, S.D. (1994). *Developmental observation checklist system: A systems approach to assessing very young children.* Austin, TX: PRO-ED.

Hughes, M., & Valle-Riestra, D. (2008). Responsibilities, preparedness, and job satisfaction of paraprofessionals: Working with young children with disabilities. *International Journal of Early Years Education, 16*(2), 163–173. doi:10.1080/09669760701516892

Johnson, S., Wolke, D., & Marlow, N. (2008). Developmental assessment of preterm infants at 2 years: Validity of parent reports. *Developmental Medicine and Child Neurology, 50*(1), 58–62. doi:10.1111/j.1469-8749.2007.02010.x

Killoran, J., Templeman, T.P., Peters, J., & Udell, T. (2001). Identifying paraprofessional competencies for early intervention and early childhood special education. *Teaching Exceptional Children, 34*(34), 68–73.

Likins, M. (2003). NCLB implications for paraprofessionals. *Principal Leadership (Middle School Education), 3*(3), 10–13.

Losardo, A., & Notari-Syverson, A. (2011). *Alternative approaches to assessing young children* (2nd ed.). Baltimore, MD: Paul H. Brookes Publishing Co.

McCann, D., Bull, R., & Winzenberg, T. (2012). The daily patterns of time use for parents of children with complex needs. *Journal of Child Health Care, 16,* 26–52.

McCormick, L., Noonan, M.J., Ogata, V., & Heck, R. (2001). Co-teacher relationship and program quality: Implications for preparing teachers for inclusive preschool settings. *Education and Training in Mental Retardation and Developmental Disabilities, 36*(2), 119–132.

McWilliam, R.A. (1992). *Family-centered intervention planning: A routines-based approach.* Tucson, AZ: Communication Skill Builders.

McWilliam, R.A. (2005). Assessing the resource needs of families in the context of early intervention. In M.J. Guralnick (Ed.), *The developmental systems approach to early intervention* (pp. 215–234). Baltimore, MD: Paul H. Brookes Publishing Co.

McWilliam, R.A. (Ed.). (2010). *Working with families of young children with special needs.* New York, NY: Guilford Press.

McWilliam, R., Casey, A.M., & Sims, J. (2009). The routine-based interview: A method for gathering information and assessing needs. *Infants and Young Children, 22*(3), 224–233.

Minondo, S., Meyer, L., & Xin, J. (2001). The roles and responsibilities of teaching assistants in inclusive education: What's appropriate? *Journal of The Association for Persons with Severe Handicaps, 26,* 114–119.

Ratcliff, N.J., Jones, C.R., Russell Vaden, S., Sheehan, H., & Hunt, G.H. (2011). Paraprofessionals in early childhood classrooms: An examination of duties and expectations. *Early Years, 31*(2), 163–179.

Salend, S.J. (2008). *Creating inclusive classrooms: Effective and reflective practices* (6th ed.). Upper Saddle River, NJ: Prentice Hall/Merrill.

Sands, D.J., Kozleski, E.B., & French, N.D. (2000). *Inclusive education for the 21st century.* Belmont, CA: Wadsworth.

Vangalder, C.J. (1997). *CARE: Caregiver assistance, resources and education. A case study of a family-centered assessment and intervention model.* Holland, MI: Holland Public School District. (ERIC Document Reproduction Service No. ED407787)

Zins, J.E., Weissberg, R.P, Wang, M.C., & Walberg, H.J. (Eds.). (2004). *Building academic success on social and emotional learning: What does the research say?* New York, NY: Teachers College Press.

Activity Matrix

Routine/activity	Skills related to the outcomes			

Family Data Collection Sheet

Child's name: _____

Target skill: _____

Date	Routine/activity	Child response	Observer

## CHAPTER 9

Blended Practices for Promoting Social-Emotional Development in Young Children

Kathleen Artman-Meeker, Elizabeth McLaren, Mary Louise Hemmeter, and Jennifer Grisham-Brown

Ms. Vicky scanned the playground as her class of 18 preschool children played outside. Although it was early in the school year, Ms. Vicky had already noticed that some children seemed to make friends right away and some children seemed to struggle. As if on cue, she heard a scuffle near the sensory table. "Here we go again," she thought to herself as she noticed Malia and Patrick arguing over yet another object in the sensory table. "These two always seem to be fighting with someone. I've got to figure out what to do about this." After restoring peace at the sensory table, Ms. Vicky heard Claire, a child with autism, begin to cry at the top of the slide. Children were moving all around her, and Claire didn't seem to know how to take her turn on the slide. Ms. Vicky was so busy with Claire that she almost didn't notice Brent, a child with a speech-language delay, sitting by himself in the grass. "He seems to be by himself a lot. I'd better watch that," she thought to herself. Ms. Vicky had tried her best to build a welcoming classroom environment, but she was confused and overwhelmed by the different social-emotional needs of the children in her classroom.

Like Ms. Vicky, many preschool teachers struggle to meet the wide range of social-emotional needs of the children in their classrooms. Children enter preschool at various developmental levels and with diverse social experiences. This chapter describes the importance of social-emotional development for young children and recommended practices for promoting social-emotional development. The chapter continues with an introduction to blended practices for promoting social-emotional development, including the scope of instruction and specific strategies for teaching social-emotional skills at the universal, targeted, and individualized level. It concludes with a case study demonstrating the application of these strategies to meet the needs of all learners.

ISSUES AND TRENDS IN THE PROMOTION OF SOCIAL-EMOTIONAL DEVELOPMENT

Since the early 2000s, research has consistently supported the importance of social-emotional development for children's school readiness and overall mental health (Bierman, Nix, Greenberg, Blair, & Domitrovich, 2008; Blair, 2002; Galinsky, 2010; Greenberg, Riggs, & Blair, 2007; Ladd, Birch, & Buhs, 1999; Ladd, Kochendorfer, & Coleman, 1997; McClelland et al., 2007; Raver, 2002; Raver & Zigler, 1997; Shonkoff & Phillips, 2000; Tzuriel & Flor-Maduel, 2010; Welsh, Nix, Blair, Bierman, & Nelson, 2010). The National Association for the Education of Young Children (NAEYC; Copple & Bredekamp, 2009) described social-emotional competence as both important in its own right and predictive of later school success. Children who get along with others, follow directions, regulate their emotions, think of appropriate solutions to problems, persist at difficult tasks, engage in social interactions, interpret others' behaviors, and have positive self-images are more likely to do well in school, at home, and in the community (Jones, Greenberg, & Crowley, 2015;

Smith, 2010). This is true not only during the early childhood years but also into adolescence. Social-emotional competence in the early years is a strong predictor of positive outcomes in elementary school and beyond (National Scientific Council on the Developing Child, 2008; Raver & Knitzer, 2002; Zins, Bloodworth, Weissberg, & Walberg, 2004). Many schools and early childhood education (ECE) programs consider social-emotional learning a key component of their curriculum (Civic Enterprises, Bridgeland, Bruce, & Hariharan, 2013). Teachers report that focusing on social-emotional learning improves the climate of their programs, reduces bullying and challenging behavior, and boosts academic performance (Civic Enterprises et al., 2013).

Prevalence of Social-Emotional Challenges in Young Children

Social-emotional challenges and challenging behavior remain a common concern among teachers and families, despite the compelling research on the importance of social-emotional development for young children (Hebbeler et al., 2007; Hemmeter, Corso, & Cheatham, 2006). Between 9.5% and 14% of young children experience social-emotional problems that negatively affect their development and ability to learn (Brauner & Stephens, 2006; Robbins, Stagman, & Smith, 2012). Furthermore, children under the age of 6 receive approximately 9% of the specialty mental health services in the United States despite accounting for less than 6% of the nation's population (U.S. Census Bureau, 2010; Warner & Pottick, 2006).

Concerns are exacerbated for children with a variety of risk factors such as poverty and disability. Children living in neighborhoods with high concentrations of poverty are more likely to experience behavioral and social-emotional challenges than are their more affluent peers (Duncan, Brooks-Gunn, & Klebanov, 1994). The prevalence of children with persistent challenging behavior in Head Start is reported to be as high as 30% (Qi & Kaiser, 2003). In a survey of Head Start teachers, more than 50% of respondents reported having children with defiance, aggression, and disruptive behavior in their classroom (Snell, Berlin, Vorhees, Stanton-Chapman, & Hadden, 2012). The same study reported that 29% of teachers had concerns with children's social skills or internalizing behaviors.

Social-emotional development is also a concern of families of children with disabilities. More than 30% of parents reported difficulties with their child's challenging behavior in one study, and 25% of parents reported that their child had social-emotional concerns such as anxiety, hyperactivity, depressive symptoms, and problems interacting with others (Hebbeler et al., 2007). About 19% of children suspended from preschool programs for challenging behavior are children with special needs served under the federal Individuals with Disabilities Education Improvement Act (IDEA) of 2004 (PL 108-446) (U.S. Department of Education Office for Civil Rights, 2014). These findings led to a federal policy statement about suspension and expulsion that urges programs to ensure that developmentally appropriate practices are in place for supporting children's social-emotional development and preventing challenging behavior. The *Policy Statement on Expulsion and Suspension Policies in Early Childhood Settings* (2014) was developed jointly by the U.S. Departments of Education and Health and Human Services.

Social-emotional development is critical for success in school and life (Shonkoff & Phillips, 2000), and there is growing evidence of negative outcomes for children who do not develop appropriate social-emotional skills. Social and behavioral disengagement at school is associated with higher rates of delinquency among youth (Hirschfield & Gasper, 2011; National Scientific Council on the Developing Child, 2008). Children who are socially rejected by their peers when they are young are more likely to experience poor outcomes in school (Coie, Lochman, Terry, & Hyman, 1992; Shonkoff & Phillips, 2000) and face lifelong mental health concerns (Cowen, Pederson, Babigian, Isso, & Trost, 1973; Shonkoff et al., 2012).

Recommended Practices in the Promotion of Social-Emotional Development

The social-emotional domain is a critical element of early childhood and preschool programs, given the long-term outcomes that are influenced by social-emotional learning during early childhood. It is a basic tenet of NAEYC's developmentally appropriate practice that 1) development across domains is interrelated and important and 2) "children develop best when they have secure, consistent relationships with responsive adults and opportunities for positive relationships with peers" (Copple & Bredekamp, 2009, p. 13). Social-emotional development occurs within the contex contexts.

Research and policy supports a three-tiered approach to promotion of social-emotional development and prevention of challenging behavior (Division for Early Childhood [DEC], 2007; Fox, Carta, Strain, Dunlap, & Hemmeter, 2009; U.S. Department of Health and Human Services, 2015; ZERO TO THREE, 2003). Teachers use practices at the universal level that promote the social-emotional well-being of all children. They use practices that improve children's communication skills, prevent challenging behavior, and help all children learn to regulate emotions, cooperate with others, and follow directions. Teachers provide focused supports at the secondary or prevention level for children who are at risk for social-emotional delays or challenging behavior. This level focuses on preventing negative outcomes through explicit instruction in social skills and emotional regulation (Fox et al., 2009). Finally, teachers and teams provide individualized supports at the tertiary level based on an understanding of an individual child's behavior.

Fox, Dunlap, Hemmeter, Joseph, and Strain (2003) described a specific application of the three-tiered approach to promoting social-emotional development. This framework is referred to as the Pyramid Model for Promoting Social Emotional Competence (see Figure 9.1) and describes practices for building relationships, designing supportive environments, promoting social skills and emotional development, and developing individual supports for

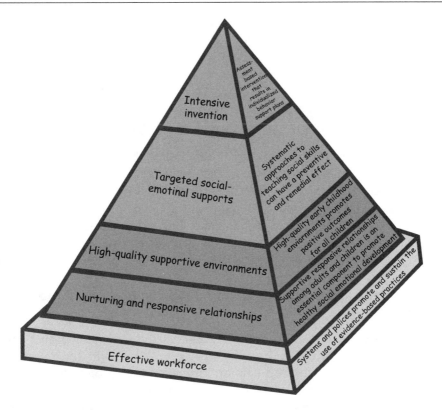

Figure 9.1. The Pyramid. (From CSEFEL. *Pyramid model: Promoting social and emotional competence in infants and young children.* Nashville, TN: CSEFEL; reprinted by permission.)

children with the most significant social-emotional needs and challenging behavior. The three tiers of practice depicted in the Pyramid Model are designed to address the social-emotional and behavioral needs of all children in inclusive preschool classrooms.

Specific strategies associated with each tier of the Pyramid Model correspond to recommended practices in early childhood education. Practices organized under the universal tier of the Pyramid Model focus on fostering nurturing relationships and creating supportive environments and are strategies to be used with all children in a preschool classroom. Supporting play, engaging with children in extended conversations, providing descriptive praise, encouraging children, providing adequate materials, balancing schedules, structuring transitions, and teaching rules are examples of research-based strategies teachers would use at this tier. Practices organized under the targeted tier of the Pyramid Model focus on providing children with targeted social-emotional instruction and supports, including teaching children problem solving, handling anger, making friends, and communicating emotions. Strategies used at this level might focus on intentional instruction for all children (e.g., formally teaching the entire class how and when to share with peers) or providing targeted instruction to a subset of students (e.g., inviting four children known to struggle with sharing to a group art project in which sharing is modeled and encouraged). Finally, teachers provide individualized, intensive interventions for the small number of children who do not respond to universal and targeted supports (Fox et al., 2009).

BLENDED PRACTICES FOR PROMOTING SOCIAL-EMOTIONAL DEVELOPMENT

Promoting children's social-emotional development requires a comprehensive and intentional approach, including a deep understanding of the specific skills children acquire during the early childhood years. It also involves careful planning to systematically support the development of these skills. This section describes the social-emotional skills children need to learn and the universal, targeted, and individualized approaches teachers can use to support this learning.

Scope of Instruction: Social-Emotional Skills and Outcomes

Although there is no universally accepted definition of *social competence,* there is agreement that social competence is a "dynamic and higher order construct in which skills and abilities categorized within the traditional domains of cognitive, communication, affective, and motor development are integrated in the service of specific interpersonal goals" (Guralnick, 1997, p. 599). These interpersonal goals include initiating and maintaining relationships with others, resolving conflicts, and building friendships. Viewing social competence from this perspective suggests a much broader set of goals than has often been addressed in preschool classrooms. This perspective moves us from focusing primarily on teaching children to initiate and respond to their peers to helping children develop friendships, express their emotions, and solve social problems (Cairone & Mackraine, 2012; Hyson, 2004; Webster-Stratton, 1999).

Table 9.1 provides an overview of the social-emotional outcomes that are important to address during the preschool years. These outcomes can be separated into three primary groups: 1) social relationship skills, 2) emotional regulation and empathy (e.g., recognizing, responding to, and expressing emotions; self-regulation), and 3) social problem solving. These categories overlap to some extent because of the integrated nature of these skills.

Universal Tier: Designing Classrooms and Experiences to Promote Social-Emotional Development

Fostering social-emotional development begins with building a secure, caring, and supportive social environment in which children learn and try new skills. The universal tier includes two distinct sets of practices (Fox et al., 2009). The first set of practices involves building positive and nurturing relationships with children and their families. Family engagement

Table 9.1.   Social-emotional outcomes for preschool children

Social relationship skills

Initiate to other children and adults
Respond to initiations from other children and adults
Take turns
Share with others
Cooperate with peers and adults
Engage in cooperative play

Emotional regulation and empathy

Recognize emotions in self and others
Express emotions in prosocial ways
Practice self-regulation
Follow routines and rules/expectations
Understand that actions affect others
Respond with sympathy to others

Social problem solving

Practice self-control
Formulate potential solutions when faced with conflict or frustration
Solve interpersonal conflicts through conversation
Implement problem-solving strategies (with adult assistance, if needed)
Exercise independence

is critical as it serves to teach children about different expectations in different settings, provides the child with more information and examples about social behavior, and changes the way significant others respond to the child's behavior. The second set of practices involves providing high-quality, supportive environments. This section describes these two sets of universal practices for promoting social-emotional development of all children.

Building Positive Relationships with and Among Children   Creating a caring, socially rich, cooperative, and responsive classroom does not happen automatically; it requires a planned approach on the part of the teacher and teaching staff. In fact, research has found that very few prosocial behaviors occur naturally in preschool classrooms (Eisenberg & Fabes, 1998). The social context of the classroom sets the stage for children to develop the social-emotional foundations that will be critical to their success in school and life, as outlined earlier in this chapter. The goal is to identify and use intentional practices that welcome teaching staff, children, and families into a caring community of learners.

Adult–child relationships may be the most powerful tool for working with young children because they set the stage for children's success by providing a secure foundation for emotional development (Downer, Sabol, & Hamre, 2010; Hyson, 2004; Shonkoff & Phillips, 2000). Relationships provide a context for the child to learn about his or her feelings and the feelings of others and to develop self-confidence and self-esteem. Children learn about the effect of their behaviors on others and begin to understand that their behavior gives them some control over their environment. These relationships are an important foundation for the teaching and learning processes.

Although the importance of relationships may seem obvious, it is often difficult to establish supportive relationships with every child either because of individual child characteristics or because of the sheer demands of running a classroom of active, eager young children. A child who needs these relationships the most is often the least likely to have access to them. Children with the most social-emotional challenges or challenging behavior would benefit greatly from ongoing, positive interactions with adults and peers, but their behaviors often interfere with the interactions that lead to these types of relationships. For example, teachers may respond to a child with persistently challenging behavior only when he or she is engaging in challenging behavior, and other children may avoid the child because they are afraid of the child or his or her behaviors. When the child is engaged in appropriate behavior, adults may not pay attention to him or her because they want to avoid further challenging behavior. Thus, this child has very few opportunities to learn from positive interactions.

Intentionally including one-to-one interactions is one powerful strategy to develop positive, supportive relationships between teacher and child (Driscoll & Pianta, 2010). These interactions should occur with regular frequency (multiple times per week) and should not be part of a rewards system contingent on the child's behavior. The child should be encouraged to take the lead and choose the activities and materials during the interactions. The teacher follows the child's lead by imitating and describing the child's play, avoiding directions and judgmental commentary on child behavior, and making statements that are supportive. Such one-to-one interactions can refocus a negative pattern of child–teacher interaction into a more positive pattern based on support and enjoyment rather than conflict. This method is referred to as *banking time* because the interactions create a resource that the child may draw on when confronted with stress or conflict throughout the day.

In addition to building positive relationships between teacher and child, teachers must be intentional in how they help children form social relationships with one another. Practices that can be used to create a caring community among children include the following (Bovey & Strain, n.d.; Gartrell, 2012a; Kaiser & Rasminsky, 2012):

- Class jobs that emphasize cooperation and helpfulness (e.g., passing out materials at mealtime or circle time, having a class "greeter" in the morning)

- Class materials that encourage peer cooperation rather than competition (e.g., puppets, wagons, floor puzzles, balls, construction materials, parachute, musical instruments)

- Pairing peers as "buddies" by placing one highly competent child with a child who is less competent (e.g., pairing students to walk in the hallway together, selecting center activities in pairs). It's important to follow child interest when using "buddies" by allowing children to separate as needed and to select activities that are appealing for both children.

- Creating partnering opportunities for typically solitary activities (e.g., place two chairs at the writing center or computer to encourage communication and cooperation)

- Catching children being good and commenting on prosocial behaviors (e.g., comment to a co-worker how well children are sharing materials, problem solving, or being helpful)

- Incorporating think-pair-share during class meeting times (e.g., ask children to talk with a friend to brainstorm ways to make a new child feel welcome to the classroom and then share the ideas with the whole group)

- Adults modeling assisting each other through teaming (e.g., in front of the children, tell your co-worker that you will set the tables for lunch while he or she reads to the children so that you can work as a team)

- Collaborating toward a class goal (e.g., creating a mural for the hallway, planting a garden, collecting donations for a food drive)

- Planning noncompetitive games and activities that encourage teamwork (e.g., playing "car wash" during outdoor play or "painting" the sidewalk with water and paintbrushes)

- Modeling and reinforcing simple manners (e.g., saying "please," "thank you," and "excuse me")

- Encouraging children to help each other and adults (e.g., encourage a child to help a peer hang up his or her backpack, help a peer clean up a messy part of the classroom, assist a teacher in cleaning the tables before mealtime)

- Incorporating class meetings for sharing thoughts, celebrating successes, and problem solving (e.g., hold a group discussion to brainstorm class rules at the beginning of the year)

Modeling social behaviors is one important way adults can help create a caring community. The role of the teacher in modeling social skills cannot be understated. Children watch teachers interact with other adults and with children throughout the day, which provide children with incidental models of social behavior. How teachers talk and interact with each other, families, and children can be a powerful intervention for teaching social skills to children.

Building Positive Relationships with Families   Families play a key role in promoting children's social-emotional development and addressing challenging behavior (Kaiser & Rasminsky, 2012). It is important to involve families in creating a caring community of learners. In addition to providing information about their child's behavior and social skills in other settings, families can provide contextual information that is useful in understanding children's behavior at school. They can also teach and reinforce social-emotional skills at home that are taught in school, thereby encouraging generalization of the skills across multiple environments. Families can support the school's expectations for children by talking about school expectations and providing children with opportunities to learn about those expectations in other settings. For example, one school expectation might be that children help others. Families can talk with their children about ways to help others, demonstrate how they can help others at home, and provide the child with feedback on helping behaviors.

Involving families requires that teachers and other program staff work to build relationships with families and clearly communicate about age appropriate social-emotional skills. If professionals want families to support children's social skills at home, then programs must provide families with information about supporting children's social skills and appropriate behaviors. This not only helps children learn about expectations but also provides families and school personnel with a common understanding. One simple strategy for supporting families is to send home a series of newsletters or tip-sheets outlining an age-appropriate social skill, realistic and easy-to-use strategies to implement at home, strategies that are being used at school, and the lifelong benefits of teaching that social-emotional skill.

Families and teachers can reinforce similar prosocial behaviors by communicating child successes at school and home. For example, a teacher might send a "happy gram" note home to describe how a child took turns with a peer on the swing during outdoor play, and a father might tell a teacher at arrival how the child shared dress-up clothes with her brother the previous night. The child who is part of this communication exchange understands that this social behavior is valued and expected by both his or her school and his or her home.

Providing High-Quality Supportive Environments   The universal tier involves the design and implementation of environments that support social-emotional development, including the physical environment, schedules and routines, and classroom rules and expectations. More information on some of these topics is provided in Chapter 5. This chapter provides an overview of how these strategies promote social-emotional development.

Physical Environment   Many features of the physical environment of classrooms promote children's prosocial behavior and prevent challenging behavior (see Table 9.2). These features relate to the physical design of the environment, the type and availability of materials and equipment, how materials are arranged, and the extent to which materials reflect different ability levels and interests. The environmental features described in Table 9.2 serve to promote social-emotional development and prevent challenging behaviors by increasing the likelihood that children will be engaged with the environment in appropriate ways. The physical design of

Table 9.2. Guidelines for designing the physical environment to promote prosocial behaviors and prevent challenging behavior

Provide a variety of materials at each learning center that address different ability levels, interests, and response modes.

Include materials in learning centers that are likely to promote children's interactions with each other.

Include materials that integrate subjects across centers (e.g., writing materials in the science area, books in the dramatic play area).

Make changes and additions to learning centers on a regular basis. Let children help determine what could be included in the learning center.

Use pictures or labels to tell children where things belong.

Limit the number of children in a given learning center.

Use picture posters and schedules to help children know what to do.

the environment helps children know where to play and makes it easier for children to move around the room without running into things or people. The size and design of learning centers can be critical. Learning centers that are too crowded can result in children fighting over toys or running into one another, which limits peer interactions. Restricting the number of children in a center encourages children to work cooperatively and gives children opportunities to practice skills such as negotiation, compromise, turn-taking, and sharing (Heroman et al., 2014).

Schedules, Routines, and Transitions   The schedule and how it is implemented is one of the single most important factors in preventing challenging behavior (Strain & Hemmeter, 1999; Yu, Meyer, & Ostrosky, 2013). Poorly designed schedules, inconsistent routines, too many transitions, and too much unengaged time lead to situations in which challenging behavior is likely to occur. Schedules and routines are discussed at length in Chapter 5; however, some issues specific to the effect of schedules, routines, and transitions on social-emotional development are discussed in this chapter. Table 9.3 provides an overview of practices related to schedules and routines that will promote social-emotional development and minimize the likelihood that challenging behavior will occur. A consistent schedule will help children feel secure and safe. Knowing what is happening next not only helps children feel secure but also helps them know what they should do. Disruptions in this routine will be problematic for some children and can lead

Table 9.3. Structuring transitions, routines, and schedules to promote child engagement and prevent challenging behavior

Observe the children, and design a schedule that works for your specific group of children.

Balance activities—quiet and noisy, active and passive, large group and small group, adult directed and child directed.

Minimize the number of transitions, especially those that require all children to make a transition at the same time.

Implement the schedule consistently.

Teach children the schedule and expectations related to the schedule.

Alert children about transitions.

Tell children when there will be changes in the schedule.

Use individually designed schedules for children who have difficulty with the schedule and routine.

Prompt children to help each other during routines and transitions.

Structure transitions so that children do not spend significant time waiting with nothing to do.

to challenging behavior if not handled appropriately. It is important that children are told about changes in routines in ways that they can understand, which helps them learn to regulate their emotions and reactions to events. For example, a stop sign could be placed next to an activity that will not occur that day or fabric could be fastened using Velcro across a shelf to indicate that the materials are not available at a given time. During opening circle, the teacher can explain any changes that might occur during the day to the children (e.g., children will do yoga in the gym rather than go to the playground due to inclement weather).

Activities Designed to Promote Engagement Table 9.4 provides an overview of key issues in designing activities to promote engagement. This is an important step in promoting social-emotional development and preventing challenging behaviors in that the activities are more likely to be engaging to the child if the child's individual goals and needs have been considered in the development of activities. By doing this, the teacher plans for individual response modes, different attention spans, and individual interests, which is particularly important when planning large-group activities.

The majority of time in many inclusive preschool classrooms is spent in either large-group teacher-directed activities (e.g., circle, story) or child-directed activities (e.g., centers, outdoor play), with relatively little time being spent in small-group activities. Although small groups may be difficult to implement because of a lack of staffing, they can be ideal for skill-building activities. Small-group activities allow for more individualized instruction and provide opportunities for promoting peer interaction. For small-group activities to be successful, teachers should keep in mind the importance of planning for high levels of student participation and should monitor children's engagement and adapt the activity accordingly based on the individual needs of each child in the group. Making sure that all children can participate in activities in meaningful ways is another key factor in promoting engagement. For example, a child who is new in the class might need a peer to help him or her follow the routine of the classroom.

Classroom Rules and Expectations Teaching rules and expectations is a universal support in terms of encouraging appropriate social-emotional behaviors and preventing challenging behavior (Copple & Bredekamp, 2009;

Table 9.4. Designing classroom activities to promote child engagement

Include large-group, small-group, and child-directed activities in the daily schedule.
Design activities with individual children's goals and interests in mind.
Have a purpose or goal for each activity.
Use peers as models during large-group activities.
Vary the topics and activities from day to day.
Monitor children's attention and adjust group activities accordingly.
Provide opportunities for active child participation.
Vary opportunities for participation based on children's skills and interests.
Give children jobs during group activities.
Assign adults to support children who have difficulty attending during group activities.

Gartrell, 2012b). Developing similar behavioral expectations across all classrooms as part of a programwide positive behavior interventions and supports (PBIS) plan helps create consistency and provides a common emphasis on prosocial behavior. Expectations should be stated positively, limited in number, and focused on behaviors that are relevant across all the settings in the program. For example, a program might set the expectations to "Be safe, Be Respectful, and Be Helpful." Staff members and families throughout the program can then remind children to follow these expectations in the hallways, classrooms, playgrounds, and homes. Figure 9.2 provides an example of one program's expectations.

As part of their programwide PBIS plan, Ms. Vicky's center developed a set of behavioral expectations for all children in the program. They developed a 1-page overview (see Figure 9.2) of the expectations and behaviors to share with families during the first round of parent–teacher conferences. As the teachers shared it with the families, they talked about how these expectations might look at home. In some cases, families raised issues about how an expectation was inconsistent with their parenting practices. Teachers used this opportunity to talk openly with families about differences in school and home expectations and to problem-solve about how they could work together to address these differences.

Intentional Teaching for Social-Emotional Development

Teachers provide intentional instruction on social-emotional skills, including relationship skills, emotional regulation and empathy, and social problem solving, at the universal tier. All young children need support to effectively use these skills during the preschool years (Fox et al., 2009). Research on effective strategies for teaching social-emotional skills clearly indicates that instruction must be comprehensive for it to be most effective (Domitrovich, Cortes, &

The Buzz about the 3 "Bees"	
Welcome to a new school year! You might have heard about the "3 Bees." This is our program's way of talking about how we treat one another in the program. Teachers, children, and families all help each other follow these important guidelines. You'll see posters in classrooms that show the 3 Bees in words and pictures. Here is what you might hear in the program:	
Be safe	Safety is our first priority. In the classroom, this means using walking feet, cleaning up toys, and using materials safely. Outdoors it means using equipment safely and listening for directions.
Be Respectful	This means using kind words, following directions, and listening to others. It means taking good care of our space and materials. It also means respecting yourself by doing your best.
Be Helpful	This means helping one another, working together, and caring about the people around us.

Figure 9.2. A program's expectations to share with families. (From Pyramid Model Research Project. [2008]. *Teaching Pyramid Teacher Implementation Guide 1*. Nashville, TN: CSEFEL; adapted by permission.)

Greenberg, 2007; Webster-Stratton & Reid, 2004). The most successful programs focus on social-emotional development on a daily basis, use a structured approach for teaching critical skills and reinforcing them in context, and provide training and support to families to support children's behavior at home (Joseph & Strain, 2003; Webster-Stratton, 1999). Although time consuming and labor intensive, this type of comprehensive approach is critical, given the effect of children's social-emotional development on their development in other areas and their later school and life success. This section begins by describing critical elements of social-emotional instruction. It then describes the systematic approaches designed to teach and support specific skills, including relationship skills, emotional regulation and empathy, and social problem solving.

Critical Elements of Social Skills Instruction   Teaching social-emotional skills requires intentional teaching that goes beyond instruction during teacher-led group activities. Effective social skill instruction should address the acquisition of new skills, the fluency of using skills with ease, and the maintenance of skills over time and generalization of skills into unique situations (Bailey & Wolery, 1992). Fox and Lentini (2006) described these three stages of learning as 1) show-and-tell, 2) practice makes perfect, and 3) maintenance and generalization. Teachers should introduce a new social skill in show-and-tell by explaining it with concrete examples, demonstrating how the skill might be used in context, and providing encouragement and feedback to children as they practice the skill. Table 9.5 provides a list of children's literature that can be used to address social-emotional

Table 9.5.   Children's books that address social-emotional development

And Here's to You (David Elliott & Randy Cecil, 2009)
The Big Book of Beautiful Babies (David Ellwand, 2001)
Feelings (Aliki, 1986)
The Feelings Book (Todd Parr, 2005)
Glad Monster, Sad Monster: A Book About Feelings (Anne Miranda & Ed Emberley, 1997)
Hands Are Not for Hitting (Martine Agassi, 2002)
How Are You Peeling? (Saxton Freymann & Joost Elffers, 2004)
I Can Share (Karen Katz, 2011)
I Like Me (Nancy Carlson, 1990)
If You Plant A Seed (Kadir Nelson, 2015)
Little Humans (Brandon Stanton, 2014)
The I'm Not Scared Book (Todd Parr, 2011)
The Kissing Hand (Audrey Penn, 2007)
My Many Colored Days (Dr. Seuss, 1996)
On Monday When It Rained (Cheryl Kachenmeister, 1989)
Quiet Loud (Leslie Patricelli, 2003)
Rainbow Fish (Marcus Pfister, 1999)
Scared Stiff (Katie Davis, 2001)
Sometimes I'm Bombaloo (Rachel Vail, 2005)
The Thankful Book (Todd Parr, 2012)
The Three Grumpies (Tamra Wright, 2003)
Today I Feel Silly (Jamie Lee Curtis, 2007)
The Way I Feel (Janan Cain, 2000)
Thunder Boy, Jr. (Sherman Alexie, 2016)
When I Feel Scared (Cornelia Maude Spelman & Kathy Parkinson, 2002)
When Sophie Gets Angry—Really, Really Angry (Molly Garrett Bang, 2004)

skills and may be useful to introduce a new skill to children during the first step of this process. Additional resources can be found at http://csefel .vanderbilt.edu/resources/strategies.html#list.

In the second step, the teacher intentionally plans structured opportunities or identifies naturally occurring opportunities for the child to practice the new skill to build fluency. For example, a teacher might plan a small-group activity to role-play common scenarios when it's appropriate to trade a toy or assist children during play to trade as needed. The teacher provides feedback and encouragement as the child gains confidence and ability. The child uses the social-emotional skill independently in new and unique situations in maintenance and generalization and depends less on external motivation from the teacher to use the skill. Box 9.1 provides an example of how to use the three-step process for teaching and supporting social skills instruction.

Teaching and Supporting Relationship Skills   Teachers explicitly instruct children how to interact with and form relationships with other children and adults at the universal tier. Social relationship skills are important in terms of setting the stage for social-emotional development.

Box 9.1.   Three-Step Process for Teaching and Supporting Social-Emotional Skill Instruction

Stage One—Acquisition—Show-and-Tell

Ms. Vicky reads the book *Sophie Gets Angry—Very, Very Angry* (Bang, 2004) at group time to talk to children about ways to calm down when they are upset. She introduces the concepts of deep breathing and spending time alone to think and calm down rather than reacting in a harmful manner.

Stage Two—Fluency—Practice Makes Perfect

During small group, Ms. Vicky has children describe a time they felt frustrated or angry and then lets the children take turns practicing taking deep breaths as they watch the fish tank in the "cool down" area of the classroom. When Ms. Vicky notices children visibly upset during free choice, she reminds them of the "cool down" strategy and sits with them as they breathe and watch the fish tank.

Stage Three—Maintenance and Generalization

The next week Ms. Vicky overhears Sarah say to her friend, "I'm so mad right now! I want some alone time!" and watches her go the fish tank and take deep, calming breaths. Ms. Vicky tells Sarah how proud she is that she remembered a great way to calm down. At dismissal, Ms. Vicky tells Sarah's mother how well she is calming her body in the classroom. Her mother reports that Sarah goes to her bedroom and cuddles with her stuffed animals as a way to calm down at home.

Relationship skills help children be successful in their interactions with others and are linked with having more friends (Tremblay, Strain, Hendrickson, & Shores, 1981) and include initiating and responding to others, turn-taking, sharing, helping others, cooperating, giving compliments, knowing how and when to apologize, and entering and exiting play. Interactions with peers provide the context for forming friendships and other relationships with both peers and adults.

Explicitly teaching and supporting children's use of relationship skills includes modeling and role playing prosocial behaviors, structuring activities that require peer interaction, selecting materials that foster cooperation rather than competition, and encouraging and praising children for using positive social interactions. Table 9.6 provides sample ideas that can be used to introduce and encourage use of these relationship skills.

Teaching and Supporting Emotional Regulation and Empathy

Emotional regulation and *empathy* refer to children's ability to recognize and express their own emotions and feelings and recognize and respond to the emotions of others (Hyson, 2004). Children who manage their own emotions well and who respond appropriately to the emotions of others will be more successful in their interactions with their peers. Emotional regulation and empathy require that children have adequate communication skills for expressing emotions, the cognitive abilities to understand and interpret their own and others' emotions, and the ability to control their own behavior. Anger management, impulse control, and the ability to calm oneself are important components of emotional regulation. The ability to identify and describe feelings and emotions is at the foundation of emotional regulation and empathy. Teaching children emotional vocabulary to label their emotions (e.g., "I am angry!") and helping them understand the subtle differences among various emotions (e.g., the differences among angry, frustrated, and disappointed) are the first steps in promoting children's emotional regulation and empathy. Next, teachers help children learn how to appropriately express emotions. A key feature of instruction on emotions and empathy is that all emotions are valid, but it is important to learn how to express those emotions in a way that is safe to self and others. Instruction related to emotion identification, emotional regulation, and empathy should include learning to identify and label emotional states in oneself (e.g., "Do you feel proud of yourself that you put your coat away all by yourself?") and then in others (e.g., "Do you see the tears on Jessie's face? How do you think she's feeling?"). In addition to planned instructional experiences that teach children socially acceptable ways to handle strong emotions (e.g., practice using calming breaths during whole-group instruction), teachers should be prepared to provide support to children as they learn to use these methods during real-life situations (e.g., modeling calming breaths when two children are in a dispute over the swing). Table 9.7 describes sample ideas for teaching children about emotional vocabulary, emotional regulation, and empathy.

Table 9.6. Introducing and promoting relationship skills

Relationship skills	Strategies to teach and promote relationship skills
Initiating and responding to others	Use a scripted social story to teach children specific phrases to use for greetings. Use puppets to model and practice initiating or responding ("Good morning" or "My name is Reid" when asked his name). Provide a communication board with appropriate communication phrases related to greetings and responses to common questions. Provide positive reinforcement when a child initiates or responds appropriately.
Turn-taking	Select materials that encourage turn-taking (e.g., balls and board games that encourage children to play together and take turns for play to be successful). Encourage children to take more frequent turns as well as increase the duration of the turn-taking.
Sharing	Intentionally structure activities so that children are encouraged to share access to all materials (e.g., provide a limited number of scissors, play games such as Go Fish that require sharing, provide each child one color of paint and he or she must trade to gain access to multiple colors). Use role play to model strategies to ask for materials (e.g., "Can I have some of the blocks?") as well as appropriate ways to refuse (e.g., "It's my turn on the computer now. You can have the next turn"). Adults model sharing materials with co-workers and children throughout daily activities. Use children's literature to provide examples of the benefits of sharing (e.g., *The Rainbow Fish* [Pfister, 1996])
Helping others	Identify a variety of class jobs that focus on helping others, such as 1) assisting peers who are putting their backpacks and coats in their cubbies during arrival time, 2) feeding the class pet, and 3) passing out snack supplies. Encourage children to ask peers for assistance or demonstrate how to do something rather than relying solely on teacher assistance.
Cooperating (working together)	Peer buddies (e.g., children are paired to play together for 5 minutes, and then they choose to continue play or find another activity) Group projects (e.g., children work cooperatively toward a common goal such as creating a collage or class book or planting a garden)
Giving compliments	Create a "compliment tree" by adding leaves over time to a tree mural with compliments children make about peers (these can be encouraged during a small-group activity or spontaneously throughout the day). Teachers model giving compliments to co-workers and children to create a positive social context.
Knowing how and when to apologize	Role-play scenarios at large and small group about one child hurting another friend's feelings and apologizing to make him or her feel better. Scenarios could be based on real-life situations observed in the classroom to make this concrete for children.
Entering and exiting play	Use a scripted social story to teach children specific phrases to use when entering play and giving "play organizer statements" (e.g., "Let's play blocks"). Use puppets to model and practice asking, "Will you play with me?" and "Thanks for playing. See you later!"

Table 9.7.   Introducing and promoting emotional regulation and empathy

Social-emotional skills	Strategies to teach and promote emotional regulation and empathy
Identify, label, and describe feelings and emotions in self and others	Use photographs and illustrations of a variety of facial expressions to directly teach what emotions look like. • Use mirrors and ask children to imitate facial expressions portrayed in the photographs. • Ask children what might have made the person in the photograph feel that way. Ask children to reflect on what makes them feel the same emotion. Teach a variety of emotion vocabulary. Children need more than the basic *happy*, *sad*, and *mad* to accurately label their emotions and the emotions of others. Focus on specific words such as *frustrated*, *disappointed*, and *proud*. Create a classroom collage related to a featured emotion. For example, cut pictures out of magazines, take photographs of children making appropriate facial expressions, and have children dictate and illustrate scenarios related to the emotion "proud." Use teachable moments to assist children in labeling the emotion they are feeling during daily activities. Use a feelings chart for children to identify the emotion they are feeling at a specific time. Encourage them to identify if and when that emotion changes throughout the day. Use children's literature to teach emotion vocabulary and possible scenarios when children might feel that way (e.g., *On Monday When It Rained* [Kachenmeister & Berthiaume, 2001]) Use happy/sad faces on popsicle sticks for children to identify how a character is feeling while reading a book (e.g., *Today I Feel Silly* [Curtis & Cornell, 2007]) or while reading a social story.
Empathy	Use role play and children's literature (*Today I Feel Silly* [Curtis & Cornell, 2007]) to assist children in taking the perspective of another child. Use illustrations or stories to encourage discussion about how a child might feel and why. Encourage children to label how a peer might be feeling during conflict resolution discussions.
Manage anger and strong emotions	Use role play to assist children in identifying times when they may feel angry or upset. Label emotions for children during situations in which they, or you, are experiencing strong emotions. Teach the four steps of the Turtle Technique (Joseph & Strain, 2010; Schneider, 1974) using a turtle puppet and encouraging children to demonstrate each step during role play. Support children in the four steps as they apply this skill during real-life scenarios. 1. Recognizing that you feel angry 2. Thinking "stop" 3. Going into your "shell," taking three deep breaths, and thinking calming, coping thoughts 4. Coming out of your "shell" when calm and thinking of solutions to the problem Teach families the Turtle Technique, and encourage children to use this in home and community settings.
Impulse control and follow directions	Use social stories and children's literature (*When Sophie Gets Angry—Very, Very Angry* [Bang, 2004]) to identify situations in which children might feel out of control and appropriate ways to respond. Incorporate games that require impulse control, such as Simon Says or Red Light, Green Light, to practice impulse control during play (Center on the Developing Child at Harvard University, 2014)

Table 9.7.   *(continued)*

Social-emotional skills	Strategies to teach and promote emotional regulation and empathy
Emotional regulation	Teach children to notice the physical differences between feeling tense and relaxed. These can be described as "tight" (tense) muscles or sensations like "butterflies" in the stomach (Webster-Stratton & Reid, 2004). Use a feelings thermometer to help children see the difference between "hot and angry" emotions and "cool and calm" emotions (Webster-Stratton & Reid, 2004, p. 103). Have them practice making physical changes in their bodies to replicate these feelings.
	Model keeping calm during frustrating/disappointing experiences during the day. Describe to children what occurred that was frustrating and what strategy is being used to calm down (e.g., "I'm so disappointed it's raining today and we can't go outside. I'm going to take some deep breaths and think about the fun things we can do inside instead").
	Model and practice deep breathing. Encourage children to take deep belly breaths and pretend they are blowing out birthday candles.
	Listen nonjudgmentally to children as you describe the emotions they are feeling. Help them label emotions, and acknowledge the validity of their feelings.

Teaching and Supporting Social Problem Solving   Social problem solving helps children resolve conflicts in nonviolent ways and develop independence and confidence (Webster-Stratton, 1999). Many of the challenging behaviors that occur in classrooms result from conflicts between children (e.g., they both want the same toy) and from instances in which children do not have the skills they need to solve a problem in an appropriate way (e.g., Simon and Indigo want to play with the same toy and are grabbing it from each other). Social problem solving requires children to have developed some of the other social-emotional competencies that are addressed in this section. For example, children have to know there is a problem in order to begin problem solving. Children generally know there is a problem because of the way they are feeling. In order to evaluate different solutions, children must learn to take the perspective of others and evaluate the potential outcome of a solution for themselves and for others.

Given the complex nature of problem solving is not a skill most children learn without a structured approach to teaching. Approaches for teaching social problem solving generally involve teaching children a series of steps such as: 1) identify the problem, 2) brainstorm solutions, 3) evaluate solutions, 4) choose a solution and try it, and 5) evaluate the outcome (Shure, 1994; Webster-Stratton, 1999). Figure 9.3 shows a visual that teachers can use to teach and reinforce steps. Children have to be taught the multistep process using a variety of teaching strategies (see Table 9.8) and then guided through the process as they use it in context.

Encouraging children to take ownership of and a leadership role in problem solving, rather than relying on the teacher to always take the lead in the process, is a critical aspect of teaching problem solving. Evans (2002) argued

Problem-Solving Steps

1. What is my problem?

2. Think, think, think
   of some solutions

3. What would happen if...?
Would it be safe? Would it be fair?
How would everyone feel?

4. Give it a try!

Figure 9.3. Problem-solving steps. (From the Center for Social and Emotional Foundations for Early Learning [CSEFEL]. *Problem-solving steps poster.* Nashville, TN: CSEFEL; reprinted by permission.)

that problem solving is a logical consequence for making a social error, and children learn from the experience when they are actively involved in the problem solving process, rather than having a solution imposed on them from an authority figure. Let's return to the previous example about Indigo and Simon, who were fighting over the toy. If they learn to figure out what they can do (e.g., trade toys) without adult intervention, then they are more likely to be able to use that in other situations. Once children experience success in solving problems, their feelings of self-efficacy increase and they will take on increasing complex problems independently and with support from peers and teachers (Pawlina & Stanford, 2011).

Targeted Tier: Supplemental Teaching, Practice, and Supports to Promote Social-Emotional Development

Some children will need additional support around the development of social-emotional skills, despite high-quality instruction at the universal tier (Fox et al., 2009). Teachers use data to identify the specific skills that children need support around and then provide targeted, systematic instruction on these skills. This section describes three key strategies for providing

Table 9.8. Introducing and promoting social problem solving

Direct teaching

Teach children problem-solving steps and provide visual cues in the classroom (see Figure 9.3) to remind and support children as they use this process in context.

Use children's literature to discuss social problems, and brainstorm possible solutions to the character's dilemma with the children.

Role-play situations with children using concrete examples of common classroom problems. Support children during these structured practice sessions as they work through the problem-solving steps and as they begin to use the steps in context.

Remind children to use calming techniques such as the Turtle Technique to deescalate before they attempt to problem-solve.

Use published curricula for role-play scenarios and visual supports.

Problematize

Teachers can intentionally sabotage or problematize situations throughout the day to encourage children to practice problem solving. For example, if three children want to join a small-group art activity, intentionally place only two chairs at the table and ask the children to help solve the problem (http://www.vanderbilt.edu/csefel).

Solution kit

Provide visual cues with common solutions to problems (e.g., wait and take turns, trade, get a teacher) to assist children in generating possible solutions when problem solving. Cues can be obtained from commercial sources, created with images from magazines or photographs from the classroom, or drawn by children.

Encourage children to try more than one idea if the first solution isn't successful or acceptable to peers.

Class meetings (Gartrell, 2012a)

Class (or community) meetings are conducted as a whole-group conversation to discuss and solve issues that involve the entire classroom. Teachers facilitate a group discussion during these meetings to make decisions in a noncompetitive and inclusive format. For example, a class meeting might be held at the beginning of the school year to generate and set classroom rules. In another situation, a meeting could be held after a teacher notices teasing on the playground and the venue would be used to discuss how the children feel when they are teased and set guidelines on how to treat each other respectfully.

- All children are allowed to speak during meetings, but they need to listen to others, be honest, and be kind.
- Teachers should support children during the problem-solving process. Once children learn the class meeting process, teachers should take less of a lead role and allow children to take on more responsibility.

Mediation steps (Evans, 2002)

The High/Scope problem-solving approach includes attending to children's emotional states. This model incorporates emotional regulation and discussion of children's feelings about the conflict during the initial stages of conflict resolution.

- Approach the situation calmly.
- Acknowledge children's feelings.
- Gather information about the situation.
- Restate the problem.
- Solicit solution ideas from the children and choose one together.
- Implement the solution and provide support as needed.

targeted instruction around social-emotional development—direct teaching, naturalistic strategies, and peer-mediated strategies.

Direct Teaching   There is an identified set of recommended practices that are useful and effective in teaching social-emotional skills to young children who need additional support (Division for Early Childhood, 2014). These strategies generally include describing, modeling, rehearsing, role playing, prompting children in naturalistic contexts, and reinforcing and acknowledging the behavior when it occurs. Many of the teaching strategies used to provide targeted instruction on social-emotional skills are similar to the strategies used for instruction across the curriculum, but they are designed and delivered with the learning goals of particular children in mind. It is important that a child learns the concept (e.g., using a personalized storybook to teach the child about what it means to help others), practices the skill (e.g., during snack, center, and other times when the child needs assistance), and has opportunities to view and talk about examples and nonexamples of the skill (e.g., during group or individual discussions with the teacher). Large- and small-group activities can be used for introducing the skill, modeling the skill, and role playing the skill, which will benefit the children who need more targeted supports and all the children in the class. Puppets, books, songs, and games can be useful in capturing the child's interest and explaining the concept to a child in ways that he or she is likely to understand (see Table 9.5 for children's books about different types of social-emotional skills). Center time and outdoor play as well as other child-directed activities provide an important context for individual or small groups of children to practice social-emotional skills and get feedback about the skills from teachers and peers.

Concrete examples and opportunities to practice skills within a meaningful context are critical to child learning. Using scripted social stories that teach behavioral expectations in a given social context is one way to provide concrete examples to young children (Gray, 2010). The stories are written from a child's perspective and include very specific statements that describe appropriate behavior within a given social situation (e.g., "Abby says, 'I want to play!' when she joins her friends on the playground") and pictures that illustrate the expected behavior. Teachers can use an individual child's name and photographs of that child to illustrate his or her personalized social story and make the stories concrete and meaningful.

Naturalistic Strategies   Naturalistic strategies are designed to help children learn to use social-emotional skills in authentic contexts and during routine interactions. Naturalistic strategies include environmental arrangement and interaction techniques (Franzone, 2009). The team should first identify a specific target behavior for a child (e.g., turn-taking) in order to use naturalistic strategies most effectively. The team can then identify ways the environment can be structured to elicit the target behavior. For example, the team may provide toys with many pieces, such as blocks or

Legos, to spark social interactions. Cooperative games may be provided during free play in the classroom, or materials may be placed out of reach so children need to make requests or engage in problem solving. In addition to environmental strategies, interactions are powerful naturalistic teaching strategies. First, adults follow children's interests. They see where, with whom, and how children choose to play. Then they use those interests to encourage conversation or socialization. They respond to children's communication attempts by repeating, expanding, or imitating the child's language or behavior. In some cases, the adult might interpret a child's social behavior for peers. An adult might say, "I think Ryan is asking to play with you." Finally, adults provide descriptive feedback to children about their social behavior. An adult might describe positive behaviors by saying, "Ryan asked to play and now you're building a road together."

> *Ms. Vicky knows that Claire has a difficult time taking turns. She also knows that Claire loves playing with collections of small objects such as counting bears and trains. Ms. Vicky replaces the classroom's manipulatives with cooperative games that include small objects (e.g., Ants in the Pants, Checkers). She hopes Claire will be drawn to the games and engage in turn-taking. Ms. Vicky stays close to Claire during free play and joins her when Claire chooses the games. She models and encourages as Claire and a peer begin playing the game.*

Peer-Mediated Strategies   Peers are natural play partners, but they can also help one another learn valuable social-emotional skills. In many studies of peer-mediated strategies, a socially skilled peer is taught to facilitate and encourage another child's social-emotional behavior during natural opportunities (Harris, Pretti-Frontczak, & Brown, 2009; Neitzel, 2008; Robertson, Green, Alper, Schloss, & Kohler, 2003; Strain & Bovey, 2011). The peer is taught specific strategies for supporting the target child. The peer might learn how to help organize play, how to share, how to offer help, or how to provide appropriate affection (Neitzel, 2008). The peer and the target child have structured opportunities to use these skills together. These interactions can begin to happen during regular routines and activities as the children become more proficient.

Peer-mediated strategies can also be classroomwide or less formal. For example, teachers can take opportunities to pair children for a variety of different activities. Children can line up in pairs, or a short period of free playtime can be dedicated to "peer buddy play." For example, children might begin the free playtime with a peer buddy in a certain interest area or learning center. Children can choose the name of a buddy randomly (e.g., from a jar) or teachers can be strategic about buddy pairings. All children can be taught simple strategies for promoting play and social interactions during buddy playtime. For example, children can be taught three strategies: stay with your buddy, play with your buddy, and talk to your buddy (Goldstein, English, Shafer, & Kaczmarek, 1997).

INDIVIDUALIZED TIER: INTENSIVE AND INDIVIDUALIZED INTERVENTIONS FOR CHILDREN WITH THE MOST SIGNIFICANT SOCIAL-EMOTIONAL AND BEHAVIORAL NEEDS

Although the strategies previously described will be adequate for promoting social-emotional development and preventing challenging behaviors in most children, a small number of children will need more intensive, individualized interventions (Fox et al., 2009; Sugai et al., 2000). Although the number of children exhibiting persistent challenging behavior or other significant social-emotional needs in a given classroom is likely to be rather small, this level of challenging behavior can seriously affect the social climate in a classroom and impede the social-emotional learning of the child with challenging behavior. When children display social-emotional challenges of this severity, it is likely to take a systematically designed and consistently implemented plan to effectively address the challenging behaviors and social-emotional challenges. This section of the chapter describes ways to assess challenging behavior and how to use that information to design interventions and strategies to target those specific behaviors, including intentional teaching of social-emotional skills.

The framework for designing and implementing interventions for challenging behaviors that is discussed in this section is consistent with an approach called *PBIS* (Horner et al., 2009; Lucyshyn, Dunlap, & Albin, 2002). This approach has a substantial database to support its effectiveness in reducing challenging behavior and increasing prosocial behaviors in children with even the most challenging behaviors. It has been effectively used with a wide range of children with and without disabilities as well as with children of different ages. PBIS is based on both behavioral research and humanistic values and is designed to result in a decrease in challenging behavior as well as the acquisition of new skills and more positive relationships with adults and peers (Iovannone et al., 2009). There has to be a commitment to a team approach and involvement of relevant people in the child's life, including teachers and family members as well as other adults who interact with the child on a regular basis (e.g., child care providers, therapists), in order to accomplish these outcomes. The effectiveness of this approach depends on the consistent implementation of the plan across natural environments (Benedict, Horner, & Squires, 2007; Bradshaw, Reinke, Brown, Bevans, & Leaf, 2008; Conroy et al., 2014) and on the provision of support and training for parents (Fox, Clarke, & Dunlap, 2013; Reinke, Splett, Robeson, & Offutt, 2009; Webster-Stratton, 1999) and other adults who are involved in the implementation of the plan.

PBIS is based on an underlying assumption that most challenging behaviors represent an attempt by the child to communicate some message (i.e., behaviors are social) (Carr et al., 1994). They serve a specific purpose for the child, and they are influenced by what happens right before the behavior as well as what happens after the behavior occurs (O'Neill, Horner, Albin, Storey, & Sprague, 1990; Reichle & Wacker, 1993). Young children's challenging behaviors generally serve the purpose of either requesting something (e.g., attention from an adult, a toy) or protesting or avoiding something (e.g., getting out of an activity the child does not want to do). The function of the behavior (requesting or protesting) is critical to identifying new skills to teach the child and developing strategies for supporting the new skills and preventing the challenging behavior. For example, if the child wants to play with another child and he or she hits the person with a toy, then the function of his or her challenging behavior is getting a friend's attention. In order to reduce his or her challenging behavior (i.e., hitting), it will be necessary to teach him or her a more appropriate behavior or relationship skill (e.g., asking, showing a picture of what he or she wants) to use when he or she wants to make a request to play. The following scenarios provide examples of how challenging behavior serves a social purpose or function for Claire and Patrick.

> *Claire does not like to go to the computer area. It is hard for her; she cannot work the mouse, and she doesn't understand how the computer works. The new student teacher who is walking with Claire and holding her hand does not know this, and she looks around the room and begins to move toward the computer area. Claire starts hitting the student teacher and crying. The student teacher assumes Claire doesn't like her. After several observations, it is determined that Claire's challenging behavior serves the purpose of avoiding activities that are too difficult for her or that she does not like. Claire needs to learn appropriate social-communication strategies for letting someone know when she doesn't want to do something.*
>
> *Patrick often pushes other children. After several observations and completing an assessment, the teacher determines that the function of Patrick's behavior is to get someone to play with him. For example, the teacher observes Patrick sitting next to two boys who are building a tower. Patrick picks up some blocks and puts them beside one of the boys; the boy does not respond. So, Patrick pushes one of the boys, who turns to him and starts asking him what he wants. Patrick needs to learn more appropriate strategies for entering play situations.*

PBIS is an individualized planning process that involves 1) identifying environmental factors (e.g., interactions, events) that trigger challenging behavior, 2) identifying the purpose that the behavior serves for the child, 3) identifying more appropriate behaviors that the child can use in place of the challenging behavior (e.g., social skills, communication skills), and 4) developing a plan that includes strategies for preventing the challenging behavior, teaching new skills, and responding to occurrences of challenging behavior (Fox et al., 2003). The primary steps of the process are described in the text that follows and include 1) gathering information, 2) developing a behavior support plan, and 3) implementing and evaluating the plan. A team that includes the family and professionals who work with the child and conducts all of the steps will be successful. Although this chapter provides an overview of the steps involved in the PBIS process, it is beyond the scope of this book to describe the PBIS process in sufficient detail for implementation. A great deal of information is available on implementing PBIS that teachers can find in additional resources (e.g., Dunlap, Wilson, Strain, & Lee, 2013; Hieneman, Childs, & Sergay, 2006; Stormont, Lewis, Beckner, & Johnson, 2007).

Gathering Information   Gathering information is the first step in dealing with children who have persistently challenging behavior. This process is often referred to as *functional behavioral assessment* (FBA; Artman-Meeker & Hemmeter, 2014; Neilsen & McEvoy, 2004; O'Neill et al., 1990) and can include interviews and observations by family members, other caregivers, and others who work or interact with the child. The interview should address issues such as when and how often the behavior occurs, the child's preferences (i.e., likes, dislikes), what strategies have been tried in terms of addressing the challenging behavior, and what has worked or not worked. The interview can also help identify social-emotional skills already in the child's repertoire.

The functional assessment process also includes observations of the child in natural environments to identify the possible function and triggers of the child's behavior. An antecedent-behavior-consequence analysis is the most common method for these observations. Antecedent is what happens before the behavior, behavior is the actual challenging behavior, and consequence is what happens after the behavior. Teacher directions, lack of attention from a peer or teacher, or a change in activity or transition are some common antecedents or triggers for children's challenging behavior. Keeping a narrative description of what the child is doing is one common way to collect this information. Figure 9.4 is an example of notes written by Noah's teachers. Although brief, this example demonstrates that Noah uses a variety of challenging behaviors (e.g., sticking his fingers in someone's ear, knocking over a tower, pushing trays off of the table), but they all serve the common purpose of getting someone's attention. They also work for Noah. Although he might initially get some negative attention, he gets attention that eventually results in positive attention. The interview will provide information about activities or routines in which the challenging behavior is most likely to occur. These activities and routines can then be used for the direct observations. It is likely to take a great deal of time and writing to complete these observations than the sample in Figure 9.4.

Developing a Behavior Support Plan   A behavior support plan is a comprehensive plan for addressing a child's challenging behaviors and has four primary components: 1) hypotheses, 2) prevention strategies, 3) replacement skills, and 4) adult responses (Fox, Lentini, & Dunlap, 2004). The inclusion of these components makes this approach comprehensive in that it focuses on providing supports to children and teaching new skills as

Times/activity	Antecedent	Behavior	Consequence	Possible function
8:45 Opening Circle	Miss Santos is reading a story using a big book. Before the circle, Miss Santos reminds the children to sit on their mats and keep their hands to themselves.	Noah taps his friend Cher on the shoulder and then sticks his finger in her ear.	Miss Patti, the assistant, comes over and sits next to Noah.	Get attention
9:15 Center Time	Charlie and Jack are playing in the block area. Noah comes over to the block area and sits next to the two boys, who continue what they are doing. Noah starts building a tower right next to them, but when he starts telling them about it, they ignore him.	Noah gets up and knocks over the structure that Charlie and Jack are building.	Miss Santos comes over and suggests that Charlie and Jack add on to the tower that Noah started building.	Get attention
10:00 Snack	Noah is sitting at a table with Hannah, José, and Jalen. Hannah and José are talking about what they are going to do on the playground today.	Noah pushes his tray into the trays of the other children, knocking their drinks over.	Miss Santos comes over, cleans up everything, tells Noah he shouldn't have done that, and sits down next to him. She proceeds to ask him about his favorite activity, reading books.	Get attention

Figure 9.4.   Observation of a child's challenging behavior.

well as including strategies for responding to challenging behavior when it occurs.

The information obtained through observations and interviews can be used to formulate hypotheses about the child's challenging behaviors. The hypotheses will then be used to develop the behavior support plan (visit http://www.vanderbilt.edu/csefel for sample behavior support plans). The behavior hypothesis will be based on the functional assessment information and will represent the team's best guess about why the behavior occurs. A sample hypothesis for Noah might be, "Noah uses aggressive behaviors (e.g., sticking his finger in another child's ear, knocking over children's toys) to initiate interactions with others, including adults and peers. When he does this, adults typically give him attention and prompt his peers to give him attention after discussing the situation with him." This example includes specific information about the child's behavior (e.g., aggressive behaviors such as sticking a finger in a friend's ear), the predictors of the behavior (i.e., when he wants to interact with another child), and what the adults do when the child exhibits the challenging behavior.

Once the hypothesis has been identified, the team generates 1) strategies that will be used to prevent the challenging behavior, 2) skills that the child will be taught to use in place of the challenging behavior, and 3) strategies for how the adults will respond when and if the challenging behavior occurs. Prevention strategies will be used during the routines and activities that are identified through the functional assessment process to be most problematic for the child. Prevention strategies are designed to reduce the likelihood that the child will engage in the challenging behavior by either making those activities and routines easier for the child to complete without challenging behavior or making the challenging behavior irrelevant. Some sample prevention strategies might include

- Adding something to the activity to make it more interesting to the child

- Giving the child a choice

- Providing the child with a picture schedule that helps him or her understand the routine of the environment

- Giving the child an individualized warning prior to a transition

- Breaking down an activity into steps the child can understand

- Providing adult attention and support during problematic routines and activities

- Using pictures or line drawings to show where materials go

Although many of these strategies are similar to those described in Chapter 5, they should be selected for the behavior support plan as they relate to the function of a child's specific challenging behavior. Let's return to the scenario involving Noah. The hypothesis statement developed for him was, "Noah uses aggressive behaviors (e.g., sticking his finger in another child's ear, knocking over children's toys) to initiate interactions with others, including adults and peers. When he does this, adults typically give him attention and prompt his peers to give him attention after discussing the situation with him."

The team would need to identify prevention strategies that would reduce Noah's need for using challenging behavior, including assigning an adult to stay near him during playtime, structuring a play space or buddy group for Noah, and giving him a role that involves interactions with peers (e.g., go around the room giving transition warning). Once the team identifies the function of the challenging behavior, a set of replacement skills can be identified. That is, the team should identify skills the child can use that serve the same purpose as the challenging behavior but that are more socially appropriate. Replacement skills should be both effective and efficient, meaning that they should result in the same outcome the challenging behavior produced. It is best to identify a replacement skill that is already in the child's repertoire but that he or she does not use in the challenging routine and activities. For example, if Noah is nonverbal, selecting a verbal skill for him is not likely to be as effective as selecting a nonverbal skill that he can already do.

Based on the observational and interview data, it is clear that Noah is not likely to get peers' attention appropriately. It is also clear that he uses a variety of behaviors (e.g., sticking fingers in people's ears, knocking over toys) to indicate he wants attention. So, the team determines that they want to teach him a more appropriate way to indicate that he wants attention. The team selects two skills on which to work. First, they are going to teach him to tap a friend on the shoulder when he is ready to play with another child. They will use a combination of questions and models to teach him to tap a friend on the shoulder. They will use these teaching strategies at times when he is not engaging in the challenging behavior by anticipating when he wants someone's attention and prompting him to tap the child's shoulder before the challenging behavior occurs. Next, they are going to teach him to show the child a picture of a play idea.

The effectiveness of the replacement skill depends not only on the child using the skill but also on the adults and peers in the environment responding to the child in positive ways. If peers and adults respond to the replacement skill more quickly and more positively than the challenging behavior, then the child will not need to use the challenging behavior. Although Noah might have the ability to tap a peer on the shoulder and show the child a picture, he will need to be taught to do that at times that are functional. It is important to teach replacement skills throughout the day at times when the child is not engaging in the challenging behavior.

Although the prevention strategies and replacement skills are designed to decrease the frequency of challenging behavior, there will most likely still be occurrences of the challenging behavior. Identifying strategies for how adults will respond to the challenging behavior when it occurs is an important step in the development of the behavior support plan. The response should make the challenging behavior ineffective. In addition, the responses for appropriate behavior should be greater or more positive than those for the challenging behavior. Noah's team decides that when the challenging behavior occurs, they will prompt him to tap the child on the shoulder. If Noah does not respond, then they will physically prompt him to use the strategy before a child plays with him.

Implementing and Evaluating the Plan The effective implementation of the plan requires that all team members are committed to the plan, relevant staff is trained to use the procedures, and strategies identified in the plan fit with the ongoing routines of the relevant environments. It is also important to identify the supports that staff and family members will need as they implement the plan. Staff and family members should understand that the initial implementation of the plan may result in a short period during which the challenging behavior escalates. This highlights the need for a system for monitoring both the implementation of the plan and the effects of the plan on the child's challenging behavior and social-emotional skills. For example, if the behavior escalates, it is important to know if the plan is being implemented correctly. Data collection should be comprehensive enough to indicate what is going on with both child and adult behavior but should also be able to be completed efficiently. Part of the plan should also involve determining who will monitor the plan and how decisions will be made if changes are needed in the plan. Strategies for monitoring the plan are similar to those strategies described in Chapters 4 and 5.

As part of the behavior support plan, individualized strategies can be used to teach all social-emotional skills described in this chapter. The tiers build on one another, with successively more intensive and individualized strategies used to support the successively smaller number of children who need support at each tier.

Curricula and Resources to Support All Tiers

A great deal of research exists on effective strategies for teaching social skills and promoting emotional development (e.g., Barnett et al., 2008; Barton et al., 2014; Domitrovich et al., 2007; Pianta, Mashburn, Downer, Hamre, & Justice, 2008; Raver et al., 2008; Webster-Stratton, Reid, & Hammond, 2004; Webster-Stratton, Reid, & Stoolmiller, 2008). In addition to research on various teaching strategies, there are also packaged curricula that focus on social-emotional development and use a variety of teaching strategies. Joseph and Strain (2003) reviewed several social-emotional curricula and identified criteria for evaluating them in terms of the effectiveness of the curricula in promoting children's skills. Barton and colleagues (2014) replicated this review and reviewed 10 classroom curricula. They found that a number of curricula address critical skills in the area of social-emotional development. Two thirds of the curricula were supported by moderate or strong empirical research. Three of the curricula were designed to operate within a tiered system of universal, targeted, and individualized supports—First Step (Walker et al., 1998), Second Step (Frey, Hirschstein, & Guzzo, 2000), and Incredible Years (Webster-Stratton, 2015). Joseph and Strain also found that a training program for parents is a critical component to the success of a social-emotional curriculum. Barton et al. found that half of the classroom curricula offered a comprehensive home component. See Table 9.9 for a sample of social-emotional curricula and resources.

Table 9.9.   Specific curricula and resources

Center on the Social and Emotional Foundations for Early Learning
http://csefel.vanderbilt.edu
Teacher- and family-friendly resources based on evidence-based practices that support social-emotional development. Resources include research summaries, video, trainings, social stories, and lesson plan ideas.

Book Nook from the Center on the Social and Emotional Foundations for Early Learning
http://csefel.vanderbilt.edu/resources/strategies.html#booknook
An in-depth list of children's literature categorized by the social-emotional skill addressed in the story. Suggested classroom activities that can be embedded into classroom routines are outlined for more than 20 children's books.

Technical Assistance Center on Social Emotional Intervention
http://challengingbehavior.fmhi.usf.edu
Collection of user-friendly resources on social-emotional development and intervention for challenging behavior. Resources include articles, videos, photographs, and free make-and-take files for visual cues and teaching materials.

Backpack Connection Series from the Technical Assistance Center on Social Emotional Intervention
http://challengingbehavior.fmhi.usf.edu
Downloadable handouts written in family-friendly language that can be used to share information with families about supporting social-emotional development at home and addressing challenging behaviors. Handouts include topics of addressing child behavior, emotions, routines and schedules, and social skills.

Head Start National Center on Quality Teaching and Learning
http://eclkc.ohs.acf.hhs.gov/hslc/tta-system/teaching/center
A collection of professional development resources for teachers, including research articles, handouts, videos, and 15-minute in-service sessions on a variety of topics, including social-emotional development of young children.

Head Start Center for Inclusion
http://depts.washington.edu/hscenter
Resources for teachers, disability coordinators, family service providers, trainers, and families that include 15-minute trainings, videos, and classroom materials (including social stories).

Center for Early Childhood Mental Health Consultation
http://www.ecmhc.org
A variety of resources for teachers, administrators, and families that provide an overview of social-emotional milestones, instructional strategies, tip sheets, classroom visuals, and a home kit to share with families.

CASE STUDY OF BLENDED PRACTICES FOR SOCIAL-EMOTIONAL ASSESSMENT AND INSTRUCTION

Assessment

Ms. Vicky administers the Assessment, Evaluation, and Programming System (AEPS®; Bricker, 2002), a curriculum-based assessment, four times per year. Ms. Vicky identified a few patterns during her team's fall assessment of the children in her class. Many children struggled with "resolving conflicts by selecting effective strategies." She realized that focusing on emotions and problem solving might help all of the children. Ms. Vicky decided to use this information and her own observations in the classroom to be more intentional about social-emotional teaching for all children in the classroom. She began thinking deeply about her curriculum and the experiences all children have in the classroom.

Scope and Sequence

Ms. Vicky began by identifying a scope and sequence for the skills she thought were most important for children in her class to learn. She reviewed her program's social-emotional curriculum and attended additional training on social-emotional teaching, with materials from the Center on the Social and Emotional Foundations for Early Learning (CSEFEL) (http:// www.vanderbilt.edu/csefel). After attending this training, she realized that she needed to continue teaching children to recognize emotions in themselves and others, make and keep friends, and solve common social problems. Her quarterly AEPS® data indicated that she needed to specifically address problem solving with a number of children in her classroom this year. She also recognized that one child, Claire, would need more individualized supports. Table 9.10 shows an abbreviated sample of the scope and sequence Ms. Vicky used for social problem solving, based on her program's curriculum.

Activities and Intervention Strategies for the Universal Level

Ms. Vicky began implementing her program's social-emotional curriculum. She used large-group activities to teach all children the critical skills they would need to be successful in solving problems. First, Ms. Vicky role-played a variety of situations with children to identify potential emotions by playing "How would you feel if?" during morning circle time. Once children became accustomed to labeling a variety of emotions, she introduced the problem-solving steps to the children during a large-group activity by reading When Sophie Gets Angry—Really, Really Angry *(Bang, 2004) to the group; in this book, the main character is upset with her sister. She helped the children identify the character's feelings and then introduced a few picture cards to help the children learn the problem-solving steps. They brainstormed potential solutions to Sophie's dilemma and talked about the potential outcomes of each solution. Then Ms. Vicky role-played a problem with her co-teacher. They both pretended they wanted to get a drink from the drinking fountain at the same time. They had the children help them figure out how to solve the problem.*

Once the concept of problem solving had been introduced at group time, Ms. Vicky planned small-group activities to give all children a chance to practice the skills with puppets, stories, and role plays. She also looked for opportunities throughout the day to talk about problem solving with individual children to aid in generalization of the skill. For example, she helped two students who wanted to ride the same bike use the problem-solving

Table 9.10. Scope and sequence for teaching interpersonal problem solving

Skill	Sequence	Ms. Vicky's notes
Joint attention	Foundational skill needed for problem solving (individual tier)	Read Claire's scripted story with focus on attending to peers and peer comments. Play Claire's video model and emphasize need to look at peers and repeat what peers say.
Problem solving	Recognize there is a problem and calm down (targeted tier)	Start with simple steps such as "stop and think," then add steps as children learn them. Encourage children to use the "calm down" area if needed. Post Tucker the Turtle images in the "calm down" area of the room. Remind Patrick, Malia, Brent, and Claire to use their individualized Tucker the Turtle cards and go to the calm down area.
	Identify the problem (universal tier)	Support children as each child tells his or her side of the story, and encourage children to listen to each other. Restate the problem before children begin generating solutions.
	Generate solutions (universal tier)	Include problem-solving steps and solution kit photographs in dramatic play area and gross motor room where conflicts typically occur. Once they get the idea of coming up with solutions, introduce the solution kit. Start with a few simple ones such as, "Get a teacher" or "Say, 'Can I play?'" Resist the urge to solve problems for the children, and support them in generating and trying solutions.

process. Sometimes she even contrived opportunities to use the process. For example, one day she purposely set out too few carpet squares at group time. She identified the situation as a problem and had the children generate solutions. Ms. Vicky and her co-teacher encouraged children to problem-solve and celebrated their efforts.

Activities and Intervention Strategies for the Targeted Level

Ms. Vicky provided additional supports for the problem-solving process for a small number of children. She or her co-teacher remained close to these children during free play and reminded them to use the strategies. She also simplified the materials: she decided to go back and focus on "stop and think." She used the Tucker the Turtle materials with these four children to help them learn to stop and calm down. Then she made small sets of picture cards for the children to carry or easily access to remind themselves of the steps. In addition, the teachers taught them to use the "calm down" area of the classroom to breathe prior to using the problem-solving strategies. She paired them up with children who were more skilled during small-group time and gave them more opportunities to practice.

Activities and Intervention Strategies for the Individualized Level

Claire still seemed to struggle, despite the additional supports. Claire was diagnosed with autism and her difficulty to take the perspective of a peer and attend to peers as they talked was interfering with her ability to use the problem-solving process. She also used challenging behavior such as running from the teacher and hiding during problematic situations. Ms. Vicky worked with the special education teacher, the speech-language pathologist, and Claire's family to gather information about Claire's behavior as part of the functional assessment and behavior support planning process. The team developed a hypothesis statement for Claire based on their data: "When Claire wants an object another peer has and is asked to use the problem-solving steps, she runs from the situation, cries, and hides in the classroom. When this happens, adults talk to Claire and give her something to play with by herself. The function of Claire's behavior is to escape or avoid problem-solving interactions and to gain access to toys." Table 9.11 shows the behavior support plan the team developed to address Claire's behavioral and social-emotional needs. It included developing a personalized scripted story for Claire about problem solving, with a special focus on the need to look at her peers, repeat her peers' suggestions, and strategies for handling disappointment. It featured pictures of Claire and her classmates and emphasized the need for Claire to attend to her peers' comments during problem solving. They also developed a video self-model of Claire solving a problem with a peer on the playground. They played it for her before the class went outside and reminded her how to use her new strategy. Ms. Vicky made note of the tiered supports she was using to help all children in her class learn problem-solving strategies (see Figure 9.5).

Table 9.11.   Excerpt from Claire's behavior support plan

Prevention strategies	New skills to teach	New responses
Ms. Vicky and her co-teacher take turns staying close to Claire during free play. Structure center time so Claire is near a preferred peer. Allow Claire to hold a comfort item or something that soothes her when stressed.	Use a scripted story to teach Claire to appropriately use the problem-solving steps (e.g., look at peer, stay close, try a different solution). Use a video model to teach Claire to complete the problem-solving process with a preferred peer.	**For challenging behavior:** Read the scripted story with Claire and prompt her through the steps. Prompt Claire to use the problem-solving cards. **For new skills:** Provide behavior-specific praise. Let Claire leave the interaction as soon as she uses the strategy. Give Claire access to the toys that she appropriately requests as part of the problem-solving process.

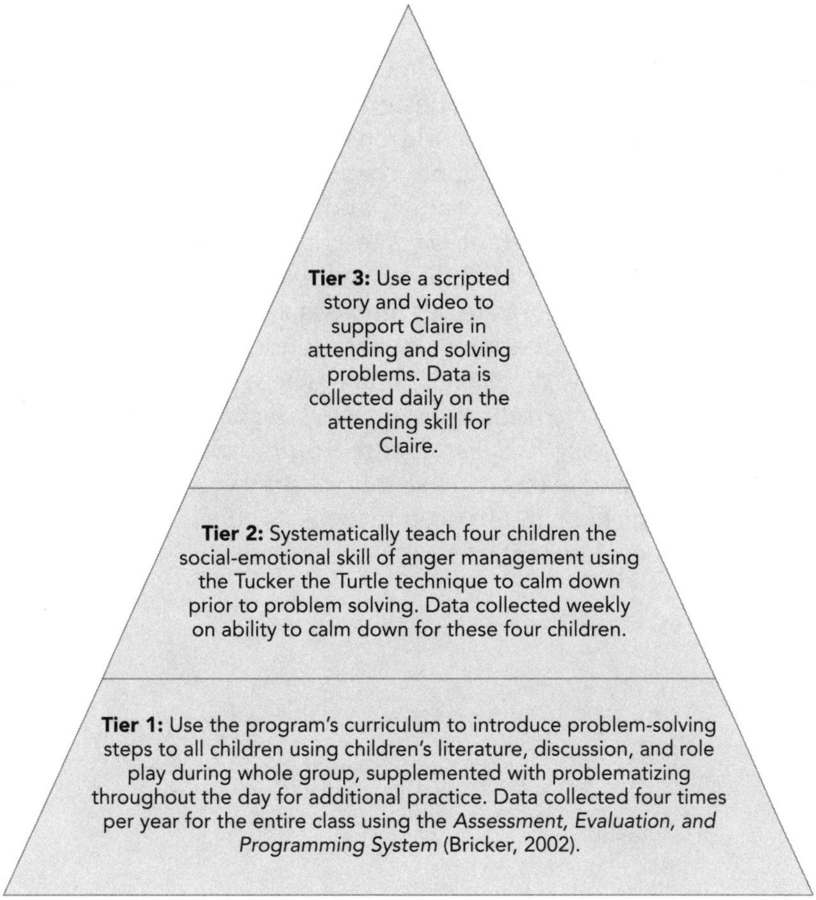

Tier 3: Use a scripted story and video to support Claire in attending and solving problems. Data is collected daily on the attending skill for Claire.

Tier 2: Systematically teach four children the social-emotional skill of anger management using the Tucker the Turtle technique to calm down prior to problem solving. Data collected weekly on ability to calm down for these four children.

Tier 1: Use the program's curriculum to introduce problem-solving steps to all children using children's literature, discussion, and role play during whole group, supplemented with problematizing throughout the day for additional practice. Data collected four times per year for the entire class using the *Assessment, Evaluation, and Programming System* (Bricker, 2002).

Figure 9.5. Tiered supports Ms. Vicky used in her classroom.

Progress Monitoring and Individualized Supports

Ms. Vicky used data to help her know whether her teaching strategies were working. She administered the AEPS® four times per year and collected regular data on children's problem-solving progress during daily activities in order to track the social-emotional development of all children in the class. She used these data to identify children such as Patrick, Malia, Brent, and Claire, who needed extra support on the specific strategies she was teaching. She collected anecdotal notes weekly on their use of "calm down" strategies until she was satisfied that they had mastered these prerequisite skills for the problem-solving steps. As previously noted, she collected daily data on Claire's individualized target skills. She noted whenever children used targeted skills such as emotion words or solving problems independently or with teacher assistance. By the end of the year, Ms. Vicky was proud of the progress her class had made.

SUMMARY

Promoting social-emotional development is an important part of the preschool curriculum. This chapter is designed to provide the reader with proactive strategies for promoting children's social-emotional development. Teaching friendship skills, emotional regulation, and social problem solving; providing a caring social context; and using effective curricula and teaching strategies are important ways teachers promote optimal development. Only a small number of children will need targeted individualized interventions when these strategies are consistently implemented with a high degree of fidelity. Teachers use data to identify children who need each tier of support. How do teachers know where to begin? CSEFEL (2010) developed an *Inventory of Practices for Promoting Social-Emotional Development and Preventing Challenging Behavior.* Figure 9.6 provides a sample from this inventory. Teachers and teams can use this inventory as a self-assessment to determine where the team might need to focus its efforts around promoting social-emotional development.

Inventory of Practices for Promoting Social Competence

Creating Supportive Environments

Skills and indicators	Consistently 3	Occasionally 2	Seldom 1	Target for training? YES	NO	Observations/evidence
6. Ensures smooth transitions						
☐ Structures transitions so children do not have to spend excessive time waiting with nothing to do						
☐ Teaches children the expectations associated with transitions						
☐ Provides warnings to children prior to transitions						
☐ Individualizes the warnings prior to transitions so that all children understand them						
Comments:						
7. Designs activities to promote engagement				YES	NO	
☐ Plans and conducts large-group activities with specific goals in mind for the children						
☐ Varies the topics and activities in the large group from day to day						
☐ Provides opportunities for children to be actively involved in large-group activities						
☐ Varies speech and intonation to maintain the children's interests in the large-group activity						
☐ Monitors children's behavior and modifies plans when children lose interest in large-group activities						
☐ Plans and conducts small-group activities with specific goals in mind for each child						
☐ Plans and conducts fun small-group activities						
☐ Uses peer as models during small-group activities						
☐ Monitors children's behavior and modifies plans when children lose interest in small-group activities						
☐ Makes adaptations and modifications to ensure that all children can be involved in a meaningful way in any activity						
☐ Uses a variety of ways to teach the expectations of specific activities so that all children understand them						
Comments:						

Date 1 Completed: _____   Date 2 Completed: _____

Figure 9.6. Selected items from Center on the Social and Emotional Foundations for Early Learning inventory of practices. (From CSEFEL. [2010]. *CSEFEL Inventory of Practices*. Nashville, TN: CSEFEL; reprinted by permission.)

Figure 9.6. (continued)

Inventory of Practices for Promoting Social Competence

Social and Emotional Teaching Strategies

Skills and indicators	Consistently	Occasionally	Seldom	Target for training?		Observations/evidence
	3	2	1	YES	NO	
23. Models appropriate expressions and labeling of their own emotions and self-regulation throughout the course of the day	3	2	1	YES	NO	
❑ Labels positive feelings						
❑ Labels negative feelings paired with actions to regulate						
Comments:						
24. Creates a planned approach for problem-solving processes within the classroom	3	2	1	YES	NO	
❑ Individualizes the planned approach to the appropriate level of the child						
❑ Systematically teaches the problem-solving steps: a What is my problem? b What are some solutions? c What would happen next? d Try out the solution.						
❑ "Problematizes" situations throughout the day to allow children opportunities to generate solutions						
❑ Takes time to support children through the problem-solving process during heated moments						
❑ Comments on and reinforces children's problem-solving efforts						
Comments:						
25. Promotes children's individualized emotional regulation that will enhance positive social interactions within the classroom	3	2	1	YES	NO	
❑ Helps children recognize cues of emotional escalation						
❑ Helps children identify appropriate choices						
❑ Helps children try solutions until the situation is appropriately resolved						
❑ Displays photographs of children working out situations						
Comments:						

Date 1 Completed: _____

Date 2 Completed: _____

LEARNING ACTIVITIES

1. Observe a classroom and list three activities or routines that promote the development of a caring and respectful community of learners. Identify one activity or routine that could be modified to encourage a more caring and respectful tone in the classroom.

2. Observe a classroom and describe several teaching practices related to rules, routines, and transitions that support prosocial behaviors and prevent challenging behaviors.

3. Identify one social skill mentioned in this chapter that is important to teach to young children. Plan activities to teach the new skill (show-and-tell), encourage fluency of using the skill with ease (practice), and generalize and maintain the skill to another context.

4. Choose a book from Table 9.5. Develop a plan that includes the following:

   • What social-emotional skills could be taught using the book?

   • Describe how you will use the book to teach the skills during group time.

   • Describe an activity you will do during small-group or center time to reinforce the skill you are teaching.

5. Brainstorm a list of 10 opportunities for "problematizing" during typical activities and routines to encourage children to solve common social problems. What would the teacher need to do to create a problem that needs to be solved? What are common solutions the children might generate? What are difficulties the children might encounter as they generate and implement solutions?

6. Identify one social skill that is discussed in this chapter. List the scope (the components and/or prerequisite skills) and sequence (the order in which the child needs to learn and demonstrate the component skills) of the social skill you identified.

7. Identify one child in an inclusive classroom who displays challenging behaviors. Based on observation of the child and interview with teaching staff, address the following:

   • Identify possible environmental factors (e.g., interactions, events) that may trigger challenging behavior.

   • Identify a potential purpose (i.e., function) that the behavior serves for that child.

   • Identify one or more appropriate behaviors that the child can use in place of the challenging behavior.

   • Briefly describe strategies to prevent the challenging behavior, teach the replacement skill you previously identified, and respond if the child repeats the challenging behavior.

REFERENCES

Artman-Meeker, K.M., & Hemmeter, M.L. (2014). Functional assessment of challenging behaviors. In M.E. McLean, M.L. Hemmeter, & P.A. Snyder (Eds.), *Essential elements for assessing infants and preschoolers with special needs* (pp. 242–270). Upper Saddle River, NJ: Pearson Education.

Agassi, M., & Heinlen, M. (2002). *Hands are not for hitting.* Golden Valley, MN: Free Spirit Publishing.

Alexie, S. (2016). *Thunder boy jr.* New York, NY: Little, Brown and Company.

Aliki (1986). *Feelings.* New York, NY: Harper-Collins-Greenwillow Books.

Bailey, D.B., & Wolery, M. (1992). *Teaching infants and preschoolers with disabilities.* Upper Saddle River, NJ: Prentice Hall.

Bang, M. (2004). *When Sophie gets angry—really, really angry.* New York, NY: Scholastic.

Barnett, S., Jung, K., Yarosz, J., Thomas, J., Hornbeck, A., Stechuk, R., & Burns, S. (2008). Educational effects of the tools of the mind curriculum: A randomized trial. *Early Childhood Research Quarterly, 23,* 299–313.

Barton, E.E., Steed, E.A., Strain, P., Dunlap, G., Powell, D., & Payne, C. (2014). An analysis of classroom-based and parent-focused social-emotional programs for young children. *Infants and Young Children, 27,* 3–29.

Benedict, E.A., Horner, R.H., & Squires, J.K. (2007). Assessment and implementation of positive behavior supports in preschool. *Topics in Early Childhood Special Education, 27,* 174–192.

Bierman, K.L., Nix, R.L., Greenberg, M.T., Blair, C., & Domitrovich, C.E. (2008). Executive functions and school readiness intervention: Impact, moderation, and mediation in the Head Start REDI program. *Development and Psychopathology, 20,* 821–843.

Blair, C. (2002). School readiness: Integrating cognition and emotion in a neurobiological conceptualization of children's functioning at school entry. *American Psychologist, 57,* 111–127.

Bovey, T., & Strain, P. (n.d.). What works brief 6: Using environmental strategies to promote positive social interactions. Retrieved from http://csefel.vanderbilt .edu/briefs/wwb6.pdf

Bradshaw, C.P., Reinke, W.M., Brown, L.D., Bevans, K.B., & Leaf, P.J. (2008). Implementation of school-wide positive behavioral interventions and supports (PBIS) in elementary schools: Observations from a randomized trial. *Education and Treatment of Children, 31,* 1–26.

Brauner, C.B., & Stephens, B.C. (2006). Estimating the prevalence of early childhood serious emotional/behavioral disorder: Challenges and recommendations. *Public Health Reports, 121,* 303–310.

Bricker, D. (Series ed.). (2002). *Assessment, Evaluation, and Programming System for Infants and Children (AEPS®)* (2nd ed.). Baltimore, MD: Paul H. Brookes Publishing Co.

Cain, J. (2000). *The way I feel.* Seattle, WA: Parenting Press.

Cairone, K., & Mackraine, M. (2012). *Promoting resilience in preschool: A strategy guide for early childhood professionals* (2nd ed.). Lewisville, NC: Kaplan Early Learning.

Carlson, N. (1990). *I like me!* New York, NY: Penguin-Puffin Books.

Carr, E.G., Levin, L., McConnachie, G., Carlson, J.I., Kemp, D.C., & Smith, C.E. (1994). *Communication-based intervention for problem behavior: A user's guide for producing positive change.* Baltimore, MD: Paul H. Brookes Publishing Co.

Center on the Developing Child at Harvard University. (2014). *Enhancing and practicing executive function skills with children from infancy to adolescence.* Retrieved from http://www.developingchild.harvard.edu/.

Center on the Social and Emotional Foundations for Early Learning. (2010). *Inventory of practices for promoting children's social emotional competence.* Champaign, IL: CSEFEL.

Civic Enterprises & Bridgeland, J., Bruce, M., & Hariharan, A. (2013). *The missing piece: A national teacher survey on how social and emotional learning can empower children and transform schools.* Chicago, IL: Author.

Coie, J.D., Lochman, J.E., Terry, R., & Hyman, C. (1992). Predicting early adolescent disorder from childhood aggression and peer rejection. *Journal of Consulting and Clinical Psychology, 60*(5), 783.

Conroy, M.A., Sutherland, K.S., Algina, J.J., Wilson, R.E., Martinez, J.R., & Whalen, K.J. (2014). Measuring teacher implementation of BEST in CLASS intervention program and corollary child outcomes. *Journal of Emotional and Behavioral Disorders, 23,* 144–155. doi:10.1177/1063426614532949

Copple, C., & Bredekamp, S. (2009). *Developmentally appropriate practice in early childhood programs serving children from birth through age 8.* Washington, DC: National Association for the Education of Young Children.

Cowen, E.L., Pederson, A., Babigian, H., Isso, L.D., & Trost, M.A. (1973). Long-term follow-up of early detected vulnerable children. *Journal of Consulting and Clinical Psychology, 41*(3), 438.

Curtis, J.L., & Cornell, L. (2007). *Today I feel silly and other moods that make my day.* New York, NY: HarperCollins.

Davis, K. (2001). *Scared stiff.* San Diego, CA: Harcourt Children's Books.

Division for Early Childhood. (2007). *Position statement: Identification and intervention with challenging behavior.* Retrieved from http://www.dec-sped.org/uploads/docs/about_dec/position_concept_papers/PositionStatement_Chal_Behav_updated_jan2009.pdf

Division for Early Childhood. (2014). *DEC recommended practices in early intervention/early childhood special education 2014.* Retrieved from http://www .dec-sped.org/recommendedpractices

Domitrovich, C.E., Cortes, R., & Greenberg, M.T. (2007). Improving young children's social and emotional competence: A randomized trial of the Preschool PATHS Program. *Journal of Primary Prevention, 28,* 67–91.

Downer, J., Sabol, T.J., & Hamre, B. (2010). Teacher-child interactions in the classroom: Toward a theory of within- and cross-domain links to children's developmental outcomes. *Early Education and Development, 21,* 699–723.

Driscoll, K.C., & Pianta, R. (2010). Banking time in Head Start: Early efficacy of an intervention designed to promote supportive teacher-child relationships. *Early Education and Development, 21,* 38–64.

Duncan, G.J., Brooks-Gunn, J., & Klebanov, P.K. (1994). Economic deprivation and early childhood development. *Child Development, 65,* 296–318.

Dunlap, G., Wilson, K., Strain, P.S., & Lee, J.K. (2013). *Prevent-teach-reinforce for young children: The early childhood model of individualized positive behavior support.* Baltimore, MD: Paul H. Brookes Publishing Co.

Elliott, D., & Cecil, R. (2009). *And here's to you.* Somerville, MA: Candlewick Press.

Ellwand, D. (2001). *The big book of beautiful babies.* New York, NY: Penguin-Dutton Children's Books.

Emberley, E., & Miranda, A. (1997). *Glad monster, sad monster: A book about feelings.* New York, NY: Hachette Book Group-LB Kids.

Eisenberg, N., & Fabes, R.A. (1998). Prosocial development. In W. Damon & N. Eisenberg (Eds.), *Handbook of child psychology: Social, emotional, and personality development* (Vol. 3, pp. 701–778). New York, NY: Wiley.

Evans, B. (2002). *You can't come to my birthday party! Conflict resolution with young children.* Ypsilanti, MI: High/Scope Press.

Fox, L., Carta, J., Strain, P., Dunlap, G., & Hemmeter, M.L. (2009). Response to intervention and the pyramid model. Tampa, FL: University of South Florida, Technical Assistance Center on Social Emotional Intervention for Young Children.

Fox, L., Clarke, S., & Dunlap, G. (2013). Helping families address challenging behavior: Using positive behavior support in early intervention. In M.M. Ostrosky & S.R. Sandall (Eds.), *Addressing young children's challenging behaviors* (Young Exceptional Children Monograph Series No. 15; pp. 59–75). Los Angeles, CA: The Division for Early Childhood of the Council for Exceptional Children.

Fox, L., Dunlap, G., Hemmeter, M.L., Joseph, G., & Strain, P. (2003). The teaching pyramid: A model for supporting social competence and preventing challenging behavior in young children. *Young Children, 58*(4), 48–52.

Fox, L., & Lentini, R.H. (2006). "You got it!" Teaching social and emotional skills. *YC Young Children, 61*(6), 36–43.

Fox, L., Lentini, R., & Dunlap, G. (2004). *Individualized intensive interventions: Developing a behavior support plan.* Unpublished training module, Center on the Social and Emotional Foundations for Early Learning, University of Illinois at Urbana-Champaign.

Franzone, E. (2009). *Naturalistic intervention: Steps for implementation.* Madison, WI: National Professional Development Center on Autism Spectrum Disorders, Waisman Center, University of Wisconsin.

Frey, K.S., Hirschstein, M.K., & Guzzo, B.A. (2000). Second step preventing aggression by promoting social competence. *Journal of Emotional and Behavioral Disorders, 8*(2), 102–112.

Freymann, S., & Elffers, J. (2004). *How are you peeling?* New York, NY: Scholastic.

Galinsky, E. (2010). *Mind in the making: The seven essential life skills every child needs.* New York, NY: HarperCollins.

Gartrell, D. (2012a). *Education for a civil society: How guidance teaches young children democratic life skills.* Washington, DC: National Association for the Education of Young Children.

Gartrell, D. (2012b). Guidance matters: From rules to guidelines. *Young Children, 1,* 56–58.

Goldstein, H., English, K., Shafer, K., & Kaczmarek, L. (1997). Interaction among preschoolers with and without disabilities: Effects of across-the-day peer intervention. *Journal of Speech, Language, and Hearing Research, 40,* 33–48.

Gray, C. (2010). *The new social story book.* Arlington, TX: Future Horizons.

Greenberg, M.T., Riggs, N.R., & Blair, C. (2007). The role of preventive interventions in enhancing neurocognitive functioning and promoting competence in adolescence. In D. Romer & E.F. Walker (Eds.), *Adolescent psychopathology and the developing brain: Integrating brain and prevention science* (pp. 441–461). New York, NY: Oxford University Press.

Gunnar, M.R., Herrera, A., & Hostinar, C.E. (2009). Stress and early brain development. In R.E. Tremblay, R. Peters, & M. Boivin (Eds.), *Encyclopedia on early childhood development* (pp. 1–8). Montreal, Quebec, Canada: Centre of Excellence for Early Childhood Development.

Guralnick, M.J. (Ed.). (1997). *The effectiveness of early intervention.* Baltimore, MD: Paul H. Brookes Publishing Co.

Harris, K.I., Pretti-Frontczak, K., & Brown, T. (2009). Peer-mediated intervention: An effective, inclusive strategy for all young children. *Young Children, 64,* 43–49.

Hebbeler, K., Spiker, D., Bailery, D., Scarborough, A., Mallik, S., Simeonsson, R., Singer, M., & Nelson, L. (2007). *Early intervention for infants and toddlers with disabilities and their families: Participants, services and outcomes.* Menlo Park, CA: SRI International.

Hemmeter, M.L., Corso, R., & Cheatham, G. (2006, February). Issues in addressing challenging behaviors in young children: A national survey of early childhood educators. Conference on Research Innovations in Early Intervention, San Diego, CA.

Heroman, C., Trister Dodge, D., Berke, K., Bickart, T., Colker, L., Jones, C., Copley, J., & Dighe, J. (2014). *The Creative Curriculum for Preschool* (5th ed.). Bethesda, MD: Teaching Strategies.

Hieneman, M., Childs, K., & Sergay, J. (2006). *Parenting with positive behavior support: A practical guide to resolving your child's difficult behavior.* Baltimore, MD: Paul H. Brookes Publishing Co.

Hirschfield, P.J., & Gasper, J. (2011). The relationship between school engagement and delinquency in late childhood and early adolescence. *Journal of Youth Adolescence, 40,* 3–22.

Horner, R., Sugai, G., Smolkowski, K., Todd, A., Nakasato, J., & Esperanza, J. (2009). A randomized, wait-list controlled effectiveness trial assessing school-wide positive behavior support in elementary schools. *Journal of Positive Behavior Interventions, 11,* 133–144.

Hyson, M. (2004). *The emotional development of young children: Building an emotion-centered curriculum* (2nd ed.). New York, NY: Teachers College Press.

Individuals with Disabilities Education Improvement Act (IDEA) of 2004, PL 108-446, 20 U.S.C. 1400 *et seq.*

Iovannone, R., Greenbaum, P.E., Wang, W., Kincaid, D., Dunlap, G., & Strain, P. (2009). Randomized controlled trial of the prevent-teach-reinforce tertiary intervention for students with problem behaviors. *Journal of Emotional and Behavioral Disorders, 17,* 213–225.

Jones, D.E., Greenberg, M., & Crowley, M. (2015). Early social-emotional functioning and public health: the relationship between kindergarten social competence and future wellness. *American Journal of Public Health, 16*(2015), e1–e8.

Joseph, G.E., & Strain, P.S. (2003). Comprehensive evidence-based social-emotional curricula for young children: An analysis of efficacious adoption potential. *Topics in Early Childhood Special Education, 23*(2), 62–73.

Joseph, G.E., & Strain, P.S. (2010). Teaching young children interpersonal problem-solving skills. *Young Exceptional Children, 13,* 28–40.

Kachenmeister, C., & Berthiaume, T. (2001). *On Monday when it rained.* New York, NY: Houghton Mifflin.

Kaiser, B., & Rasminsky, J.S. (2012). *Challenging behavior in young children* (3rd ed.). Upper Saddle River, NJ: Pearson Education.

Katz, K. (2011). *I can share.* New York, NY: Penguin-Grosset & Dunlap.

Ladd, G.W., Birch, S.H., & Buhs, E.S. (1999). Children's social and scholastic lives in kindergarten: Related spheres of influence? *Child Development, 70*(6), 1373–1400.

Ladd, G.W., Kochenderfer, B.J., & Coleman, C.C. (1997). Classroom peer acceptance, friendship, and victimization: Distinct relation systems that contribute uniquely to children's school adjustment? *Child Development, 68*(6), 1181–1197.

Lucyshyn, J.M., Dunlap, G., & Albin, R.W. (2002). *Families and positive behavior support: Addressing problem behavior in family contexts*. Baltimore, MD: Paul H. Brookes Publishing Co.

McClelland, M.M., Cameron, C.E., Connor, C.M., Farris, C.I., Jewkes, A.M., & Morrison, F.J. (2007). Links between behavioral regulation and preschoolers' literacy, vocabulary, and math skills. *Developmental Psychology, 43,* 947–959.

National Center for Children in Poverty. (2009). *Low-income children in the united states national and state trend data, 1998–2008.* New York, NY: National Center for Children in Poverty.

National Scientific Council on the Developing Child. (2008). *Mental health problems in early childhood can impair learning and behavior for life: Working paper no. 6.* Retrieved from http://www.developingchild.net

Neilsen, S., & McEvoy, M. (2004). Functional behavioral assessment in early education settings. *Journal of Early Intervention, 26*(2), 115–131.

Neitzel, J. (2008). *Steps for implementation: PMII for early childhood.* Chapel Hill, NC: National Professional Development Center on ASD, Frank Porter Graham Child Development Institute, University of North Carolina.

Nelson, K. (2015). *If you plant a seed.* New York, NY: HarperCollins.

O'Neill, R.E., Horner, R.H., Albin, R., Storey, K., & Sprague, J. (1990). *Functional assessment of problem behavior: A practical assessment guide.* Baltimore, MD: Paul H. Brookes Publishing Co.

Parr, T. (2005). *The feelings book.* New York, NY: Hachette Book Group-LB Kids.

Parr, T. (2011). *The I'm not scared book.* New York, NY: Little, Brown and Company.

Parr, T. (2012). *The thankful book.* New York, NY: Little, Brown and Company.

Patricelli, L. (2003). *Quiet loud.* Somerville, MA: Candlewick Press.

Pawlina, S., & Stanford, C. (2011). Preschoolers grow their brains: Shifting mindsets for greater resiliency and better problem solving. *YC Young Children, 66*(5), 30.

Penn, A. (2007). *The kissing hand.* Indianapolis, IN: Tanglewood Publishing.

Pfister, M. (1996). *The Rainbow fish.* New York, NY: North-South Books.

Pianta, R.C., Mashburn, A.J., Downer, J.T., Hamre, B.K., & Justice, L. (2008). Effects of web-mediated professional development resources on teacher-child interactions in pre-kindergarten classrooms. *Early Childhood Research Quarterly, 23,* 431–451.

Pyramid Model Research Project. (2008). *Teaching Pyramid Teacher Implementation Guide 1.* Nashville, TN: CSEFEL.

Qi, C.H., & Kaiser, A. (2003). Behavior problems of preschool children from low-income families. *Topics in Early Childhood Special Education, 23,* 188–216.

Raver, C. (2002). Emotions matter: Making the case for the role of young children's emotional development for early school readiness. *Social Policy Report of the Society for Research in Child Development, 16*(3), 1–20.

Raver, C., & Knitzer, J. (2002). *Ready to enter: What research tells policymakers about strategies to promote social and emotional school readiness among three- and four-year old children.* New York, NY: National Center for Children in Poverty.

Raver, C.C., Jones, S.M., Li-Grining, C.P., Metzger, M., Champion, K.M., & Sardin, L. (2008). Improving preschool classroom processes: Preliminary findings from a randomized trial implemented in Head Start settings. *Early Childhood Research Quarterly, 23,* 10–26.

Raver, C.C., & Zigler, E.F. (1997). Social competence: An untapped dimension in evaluating Head Start's success. *Early Childhood Research Quarterly, 12*(4), 363–385.

Reichle, J., & Wacker, D. (1993). *Communicative alternatives to challenging behavior: Integrating functional assessment and intervention strategies.* Baltimore, MD: Paul H. Brookes Publishing Co.

Reinke, W.M., Splett, J.D., Robeson, E.N., & Offutt, C.A. (2009). Combining school and family interventions for the prevention and early intervention of disruptive behavior problems in children: A public health perspective. *Psychology in the Schools, 46,* 33–43.

Robbins, T., Stagman, S., & Smith, S. (2012). *Young children at risk: National and state prevalence of risk factors.* New York, NY: Columbia University National Center for Children in Poverty.

Robertson, J., Green, K., Alper, S., Schloss, P.J., & Kohler, F. (2003). Using peer-mediated intervention to facilitate children's participation in inclusive child care activities. *Education and Treatment of Children, 26,* 182–197.

Seuss, D. (1996). *My many colored days.* New York, NY: Knopf Books for Young Readers.

Schneider, M.R. (1974). Turtle technique in the classroom. *Teaching Exceptional Children, 7*(1), 22–24.

Shonkoff, J.P., Garner, A.S., Siegel, B.S., Dobbins, M.I., Earls, M.F., McGuinn, L., ... & Wood, D.L. (2012). The lifelong effects of early childhood adversity and toxic stress. *Pediatrics, 129*(1), e232–e246.

Shonkoff, J., & Phillips, D.A. (Eds.). (2000). *From neurons to neighborhoods: The science of early childhood development*. Washington, DC: National Academies Press.

Shure, M.B. (1994). *I Can Problem Solve (ICPS): A cognitive approach to preventing early high risk behaviors*. Champaign, IL: Research Press Publishers.

Smith, B.J. (2010). *Recommended practices: Linking social development and behavior to school readiness*. Nashville, TN: Vanderbilt University Center for the Social on the Social and Emotional Foundations for Early Learning.

Smith, B., & Fox, L. (2002). *Systems of service delivery: A synthesis of evidence relevant to young children at risk for or who have challenging behavior*. Tampa, FL: University of South Florida, Center for Evidence-Based Practice: Young Children with Challenging Behavior.

Snell, M.E., Berlin, R.A., Vorhees, M.D., Stanton-Chapman, T.L., & Hadden, S. (2012). A survey of preschool staff concerning problem behavior and its prevention in Head Start classrooms. *Journal of Positive Behavior Interventions, 14*, 98–107.

Spelman, C.M. (2002). *When I feel scared*. Park Ridge, IL: Albert Whitman and Company.

Stanton, B. (2014). *Little humans*. New York, NY: Macmillan-Farrar, Straus, and Giroux.

Stormont, M., Lewis, T.J., Beckner, R., & Johnson, N.W. (Eds.). (2007). *Implementing positive behavior support systems in early childhood and elementary settings*. Thousand Oaks, CA: Corwin Press.

Strain, P.S., & Bovey, E.H. (2011). Randomized, controlled trial of the LEAP model of early intervention for young children with autism spectrum disorders. *Topics in Early Childhood Special Education, 31*, 133–154.

Strain, P., & Hemmeter, M.L. (1999). Keys to being successful. In S. Sandall & M. Ostrosky, (Eds.), *Young exceptional children: Practical ideas for addressing challenging behaviors* (Young Exceptional Children Monograph Series No. 1; pp. 17–28). Longmont, CO: Sopris West Educational Services and Denver, CO: DEC.

Sugai, G., Horner, R.H., Dunlap, G., Hieneman, M., Lewis, T.J., Nelson, C.M.,. . . Reuf, M. (2000). Applying positive behavior support and functional assessment in schools. *Journal of Positive Behavioral Interventions, 2*(3), 131–143.

Tremblay, A., Strain, P.S., Hendrickson, J.M., & Shores, R.E. (1981). Social interactions of normal preschool children using normative data for subject and target behavior selection. *Behavior Modification, 5*(2), 237–253.

Tzuriel, D., & Flor-Maduel, H. (2010). Prediction of early literacy by analogical thinking modifiability among kindergarten children. *Journal of Cognitive Education and Psychology, 9*, 207–226.

U.S. Census Bureau. (2010). *Age and sex composition: 2010*. Retrieved from http://www.census.gov/prod/cen2010/briefs/c2010br-03.pdf

U.S. Department of Education Office for Civil Rights. (2014). *Civil rights data collection data snapshot: School discipline*. Retrieved from http://www2.ed.gov/about/offices/list/ocr/docs/crdc-discipline-snapshot.pdf

U.S. Department of Health and Human Services. (2015). *Draft policy statement on inclusion of children with disabilities in early childhood programs*. Accessed from http://www2.ed.gov/policy/speced/guid/idea/memosdcltrs/inclusion-policy-statement-draft-5-15-2015.pdf

Stanton, B. (2014). *Little humans*. New York, NY: Macmillan-Farrar, Straus, and Giroux.

Walker, H.M., Kavanagh, K., Stiller, B., Golly, A., Severson, H.H., & Feil, E.G. (1998). First step to success an early intervention approach for preventing school antisocial behavior. *Journal of Emotional and Behavioral Disorders, 6*(2), 66–80.

Warner, L.A., & Pottick, K. (2006). Functional impairment among preschoolers using mental health services. *Child and Youth Services Review, 28*, 473–486.

Webster-Stratton, C. (1999). *How to promote children's social-emotional competence*. London, England: Paul Chapman.

Webster-Stratton, C. (2015). The incredible years series. In M.J. Van Ryzin, K.L. Kumpfer, G.M. Fosco, & M.T. Greenberg (Eds.), *Family-based prevention programs for children and adolescents: Theory, research, and large-scale dissemination* (pp. 42–67). New York, NY: Psychology Press.

Webster-Stratton, C., & Reid, M.J. (2004). Strengthening the social-emotional competence in young children—the foundation for early school readiness and success: Incredible Years classroom social skills and problem solving curriculum. *Infants and Young Children, 17*, 96–113.

Webster-Stratton, C., Reid, M.J., & Hammond, M. (2004). Treating children with early-onset conduct problems: Intervention outcomes for parent, child, and teacher training. *Journal of Clinical Child and Adolescent Psychology, 33*, 105–124. doi:10.1207/S15374424JCCP3301_11

Webster-Stratton, C., Reid, M.J., & Stoolmiller, M. (2008). Preventing conduct problems and improving school readiness: Evaluation of the Incredible Years teacher and child training programs in high-risk schools. *Journal of Child Psychology and Psychiatry, 49,* 471–488.

Welsh, J.A., Nix, R.L., Blair, C., Bierman, K.L., & Nelson, K.E. (2010). The development of cognitive skills and gains in academic school readiness for children from low-income families. *Journal of Educational Psychology, 102,* 43–53.

Wright, T. (2003). *The three grumpies.* New York, NY: Bloomsbury Publishing.

Yu, Y., Meyer, L.E., & Ostrosky, M. (2013). Creating accepting classroom environments: Promoting positive attitudes towards peers with challenging behavior. In M.M. Ostrosky & S.R. Sandall (Eds.), *Addressing young children's challenging behaviors* (Young Exceptional Children Monograph Series No. 15; pp. 14–28). Los Angeles, CA: The Division for Early Childhood of the Council for Exceptional Children.

ZERO TO THREE. (2003). *Assuring school readiness by promoting healthy social and emotional development.* Washington, DC: Author.

Zins, J., Bloodworth, M., Weissberg, R., & Walberg, H. (2004). The scientific base linking social and emotional learning to school success. In J. Zins, R. Weissberg, M. Wang, & H.J. Walberg (Eds.), *Building academic success on social and emotional learning: What does the research say?* (pp. 1–22). New York, NY: Teachers College Press.

## CHAPTER 10

Blended Practices for Promoting Literacy Skills

Ragan H. McLeod, Jill F. Grifenhagen, Anna H. Hall, Mary Louise Hemmeter, and Jennifer Grisham-Brown

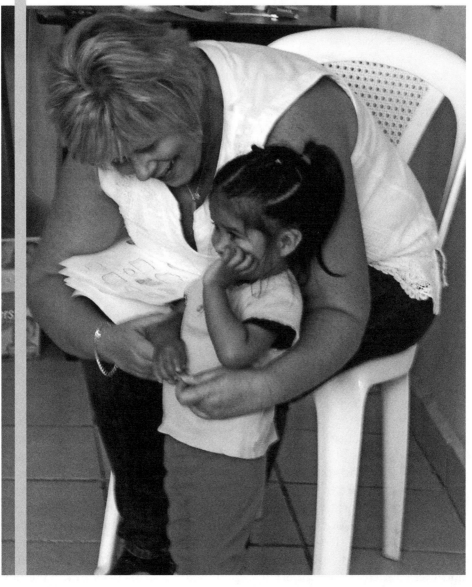

Ms. Anaya and her assistant, Mrs. Getty, are teachers in an inclusive public prekindergarten (pre-K) classroom. Children attend half-day sessions, and the class includes children with identified disabilities, children living in poverty, and children who are English language learners (ELLs). The classroom also includes children who have not been identified as having any risk factors for later academic or reading delays. There are 15 children in the class, and a speech-language pathologist (SLP) spends 1 day a week in the class and an occupational therapist spends a separate day in the classroom. The team uses an integrated services model so that all adults work with all children and the team collaborates to incorporate individual child goals in the planned classroom activities.

Ms. Anaya recently received workshop training on promoting language and literacy skills due to a literacy initiative in her school system. After reviewing data on her children from the previous school year, Ms. Anaya is concerned about how her instruction meets children's language and literacy needs. Ms. Anaya had a daily storytime in previous years and generally chose high-quality books such as Newbury Award winning books or classics from authors such as Eric Carle. Children were often unengaged and disinterested in listening to the story, however. Children rarely chose to visit the library center during choice time and had little interest in interacting with reading and writing materials. Ms. Anaya knows that there is a range of alphabet knowledge in her class, from children who know all of their letters and some letter sounds to children who have no alphabet knowledge. There is also wide variability in children's skills when the class plays rhyming games and participates in syllable counting. Ms. Anaya feels overwhelmed about how to best support language and literacy knowledge and skills for the range of children in her classroom.

Early literacy development has become a focus of early childhood education (ECE) programs in recent years, with increasing research on the importance of developing literacy skills in early childhood for later academic success (National Early Literacy Panel, 2008; National Reading Panel, 2000; Snow, Burns, & Griffin, 1998). In turn, education policy has increasingly focused on promoting these skills during pre-K and the primary grades. Thus, ECE teachers are increasingly focused on practices that promote literacy skills.

Literacy-building practices can be complex to implement as a classroom teacher because early literacy consists of several domains that need to be addressed as building blocks for later reading and writing. Teaching children with a range of initial skill levels in literacy and a variety of unique needs adds to these demands. Teachers can effectively meet children's needs and prepare them for the literacy demands that lie ahead by focusing on the building blocks of literacy and ensuring all children have many opportunities to practice these skills in the early childhood classroom. Current issues and trends in early literacy development, how to create a language- and literacy-rich classroom environment, and key practices in the literacy domains of vocabulary development, book appreciation, print concepts, alphabet knowledge, phonological awareness, and prewriting skills are discussed in the following sections.

ISSUES AND TRENDS IN LITERACY DEVELOPMENT

Literacy development begins with language development, and although most children follow common developmental paths in both of these skill sets, there are children who experience delays in language and literacy. Language and literacy development as well as the risk factors for delays in these areas are discussed next.

Language as a Foundation

Learning to read hinges on general language skill development in the early years. Oral language skills are a key element in reading development. Early and persistent language delays are linked to later reading deficits (Catts, Fey, Tomblin, & Zhang, 2002; Nathan, Stackhouse, Goulandris, & Snowling, 2004). Oral language includes phonological awareness, syntax/grammar, social/pragmatics, and lexicon/vocabulary, all necessary for building literacy and academic success. Phonological awareness and vocabulary knowledge are the language domains most closely tied to early literacy skills.

Phonological awareness is the broad term for identifying and manipulating parts of spoken language. Phonological awareness skills include syllable segmentation, rhyming, and alliteration skills. A child may be asked to produce a word that rhymes with *snack* or to clap the number of syllables in *snack* to demonstrate phonological awareness. Spoken language can be segmented into different chunks such as words, syllables, onsets, rimes, and phonemes. Phonemes are individual sounds in words. For example, there are three phonemes in *hat* (/h/ /a/ /t/) and *chip* (/ch/ /i/ /p/). Phonemic awareness, a subcategory of phonological awareness, entails manipulating phonemes in words. The child may be asked to say all the sounds he or she hears in *snack* (/s/ /n/ /a/ /k/) to demonstrate phonetic awareness. Phonics is the ability to match the phoneme to the written language. In other words, phonics knowledge requires phonological awareness and letter–sound correspondence. A child may demonstrate phonics knowledge by correctly identifying the letter *f* as the beginning sound in *fox* or writing the letters *i, n,* and *g* for the rime in *ring.* Phonological awareness and, more specifically, phonemic awareness, support the child's phonics knowledge. Phonics knowledge, in turn, supports children's later literacy skills of decoding and spelling.

Vocabulary knowledge is important to later reading comprehension. Research has demonstrated that the amount of vocabulary that children are exposed to is related to the vocabulary growth of children (Hart & Risley, 1995), and classrooms teachers' complexity and variety of language use affects children's vocabulary, even when taking parent language and socioeconomic status, two variables that have also been shown to affect child language, into account. Vocabulary knowledge includes both listening (receptive) vocabulary—words a child understands—and speaking (expressive) vocabulary—words the child uses when he or she speaks. Typically developing children have 4,000–6,000 expressive words by the age of 5. Both the number of words known and the understanding of the meaning of those words are important to learning to read. If a child does not have a working vocabulary when learning to read, then he or she cannot comprehend sentences (i.e., strings of words) and cannot use the context of word meanings to learn new words.

Variability in Early Language and Literacy Skills

Development of oral language skills follows a predictable progression for most children. Some children, however, experience delays in oral language development that can lead to delays in learning to read. Any delays in early development may affect oral language and, consequently, reading skills because reading depends on cognitive, motor, and social skills.

Children with language delays may have only expressive delays or expressive and receptive delays. Children rarely have only receptive delays because receptive delays lead to expressive delays (i.e., if a child understands fewer words than same-age peers, he or she will also produce fewer words). The co-occurrence of receptive and expressive delays is much more concerning because of the potential effect on language development and later reading. A review of the literature indicates that approximately 3% of 3-year-olds exhibit both receptive and expressive delays, and about 75% of these children continue to have language delays through childhood (Law, Boyle, Harris, Harkness, & Nye, 2000). Many children who are diagnosed solely or primarily with early language delays have typical cognitive skills (Tomblin, Zhang, Buckwalter, & Catts, 2000), but children who have both types of language delays and cognitive skills in the low normal range (i.e., IQ of 70–85) are at high risk for ongoing language and future reading delays.

Children who are diagnosed with delays or disabilities other than, or in addition to, language delays are also at risk for language-related reading difficulties in the early grades and beyond. The definition of developmental delay varies from state to state. The majority of states identify developmental delay using either a discrepancy between chronological and developmental age or standard deviation scores. An example for the latter would be identifying a child with a developmental delay if he or she scored 1.5 standard deviations below the mean in one area or domain of development (e.g., communication, motor, language) (Rosenberg, Zhang, & Robinson, 2008). Nearly all children with significant developmental disabilities experience delays in language development.

Type of disability may influence the type of language delays a child experiences. Receptive and expressive language delays are often apparent in children with intellectual disabilities (i.e., IQ of 70 or below). The extent of the delay varies based on a number of factors, including the source of the delay, the severity of the delay, and the co-occurrence of other developmental delays. The source of the delay could result from a genetic condition, trauma during birth, or trauma in early childhood, such as traumatic brain injury. For example, children with autism spectrum disorder have more difficulty with the social aspects of language (e.g., asking and answering questions) than with phonemic awareness or vocabulary learning, although this is often hard to assess due to the behavior and social delays that children with autism spectrum disorder often display. Hearing impairments affect early speech-language development even when no cognitive delays are apparent. The language delay exhibited by a child with a disability will also depend on the early intervention received—when it began, how much the child received, and the quality of intervention services (Campbell & Ramey, 1994). Delays in areas of development, whether those are language specific, often affect reading skills later in life. These delays most likely affect children's reading abilities if they are not remediated early through intervention. A study of children who had language impairments of some kind in kindergarten showed that 50% of these children also tested as having a reading disability in second and fourth grade (Catts et al., 2002).

In addition to children who have disabilities, young children from low-income families have risk factors for later reading difficulties. Family education level, family stress, and family structure may mediate the relationship between poverty and later reading delays (Stanton-Chapman, Chapman, Kaiser, & Hancock, 2004). Research indicates that children from low-income families may experience home literacy practices that differ from the early literacy practices typically found in school settings (Dickinson & Tabors, 2001; Payne, Whitehurst, & Angell, 1994). These differences may lead to children from poverty performing below their peers on measures of early literacy achievement. According to the National Head Start 2004 Family and Child Experiences Survey, 50% of 4-year-olds entering Head Start were a year behind in vocabulary knowledge, and 75% knew fewer than 10 letters (U.S. Department of Health and Human Services, 2004).

Children who enter school and are not proficient English speakers struggle to read at grade level (Donahue, Daane, & Jin, 2005). Dual language learners are a diverse group and include children with a multitude of first languages, home environments, and literacy support. Children who are dual language learners can range from monolingual in their native language to close to monolingual in English (Tabors & Snow, 2001), an important factor for teachers as they plan language and literacy instruction. Strong language skills in the first language relate to ease of learning English. It is important for dual language learners, as well as all children, to be exposed to literacy activities by the family in the home because home exposure to language and literacy is critical to development of early literacy skills (Dickinson & Tabors, 2001). Families should be encouraged to converse and engage in early literacy practices with their children in the language that is most comfortable and fluent for the family (Ballantyne, Sanderman, & McLaughlin, 2008). Overall, dual language learners' growth in oral language skills in early childhood settings is predictive of kindergarten literacy skills (Hammer, Scarpino, & Davison, 2011). Some preliteracy skills such as rhyming, alliteration, the alphabetic principle, and syntactic knowledge when known in one language easily transfer to the second language (Tabors & Snow, 2001). Vocabulary knowledge for dual language learners is similar to that of monolingual children when it is combined for both languages, but vocabulary knowledge is less than that of monolingual peers when each individualized language is analyzed (Hammer et al., 2011). Debates continue about the best instruction for dual language learners, but it is clear that the language and preliteracy skills of these children should be closely monitored during the pre-K years (see Chapter 11 further information on blended practices for dual language learners).

All children bring unique strengths and needs to the classroom. Learning preliteracy skills in pre-K and reading in school is not a problem for some children. Some children, however, face difficulties in learning the skills necessary for reading. Children face hurdles in achieving preliteracy skills when multiple risk factors are present. Early intervention and support at the early childhood level is necessary and can be effective in supporting skill development that has a lasting impact on academic outcomes (Campbell, Ramey, Pungello, Sparling, & Miller-Johnson, 2002; Reynolds, Temple, Robertson, & Mann, 2001). Support for preliteracy skills in early childhood settings begins by creating a language- and literacy-rich environment.

CREATING A LANGUAGE- AND LITERACY-RICH EARLY CHILDHOOD EDUCATION ENVIRONMENT

Children are born with a natural desire to communicate and participate in social systems (Kampmann & Bowne, 2011; Vygotsky, 1978). As young children communicate and interact with others, their language and literacy skills help them make sense of their world (Kampmann & Bowne, 2011) and contribute to their future ability to read and write (Strickland et al., 2004). It is critical that early childhood classrooms provide regular and active interactions with language and print (Morrow & Gambrell, 2004), quality materials and centers, and adult involvement to guide and extend children's learning (Bernhard, Winsler, Bleiker, Ginieniewicz, & Madigan, 2008; Justice, Chow, Capellini, Flanigan, & Colton, 2003) in order to foster important early literacy skills (e.g., concepts of print, alphabet knowledge, phonemic awareness).

High-quality language and literacy environments provide a variety of instructional approaches that build on what children already know to scaffold their learning and provide additional knowledge (Morrow & Gambrell, 2004). Focusing on meaningful activities that involve fundamental concepts about literacy and language growth, rather than extensive practice of skills in isolation or teacher-directed paper-and-pencil tasks, is another important quality of these environments (Clark & Kragler, 2005; Morrow &

Gambrell, 2004). Children are motivated to question and interact with their environment through exposure to contextualized learning experiences and high-quality materials, which sparks their interests and supports their passions (Clark & Kragler, 2005; Justice, 2004; Kampmann & Bowne, 2011). The following two sections of this chapter provide practical suggestions for designing environments and providing activities that promote language development and literacy skills for young children.

Promoting Language Skills

Language development flourishes in classroom environments that value home and school languages and provide frequent meaning-centered interactions (Bauer & Manyak, 2008). As children listen and speak in classrooms where they feel safe to take linguistic risks, they develop a sense of words and build sensitivity to sounds, which leads to acquisition of phonological awareness and phonics skills (Bauer & Manyak, 2008; Strickland et al., 2004). It is important for ECE teachers to provide opportunities for children to engage in oral language activities, such as sharing and problem solving (Kampmann & Bowne, 2011), because of the relationship between language development and later literacy achievement. For example, if the teacher notices that the children are having difficulty sharing the swings at recess, he or she may call a class meeting and invite the children to brainstorm solutions to the problem. Another example would be meeting with children in small groups to talk about plans for an upcoming classroom celebration. As children share their thoughts during this type of purposeful discussion, teachers can record their ideas through shared writing and invite children to participate in a shared rereading of the short, meaningful text to help children make connections between oral language and written symbols.

Positive communication opportunities occur naturally in learning centers when children are invited to create, take turns, and solve problems and when teachers are actively involved in facilitating play. "The materials and their use should be discussed, and the teacher should offer additional help by modeling literacy behaviors and playing along with the children" (Morrow & Rand, 1991, p. 401). For example, the teacher could demonstrate purposeful writing by building a house in the block center and then writing his or her home address on a notecard and taping it to her house. Literature on learning centers also suggests the importance of incorporating items that children are familiar with in their daily lives (Van Hoorn, Nourot, Scales, & Alward, 2006). For example, dramatic play areas could include empty boxes or containers of food that children bring from home and props (e.g., menus from local restaurants, city newspaper) to help children draw on their background and experiences as they interact with their classmates.

In addition to providing opportunities for children to communicate and develop language through play, teachers can enrich the language environment by exposing children to sophisticated language, including varied vocabulary, complex syntax, and a variety of social uses of language.

Meaningful activities such as storytelling, drama, and read-alouds allow students to use language in new ways and experience new models of language from their teacher and peers (McCarrier, Pinnell, & Fountas, 2000). For example, children are able to practice using language to express ideas and different grammatical structures for a variety of purposes when they share a family tradition through a personal story or act out a poem they have recently heard. Teachers can also share a variety of literature and make books accessible to students throughout the day to provide additional exposure to new vocabulary (Strickland et al., 2004).

Meaningful talk occurs not only during play and structured language activities, but it also happens throughout the day when teachers and children engage in informal and formal conversations. Children are introduced to new subjects for discussion and are able to comprehend and use increasingly complex and varied language when they are allowed time to talk and are guided in conversation by their teacher. Teachers can provide students with ample time to respond to questions, support instructional conversations that focus on thematic units, establish a habit of responding to children's comments about their personal experiences, and ask children open-ended questions (i.e., questions that cannot be answered with a "yes" or "no") (Bauer & Manyak, 2008; Pinnell & Fountas, 2011; Strickland et al., 2004) in order to encourage children to converse.

In addition to meaningful conversations, it is important for language-rich classrooms to include student-led interactions and build on collective knowledge to promote meaningful conversations. During classroom inquiries, children can be asked to search for information, explain findings to their peers, give and receive directions, and work together to design and complete projects. As children work together and share discourse, they gain confidence in using their language skills in addition to creating meaningful bonds with their classmates as coinvestigators (Bauer & Manyak, 2008; Pinnell & Fountas, 2011). Children should be given plenty of opportunities for child-directed activities in which the teacher follows their lead in terms of interest and attention (Girolametto & Weitzman, 2002; Snow, 1983).

Promoting Literacy Skills

"What children learn from listening and talking contributes to the ability to read and write and vice versa" (Strickland et al., 2004, p. 86). It is critical to consider the importance of providing dynamic print-rich use in conjunction with language resources and opportunities because of the important relationship between the development of oral language and literacy (Tao & Robinson, 2005). Strickland and Morrow noted,

> A rich literacy classroom environment will include a library corner and writing center with an abundant supply of materials for reading, writing, and oral language; it integrates well with content area teaching and is designed to emulate functional life experiences. (1988, p. 156)

Literacy-rich environments should include a variety of print materials, and teachers should model meaningful use of the materials in children's daily classroom experiences (Bauer & Manyak, 2008; Tao & Robinson, 2005). Just as children need exposure to varied vocabulary and language experiences, children need exposure to a variety of texts and literacy experiences (Tao & Robinson, 2005). Literacy-rich classrooms provide access to fiction and nonfiction books (in home languages and in English), poetry, magazines, student-created print, teacher writing, commercial print, and other examples of writing and drawing that reflect children's cultures, curiosities, and experiences (Bauer & Manyak, 2008; Tao & Robinson, 2005).

Teachers in literacy-rich classrooms help children engage in active participation and use of the various literacy tools in their environment in order to extend content knowledge and expose children to the functional and meaningful uses of print (Strickland & Morrow, 1988; Tao & Robinson, 2005). For example, when children observe the relevance of print by participating in a group letter-writing activity to the local fire department and receive a letter in return from the fire chief, they are more likely to experiment with writing to communicate their thoughts and questions in the future. Bulletin boards in which children can record their lunch choices, sign-in sheets for attendance, and shopping lists for classroom cooking projects (Axelrod, Hall, & McNair, 2015) are additional examples of functional print opportunities.

The classroom library is an invaluable resource in providing opportunities for children to freely and independently gain access to books and other print materials in a literacy-rich environment (see Figure 10.1).

Figure 10.1. Classroom library.

The classroom library should be distinct from other areas of the classroom and provide an attractive and comfortable space for children to select, read, and replace books of their choosing (Smith, Brady, & Anastasopoulos, 2008). It is helpful to shelve books on open displays (so children can easily see each cover) and provide carpeting, pillows, and child-size furniture for a comfortable reading experience. The library should also include an ample supply of books from different genres (e.g., informational, narrative, poetry) that cover a range of topics and are relevant to the children in the class. A balance of commercial texts and student-made books should be included that reflect diverse representations of characters, cultures, and family structures in order to honor the home languages and literacy experiences of the children. (Axelrod et al., 2015; Smith et al., 2008). Children can be involved in organizing the library as well as adding to the library with books and poems they have created in the writing center.

The writing center is also an important area of any literacy-rich environment because it allows children the freedom to explore and use print in meaningful ways (see Figure 10.2; Hansen, Davis, Evertson, & Freeman, 2011). Young children are more likely to show interest in expressing their feelings during independent and shared writing times when they observe their teacher engaging in writing and participate themselves in functional uses of print throughout the day (Tao & Robinson, 2005). By providing time in the day for free-choice writing, myriad writing materials, and personalized resources, children may voluntarily and enthusiastically visit the writing center to apply the skills they are learning. Writing centers should

Figure 10.2. Classroom writing center.

include open-ended materials such as blank paper, dry erase boards, markers, scissors, glue sticks, hole punches, crayons, and envelopes that allow children to create a variety of self-directed writing projects. Word lists and personalized dictionaries can provide children with resources for selecting and spelling new words. Personal writing folders can also be provided to help children organize their writing and encourage children to continue writing projects over time (Axelrod et al., 2015). Mailboxes for each child can also be provided to encourage children to communicate with each other through writing.

In addition to a classroom library and writing center, print materials for writing and reading can be made available in every part of the classroom and naturally integrated into other activities. For example, a menu could be placed in the restaurant of a dramatic play center, or a notepad for recording growth and changes could be placed near a class pet or plant in a science center. Clipboards with pens attached by string could be used to record observations during outdoor adventures (e.g., illustrations of different tree varieties found on a nature walk, measurements of plants in the school garden). Children could also be allowed to choose centers by signing their names on sign-up sheets near each center.

Language- and literacy-rich ECE environments require careful planning and instruction (Morrow & Gambrell, 2004). Environments rich in print or language experiences alone are not sufficient; however, they can be powerful for promoting literacy development and achievement when combined and accompanied by teachers involved in supporting children's participation. Teachers make academic content meaningful and build on children's prior knowledge by providing high-quality materials and activities, along with intentional instruction, within a supportive and motivating environment. Creating a language- and literacy-rich environment affords opportunities for teachers to provide instruction in the key areas of literacy learning—vocabulary, book appreciation, print concepts, alphabet knowledge, phonological awareness, and prewriting.

BLENDED PRACTICES FOR KEY AREAS OF LITERACY

Ms. Anaya and Mrs. Getty decide that reevaluating their classroom environment with a lens toward language and literacy is the first step to enhance children's language and literacy skills. They enlist the help of the school's literacy coach to gather resources and plan their approach.

The literacy coach provides the teachers with some bright, new nonfiction books to include in the classroom library. She helps them organize the center with baskets that show the book covers and comfortable pillows to sit on while reading. They create a post office in the writing center by turning a shoe organizer into mailboxes for each child and adding a variety of stationary and envelopes. Ms. Anaya and Mrs. Getty find literacy materials to incorporate into other centers as well. For example, farm-related building materials and animals are in in the block center. The teachers have also included nonfiction books about farms and farm animals as well as child-focused magazines that are focused on farms. They add clipboards with waiting lists to popular centers so children can sign up to wait for their turn.

The literacy coach also helps Ms. Anaya and Mrs. Getty make several plans for changes to their instructional approaches. They plan for oral language practice several times during the day, including sharing time during their small-group activities and snack time discussions. Ms. Anaya plans to add a quick poem or song to their daily large-group time that features rhymes, letters, and sounds. During closing circle, the teachers plan to have each child tell a friend about what he or she did today in class. Mrs. Getty suggests coming up with a daily conversation starter related to the class theme, and each teacher plans to open up that discussion at one center during center time.

The National Early Literacy Panel (2008) released a report on the development of early literacy and the home and school influences on early literacy learning based on a systematic review of research. The report indicated that key areas of literacy knowledge in early childhood are strongly related to later reading and writing skills. Alphabet knowledge, phonological awareness, and writing skills were strong predictors of the literacy outcomes measured—decoding, reading comprehension, and spelling. In addition, oral language skills, including vocabulary and concepts of print, were also significantly related to decoding, reading comprehension, and spelling for children. Evidence-based teaching strategies in each of these key areas, as well as book appreciation or exposure to literature, are discussed in the following section.

Blended Practices for Vocabulary Development

Children need knowledge of a diverse vocabulary, including both receptive or listening vocabulary and expressive or speaking vocabulary, to effectively communicate. Both listening and speaking vocabulary are vital to comprehension when learning to read. Vocabulary knowledge develops along a continuum. Children's understanding of a vocabulary word ranges from inaccurate to precise. The depth of understanding of a word varies as does a child's ability to produce and use the word when he or she understands it receptively (Henriksen, 1999).

Teachers promote vocabulary development by providing opportunities for children to experience a varied vocabulary that is meaningfully connected to their experiences and interests. Teachers can support vocabulary development explicitly through direct instruction or implicitly through exposure across the day. Teachers also provide clear information about vocabulary words and opportunities for children to use vocabulary and receive feedback about vocabulary use.

Teachers should choose specific vocabulary words for instruction to ensure children are exposed to a varied vocabulary. Beck, McKeown, and

Kucan (2013) provided some guidance for choosing words to teach. Words fall into three categories—Tier 1 words are the most basic (e.g., *boy, run, sad*), whereas Tier 3 words are domain specific (e.g., *cosine, anaphylactic*) and are infrequently used. Tier 3 words are typically learned in subject-specific courses in secondary school or higher education. Tier 2 words are common words for experienced language users, are used across domains, and are recommended for instruction (e.g., *exchange, anxious, determine, spoil*).

In addition to exposure to varied vocabulary, children need multiple exposures to the same words in different contexts. Book reading and guided play are opportunities for vocabulary exposure and instruction. Repeated readings of the same book provide an opportunity to expose children to new or unknown words and to teach about those words before, during, and after reading (Dickinson & Tabors, 2001). The more children have opportunities to hear and use words, the more likely they are to have deeper knowledge and better ability to use the words. Multiple exposures to a vocabulary word should be meaningfully connected. For example, a teacher may introduce the word *grumpy* during a reading of *Hooray for Hat!* (Won, 2014) and also use this word when children are working in centers by labeling the feeling when children exhibit grumpy characteristics or acting out the story with animal puppets in the dramatic play center. For a deeper understanding of *grumpy*, the teacher could talk about when he or she felt grumpy and have children share stories or create pictures of when they were grumpy. Teachers could include other books in which characters act or feel grumpy. Introducing words in this integrated way supports learning better than introducing them as isolated words or in isolated experiences (i.e., only in book reading). Automated or computer-assisted learning programs may provide additional opportunities for children to experience and practice vocabulary (Spencer et al., 2012).

Conversations are an important context for learning vocabulary (Howes, 2000; Tomasello & Farrar, 1986). Responsive adults who provide opportunities for children to use new vocabulary and provide feedback about that use in conversation support vocabulary learning (Girolametto & Weitzman, 2002). This is true in book reading and in free play. It is important that the definitions teachers provide to children are meaningful and relatable to the child. For example, the definition for *knead* might be provided as "to mix by pressing, folding, or pulling with your hands." The teacher makes this definition meaningful by presenting it in the context of the story in which the character kneads the dough and providing children an opportunity to knead pretend dough or playdough in the dramatic play area. Also, categorizing words helps children connect to known words and learn new vocabulary better. For example, by connecting knead to *fold, pull,* and *press,* words the children are familiar with, the teacher supports children's connections between the new word and the familiar actions one can do with dough.

Adaptations for the Blended Classroom Additional explicit instruction in vocabulary may be necessary for children who are having difficulty learning vocabulary or who enter a classroom with limited vocabularies, including more frequent exposure or more opportunities to use the vocabulary words they are using. Additional or different target words for vocabulary instruction may be chosen for some children, including words that are useful for classroom interactions (e.g., activity or center names, classmates' names) or common vocabulary. Children who are having difficulty learning new vocabulary may benefit from additional supports such as visual or physical cues or additional definitions or experiences with words (McLeod, 2010; Weizman & Snow, 2001). For example, the teacher may provide a picture of a person kneading dough or having a consistent action that simulates kneading that is used whenever he or she says "knead." If a child uses an augmentative and alternative communication (AAC) system, special consideration needs to be given to programming vocabulary words that allow the child to practice vocabulary and participate in the planned activities around vocabulary.

Blended Practices for Developing Book Appreciation

Teachers have many elements to consider when choosing books to share with children. Books should be relevant to the children in the classroom and represent the diversity within the classroom and the community, including diverse ethnicities and cultures, family structures, gender roles, and abilities and should be reviewed for possible stereotypes. For example, teachers may look for whether men and women are portrayed in clichéd ways, such as one gender always portrayed as doctors or teachers. Portrayals of children with disabilities should be positive, which, according to Dyches and Prater includes

> (a) emphasiz[ing] strengths rather than weaknesses, (b) represent[ing] high expectations of the character with [a developmental disability], (c) enhanc[ing] positive contributions, (d) show[ing] the character acting on his/her choices, (e) [obtaining] full citizenship in the home and community, and (f) enjoy[ing] reciprocal relationships. (2005, p. 208)

Using a checklist to evaluate books for positive portrayals of children with disabilities can be effective in determining which books to share with children (Nasatir & Horn, 2003).

Translating key words in the text to the home languages of children and color-coding these key words across books to each language may be necessary in classrooms in which multiple languages are represented. For example, words in Spanish might always be in blue, whereas words in Arabic would be written in green. This addition of native language in books supports children's linguistic development (Minaya-Rowe, 2004). When possible, classrooms should also include a selection of books in children's home language. Children should be given opportunities throughout the day to read and enjoy books and other materials. It is helpful to have multiple times during the daily schedule in which children may gain access to books in the classroom library and other centers, both independently and with the support of their teachers. Teachers can build excitement around a variety of books by previewing the books before placing them in accessible areas of the room. Beyond exposing children to a variety of texts, teachers introduce the purpose of and ways to use the different materials. For example, a teacher may show a group of children how to find information about a specific animal in a reference guide using the table of contents or index or finding and reading select poems in a poetry collection.

Sharing books with children during read-alouds is an excellent way to foster a love of reading and print. Teachers have an opportunity to share their own love of reading and enjoyment of books during shared reading through positive affect, animated reading, and personal interest. Books can be shared in whole-group or small-group settings or individually with children. Teachers can share rich stories that most young children may not be able to read themselves. Reading books that children enjoy repeatedly supports their interest in viewing these books independently (Dennis, Lynch, & Stockall, 2012). To engage children during reading, teachers can consider prompts to use before, during, and after that allow children to participate and respond (Morrow & Gambrell, 2004). Dialogic reading, an interactive method of shared reading, includes the acronym CROWD (completion prompts, recall prompts, open ended prompts, "wh-" question prompts, and distancing prompts) to remind teachers of specific prompts to engage children through conversations about texts (see http://www.readingrockets.org/article/400 for more information). Teachers should read books prior to shared reading to determine possible prompts that will support children's engagement.

Adaptations for the Blended Classroom   It is important that all children be able to gain access to books and other written materials. Adaptations and modifications should be provided to meet the needs of children with disabilities. For example, children with visual impairments may benefit from braille overlays for books, large-print materials, or access to audiobooks, depending on their individual learning media needs. Slant boards, book stabilizers, or book holders provide access for children with motor needs. Providing supports such as picture references, objects that children can hold that relate to events or objects in the story, can engage children as well as provide support for connecting to and comprehending the story. A teacher could provide toy construction vehicles for children to identify the various parts or actions of the diggers in *Dazzling Diggers* (Mitton & Parker, 2000). Teachers also need to be aware of abstract language that is used in books that may be confusing to children with language delays or who have hearing impairments. For example, idioms such as "pulling my leg" or "in a pickle" may be confusing because the literal meaning does not equate to the common usage. Comprehension of abstract language in books may be supported through additional examples (e.g., "Sam was pulling your leg when he said he flew to the moon yesterday") or references to the pictures or actions in the story (e.g., "*In a pickle* means in trouble. I can tell the puppy in this story is in a pickle because he can't find his way home and he looks scared").

Blended Practices for Print Concepts

Understanding print concepts is a foundational early literacy skill necessary to reading acquisition. Children need to know print conventions (e.g., print is read left to right and top to bottom, there are spaces between words) as well as general concepts about print (e.g., book cover, author, text). A child with well-developed print concepts knows that print tells a story and recognizes that print conveys meaning.

Substantial evidence shows that print concepts relate to later reading achievement. A young child's understanding of print concepts has successfully predicted his or her future reading success (Adams, 1990; Clay, 1993; Scarborough, 1998). The National Early Literacy Panel (2008) conducted a comprehensive review of early literacy research and found concepts about print and print awareness in early childhood or kindergarten were significantly related to later literacy achievement, particularly reading comprehension.

Understanding print concepts is fostered through teaching practices and instructional interventions that can be built into the literacy routines of the ECE classroom. Combining shared, interactive reading with attention to print conventions or print referencing is an effective strategy. This approach may be used in whole-class read-alouds or through shared reading with individuals or small groups of children. Begin by choosing books with salient print features such as large narrative print, redundant text, or contextualized print embedded within the illustrations (Justice & Kaderavek, 2002). Children are more likely to visually attend to print when they are reading books in which print is a salient feature (Justice & Lankford, 2002). Electronic storybooks presented on computers or tablets can be another beneficial tool because they feature print made particularly salient through graphic means (e.g., highlighted links) and appear to help children internalize knowledge of print concepts and features (de Jong & Bus, 2002). Teachers can read aloud using print-referencing strategies such as pointing to print and talking about print. This may be as simple as tracking print while reading, pointing out salient text features, or thinking aloud about aspects of print (e.g., "I'm going to start reading right here at the top of the page." "I can tell the character is shouting because these words are in all capital letters"). Researchers demonstrated that pre-K children made substantial gains on a variety of print awareness measures when teachers implemented these simple strategies during shared book reading. The use of print-referencing strategies has been especially effective for children with language impairments or children who are at risk for reading difficulties (Justice, Pullen, & Pence, 2008; Lovelace & Stewart, 2007; McGinty, Breit-Smith, Fan, Justice, & Kaderavek, 2011).

Print awareness may also be built into an ECE classroom through the print-focused play interactions characteristic of a literacy-rich environment.

Studies have demonstrated that integrating literacy materials, including functional signs such as building labels (e.g., library, restaurant), familiar meaningful texts (e.g., telephone books, menus), and literacy tools (e.g., paper, pencils), into children's play settings can encourage children's print awareness (Neuman & Roskos, 1990, 1992). Children often naturally integrate these materials into their play when made available, although adult modeling and encouragement can increase their use and may be necessary for some children. Adults can play an important role in encouraging children to include literacy materials and activities into their play, which can produce more powerful effects on print awareness (Christie & Enz, 1992; Neuman & Roskos, 1993; Roskos, Christie, Widman, & Holding, 2010). Teachers can guide children in how to use print materials during play (e.g., typing an e-mail, reading a menu at a restaurant). These supportive opportunities to practice with print-enriched play lead to children's increased understanding of the forms and functions of print.

Targeted activities and instruction may also be necessary for some children and can be effective at building print concepts. Overall, letter-focused interventions have demonstrated a significant effect on print knowledge (National Early Literacy Panel, 2008). Targeted letter-focused interventions include games and activities that focus on letter and words and are often delivered in a small-group setting or individually. Research has demonstrated that short, explicit lessons and activities are most effective at increasing print awareness (Justice, 2006; Reutzel, Oda, & Moore, 1989). Lessons should explicitly articulate technical language about print concepts (e.g., *top, bottom; letter, word; title, author*) and can be built into other literacy activities including book reading and modeled or shared writing. Technology-based games and activities are another high-interest means of delivering instruction on print concepts.

Adaptations for the Blended Classroom   Print-referencing strategies may be used more frequently or intensively (e.g., in one-to-one shared reading sessions) for children who need more support acquiring print concepts. Teachers should pay extra attention to choosing traditional or electronic texts that feature salient print features and ensure that these texts are accessible to all children in the classroom. Teachers may scaffold play interactions involving print through modeling or prompting children to talk about and use print in play situations. Opportunities to practice with print concepts can be naturally built into occurring classroom activities and routines, offering intensive instruction without segregating the children who are still building these skills (Grisham-Brown, Pretti-Frontczak, Hawkins, & Winchell, 2009; Grisham-Brown, Ridgley, Pretti-Frontczak, Litt, & Nielson, 2006).

Blended Practices for Alphabet Knowledge

Alphabet knowledge is the knowledge of letter names, forms, and the associated sounds. This skill set includes the ability to recite the alphabet, identify letters, print letters, and match letters to sounds. Early literacy experts agree that alphabet knowledge is an essential building block of literacy. Snow et al. (1998) reported on preventing reading difficulties in young children and identified weaknesses in alphabet knowledge as a prime area for intervention to prevent later reading problems. Alphabet knowledge is a strong predictor of later literacy achievement, including decoding, comprehension, and spelling (Adams, 1990; Catts et al., 2002; Whitehurst & Lonigan, 1998). Pre-K and kindergarten students with poor knowledge of letter names and sounds are more likely to struggle with learning to read and be classified as having reading disabilities (Gallagher, Frith, & Snowling, 2000; O'Connor & Jenkins, 1999).

Many teaching strategies have been linked to effectively building alphabet knowledge. One place to start is with children's own names, which are typically highly visible and meaningful in their daily lives (Bloodgood, 1999; Treiman & Broderick, 1998). Children may practice identifying the letters in their name, building their name with letter cards or magnetic letters, and writing the letters in their name. Alphabet knowledge is another skill enhanced by interactive book reading (Mol, Bus, & de Jong, 2009). Reading a variety of books can be effective, although alphabet books specifically (e.g., *Dr. Seuss' ABCs* [Seuss, 1996], *Chicka Chicka Boom Boom* [Martin & Archambault, 1989]) can be introduced through teacher reading and made accessible in the classroom library. Research demonstrated that alphabet knowledge is increased with exposure to alphabet books (Bradley & Jones, 2007; Murray, Stahl, & Ivey, 1996).

Highly engaging literacy activities across the school day can build children's knowledge of the letters and their sounds (Aram, 2006; Connor, Morrison, & Slominski, 2006). Teachers may use a variety of songs and rhymes that teach the alphabet and the sounds that correspond to each letter; many early childhood curricula feature songs and materials that emphasize these skills. Songs and rhymes that feature movement are helpful in building children's memory for letters and their sounds, particularly for ELLs (Paquette & Rieg, 2008). Other types of hands-on activities, particularly those that feature sensory materials (e.g., writing letters in finger paint, textured letters), can be especially powerful for some children. Letter games can be implemented in large-group, small-group, or free play settings, and many are available through technology. Alphabet knowledge may be integrated into modeled and interactive writing activities when the teacher calls the children's attention to the letters, how the letters are formed, and corresponding sounds. Children also build alphabet knowledge by participating in emergent and invented writing activities. In fact, experts warn against having children wait to write until they know all the letters of the alphabet because children get a sense of letters and their sounds by engaging in daily writing activities (Fountas & Pinnell, 1996; Wagstaff, 1998). Encourage children to explore letters through meaningful writing activities to build alphabet knowledge.

After learning letters, research suggests that some children require direct instruction to learn the corresponding sounds (Bergeron, Lederberg, Easterbrooks, Miller, & Connor, 2009; Wasik, 2001). Targeted instructional programs such as Reading Recovery (an intensive one-to-one intervention; Clay, 1993) focus on making the letter–sound connection in first grade. Curricula designed to facilitate early literacy skills vary considerably in how alphabet knowledge is taught (Justice, Pence, Bowles, & Wiggins, 2006), especially with respect to whether instruction targets letter names and sounds or only letter sounds. Table 10.1 outlines a few early childhood curricula that feature activities and materials focused on alphabet knowledge. Studies suggest activities and instruction on the alphabet is most effective when combined with phonological awareness training (Bus & van IJzendoorn, 1999; National Early Literacy Panel, 2008). See the next section for combining teaching strategies addressing both sets of skills.

Adaptations for the Blended Classroom Some children in a blended classroom may need additional exposure to and practice with letters. These children may benefit from targeted instruction involving modeling, practice, and immediate feedback (Aram, 2006; Bergeron et al., 2009; van Bysterveldt, Gillon, & Moran, 2006). Teachers can provide extra opportunities to work with the letters in a child's name or embed instruction on letters throughout the school day. Various children in the classroom may have different targets for letter knowledge, both in terms of the number of letters they are working on and the complexity of the alphabet skill (identify, name, or write letters).

Blended Practices for Phonological Awareness

As previously described, phonological awareness is the ability to detect, manipulate, or analyze parts of spoken language, independent of meaning. Phonological awareness is often seen as developing along a continuum, starting with sensitivity to large and concrete units of sounds (i.e., words, syllables) and progressing to sensitivity to small and abstract units of sounds (i.e., phonemes) (Lonigan, 2006). These skills are typically acquired during the early childhood years, and phonological awareness is a key prerequisite for reading and an important part of early literacy instruction. Phonological awareness skills are a significant predictor of children's later literacy achievement in spelling, comprehension, and decoding (National Early Literacy Panel, 2008). The National Research Council's panel on preventing reading difficulties in young children recommends targeting phonological awareness to prevent the occurrence of significant reading problems (Snow et al., 1998). Relatedly, deficits in phonological awareness in older children are considered one of the primary causes of developmental dyslexia (Stanovich, 1988; Stanovich & Siegel, 1994).

Early literacy experts recommend that teachers start with less complex skills (e.g., rhyming and alliteration—identifying words with the same

Table 10.1 Literacy curricula and resources

Curricula	Areas of focus					For further information
	Vocabulary	Book appreciation	Print concepts	Phonemic awareness	Prewriting	
DLM Express plus Open Court	X	X	X	X	X	https://www.mheonline.com/earlychildhood connection/inside.php?page=dlm http://opencourtreading.com/
Ladders to Literacy	X	X	X	X		http://www.products.brookespublishing.com/Ladders-to-Literacy-P201.aspx
Let's Begin with the Letter People	X	X	X	X	X	http://www.abramslearningtrends.com/lets_begin_with_letter_people.aspx
Waterford Early Reading Program (computer-assisted instruction)	X	X	X	X		http://www.waterfordearlylearning.org

Resources	Areas of focus					Authors or web site
	Vocabulary	Book appreciation	Print concepts	Phonemic awareness	Prewriting	
Bringing Words to Life	X					Beck, McKeown, and Kucan (2013)
Direct Instruction	X		X		X	http://www.nifdi.org
Lindamood Phoneme Sequencing Program For Reading, Spelling, and Speech				X		Lindamood and Lindamood (1998)
Phonemic Awareness In Young Children				X		Adams, Foorman, Lundburg, and Beeler (1997)
Phonological Awareness Training For Reading				X		Torgesen and Bryant (1993)
Promoting Literacy Development: 50 Research-Based Strategies for K–8 Learners				X		Antonacci and Callaghan (2011)
Speech to Print: Language Essentials for Teachers			X			Moats (2000)
Sound Foundations				X		Byrne and Fielding-Barnsley (1991)
Sounds Abound				X		Catts and Williamson (1993)
The Phonological Awareness Kit				X		Robertson and Salter (1995)

initial sound) during pre-K, then progress to more complex skills (Anthony & Lonigan, 2004; Carroll, Snowling, Stevenson, & Hulme, 2003). Phonological awareness is best addressed through short, focused instructional sessions. Instruction in small-group settings is particularly effective (National Reading Panel, 2000). A number of classroom activities and routines can be used to foster young children's phonological awareness. These activities should be age appropriate, highly engaging, and repeated as part of a predictable routine. Reading poems, reciting rhymes, and singing songs with children all provide practice with these skills. The rhymes and word play involved in these types of activities can call attention to rhyming, syllables, and sounds (Yopp & Yopp, 2000). Classroom book reading may also feature texts that rhyme or include predictable word play (e.g., *Brown Bear, Brown Bear, What Do You See?* [Carle, 1967]) because children are more likely to attend to the phonological properties of speech when hearing these types of texts read aloud. Rhyming concepts can be difficult for children to acquire, especially for young children with weak oral language skills (Boudreau & Hedberg, 1999). Repeated practice may be necessary to promote the development of these skills. Rhyming activities should begin with easier tasks such as recognizing rhyming words and move to more difficult tasks such as generating rhyming words. The same holds true for alliteration, or recognizing and generating words that begin with the same initial sound. Multiple exposures and opportunities for practice should be provided.

More targeted instruction may be necessary as children progress to more complex phonological skills or if they are having difficulty with phonological awareness. Experts concluded that phonological awareness training for children with or at risk for reading disabilities must be more explicit or more intense than the general age-appropriate activities (Torgesen et al., 2001; Wagner, Torgesen, & Rashotte, 1994). This training includes strategic Tier 2 instruction in segmenting and blending at the phoneme level (Koutsoftas, Harmon, & Gray, 2009; Roth, Troia, Worthington, & Handy, 2006). Ample evidence shows that phonological awareness training is beneficial for beginning readers starting as early as age 4 (Byrne & Fielding-Barnsley, 1991; Koutsoftas et al., 2009). Instruction at the pre-K level should begin with easier blending tasks, such as blending syllables (/win/ + /do/ → *window*) or blending onsets and rimes (the initial sound and the vowel sound and the rest of the syllable that follows: /fl/ + /ash/ → *flash*) into words. Segmenting tasks can focus on tapping and counting syllables in words or words in sentences or segmenting words into onsets and rimes. Further training typically includes explicit modeling and practice with phoneme segmentation (/cat/ → /c/ /a/ /t/), blending (/c/ /a/ /t/ → /cat/), deleting (/cat/ − /c/ = /at/), or substitution (/cat/, /c/ → /b/ = /bat/). Blending and segmenting activities have been shown to improve the skills of kindergarten children with low phonological awareness (Fox & Routh, 1984; O'Connor, Jenkins, & Slocum, 1995; Torgesen, Morgan, & Davis, 1992). In a synthesis of research, phonological training itself yielded significant effects on phonological awareness, yet it was more effective when combined with letter training (Bus & van IJzendoorn, 1999).

Adaptations for the Blended Classroom   Although phonological awareness is typically built through oral language activities, many children will benefit from combining this practice with visual cues or print, such as tracking large print in poetry that emphasizes rhyme or using colored square cards to represent individual phonemes in words. Additional opportunities for children with difficulties in this area to practice may be built into shared book reading sessions through teacher modeling and eliciting child responses. Finally, teachers should match practice activities to individual children's level of skill and targets because phonological awareness includes a number of skills at varying levels of complexity. Small-group phonological awareness activities are ideal for the blended classroom (Koutsoftas et al., 2009).

Blended Practices for Developing Prewriting Skills

Early writing is defined by Head Start as the familiarity with writing implements, conventions, and emerging skills to communicate attitudes and ideas through written representations, symbols, and letters (U.S. Department of Health and Human Services, 2010). Writing instruction in the pre-K setting typically targets procedural knowledge (e.g., motor skills, letter formation, perceptual features of writing) rather than functional roles of writing (e.g., communication, graphic representations, recording ideas) (Molfese et al., 2011). Name-writing activities are frequently used in pre-K classrooms to help children learn to copy and trace letters and progress toward independently writing some or all of the letters in their names (Diamond, Gerde, & Powell, 2008; Levin, Both-DeVries, Aram, & Bus, 2005).

Although procedural knowledge related to writing is important in the development of fine motor skills, print concepts, and alphabet knowledge, teaching children about the functions and craft of writing is equally important in promoting language and literacy development (Fletcher & Portalupi, 1998; Graves, 1983; Sterling, 2003). Researchers concluded that children come to school with prewriting skills (e.g., scribbling, invented spelling, understanding that print carries meaning) along with prereading skills (Clay, 1975, 1998), and Cramer (1998) suggested that school instruction should begin with writing because pre-K children naturally experiment with writing prior to entering school.

Calkins (1983, 1986) described children's natural excitement about writing and stated that children experience the powerful discovery that print carries meaning as they move through the developmental stages of writing. Early writing requires children to combine knowledge of letter names and letter sounds with concepts such as directionality and spacing (Clay, 2002; Tolchinsky, 2006) and allows them to freely demonstrate these skills through invented spelling and written messages.

Researchers advocate using a variety of meaningful strategies to provide writing opportunities across the early childhood curriculum and throughout the school day. These strategies vary in format and degree of teacher direction needed. First, it is important to include activities in which the teacher has total control of the writing process and can model the functions and processes involved in writing. For example, teachers may write the morning message each day during circle time to inform the children of the daily news. As teachers model writing and think aloud, they can include picture cues, draw attention to cognates or words that have similar spellings and meanings in different languages (e.g., *family, familia*), and check for comprehension through group and individual signals such as children putting their thumbs up, repeating the answer, or nodding their head (Allison & Rehm, 2007; Brown-Jeffy & Cooper, 2011; Williams & Pilonieta, 2012).

Second, shared writing allows teachers to invite children to help create the text orally through teacher–child discussions while the teacher acts as the scribe to record children's ideas (Roth, 2009). Interactive writing is another strategy that allows teachers and students to work together as coauthors. Unlike shared writing, interactive writing invites children to take an active role in the planning and writing process by taking turns with his or her teacher and peers to copy, trace, or independently write letters on the group text (McCarrier et al., 2000; Rubadue, 2002).

Finally, it is important for children to have opportunities to transfer new understandings of early writing skills gained from group lessons to their independent writing. By providing students time to write in daily journals and engage in bookmaking in the writing center, children discover the many functions of writing and begin to understand that writing is more than a procedural skill. The blank pages present children with an invitation to express their ideas and make meaning, helping them develop a comfortable familiarity with communicating through text, which will help them successfully negotiate the demands of writing beyond the early childhood years (Ray & Glover, 2008).

Adaptations for the Blended Classroom   It is important for teachers who are modeling writing to limit the amount of text and think aloud while writing each letter (e.g., "I am writing the letter *a*, it has a circle and a stick"). It is important to consider adapting instruction for children of varying ability levels when co-composing and constructing texts (e.g., accepting emergent writing contributions including scribbles and letter strings, assistance with letter formation through hand-over-hand support, targeting a mixture of high- and low-level writing skills) (Wolbers, Dostal, & Bowers, 2012). Teachers should continually monitor and assess the engagement level of each child and provide assistance through one-to-one conferencing when children are writing on their own. Teachers may incorporate opportunities for intensive instruction on individual prewriting goals into daily activities such as centers or small-group lessons (Grisham-Brown et al., 2006, 2009).

LITERACY IN EARLY CHILDHOOD EDUCATION CLASSROOMS: A CASE STUDY

Ms. Anaya has already taken steps to better incorporate language and literacy instruction into her classroom this year by providing a language- and literacy-rich environment for the children in her class. She also wants to meet the individual needs of her students and knows that she will need to use ongoing assessment to do so. With help from their literacy coach, Ms. Anaya and Mrs. Getty begin planning for their year.

Assessment

The teachers administered the Individual Growth and Development Indicators (IGDIs; Early Childhood Research Institute on Measuring Growth and Development, 1998), which are a series of quick measures that are periodically given to assess growth in various developmental areas, to all children at the beginning of the year. Ms. Anaya and Mrs. Getty administer the Picture Naming, Alliteration, and Rhyming subtests, as well as a letter naming and letter sounds assessment, to assess language and literacy development. These assessments provide a baseline for the beginning of the year and show relative strengths and needs of children in the language and literacy areas. Ms. Anaya plans her large- and small-group instruction to target skills that many children have not mastered as well as opportunities for individual children to practice skills based on identified needs. For example, Jayla recognized all upper- and lowercase letters, 14 letter sounds, and scored a 17 on the Picture Naming task, all of which indicated she was at or above expected performance on these tasks. She did not have any correct responses on the Alliteration or Rhyming subtests, however. Alex recognized only four upper- and lowercase letters, no letter sounds, and showed emerging understanding of the Alliteration and Rhyming skills by scoring a 3 on each. Ms. Anaya chose to also administer the Communication subtest of the Infant and Toddler IGDIs to Craig. It gives a total communication score rather than the pre-K subtests because one of his individualized education program goals was to use two- and three-word sentences.

Ms. Anaya uses all of the information gathered to guide her ongoing assessment and instruction for the whole group and individual children. She notes the letter sounds Jayla did not identify as well as rhyming and phonemic awareness skills as areas of instruction. She notes that letter naming and letter–sound correspondence are highest priority of instruction for Alex, but he needs additional experience with phonemic awareness and rhyming. Opportunities to use language and learn vocabulary is the instructional priority for Craig. Ms. Anaya and Mrs. Getty assess all children on all literacy subtests in the fall, the winter, and the spring to document growth in these areas. For areas of need, Ms. Anaya assesses children on a monthly basis to determine whether the children are receiving the correct amount of support to make expected progress. This means Ms. Anaya or Mrs. Getty will be assessing Jayla using the Alliteration and Rhyming subtests each month as well as the letter–sound identification assessment. The Picture Naming subtest and the Letter Recognition and Letter–Sound Correspondence Subtests will only be given at the three time points.

Scope and Sequence

The literacy concepts and skills that the children in Ms. Anaya and Mrs. Getty's classroom are expected to achieve by the end of the year are outlined in the state early learning standards. Ms. Anaya realizes, however, that the children in her classroom enter with a variety of skills and abilities and that some children will exceed these expectations, whereas some will continue to need support to achieve these expectations after they leave her classroom. Ms. Anaya and Mrs. Getty hold high expectations for all children in their language and literacy development. The expectation for most children is that they will achieve the state early learning standards by the end of the year (Tier 1). The assessments that Ms. Anaya and Mrs. Getty administer provide information about what supports are needed for individual children to meet these expectations. The standards include the following:

- *Use complete sentences to express a thought or idea through adult modeling, guidance, and support (vocabulary/oral language).*

- *Participate in collaborative conversations that include book reading and theme-related vocabulary with adults and other children during transitions and routine daily activities, including free play (vocabulary/oral language).*

- *Demonstrate concepts of print, including identifying title, author, and illustrator; distinguishing between words and pictures; holding a book correctly; and reading from left to right (print concepts).*

- *Actively listen and participate in small- and large-group activities when common types of texts (e.g., storybooks, nursery rhymes, poetry) are read aloud or discussed (book appreciation).*

- *Recognize frequently occurring uppercase letters and some of the most frequently occurring lowercase letters. Demonstrate basic knowledge of letter–sound correspondence association by beginning to match the name and initial sound of some consonant letters in words (alphabet knowledge).*

- *Demonstrate increasing understanding of spoken words, syllables, and sounds, including rhyming and matching beginning sounds (phonological awareness).*

- *With modeling and support, use a combination of drawing, dictating, and emergent writing to express an idea, tell a story, or explain information (prewriting).*

Activities and Instruction

The children attend the program for 3½ hours. Ms. Anaya and Mrs. Getty begin each session with a short large-group time that includes a greeting activity, book sharing time, and shared writing experience. The primary content for the large-group time is based on the research-based curriculum that the district has chosen for all pre-K classrooms to use. Today, Ms. Anaya is reading The Little Red Hen Makes a Pizza *(Sturges, 2002), a predictable book with repetitive text that she has read to the children once before. Three vocabulary words with child-friendly definitions are introduced before reading:* apron *(something you wear over your clothes to keep them clean),* delicatessen *(a store where you buy meat or cheese), and* rummage *(to look for something by moving things around). Ms. Anaya has also printed these words on cards with identifying pictures that she adds to a "vocabulary stars" board. A star is added to the board whenever children use the word. The class gets to celebrate with a special song that they have chosen when they receive five stars. This is a curriculum activity that Ms. Anaya has found particularly successful for her class because the majority of children need to increase their vocabulary knowledge.*

The children join in on the repetitive lines (e.g., "'Not I,' said the cat") during reading. Mrs. Getty provides a verbal cue to two other students who need reminders of what to say. Jayden, a child with cerebral palsy, has the lines programmed into his voice output communication aid so he can join in the chorus. Ms. Anaya asks questions such as, "Why are the hen's friends not helping her make the pizza?" throughout the book to engage the children.

In planning for the activity, Ms. Anaya has considered embedded learning opportunities for individual children based on their areas of need. (See Hemmeter, McCollum, & Hsieh, 2005, for further information about embedding literacy learning opportunities). She provides opportunities for the children to identify letter names and sounds (e.g., "Hen starts with an H, just like Henry"). She provides multiple opportunities for children who need additional support. For example, she asks Jayla to identify a word that starts with the /d/ sound "like in dog" from the text. Ms. Anaya has the children participate in a shared writing activity in which they make a list of their favorite pizza toppings. Mrs. Getty provides three visual choices (e.g., pepperoni, peppers, cheese) for children who need additional support.

Children choose one of six centers after large group—dramatic play, library, blocks, writing, math, and science. Ms. Anaya and Mrs. Getty use a zoning approach during center time so that they each monitor three centers. Each teacher engages children in conversation about what they are doing in the center. Again, Ms. Anaya and Mrs. Getty have considered embedded learning opportunities to work on identified needs for children. For example, Mrs. Getty plays with the four children in dramatic play as they reenact The Little Red Hen Makes a Pizza *(Sturges, 2002). She encourages the children to write a grocery list. Mrs. Getty provides opportunities for*

Alex to identify the letter sounds that begin words on the list. She is able to emphasize two of the vocabulary words—apron and delicatessen—for all children as they gather the ingredients and make their pizza. She also provides Craig with opportunities to practice his language by engaging him in conversation about what he is making in the kitchen and providing prompts. For example, Mrs. Getty says, "Craig, what are you making?" Craig says, "Dough." Mrs. Getty prompts, "Say, 'I'm making dough.'"

The class divides into three small groups of five children each after center time. Each adult runs a group on the days that a third adult is in the room. Ms. Anaya leads a group following a recipe for pizza dough. She has the recipe on a large piece of chart paper with picture cues for each step. She is reinforcing math concepts of number recognition (e.g., 2 cups of flour) and measuring (e.g., amounts of each ingredient) in this activity. She also has the children read each step of the recipe, reinforcing print concepts of left-to-right and top-to-bottom reading as well as letter–sound correspondence. She reinforces the letter–sound correspondence by labeling each ingredient (e.g., "flour" and "butter" signs on the packages) and having children find the ingredients. After the small groups are completed, Ms. Anaya puts the chart paper recipe in the dramatic play center for continued use.

They have closing circle before children leave for the day. Mrs. Getty or Ms. Anaya preplan for this activity for children who need additional support by talking about it with individual children before group. They model language (e.g., "I made a pepperoni pizza!"), provide visual supports (i.e., pictures of centers they visited or small-group activities), or help program language in AAC devices. The children sing a good-bye song after the sharing time and move their names from the "hello" board to the "good-bye" board.

Progress Monitoring

Ms. Anaya, Mrs. Getty, and the therapists regularly review all children's progress toward the language and literacy goals they have identified. After the monthly administration of assessments, they meet to discuss how individual children are progressing on the identified areas of need. For example, after the first monthly assessments, they note that Jayla is identifying an additional six letter sounds but is continuing to struggle with the Alliteration and Rhyming subtests. They decide that Mrs. Getty will work individually with Jayla twice a week on the phonological awareness skills through structured games. Alex scored well on the Letter Naming, Alliteration, and Rhyming assessments, so Ms. Anaya will monitor this for 1 more month but may return to the less frequent assessments for Alex (i.e., three times a year). The SLP continues to work with Craig and provide additional ideas for encouraging his language with Ms. Anaya and Mrs. Getty when the SLP is not in the classroom. The team believes that this consistent communication about the progress of each child and plans for supporting any new or continued need is vital to the success of all children in their classroom.

SUMMARY

The significant and lasting relationship between language and literacy development in early childhood has been well established. Early childhood teachers need to be intentional about creating language- and literacy-rich classroom environments to broadly promote these skills. The variety of skills in language and literacy development—vocabulary, book appreciation, print concepts, alphabet knowledge, phonological awareness, and pre-writing—should be addressed across the day with young children. Young children with and without disabilities come to pre-K with various strengths and areas for growth across these domains. Activities should be adapted and teaching strategies implemented to allow all children to access and learn from the language and literacy curriculum.

LEARNING ACTIVITIES

1. Language- and literacy-rich classroom environments are described on pages 252–257. Observe a pre-K classroom and describe how language and literacy skills are promoted in the classroom. What materials are used to support literacy instruction? What teaching practices do you observe that support language development? What additional materials or teaching opportunities could be used to support language and literacy skills?

2. List the five key areas of literacy instruction. Do the following for each area:

   • Identify materials that support instruction in this literacy area.

   • Identify teaching practices that support this literacy area.

   • Identify adaptations for supporting this area in an inclusive classroom.

3. Examine a set of curriculum materials for the ECE classroom.

   • To what degree are the five key areas of early literacy instruction addressed?

   • What key practices could be added to strengthen the curriculum?

   • What types of adaptations are included for students with disabilities?

   • What additional resources or materials might be needed to make a comprehensive literacy curriculum for an ECE classroom?

REFERENCES

Adams, M.J. (1990). *Learning to read: Thinking and learning about print.* Cambridge, MA: The MIT Press.

Adams, M.J., Foorman, B.R., Lundberg, I., & Beeler, T. (1998). *Phonemic awareness in young children: A classroom curriculum.* Baltimore, MD: Paul H. Brookes Publishing Co.

Allison, B.N., & Rehm, M.L. (2007). Effective teaching strategies for middle school learners in multicultural, multilingual classrooms. *Middle School Journal, 39*(2), 12–18.

Anthony, J.L., & Lonigan, C.J. (2004). The nature of phonological awareness: Converging evidence from four studies of preschool and early grade school children. *Journal of Educational Psychology, 96*(1), 43–55.

Antonacci, P.A., & Callaghan, C.M. (2011). *Promoting literacy development: 50 research-based strategies for K–8 learners.* Thousand Oaks, CA: Sage Publications.

Aram, D. (2006). Early literacy interventions: The relative roles of storybook reading, alphabetic activities, and their combination. *Reading and Writing, 19*(5), 489–515.

Axelrod, Y., Hall, A.H., & McNair, J.C. (2015). A is burrito and B is sloppy joe: Creating print-rich environments for children in K-3 classrooms. *YC Young Children, 70*(4), 16–25.

Ballantyne, K.G., Sanderman, A.R., & McLaughlin, N. (2008). Dual language learners in the early years: Getting ready to succeed in school. *National Clearinghouse for English Language Acquisition and Language Instruction Educational Programs.* Retrieved from: http://www.ncela.gwu.edu/resabout/ecell/earlyyears.pdf

Bauer, E.B., & Manyak, P.C. (2008). Creating language-rich instruction for English-language learners. *The Reading Teacher, 62*(2), 176–178. doi:10.1598/RT.62.2.10

Beck, I.L., McKeown, M.G., & Kucan, L. (2013). *Bringing words to life: Robust vocabulary instruction.* New York, NY: Guilford Press.

Bergeron, J.P., Lederberg, A.R., Easterbrooks, S.R., Miller, E.M., & Connor, C.M. (2009). Building the alphabetic principle in young children who are deaf or hard of hearing. *Volta Review, 109*(2–3), 87–119.

Bernhard, J.K., Winsler, A., Bleiker, C., Ginieniewicz, J., & Madigan, A.L. (2008). "Read my story!" Using the early authors program to promote early literacy among diverse, urban preschool children in poverty. *Journal of Education for Students Placed at Risk, 13*(1), 76–105.

Bloodgood, J.W. (1999). What's in a name? Children's name writing and literacy acquisition. *Reading Research Quarterly, 34*(3), 342–367.

Boudreau, D.M., & Hedberg, N.L. (1999). A comparison of early literacy skills in children with specific language impairment and their typically developing peers. *American Journal of Speech-Language Pathology, 8*(3), 249–260.

Bradley, B.A., & Jones, J. (2007). Sharing alphabet books in early childhood classrooms. *The Reading Teacher, 60*(5), 452–463.

Brown-Jeffy, S., & Cooper, J.E. (2011). Toward a conceptual framework of cultural relevant pedagogy: An overview of the conceptual and theoretical literature. *Teacher Education Quarterly, 38*(1), 65–84.

Bus, A.G., & van IJzendoorn, M.H. (1999). Phonological awareness and early reading: A meta-analysis of experimental training studies. *Journal of Educational Psychology, 91*(3), 403–414.

Byrne, B., & Fielding-Barnsley, R. (1991). Evaluation of a program to teach phonemic awareness to young children. *Journal of Educational Psychology, 83*(4), 451–455.

Calkins, L.M. (1983). *Lessons from a child: On the teaching and learning of writing.* Portsmouth, NH: Heinemann.

Calkins, L.M. (1986). *The art of teaching writing.* Portsmouth, NH: Heinemann.

Campbell, F.A., & Ramey, C.T. (1994). Effects of early intervention on intellectual and academic achievement: A follow-up study of children from low-income families. *Child Development, 65,* 684–698. doi:10.1111/j.1467-8624.1994.tb00777.x

Campbell, F.A., Ramey, C.T., Pungello, E., Sparling, J., & Miller-Johnson, S. (2002). Early childhood education: Young adult outcomes from the Abecedarian Project. *Applied Developmental Science, 6*(1), 42–57.

Carle, E. (1967). *Brown bear, brown bear, what do you see?* New York, NY: Henry Holt and Company.

Carroll, J.M., Snowling, M.J., Stevenson, J., & Hulme, C. (2003). The development of phonological awareness in preschool children. *Developmental Psychology, 39*(5), 913–923.

Catts, H.W., Fey, E., Tomblin, J.B., & Zhang, X. (2002). A longitudinal investigation of reading outcomes in children with language impairments. *Journal of*

Speech, Language, and Hearing Research, 45, 1142–1157.

Catts, H.W., Fey, M.E., Zhang, X., & Tomblin, J.B. (1999). Language basis of reading and reading disabilities: Evidence from a longitudinal investigation. *Scientific Studies of Reading, 3*(4), 331–361.

Catts, H.W., & Williamson, T. (1993). *Sounds abound: Listening, rhyming, and reading.* Austin, TX: Pro Ed.

Christie, J.F., & Enz, B. (1992). The effects of literacy play interventions on preschoolers' play patterns and literacy development. *Early Education and Development, 3*(3), 205–220.

Clark, P., & Kragler, S. (2005). The impact of including writing materials in early childhood classrooms on the early literacy development of children from low-income families. *Early Child Development and Care, 175*(4), 285–301. doi:10.1080/0300443042000266295

Clay, M.M. (1975). *What did I write? Beginning writing behavior.* Portsmouth, NH: Heinemann.

Clay, M.M. (1993). *Reading recovery: A guidebook for teachers in training.* Portsmouth, NH: Heinemann.

Clay, M.M. (1998). *By different paths to common outcomes.* York, ME: Stenhouse Publishers.

Clay, M.M. (2002). *An observation survey of early literacy achievement* (2nd ed.). Portsmouth, NH: Heinemann.

Connor, C.M., Morrison, F.J., & Slominski, L. (2006). Preschool instruction and children's emergent literacy growth. *Journal of Educational Psychology, 98*(4), 665–689.

Cramer, R.L. (1998). *The spelling connection: Integrating reading, writing, and spelling instruction.* New York, NY: Guilford Press.

de Jong, M.T., & Bus, A.G. (2002). Quality of book-reading matters for emergent readers: An experiment with the same book in a regular or electronic format. *Journal of Educational Psychology, 94*(1), 145–155.

Dennis, L., Lynch, Lynch, S. & Stockall, N. (2012). Planning literacy environments for diverse preschoolers. *Young Exceptional Children 15*(3), 3–19. doi:10.1177/1096250612437745

Diamond, K., Gerde, H., & Powell, D. (2008). Development in early literacy skills during the prekindergarten year in head start: Relations between growth in children's writing and understanding of letters. *Early Childhood Research Quarterly, 23,* 467–478.

Dickinson, D.K., & Tabors, P.O. (2001). *Beginning literacy with language: Young children learning at home and school.* Baltimore, MD: Paul H. Brookes Publishing Co.

Donahue, P.L., Daane, M.C., & Jin, Y. (2005). *The nation's report card: Reading 2003* (NCES 2005–453). Washington, DC: U.S. Government Printing Office.

Dr. Seuss. (1996). *Dr. Seuss's ABC.* New York, NY: Random House.

Dyches, T.T., & Prater, M.A. (2005). Characterization of developmental disability in children's fiction. *Education and Training in Developmental Disabilities, 40*(3), 202–216.

Early Childhood Research Institute on Measuring Growth and Development. (1998). *Research and development of individual growth and development indicators for children between birth and age eight.* Minneapolis, MN: Center for Early Education and Development, University of Minnesota.

Fletcher, R., & Portalupi, J. (1998). *Craft lessons.* York, ME: Stenhouse Publishers.

Fountas, I.C., & Pinnell, G.S. (1996). *Guided reading: Good first teaching for all children.* Portsmouth, NH: Heinemann.

Fox, B., & Routh, D.K. (1984). Phonemic analysis and synthesis as word attack skills: Revisited. *Journal of Educational Psychology, 76*(6), 1059–1064.

Gallagher, A., Frith, U., & Snowling, M.J. (2000). Precursors of literacy delay among children at genetic risk of dyslexia. *Journal of Child Psychology and Psychiatry, 41*(2), 203–213.

Girolametto, L., & Weitzman, E. (2002). Responsiveness of child care providers in interactions with toddlers and preschoolers. *Language, Speech, and Hearing Services in Schools, 33,* 268–281.

Graves, D.H. (1983). *Writing: Teachers and children at work.* London, England: Heinemann Educational Books.

Grisham-Brown, J., Pretti-Frontczak, K., Hawkins, S.R., & Winchell, B.N. (2009). Addressing early learning standards for all children within blended preschool classrooms. *Topics in Early Childhood Special Education, 29*(3), 131–142.

Grisham-Brown, J., Ridgley, R., Pretti-Frontczak, K., Litt, C., & Nielson, A. (2006). Promoting positive learning outcomes for young children in inclusive classrooms: A preliminary study of children's progress toward pre-writing standards. *Journal of Early and Intensive Behavior Intervention, 3*(1), 171–183

Hammer, C.S., Scarpino, S., & Davison, M.D. (2011). Beginning with language: Spanish-English bilingual preschoolers' early literacy development. In S.B. Neuman & D.K. Dickinson (Eds.), *Handbook of early literacy research* (Vol. 3, pp. 118–135). New York, NY: Guilford Press.

Hansen, J., Davis, R., Evertson, J., & Freeman, T. (2011). *The prek-2 writing classroom: Growing confident writers.* New York, NY: Scholastic.

Hart, B., & Risley, T.R. (1995). *Meaningful differences in the everyday experience of young American children.* Baltimore, MD: Paul H. Brookes Publishing Co.

Hemmeter, M.L., McCollum, J., & Hsieh, W.Y. (2005). Practical strategies for supporting emergent literacy in the preschool classroom. In E.M. Horn & H. Jones (Eds.), *Supporting early literacy development in young children* (Young Exceptional Children Monograph Series No. 7; pp. 59–74). Longmont, CO: Sopris West Educational Services.

Henriksen, B. (1999). Three dimensions of vocabulary development. *Studies in Second Language Acquisition, 21*(2), 303–317.

Howes, C. (2000). Social-emotional classroom climate in childcare, child-teacher relationships and children's second grade peer relations. *Social Development, 9,* 191–204.

Justice, L.M. (2004). Creating language-rich preschool classroom environments. *Teaching Exceptional Children, 37*(2), 36–44.

Justice, L.M. (2006). Measuring preschool attainment of print-concept knowledge: A study of typical and at-risk 3- to 5-year-old children using item response theory. *Language, Speech, and Hearing Services in Schools, 37*(3), 224–235.

Justice, L.M., Chow, S.M., Capellini, C., Flanigan, K., & Colton, S. (2003). Emergent literacy intervention for vulnerable preschoolers: Relative effects of two approaches. *American Journal of Speech-Language Pathology, 12*(3), 320–332.

Justice, L.M., & Kaderavek, J. (2002). Using shared storybook reading to promote emergent literacy. *Teaching Exceptional Children, 34*(4), 8–13.

Justice, L.M., & Lankford, C. (2002). Pilot findings. *Communication Disorders Quarterly, 24*(1), 11–21.

Justice, L.M., Pence, K., Bowles, R.B., & Wiggins, A. (2006). An investigation of four hypotheses concerning the order by which 4-year-old children learn the alphabet letters. *Early Childhood Research Quarterly, 21*(3), 374–389.

Justice, L.M., Pullen, P.C., & Pence, K. (2008). Influence of verbal and nonverbal references to print on preschoolers' visual attention to print during storybook

reading. *Developmental Psychology, 44*(3), 855–866.

Kampmann, J.A., & Bowne, M.T. (2011). "Teacher, there's an elephant in the room!" An inquiry approach to preschoolers' early language learning. *Young Children, 66*(5), 84–89.

Koutsoftas, A.D., Harmon, M.T., & Gray, S. (2009). The effect of tier 2 intervention for phonemic awareness in a response-to-intervention model in low-income preschool classrooms. *Language, Speech, and Hearing Services in Schools, 40*(2), 116–130.

Law, J., Boyle, J., Harris, F., Harkness, A., & Nye, C. (2000). Prevalence and natural history of speech and language delay: Findings from a systematic review of the literature. *International Journal of Communication Disorders, 35,* 165–188.

Levin, R., Both-DeVries, A., Aram, D., & Bus, A. (2005). Writing starts with own name writing: From scribbling to conventional spelling in Israeli and Dutch children. *Applied Psycholinguistics, 26,* 463–477.

Lindamood, P., & Lindamood, P. (1998). *The Lindamood phoneme sequencing program for reading, spelling, and speech: Lips. Teacher's manual for the classroom and clinic.* Austin, TX: PRO-ED.

Lonigan, C.J. (2006). Conceptualizing phonological processing skills in prereaders. In S.B. Neuman & D.K. Dickinson (Eds.), *Handbook of early literacy research* (Vol. 2, pp. 77–89). New York, NY: Guilford Press.

Lovelace, S., & Stewart, S.R. (2007). Increasing print awareness in preschoolers with language impairment using non-evocative print referencing. *Language, Speech, and Hearing Services in Schools, 38*(1), 16–30.

Martin, B., & Archambault, J. (1989). *Chicka chicka boom boom.* New York, NY: Simon & Schuster.

McCarrier, A., Pinnell, G.S., & Fountas, I.C. (2000). *Interactive writing: How language and literacy come together, K-2.* Portsmouth, NH: Heinemann.

McGinty, A.S., Breit-Smith, A., Fan, X., Justice, L.M., & Kaderavek, J.N. (2011). Does intensity matter? Preschoolers' print knowledge development within a classroom-based intervention. *Early Childhood Research Quarterly, 26*(3), 255–267.

McLeod, R.H. (2010). *The relationship between teacher language use in enhanced milieu teaching sessions and child language outcomes* (Doctoral dissertation). Retrieved from http://search.proquest.com/docview/851890228

Minaya-Rowe, L. (2004). Training teachers of English language learners using their student's first language. *Journal of Latinos and Education, 3*(1), 3–24.

Mitton, T., & Parker, A. (2000). *Dazzling diggers.* New York, NY: Kingfisher.

Moats, L.C. (2000). *Speech to print: Language essentials for teachers.* Baltimore, MD: Paul H. Brookes Publishing Co.

Mol, S.E., Bus, A.G., & de Jong, M.T. (2009). Interactive book reading in early education: A tool to stimulate print knowledge as well as oral language. *Review of Educational Research, 79*(2), 979–1007.

Molfese, V.J., Beswick, J.L., Jacobi-Vessels, J.L., Armstrong, N.E., Culver, B.L., White, J.M., & Molfese, D.L. (2011). Evidence of alphabetic knowledge in writing: Connections to letter and word identification skills in preschool and kindergarten. *Reading and Writing, 24,* 133–150. doi:10.1007/s11145-010-9265-8

Morrow, L.M., & Gambrell, L.B. (2004). *Using children's literature in preschool: Comprehending and enjoying books.* Newark, DE: International Reading Association.

Morrow, L.M., & Rand, M.K. (1991). Promoting literacy during play by designing early childhood classroom environments. *The Reading Teacher, 44*(6), 396–402.

Murray, B.A., Stahl, S.A., & Ivey, M.G. (1996). Developing phoneme awareness through alphabet books. *Reading and Writing, 8*(4), 307–322.

Nasatir, D., & Horn, E. (2003). Addressing disability as a part of diversity through classroom children's literature. *Young Exceptional Children, 6*(4), 2–10.

Nathan, L., Stackhouse, J., Goulandris, N., & Snowling, M.J. (2004). The development of early literacy skills among children with speech difficulties: A test of the critical age hypothesis. *Journal of Speech, Language, and Hearing Research, 47*(2), 377–391.

National Early Literacy Panel. (2008). *Developing early literacy: Report of the National Early Literacy Panel.* Washington, DC: National Institute for Literacy.

National Reading Panel. (2000). *Report of the National Reading Panel: Teaching children to read: An evidence-based assessment of the scientific research literature on reading and its implications for reading instruction: Reports of the subgroups.* Washington, DC: National Institute of Child Health and Human Development, National Institutes of Health.

Neuman, S.B., & Roskos, K. (1990). Play, print, and purpose: Enriching play environments for literacy development. *The Reading Teacher, 44*(3), 214–221.

Neuman, S.B., & Roskos, K. (1992). Literacy objects as cultural tools: Effects on children's literacy behaviors in play. *Reading Research Quarterly, 27*(3), 203–225.

Neuman, S.B., & Roskos, K. (1993). Access to print for children of poverty: Differential effects of adult mediation and literacy-enriched play settings on environmental and functional print tasks. *American Educational Research Journal, 30*(1), 95–122.

O'Connor, R.E., & Jenkins, J.R. (1999). Prediction of reading disabilities in kindergarten and first grade. *Scientific Studies of Reading, 3*(2), 159–197.

O'Connor, R.E., Jenkins, J.R., & Slocum, T.A. (1995). Transfer among phonological tasks in kindergarten: Essential instructional content. *Journal of Educational Psychology, 87*(2), 202–217.

Paquette, K.R., & Rieg, S.A. (2008). Using music to support the literacy development of young English language learners. *Early Childhood Education Journal, 36*(3), 227–232.

Payne, A.C., Whitehurst, G.J., & Angell, A.L. (1994). The role of home literacy environment in the development of language ability in preschool children from low-income families. *Early Childhood Research Quarterly, 9*(3), 427–440.

Pinnell, G.S., & Fountas, I.C. (2011). *Literacy beginnings: A prekindergarten handbook.* Portsmouth, NH: Heinemann.

Ray, K.W., & Glover, M. (2008). *Already ready.* Portsmouth, NH: Heinemann.

Reutzel, D.R., Oda, L.K., & Moore, B.H. (1989). Developing print awareness: The effect of three instructional approaches on kindergarteners' print awareness, reading readiness, and word reading. *Journal of Literacy Research, 21*(3), 197–217.

Reynolds, A.J., Temple, J.A., Robertson, D.L., & Mann, E.A. (2001). Long-term effects of an early childhood intervention on educational achievement and juvenile arrest: A 15-year follow-up of low-income children in public schools. *Journal of the American Medical Association, 285*(18), 2339–2346.

Robertson, C., & Salter, W. (1995). *The phonological awareness kit.* East Moline, IL: LinguiSystems.

Rosenberg, S.A., Zhang, D., & Robinson, C.C. (2008). Prevalence of developmental delays and participation in early intervention services for young children. *Pediatrics, 121,* 1503–1509.

Roskos, K.A., Christie, J.F., Widman, S., & Holding, A. (2010). Three decades in: Priming for meta-analysis in play-literacy research. *Journal of Early Childhood Literacy, 10*(1), 55–96.

Roth, F.P., Troia, G.A., Worthington, C.K., & Handy, D. (2006). Promoting Awareness of Sounds in Speech (PASS): The effects of intervention and stimulus characteristics on the blending performance of preschool children with communication impairments. *Learning Disability Quarterly, 29*(2), 67–88.

Roth, K. (2009). *Interactive writing: Investigating the effectiveness of a dynamic approach to writing instruction for first graders* (Doctoral dissertation). Retrieved from http://search.proquest.com/docview/304894167

Rubadue, A. (2002). Sharing the pen. *Teaching PreK-8, 32*(6), 58–60.

Scarborough, H.S. (1998). Predicting the future achievement of second graders with reading disabilities: Contributions of phonemic awareness, verbal memory, rapid naming, and IQ. *Annals of Dyslexia, 48*(1), 115–136.

Smith, M.W., Brady, J.P., & Anastasopoulos, L. (2008). *Early Language and Literacy Classroom Observation Tool, Pre-K (ELLCO Pre-K)*. Baltimore, MD: Paul H. Brookes Publishing Co.

Snow, C.E. (1983). Literacy and language: Relationships during the preschool years. *Harvard Educational Review, 53*(2), 165–189.

Snow, C.E., Burns, M.S., & Griffin, P. (Eds.). (1998). *Preventing reading difficulties in young children*. Washington, DC: National Academies Press.

Spencer, E., Goldstein, H., Sherman, A., Noe, S., Tabbah, R., Zoilkowski, R., & Schneider, N. (2012). Effects of an automated vocabulary and comprehension intervention: An early efficacy study. *Journal of Early Intervention, 34*(4), 195–221.

Stanovich, K.E. (1988). Explaining the differences between the dyslexic and the garden-variety poor reader: The phonological-core variable-difference model. *Journal of Learning Disabilities, 21*(10), 590–604.

Stanovich, K.E., & Siegel, L.S. (1994). Phenotypic performance profile of children with reading disabilities: A regression-based test of the phonological-core variable-difference model. *Journal of Educational Psychology, 86*(1), 24–53.

Stanton-Chapman, T.L., Chapman, D.A., Kaiser, A.P., & Hancock, T.B. (2004). Cumulative risk and low income children's language development. *Topics in Early Childhood Special Education, 24*(4), 227–237.

Sterling, R. (2003). Why writing matters: An invitation to share your ideas about writing in the 21st century. *Voices from the Middle, 11*(2), 5–7.

Strickland, D.S., & Morrow, L.M. (1988). Emerging readers and writers: Creating a print rich environment. *The Reading Teacher, 42*(2), 156–157.

Strickland, D.S., Morrow, L.M., Neuman, S.B., Roskos, K., Schickedanz, J.A., & Vukelich, C. (2004). The role of literacy in early childhood education. *The Reading Teacher, 58*(1), 86–103.

Sturges, P. (2002). *The little red hen makes a pizza*. New York, NY: Puffin Books.

Suen, A. (2011). *Road work ahead*. New York, NY: Penguin Books.

Tabors, P.O., & Snow, C.E. (2001). Young bilingual children and early literacy development. In S.B. Neuman & D.K. Dickinson (Eds.), *Handbook of early literacy research* (Vol. 1, pp. 159–178). New York, NY: Guilford Press.

Tao, L., & Robinson, H. (2005). Print rich environments: Our pre-service teachers' report of what they observed in their field experiences. *Reading Horizons, 45*(4), 349–366.

Tolchinsky, L. (2006). The emergence of writing. In C. MacArthur, S. Graham, & J. Fitzgerald (Eds.), *Handbook of writing research* (pp. 83–95). New York, NY: Guilford Press.

Tomasello, M., & Farrar, M.J. (1986). Joint attention and early language. *Child Development, 57*, 1454–1463.

Tomblin, J.B., Zhang, X., Buckwalter, P., & Catts, H. (2000). The association of reading disability, behavioral disorders, and language impairment among second-grade children. *Journal of Child Psychology and Psychiatry and Allied Disciplines, 41*, 473–482.

Torgesen, J.K., Alexander, A.W., Wagner, R.K., Rashotte, C.A., Voeller, K.K., & Conway, T. (2001). Intensive remedial instruction for children with severe reading disabilities: Immediate and long-term outcomes from two instructional approaches. *Journal of Learning Disabilities, 34*(1), 33–58.

Torgesen, J.K., & Bryant, B.R. (1994). *Phonological awareness for reading*. Austin, TX: PRO-ED.

Torgesen, J.K., Morgan, S.T., & Davis, C. (1992). Effects of two types of phonological awareness training on word learning in kindergarten children. *Journal of Educational Psychology, 84*(3), 364–370.

Treiman, R., & Broderick, V. (1998). What's in a name: Children's knowledge about the letters in their own names. *Journal of Experimental Child Psychology, 70*(2), 97–116.

U.S. Department of Health and Human Services. (2004). *Family and child experiences survey (FACES)*. Washington, DC: Author.

U.S. Department of Health and Human Services. (2010). *Head Start impact study final report: Executive summary*. Retrieved from http://www.acf.hhs.gov/opre/resource/head-start-impact-study-final-report-executive-summary

van Bysterveldt, A.K., Gillon, G.T., & Moran, C. (2006). Enhancing phonological awareness and letter knowledge in preschool children with Down syndrome. *International Journal of Disability, Development and Education, 53*(3), 301–329.

Van Hoorn, J., Nourot, P.M., Scales, B., & Alward, K.R. (2006). *Play at the center of the curriculum* (4th ed.). Upper Saddle River, NJ: Prentice Hall.

Vygotsky, L.S. (1978). *Mind in society: The development of higher psychological processes*. Cambridge, MA: Harvard University Press.

Wagner, R.K., Torgesen, J.K., & Rashotte, C.A. (1994). Development of reading-related phonological processing abilities: New evidence of bidirectional causality from a latent variable longitudinal study. *Developmental Psychology, 30*(1), 73–87.

Wagstaff, J.M. (1998). Building practical knowledge of letter-sound correspondences: A beginner's word wall and beyond. *The Reading Teacher, 51*(4), 298–304.

Wasik, B.A. (2001). Phonemic awareness and young children. *Childhood Education, 77*(3), 128–133.

Weizman, Z.O., & Snow, C.E. (2001). Lexical input as related to children's vocabulary acquisition: Effects of sophisticated exposure and support for meaning. *Developmental Psychology, 37*(2), 265–279.

Whitehurst, G.J., & Lonigan, C.J. (1998). Child development and emergent literacy. *Child Development, 69*(3), 848–872.

Williams, C., & Pilonieta, P. (2012). Using interactive writing instruction with kindergarten and first-grade English language learners. *Early Childhood Education Journal, 40*(3), 145–150.

Wolbers, K.A., Dostal, H.M., & Bowers, L.M. (2012). "I was born full deaf": Written language outcomes after 1 year of strategic and interactive writing instruction. *Journal of Deaf Studies and Deaf Education, 17*(1), 19–38. doi:0.1093/deafed/enr018

Won, B. (2014). *Hooray for hat!* Boston, MA: Houghton Mifflin.

Yopp, H.K., & Yopp, R.H. (2000). Supporting phonemic awareness development in the classroom. *The Reading Teacher, 54*(2), 130–143.

## CHAPTER 11

Promoting the Language and Literacy Skills of Dual Language Learners

Lillian K. Durán, Jennifer Grisham-Brown, and Mary Louise Hemmeter

Ann, a veteran Head Start teacher, looks around her classroom as the children explore the centers at the beginning of a new school year in a small town in the northern Midwest. She has 18 children in her preschool classroom, with three children from Sudan, two from Somalia, one from Ethiopia, and five students whose families are from Mexico. She also has four children receiving special education services in her classroom, and one of them is Somali. The languages spoken by the children in her classroom include Arabic, Amharic, Anuyak, Oromo, Somali, and Spanish. She reflects on her time at this center and how much her population of students has changed over the last 10 years. How will she meet all of these children's needs this year?

Vivian is a new early childhood special education teacher who is working as an itinerant teacher serving local Head Start and public school district preschool programs in a nearby city. She reviews this year's caseload. Half of her students speak some Spanish at home. She has one student, Zaj, whose family speaks Hmong and two students who speak Somali, Amiin, and Halgan. She wonders how she will address their special education needs in inclusive settings when she only speaks English and she will only visit them once a week for an hour. Two other students, Xavier and Amaal, have also been referred for a special education evaluation. Xavier speaks Spanish and English at home, and Amaal speaks Somali. Vivian has not received training on conducting evaluations in languages other than English, and she questions whether she will be able to differentiate between language delay and language differences related to bilingual development and second language acquisition.

ISSUES AND TRENDS

Young dual language learners are one of the fastest-growing populations in the United States (Ballantyne, Sanderman, & McLaughlin, 2008; U.S. Census Bureau, 2010). The term *dual language learners* encompasses other frequently used terms such as limited English proficient, bilingual, English language learners (ELLs), English learners, and children who speak a language other than English. This chapter defines *dual language learners* as both simultaneous and sequential bilinguals. Simultaneous bilinguals are those children who have generally been exposed to two (or more) languages since birth. Sequential bilinguals are those children introduced to a second language around the age of 3 (Paradis, Genesee, & Crago, 2011). These are usually children in the United States who speak one language at home but are formally exposed to English when they enter preschool (Paradis et al., 2011; U.S. Department of Health and Human Services, 2013). A considerable amount of variation generally exists in the exposure dual language learners have to both their home language and English in the United States, which leads to wide variation in children's language abilities in both of their languages (Kohnert & Bates, 2002; Kohnert, Bates, & Hernandez, 1999; Lonigan, Goodrich, & Farver, 2014).

More than 300 languages are spoken in the United States today (U.S. Census Bureau, 2010), with 140 languages being spoken by children enrolled in Head Start alone (Ballantyne, Sanderman, & Levy, 2008; U.S. Department of Health and Human Services, 2013). A language other than English is generally spoken in more than 20% of U.S. households, with Spanish being the most common (U.S. Census Bureau, 2010). Furthermore, dual language learners vary not only in terms of abilities in each language and the many different languages that are spoken but also by home cultures and levels of acculturation to the United States. For example, dual language learners can be born to parents who immigrated to the United States or to families who have lived in the United States for generations but continue to speak their native language (Hammer & Rodriguez, 2012; Paradis et al., 2011).

Practitioners responsible for the education of dual language learners must be aware of these demographic factors and their potential impact on classroom performance. Young dual language learners are a heterogeneous population that vary in terms of languages spoken, the quantity of exposure to each of their languages, the timing of that exposure, and their cultural backgrounds (Hammer & Rodriguez, 2012). Four diversity principles are articulated in this book's introduction. The first is recognizing that promoting diversity takes teaching staff, administrators, and parents working together toward common goals for the program. Second, teacher preparation needs to include significant training in working with diverse populations so that teachers can realize the third goal of honoring the diverse languages, beliefs, and cultures of the children and families they serve. The final goal is identifying, using, and evaluating resources and strategies that are culturally, linguistically, and developmentally appropriate. This chapter addresses all of these areas and provides a basic foundation in the knowledge and skills that are necessary to bring many of these goals into practice.

IMPLICATIONS FOR DEVELOPMENT AND LEARNING

An achievement gap between dual language learners and their monolingual English-speaking peers in kindergarten readiness and reading achievement continues to persist, despite years of research and educational reforms to improve academic outcomes (Garcia & Miller, 2008; The Nation's Report Card, 2012). A multitude of factors contribute to the academic challenges of dual language learners, such as a higher incidence of poverty, lower levels of parental education, marginalization within the dominant culture, low participation in preschool programs, and a poor fit between dual language learner children's instructional needs and the programs available to them (Children's Defense Fund, 2011; Hammer, Scarpino, & Davison, 2011). Most preschool classrooms in the United States use English as the primary language of instruction with little instructional differentiation to support the learning of children with low English proficiency (U.S. Department of Health and Human Services, 2013). This sink-or-swim approach is not the most effective at improving the long-term academic outcomes of dual language learners (Goldenberg, 2008; Rolstad, Mahoney, & Glass, 2005; Slavin & Cheung, 2005). If English language instruction is the only option available, then teachers need to intentionally scaffold instruction so that dual language learners do not fall behind simply because they do not understand the language of instruction.

Bilingual instruction in preschool is an alternative and has been shown to improve the school readiness and language and early literacy development of dual language learners (Barnett, Yarosz, Thomas, Jung, & Blanco, 2007; Center for Early Care and Education Research-Dual Language Learners [CECER-DLL], 2011; Durán, Roseth, Hoffman, & Robertshaw, 2013). The Office of Head Start published a report that evaluated the current state of practice with dual language learners and emphasized areas to target for improvement (U.S. Department of Health and Human Services, 2008). The authors of this report specifically provided guidance to Head Start administrators, teachers, and staff on recommended practices that are based on findings from leading researchers in early bilingual language development and education (e.g., Garcia & Frede, 2010). The report emphasized supporting native language development, explicitly stating, "Research unequivocally shows the importance of intentionally supporting the acquisition of English *and* the home language in young children" (U.S. Department of Health and Human Services, 2008, p. 1).

Bilingual programs often use 50/50 or 90/10 models for instruction (Cloud, Genesee, & Hamayan 2000). In 50/50 models, 50% of the classroom time is spent in English and the other 50% in the target language. Bilingual instruction can also be delivered in a 90/10 model, with 90% of the day spent in the target language and 10% in English. Programs can also be one-way or two-way. A one-way program is when all of the students in the classroom share a home language (e.g., all children in the classroom speak Spanish in a 50/50 or 90/10 model using Spanish/English). A program can be a two-way model in which approximately half of the children speak only English and the other half speak the target home language (e.g., in a 50/50 or 90/10 classroom using French and English in which 50% of the children speak only English and the other half speak French). (See the Center for Applied Linguistics glossary of terms at http://www.cal.org/twi/glossary.htm or Cloud et al., 2000, for a full discussion of program models and terminology.) In practice, programs that define themselves as bilingual or language immersion vary significantly, and there is insufficient research to definitively suggest which is the best approach (Rolstad et al., 2005). A 50/50 two-way program (Barnett et al., 2007) and a 90/10 one-way program (Durán et al., 2013) can be more effective at improving the language and literacy development of dual language learners in preschool, however, when compared with English-only instruction.

Programs also can offer more limited native language instructional opportunities by having bilingual staff lead certain activities or lessons in the children's home language or using their first language to intentionally bootstrap the acquisition of English (Farver, Lonigan, & Eppe, 2009; Lugo-Neris, Jackson, & Goldstein, 2010). These strategies are discussed later in the chapter.

RECOMMENDED PRACTICES

Many of the practices addressed in other chapters—assessment, scope and sequence, instruction and activities, and progress monitoring—also apply to dual language learners. The intent of this chapter is to describe additional considerations in designing high-quality and effective learning environments for dual language learners. Key considerations that are central to dual language learners include the following:

- Gathering both formal and informal data regarding a child's language proficiency in both English and home language

- Supporting home language acquisition in addition to English in the classroom and through family support

- Implementing culturally responsive practice with children and their families

Gathering Formal and Informal Data About Language Proficiency

Two important issues should be addressed when gathering formal and informal data about the language proficiency of young children. These include the child's current language exposure, age at which he or she was introduced to language, and the tools that should be used to test for language proficiency.

Current Language Exposure and Age of Introduction   It is important that teachers gather information about children's current language exposure and the age at which they were introduced to all of the languages that they speak. Emerging evidence shows that a parent report of a child's current level of language exposure to all of his or her languages across a typical day is a good predictor of the child's language proficiency in each of those languages (Bedore et al., 2012). Teachers can use the Family Language Questionnaire to gather this information. A reproducible copy of this form can be found in Appendix 11A. It is important to remember that an interpreter may be needed to help the family complete the form.

Testing for Language Proficiency   Parent and teacher reports provide good information regarding children's language backgrounds and are often sufficient in general education environments to make decisions regarding the instructional language to use with children and what level of support they may need in English-only settings (Bedore, Peña, Joyner, & Macken, 2011). A parent report may not provide enough information about children's language proficiency, however, and a more formal measure of language proficiency in English or the home language is required. The Pre-IDEA Language Proficiency Test (Ballard, Tighe, & Dalton, 2010) and the Pre-Language Assessment Scale (Duncan & De Avila, 2000) are two instruments that can be used to determine English proficiency. These two tests are also available in Spanish and can provide a measure of Spanish language proficiency as well. It is important to note, however, that there are some concerns about the validity of language proficiency testing, especially in early childhood (MacSwan, Rolstad, & Glass, 2002). Therefore, multiple sources of data are likely to yield the most accurate estimates of a child's language proficiency. Table 11.1 shows the stages of English proficiency.

Measures are not currently available for children who speak languages other than English or Spanish; however, teachers can use interpreters to gather language samples, interview families, and conduct observations to gather more information about their language proficiency in their home language. This is a significant gap in practice. More practical and scalable solutions will hopefully be developed over time as linguistic diversity increases in the United States.

It is critical that each language is assessed separately and, if possible, by different assessors when testing for language proficiency. Young dual language learners are sensitive about which language to speak with different communicative partners and in different contexts, which is called

Table 11.1. Stages of English proficiency

Stage	Characteristics	Instructional prompts
Preproduction	Has little comprehension Does not yet verbalize in English	Use prompts that require a physical response, such as *Show me...* *Point to the...* *Where is...*
Early production	Has limited but increasing comprehension May produce one- or two-word responses Repeats common phrases	Use prompts that require only one- or two-word responses, such as *Yes/no questions* *Is it _____ or _____?* *What is her name?*
Speech emergence	Comprehension improves Can produce simple sentences but often with grammatical and pronunciation errors	Use prompts that will elicit slightly longer responses, such as *Why did...* *Tell me what happened when...*
Intermediate fluency	Comprehension is excellent Uses sentences but may still make a few errors	Use prompts that require independent and novel responses that may take a few simple sentences to answer, such as *What do you think will happen next?* *What would you do if...* *Tell me happened on this page?*
Advanced fluency	Child understands and speaks with near native-like proficiency	Use prompts as you would with native English-speaking students

From Hill, J.D. & Flynn, K. (2006). *Classroom instruction that works with English language learners.* Alexandria, VA: Association for Supervision and Curriculum Development; reprinted by permission.

interlocutor sensitivity (Pettito, Levy, Guana, Tetrault, & Ferraro, 2001). If the examiner switches back and forth between languages with children, the children may be unclear as to which language to speak and this approach may not elicit their best performance in either language (U.S. Department of Health and Human Services, 2013).

Supporting Home Language Maintenance

Effective instruction for dual language learners capitalizes on and continues to strengthen the cognitive-linguistic resources children have stored in their first language. Rapid transitions to English-only environments can lead to a plateau or loss of children's first language, which can have detrimental social, cognitive, and linguistic consequences (Anderson, 2012). Children need their first language to communicate with their families and within their communities (Wong Fillmore, 1991). Parents need to be able to effectively engage with their children in the language they know best. Interrupting home communication patterns can have detrimental effects on family relationships and on children's ability to benefit from all of the natural language that surrounds them in their homes and communities (Anderson, 2012).

Cognitive benefits have been associated with bilingualism, specifically in executive control. Individuals who are bilingual have been found to have higher planning, initiation of activity, working memory, inhibition, mental flexibility, and self-monitoring skills when compared with monolinguals (Bialystok, Barac, Blaye, & Poulin-Dubois, 2010). These cognitive benefits are associated with high levels of proficiency in both languages, however. Therefore, children need to maintain both languages to reap the cognitive benefits of bilingualism. In addition, when young children's home language begins to plateau while they are still in the earlier stages of English acquisition, they will face challenges in their ability to build new concept knowledge in either language, which places them at risk for falling behind developmentally and academically.

Finally, there is significant evidence that higher language and literacy skills in first language are correlated with higher long-term reading and academic achievement in English (August & Shanahan, 2006; Escamilla & Hopewell, 2010; Slavin & Cheung, 2005). Therefore, the loss or plateau of children's first language reduces the resources children can draw on to bootstrap their acquisition of English. For example, Spanish and English share many cognates, or words that sound similar and share a meaning (i.e., *elephant* and *elefante*). Researchers have found that Spanish-speaking children will learn more English cognates than noncognates (Kelley & Kohnert, 2012), providing evidence that Spanish can support English vocabulary learning. There is also significant evidence that early literacy skills such as rhyming, alliteration, elision, and blending can be transferred across languages (August & Shanahan, 2006). If children begin to lose their Spanish, there is simply less for them to draw on to transfer to English language and literacy development.

Culturally Responsive Practice

Language and culture are inextricably linked (Hammer & Rodríguez, 2012; Lynch & Hanson, 2011; Paradis et al., 2011). Not only does the United States have about 300 different languages spoken, but each of these languages also has a cultural history and identity associated with it. Teachers need to be culturally competent and responsive in a highly diverse society such as the United States. Lynch and Hanson outlined five aspects of cultural competence:

1. An awareness of one's own cultural limitations and the judgments that may be made from one's own cultural lens

2. Openness, appreciation, and respect for cultural differences

3. A view of intercultural interactions as learning opportunities

4. The ability to use cultural resources in interventions

5. An acknowledgment of the integrity and value of all cultures

It is critical that teachers in the field are able to actively engage with families to support the educational experiences of their young children. Families should feel welcomed, valued, and heard. Teachers need to have the ability to critically analyze their own cultural lens in the interest of examining biases, judgments, and potential barriers to effective relationship building and communication, particularly when the cultural values of a particular family may conflict with their own. Honesty and self-reflection are the cornerstones of cultural competence and lead to the ability to implement culturally responsive practices with the diverse range of children and families with which practitioners will work over the course of their careers.

Teachers also need guidance in understanding what questions to ask families in order to gather relevant information with which to guide culturally responsive practices. Appendix 11B provides a list of questions that can be selected from in order to learn more about children, their families, and their daily routines.

Working with interpreters is also a part of culturally and linguistically responsive practice. An interpreter may be necessary when interviewing a family or conducting a meeting. Teachers should spend time with interpreters before meetings to make sure they understand confidentiality, their role in the meeting, and the purpose of the meeting. Interpreters, as well as the early childhood education (ECE) staff, should be reminded to refrain from side conversations so that there is full communication and participation of all those present. ECE staff should maintain eye contact with the family as much as possible during the meeting to support relationship building. Many interpreters who work with ECE teams are not professionally trained interpreters but are community members who speak the target language and are available for part-time intermittent employment (Cheatham, 2011). Therefore, teachers are often responsible for providing guidance to the interpreter to facilitate high-quality, accurate, and professional interpretation services to the family.

BLENDED PRACTICES FOR TEACHING CHILDREN WHO ARE DUAL LANGUAGE LEARNERS

The linked system that is foundational in this book includes connections among assessment, scope and sequence, activities and interventions, and progress monitoring. Teachers also need to be prepared to work in inclusive settings with children who not only represent diverse languages and cultures but also present with diverse developmental levels and abilities. This book is built on providing teachers with the knowledge and skills necessary to successfully support the growth and learning of young children within this context. The following section is structured to highlight universal practices that will benefit all dual language learners. Then, more targeted and intensive supports are recommended.

Universal Strategies

The following section provides universal teaching strategies that should be implemented to best address the learning needs of dual language learners. Seven basic approaches are described in the following section:

1. Differentiating instruction based on English proficiency

2. Incorporating second language scaffolding strategies into English instruction

3. Using a suite of read-aloud strategies, including dialogic book reading, repeated readings, and book walk-throughs

4. Providing systematic vocabulary instruction

5. Incorporating the child's native language into instruction whenever possible

6. Encouraging family book reading or book walk-throughs in the child's native language

7. Assessing and progress monitoring in more than one language to capture all of the child's abilities

Differentiating Instruction   Understanding the English proficiency of the children in your setting is an important initial step in differentiating instruction for dual language learners. Teachers should adapt the level of their English to maximize comprehension and scaffold children's emerging ability to use English to communicate. Parents can provide information about children's language exposure across the day to English and their home language. Parent report has been found to provide accurate estimates of a child's language proficiency in the home language. Teachers have also been found to be good reporters of English proficiency (Bedore et al., 2011). Language proficiency testing also can be conducted, if necessary. Once teachers have language background information, they can group dual language learners into one of five English proficiency groups to guide instructional decision making (Bedore et al., 2012; Hill & Flynn, 2006).

> *Example 1: Xavier's parents are second generation Mexican Americans and speak both Spanish and English equally well. His parents filled out the Family Language Questionnaire and indicated that Xavier spends about 3 hours with his Spanish-speaking grandmother every day after school until his parents return home from work. His cousins often come over for dinner in the evenings, and they generally switch to speaking English while playing and watching television. You have observed that Xavier can communicate well with the Spanish-speaking paraprofessional as well as the other Spanish-speaking children in the classroom. He can also carry on an age-appropriate conversation in English. You would place Xavier in the intermediate to advanced English category based on the family report.*
>
> *Example 2: Amaal is an only child who spends most of her time outside of preschool with her mother who speaks Somali. Her mother reports that Amaal speaks Somali well and she has no concerns about her language. It is September and this is Amaal's first year of preschool. All of the preschool staff speak only English. You would place Amaal in the pre-production stage of English language proficiency based on the information from the Family Language Questionnaire and observing that Amaal does not talk at school.*
>
> *Discussion: What might be different between Amaal and Xavier on the first day of preschool in a predominantly English language environment? Xavier has had years of exposure to English, in addition to Spanish. Although he may have vocabulary distributed across both languages, he will be able to communicate in English with the teacher and with the other children. Amaal, however, has had limited exposure to English. All of her stored knowledge will be in Somali, and she will have no way to communicate with the teacher or other children.*

The examples in the previous case study are common scenarios across the United States. Understanding the language backgrounds of students can help teachers prepare for the children they will be teaching. The teacher might want more information about Xavier's language proficiency in both English and Spanish. Xavier will know some words in both languages and other words in one language or the other because he has been exposed to both languages since birth. The teacher also will have to be careful not to overlook his Spanish language development, especially in a predominantly English environment. The teacher will need to intentionally support his parents to continue to use Spanish at home with targeted activities that mirror what he is learning in the classroom, and the teacher should maintain regular contact with his family to monitor his progress in Spanish.

Amaal's teacher could arrange for an interpreter to meet with the family prior to the first day of school to explain what to expect when she comes to school, or they could visit the preschool program to learn firsthand what to expect. The teacher could send home simple symbols for *bathroom, water, food, help me,* and *I'm hurt,* and Amaal's mother could explain the meaning of the symbols to her daughter in Somali so that when she is in school she could use these symbols to communicate basic needs. Amaal's mother could even accompany her to school the first week to assist with the transition in order to help her feel safe in her new setting, especially if there are no Somali-speaking staff available.

Second Language Acquisition Scaffolding Strategies   Two scaffolding strategies are discussed, including total physical response and using visual and graphic cues and real items.

Total Physical Response   Total physical response (Asher 1977; Breckinridge Church, Ayman-Nolley, & Mahootian, 2004; Roberts & Neal, 2004) involves acting out words or scenes in order to support understanding and is based on the coordination of language and physical movement. Instructors give commands to students in the target language, and students respond with whole-body actions. The method is an example of the comprehension approach to language teaching (Krashen & Terrell, 1983). The listening and responding (with actions) serves two purposes—it is a means of quickly recognizing meaning in the language being learned and a means of passively learning the structure of the language itself. Examples in an ECE classroom might include acting out a story instead of reading it or acting out vocabulary words in order to facilitate learning new words.

Visual and Graphic Cues and Real Items   Visual cues and real items can be used during lessons in order to scaffold the comprehension of dual language learners, reinforce vocabulary, and teach new concepts (Beck, McKeown, & Kucan, 2013; Collins, 2010; Roberts & Neal, 2004). For example, a teacher who is reading *The Very Hungry Caterpillar* (Carle, 1969) can bring in different food items from the book for the children to sample and then name. Having direct experience with items and being shown images of target vocabulary does improve vocabulary learning (Collins, 2010; Roberts & Neal, 2004).

Use a Suite of Read-Aloud Strategies   Dialogic reading, interactive book walk-throughs (Gillanders & Castro, 2011), and repeated readings (Gillanders & Castro, 2011; Graves, August, & Mancilla-Martinez, 2013) have been found to improve the vocabulary learning of dual language learners. Dialogic reading has strong evidence indicating its effectiveness in enhancing vocabulary acquisition in a broad range of children (see U.S. Department of Education, 2007, for a review). Dialogic reading focuses on making children active participants in the book-reading experience. The adult reader prompts the child through open-ended questions to elicit interaction and dialogue centered on themes or vocabulary related to the text or illustrations in the book. The acronym CROWD is used in dialogic reading to explain the five types of questions that are integral to the strategy: *completion* prompts ("The caterpillar turned into a...?"), *recall* prompts ("Tell me two foods the caterpillar ate"), *open-ended* prompts ("What would happen if you ate all of that food?"), "*Wh-*" prompts ("What did the caterpillar eat last?"), and *distancing* prompts ("Have you eaten so much that your stomach hurt?"). In addition, Whitehurst et al. (1994) detailed how the adult reader should respond once children have responded to the initial question in order to encourage interactional sequences that go beyond one turn for each conversational partner. The acronym PEER was used to outline these extension strategies and include *prompting* the child to look at the book for more information ("Look at this page. What did the caterpillar build around himself?"), *evaluating* the child's response (child says, "A brown thing"), *expanding* on the child's response (Teacher says, "A brown thing called a *cocoon*"), and encouraging the child to *repeat* the expanded response offered by the adult reader ("What did the caterpillar build around himself?"). Using dialogic reading strategies increases the number of opportunities the child has to respond to inquiries and prompts that elicit more sophisticated thinking and language from the child. Both English- and Spanish-speaking children have shown an increase in verbal participation and complexity of language during dialogic reading episodes (Blom-Hoffman, O'Neil-Pirozzi, Volpe, Cutting, & Bissinger, 2006; Jiménez, Filippini, & Gerber, 2006; Whitehurst et al., 1988).

Book walk-throughs include discussing the book by looking at the pictures and describing the storyline (Gillanders & Castro, 2011). Book walk-throughs also involve looking at the pictures in the book and making predictions about what might happen in the story. This gives children the opportunity to preview the story and have exposure to some of the key vocabulary in the book.

Repeated book reading is also an effective practice (Graves et al., 2013) because it allows children to have multiple opportunities to comprehend the storyline and have exposure to the vocabulary in the book. In addition, young children tend to enjoy having favorite books read repeatedly.

Vocabulary Instruction Directly teaching vocabulary through multiple methods is a central emphasis in teaching dual language learners as they acquire a second language. Following are examples of vocabulary teaching techniques that have been effective with dual language learners:

• Extension activities that embed target vocabulary into other classroom activities throughout the day for repeated exposure (e.g., the teacher sets up a butterfly house in the science center and has a caterpillar that changes into a butterfly that the children can track) (Beck et al., 2013; Graves et al., 2013)

• Word walls (e.g., the teacher posts pictures with key vocabulary words from *The Very Hungry Caterpillar* [Carle, 1969] on a word wall in the writing center so children can practice writing *caterpillar [oruga], butterfly [mariposa], leaf [hoja]*) (Ballantyne, Sanderman, & Levy, 2008; Graves et al., 2013)

- Vocabulary preview and review (e.g., the teacher shows pictures of a caterpillar, cocoon, butterfly, and so forth before he or she reads *The Very Hungry Caterpillar* [Carle, 1969] and has children play a game in which they pull pictures out of a hat and name the picture; after reading the book, the children engage in the same game) (August, Carlo, Dressler, & Snow, 2005; Goldenberg, 2008; Graves et al., 2013)

- Provision of developmentally appropriate definitions for target vocabulary words (e.g., a cocoon is a little house the caterpillar builds around himself) (Beck et al., 2013; Collins, 2010; Graves et al., 2013; Lugo-Neris et al., 2010)

- Strategic use of questions to foster discussion of target vocabulary (e.g., use the dialogic reading prompts described earlier in the chapter) (Beck et al., 2013; Collins, 2010; Graves et al., 2013)

Incorporating the Child's Native Language into Instruction Whenever Possible   Using children's native language in instruction is a recommended approach to improving language and literacy development (Castro, Páez, Dickinson, & Frede, 2011; CECER-DLL, 2011; U.S. Department of Health and Human Services, 2013). Bilingual staff are often underutilized and only use children's native language for transitions or to interpret for the English-speaking teacher. It is important to recognize that this level of native language support is unlikely to support home language maintenance and growth (Garcia & Frede, 2010; Kan & Kohnert, 2005).

Bilingual staff should lead group activities in the children's native language to complement the instruction they receive in English (U.S. Department of Health and Human Services, 2013). These activities can include dialogic book reading, early literacy and numeracy activities, science, or any other activity that will teach new concepts and content in the child's home language. The same strategies for teaching English vocabulary previously listed can also be used to teach home language vocabulary. See Table 11.2 for a list of available Spanish-language curricula that could be used to guide instruction with Spanish-speaking students.

Native Language Bridging   Native language bridging strategies can also be used to facilitate English language development. These bridging strategies include 1) previewing key vocabulary in the child's native language before a lesson in English (e.g., the bilingual teacher reviews the words *caterpillar [oruga], butterfly [mariposa],* and *hungry [hambriente]* in Spanish before the book is read in English), 2) providing definitions for target vocabulary in the child's native language (e.g., a cocoon es una casita que contruyó una oruga su alrededor) (Lugo-Neris et al., 2010), and 3) intentionally teaching cognates, which are words in two languages that are from the same

Table 11.2. English–Spanish early literacy preschool curricula

Curriculum/cost*	Areas
The Creative Curriculum for Preschool (Bilingual Edition) (Teaching Strategies, 2010)	Prekindergarten (pre-K) comprehensive curriculum: literacy, social-emotional, science, math, and technology
DLM Early Childhood Express (Dukes, Clements, Sarama, & Teale, 2011)	Pre-K comprehensive curriculum: literacy, social-emotional, science, math, and technology
Opening the World of Learning (Dickinson et al., 2012)	Language, literacy, and social-emotional
Scholastic Early Childhood Program (Block, Canizares, Church, & Lobo, 2002)	Language and early literacy
Read It Again: Dual Language Curriculum (available from http://www.myreaditagain.com)	Supplemental early literacy curriculum focused on oral language, phonological awareness, print knowledge, and narrative

*Costs include materials, books, printing, parent resources, and any other materials necessary to implement the curriculum.

Adapted from Pearson Education. (2009). *Pearson research overview: Opening the world of learning* [PDF document]. Retrieved from http://www.pearsonlearning.com/microsites/owl/research.cfm.

root and therefore sound very similar and share the same meaning (*peras/ pears, salame/salami, estómago/stomach, tremendo/tremendous*). Spanish and English have many cognates, and evidence shows that Spanish-speaking children learn more cognates in English than noncognates (e.g., *accident/ accidente, dinosaur/dinosaurio*) (Dressler & Kamil, 2006; Kelley & Kohnert, 2012; Perez, Peña, & Bedore, 2010). See http://www.colorincolorado.org/ pdfs/articles/cognates.pdf for a list of common cognates.

Family Book Reading/Book Walk-throughs in the Child's Native Language Children who participate in shared reading experiences with their families in their home language have been found to gain significantly more English vocabulary in addition to vocabulary in their home language than the control groups who did not have this experience (Huennekens & Xu, 2010; Roberts, 2008; Tysbina & Eriks-Brophy, 2010). Roberts compared home storybook reading in the child's primary language with home story-book reading only in English and measured gains in English vocabulary. Storybook reading in the home language was found to improve English vocabulary acquisition over reading the same books in only English at home. Families should be encouraged to read books in their native language to their child, and if the family cannot read or there are no books available in the family's home language, then families can conduct picture walk-throughs of books even if they are written in English or simply tell the story in their native language. Making books with pictures of the family and then sending them home has also been found to be an effective strategy to increase home reading and improve vocabulary acquisition (Boyce, Innocenti, Roggman, Norman, & Ortiz, 2011).

Progress Monitoring in English and in the Home Language Even if instruction is only provided in English, documenting bilingual children's growth over time in both languages is important to better understand overall language and literacy development (Hammer, Lawrence, & Miccio, 2007). A few formal progress monitoring measures are available in Spanish, including the Circle Phonological Awareness, Language and Literacy Screener (Landry, Assel, Gunewig, & Swank, 2004) and Get Ready to Read! (Whitehurst & Lonigan, 2001). The Spanish version of the Individual Growth and Development Indicators are also under development (Wackerle-Hollman, Durán, & Rodri, 2014) and will be publicly available. No progress monitoring measures are available in other languages at this point.

Teachers should consider gathering informal language and literacy data in the children's native language to measure progress. Teachers could collect language samples, parent report of language use in the home, video-recorded sessions of play with peers who speak the same language, and story retells in their native language.

Targeted and Intensive Instruction

Some children who are dual language learners will be identified as needing higher levels of instructional supports for various reasons. There is currently not enough research to know exactly what skills to focus on or what strategies to use for Tier 2 and Tier 3 interventions with dual language learners. Small-group instruction focused on language development, vocabulary, phonological and print awareness, narrative, and alphabet knowledge with some mix of native language and English instruction is likely to yield improved outcomes (LaForett, Peisner-Feinberg, & Buysse, 2013). For example, LaForett and colleagues developed a response to intervention approach with dual language learners that included small-group instruction focused on language and literacy development with language bridging techniques such as providing definitions for English vocabulary words in Spanish.

Ultimately, differentiating instruction for dual language learners is critical, as well as having a solid understanding of how children's English language proficiency may be influencing their progress. Children with limited English proficiency in English-only environments may not make adequate progress because they do not understand the language of instruction and sufficient or effective instructional scaffolds are not in place to support their successful acquisition of new skills (Goldenberg, 2008).

Special Education Referral If children who are dual language learners are not making adequate progress or families have concerns, they may be referred for a special education evaluation. Many practitioners find it difficult to tell the difference between language delay and issues associated with second language acquisition (Banerjee & Luckner, 2013). No single instrument should be used to make special education eligibility decisions. Data collected from multiple sources should be used to create a developmental and linguistic profile for the child (Oller, Pearson, & Cobo-Lewis, 2007). It is necessary for the team to have a measure of the relative amount of input and interaction children receive in each of their languages, an observation in a natural setting, reports on children's development from parents and teachers (e.g., Head Start teacher, child care provider), and possibly a criterion-based measure in addition to standardized test results. Multiple sources of data provide the team with the opportunity to corroborate results and take note of patterns that may emerge across the different contexts, reporters, and assessments.

If a child has developmental delays, then one would expect similar scores or reports from multiple data sources. Interpreting and analyzing bilingual data and assessment scores is not an exact science. Most of the assessment tools available on the market were primarily normed on monolinguals and will need to be interpreted with caution (Barrueco, López, Ong, & Lozano, 2012; Peña, 2007). Dual language learners are known to generally score lower when each of their languages is compared with monolingual norms (Peña, Kester, & Sheng, 2012). Thus, the evaluation team needs to closely examine multiple sources of information about children's development in order to make an informed decision regarding a dual language learner's need for special education services.

Once children qualify for special education services, many of the same instructional recommendations described in this chapter apply to dual language learners with disabilities (Kohnert & Derr, 2012; Kohnert, Yim, Nett, Kan, & Duran, 2005; Santos, Cheatham, & Durán, 2012). Children with cognitive disabilities, autism, Down syndrome, and speech-language impairments growing up in bilingual environments have been found to have the capacity to learn two languages, and being bilingual does not cause more delays than being monolingual (Cheatham, Santos, & Kerkutluoglu, 2012; Paradis et al., 2011). Therefore, it is important for teachers who serve children with disabilities to reassure families that it is appropriate for them to continue speaking their native language with their child. There is no scientific evidence that this will inhibit their language development or cause them to struggle to learn English (Kohnert & Derr, 2012; Paradis et al., 2011). Families need to be able to communicate freely and efficiently with their children in the language they know best to provide quality language models. The special education team should also consider bilingual intervention, if possible (Kohnert & Derr, 2012).

SUMMARY

This chapter provides many suggestions for supporting the language and literacy development of dual language learners. The cornerstone of practice with dual language learners is considering how language proficiency in both their home language and English will affect their classroom performance and learning. Dual language learners should be provided with strategic and intentional language scaffolds in order to support their English language development and cognitive growth and to maximize the benefit they may receive from participating in preschool programs. Dual language learners should also receive native language instructional support, whenever possible, to continue home language growth and concept development.

Teaching young dual language learners and working with their families provides an exciting opportunity to learn more about the world's languages and cultures. Being bilingual and bicultural is an asset in today's global economy, and it is important that we value the cultural and linguistic capital these children and families bring to society. It is imperative that early education outcomes are improved and the potential in the young dual language learner population is realized because of the ever-increasing diversity in the United States and the rapid growth of the dual language learner population.

LEARNING ACTIVITIES

1. Observe a dual language learner who has limited English proficiency in a local inclusive preschool classroom during a large-group activity conducted all in English. Does the child respond to questions? How well does the child attend during the activities? What instructional supports does the teacher use to facilitate this child's learning in English?

2. Imagine that you are a monolingual English-speaking teacher in an inclusive preschool classroom and half of your students speak Spanish as their primary language. Describe three language scaffolding strategies you would incorporate into your instruction during English instruction. What strategies could you use to incorporate Spanish instruction and language interaction into your classroom routine? Describe a system you might develop to communicate with their families. How would you monitor the progress of your Spanish-speaking students?

3. It is the beginning of the school year and you are a monolingual English-speaking teacher in a large urban inclusive preschool program. There are five different home languages spoken in your classroom—Arabic, Mandarin Chinese, Somali, Spanish, and Vietnamese. Describe how you will set up a culturally responsive environment in your classroom. You are also meeting with every family. How will you facilitate communication? Develop a list of questions you might ask the family to get to know them and their child better. What message will you give to the family regarding the use of their home language?

4. Interview a teacher who works with dual language learners. Ask the teacher the following questions. How do you know how much English a child who speaks a language other than English at home understands and uses at the beginning of the year? What strategies have you found to be effective when teaching dual language learners? What strategies do you use to maintain contact with families with whom you do not share a language? Evaluate the teacher's responses. Based on information provided in this chapter, what else could the teacher do to offer high-quality early learning experiences to the dual language learners in his or her classroom?

REFERENCES

Anderson, R.T. (2012). First language loss in Spanish-speaking children: Patterns of loss and implications for clinical practice. In B.A. Goldstein (Ed.), *Bilingual language development and disorders in Spanish-English speakers* (2nd ed., pp. 187–212). Baltimore, MD: Paul H. Brookes Publishing Co.

Asher, J.J. (1977). *Learning another language through actions: The complete teacher's guide book* (6th ed.). Los Gatos: CA, Sky Oaks Productions.

August, D., Carlo, M., Dressler, C., & Snow, C. (2005). The critical role of vocabulary development in English language learners. *Learning Disabilities Research and Practice, 20*(1), 50–57.

August, D., & Shanahan, T. (Eds.). (2006). *Developing literacy in second language learners.* Mahwah, NJ: Lawrence Erlbaum Associates.

Ballantyne, K.G., Sanderman, A.R., & Levy, J. (2008). *Educating English language learners: Building teacher capacity.* Washington, DC: National Clearinghouse for English Language Acquisition.

Ballantyne, K.G., Sanderman, A.R., & McLaughlin, N. (2008). *Dual language learners in the early years: Getting ready to succeed in school.* Washington, DC: National Clearinghouse for English Language Acquisition.

Ballard, W.S., Tighe, P.L., & Dalton, E.F. (2010). Pre-*IDEA* language proficiency test. Brea, CA: Ballard & Tighe.

Banerjee, R., & Luckner, J. (2013). Assessment practices and training needs of early childhood professionals. *Journal of Early Childhood Teacher Education, 34*(3), 231–248.

Barnett, W.S., Yarosz, D.J., Thomas, J., Jung, K., & Blanco, D. (2007). Two way and monolingual English immersion in preschool education: An experimental comparison. *Early Childhood Research Quarterly, 22*, 277–293.

Barrera, I., & Kramer, L. (2009). *Using skilled dialogue to transform challenging interactions: Honoring identity, voice, and connection.* Baltimore, MD: Paul H. Brookes Publishing Co.

Barrueco, S., López, M., Ong, C., & Lozano, P. (2012). *Assessing Spanish-English bilingual preschoolers: A guide to best approaches and measures.* Baltimore, MD: Paul H. Brookes Publishing Co.

Beck, I.L., McKeown, M.G., & Kucan, L. (2013). *Bringing words to life: Robust vocabulary instruction.* New York, NY: Guilford Press.

Bedore, L., Peña, E.D., Joyner, D., & Macken, C. (2011). Parent and teacher rating of bilingual proficiency and language development concerns. *International Journal of Bilingual Education and Bilingualism, 14*(5), 489–511.

Bedore, L., Peña, E.D., Summers, C.L., Boerger, K.M., Resendiz, M.D., Greene, K.,...Gillam, R.B. (2012). The measure matters: Language dominance profiles across measures in Spanish-English bilingual children. *Bilingualism: Language and Cognition, 15*(3), 616–629. doi:10.1017/S1366789120000090

Bialystok, E., Barac, R., Blaye, A., & Poulin-Dubois, D. (2010). Word mapping and executive functioning in young monolingual and bilingual children. *Journal of Cognition and Development, 11*(4), 485–508.

Block, C.C., Canizares, S., Church, E.B., & Lobo, B. (2002). *Scholastic early childhood program.* New York, NY: Scholastic.

Blom-Hoffman, J., O'Neil-Pirozzi, T.M., Volpe, R., Cutting, J., & Bissinger, E. (2006). Instructing parents to use dialogic reading strategies with preschool children: Impact of a video-based training program on caregiver reading behaviors. *Journal of Applied School Psychology, 23*(1), 117–131.

Boyce, L.K., Innocenti, M.S., Roggman, L.A., Norman, V.K., & Ortiz, E. (2010). Telling stories and making books: Evidence for an intervention to help parents in migrant Head Start support their children's language and literacy. *Early Education and Development, 21*(3), 343–371. doi:10.1080/10409281003631142

Breckinridge Church, R., Ayman-Nolley, S., & Mahootian, S. (2004). The role of gesture in bilingual education: Does gesture enhance learning? *International Journal of Bilingual Education and Bilingualism, 7*(4), 303–319.

Carle, E. (1969). *The very hungry caterpillar.* New York, NY: Philomel Publishing.

Castro, D.C., Ayankoya, B., & Kasprzak, C. (2011). *The new voices-nuevas voces: Guide to cultural and linguistic diversity in early childhood.* Baltimore, MD: Paul H. Brookes Publishing Co.

Castro, D., Páez, M.M., Dickinson, D.K., & Frede, E. (2011). Promoting language and literacy in young dual language learners: Research, practice, and policy. *Child Development Perspectives, 5*(1), 15–21.

Center for Early Care and Education Research-Dual Language Learners. (2011). *Language and literacy development in dual language learners: A critical review of the research.* Chapel Hill, NC: University of North Carolina, FPG Child Development Institute.

Cheatham, G.A. (2011). Language interpretation, parent participation and young children with disabilities. *Topics in Early Childhood Special Education, 31,* 78–88.

Cheatham, G.A., Santos, R.M., & Kerkutluoglu, A. (2012). Review of comparison studies investigating bilingualism and bilingual instruction for students with disabilities. *Focus on Exceptional Children, 45*(3), 1–12.

Children's Defense Fund. (2011). *The state of America's children* [PDF document]. Retrieved from http://www.childrensdefense.org/library/archives/state-of-americas-children/state-of-americas-children-2011/2011/

Cloud, N., Genesee, F., & Hamayan, E. (2000). *Dual language instruction: A handbook for enriched education.* Boston, MA: Heinle & Heinle Publishers.

Collins, M.C. (2010). ELL preschoolers' English vocabulary acquisition from story book reading. *Early Childhood Research Quarterly, 25*(1), 84–97.

Dickinson, D.K., Copley, J.V., Izquierdo, E., Lederman, J.S., Schickedanz, J., & Wright, L. (2012). *Opening the world of learning.* Glenview, CA: Scott Foresman.

Dressler, C., & Kamil, M.L. (2006). First-and second-language literacy. In D. August & T. Shanahan (Eds.), *Developing literacy in second language learners: Report of the national literacy panel on language-minority children and youth* (pp. 197–238). Mahwah, NJ: Lawrence Erlbaum Associates.

Dukes, N., Clements, D.H., Sarama, J., & Teale, W.H. (2011). *The DLM early childhood express curriculum.* New York, NY: McGraw-Hill.

Duncan, S.E., & De Avila, E.A. (2000). *PreLAS 2000 examiner's manual.* Monterey, CA: CTB/McGraw-Hill.

Durán, L.K., Roseth, C., Hoffman, P., & Robertshaw, M.B. (2013). An experimental study comparing predominantly English and transitional bilingual education on Spanish-speaking preschoolers' early literacy development: Year three results. *Bilingual Research Journal, 36*(1), 6–34.

Escamilla, K., & Hopewell, S. (2010). Transitions to biliteracy: Creating positive academic trajectories for emerging bilinguals in the United States. In J. Petrovic (Ed.), *International perspectives on bilingual education: Policy, practice, controversy* (pp. 69–93). Charlotte, NC: Information Age Publishing.

Farver, J.M., Lonigan, C., & Eppe, S. (2009). Effective early literacy skill development for young Spanish-speaking English language learners: An experimental study of two methods. *Child Development, 80,* 703–719.

García, E., & Frede, E. (2010). *Young English language learners: Current research and emerging directions for practice and policy.* New York, NY: Teachers College Press.

Garcia, E.E., & Miller, L.S. (2008). Findings and recommendations of the National Task Force on Early Childhood Education for Hispanics. *Child Development Perspectives, 2,* 52–58.

Gillanders, C., & Castro, D.C. (2011). Storybook reading for young dual language learners. *Young Children, 66*(1), 91–95.

Goldenberg, C. (2008). Improving achievement for English language learners. In S.B. Neuman (Ed.), *Educating the other America: Top experts tackle poverty, literacy, and achievement in our schools* (pp. 139–162). Baltimore, MD: Paul H. Brookes Publishing Co.

Graves, M.F., August, D., & Mancilla-Martinez, J. (2013). *Teaching vocabulary to English language learners.* New York, NY: Teachers College Press.

Hammer, C., Lawrence, F.R., & Miccio, A.W. (2007). Bilingual children's language abilities and early reading outcomes in Head Start and kindergarten. *Language, Speech, and Hearing Services in Schools, 38,* 237–248. doi:10.1044/0161-1461(2007/025)

Hammer, C.S., & Rodríguez, B. (2012). Bilingual language acquisition and the child socialization process. In B.A. Goldstein (Ed.), *Bilingual language development and disorders in Spanish-English speakers* (2nd ed., pp. 31–46). Baltimore, MD: Paul H. Brookes Publishing Co.

Hammer, C., Scarpino, S., & Davison, M. (2011). Beginning with language: Spanish-English bilingual preschoolers' early literacy development. In S.B. Neuman & D.K. Dickinson (Eds.), *Handbook of early literacy research* (Vol. 3, pp. 118–135). New York, NY: Guilford Press.

Hill, J.D., & Flynn, K.M. (2006). *Classroom instruction that works with English language learners.* Alexandria, VA: Association for Supervision and Curriculum Development.

Huennekens, M.E., & Xu, Y. (2010). Effects of a cross-linguistic storybook intervention on the second language development of two preschool English language learners. *Early Childhood Education Journal, 38*(1), 19–26. doi:10.1007/s10643-010-0385-1

Jiménez, T.C., Filippini, A.L., & Gerber, M.M. (2006). Shared reading within Latino families: An analysis of reading interactions and language use. *Bilingual Research Journal, 30*(2), 431–452.

Kan, P.F., & Kohnert, K. (2005). Preschoolers learning Hmong and English: Lexical-semantic processing in L1 and L2. *Journal of Speech, Language, and Hearing Research, 48*(2), 372–383.

Kelley, A., & Kohnert, K. (2012). Is there a cognate advantage for typically developing Spanish-speaking English-language learners? *Language, Speech, and Hearing Services in Schools, 43*, 191–204.

Kohnert, K., & Bates, E. (2002). Balancing bilinguals II: Lexical comprehension and cognitive processing in children learning Spanish and English. *Journal of Speech, Language, and Hearing Research, 45*, 347–359.

Kohnert, K., Bates, E., & Hernandez, A. (1999). Balancing bilinguals: Lexical-semantic production and cognitive processing in children learning Spanish and English. *Journal of Speech, Language, and Hearing Research, 42*, 1400–1413.

Kohnert, K., & Derr, A. (2012). Language intervention with bilingual children. In B.A. Goldstein (Ed.), *Bilingual language development and disorders in Spanish-English speakers* (2nd ed., pp. 315–343). Baltimore, MD: Paul H. Brookes Publishing Co.

Kohnert, K., Yim, D., Nett, K., Kan, P., & Duran, L. (2005). Intervention with linguistically diverse preschool children: A focus on developing home language(s). *Language, Speech, and Hearing Services in the Schools, 36*, 251–267.

Krashen, S., & Terrell, T. (1983). *The natural approach: Language acquisition in the classroom.* Oxford, England: Pergamon.

LaForett, D.R., Peisner-Feinberg, E.S., & Buysse, V. (2013). Recognition & response for dual language learners. In V. Buysse, E.S. Peisner-Feinberg, & H.P. Ginsburg (Eds.), *Handbook of response to intervention on early childhood* (pp. 355–370). Baltimore, MD: Paul H. Brookes Publishing Co.

Landry, S., Assel, M., Gunewig, S., & Swank, P. (2004). *Circle phonological awareness language and literacy screener.* Houston, TX: Ridgeways.

Lonigan, C.J., Goodrich, J.M., & Farver, J.A. (2014, July). *Patterns of development of early literacy skills of Spanish-speaking dual-language learner preschool children.* Paper presented at 21st Annual Meeting of the Society for the Scientific Study of Reading, Santa Fe, NM.

Lugo-Neris, M.J., Jackson, C.W., & Goldstein, H. (2010). Facilitating vocabulary acquisition of young English language learners. *Language, Speech, and Hearing Services in Schools, 41*(3), 314–327.

Lynch, E.W., & Hanson, M.J. (2011). *Developing cross-cultural competence: A guide for working with children and their families* (4th ed.). Baltimore, MD: Paul H. Brookes Publishing Co.

MacSwan, J., Rolstad, K., & Glass, G.V. (2002). Do some school-age children have no language? Some problems of construct validity in the Pre-Las Espanol. *Bilingual Research Journal, 26*(2), 213–238.

Oller, D.K., Pearson, B.Z., & Cobo-Lewis, A.B. (2007). Profile effects in early bilingual language and literacy. *Applied Psycholinguistics, 28*(2), 191–230.

Paradis, J., Genesee, F., & Crago, M.B. (2011). *Dual language development & disorders: A handbook on bilingualism & second language learning* (2nd ed.). Baltimore, MD: Paul H. Brookes Publishing Co.

Pearson Education. (2009). *Pearson research overview: Opening the world of learning.* Retrieved from http://www.pearsonlearning.com/microsites/owl/research.cfm

Peña, E. (2007). Lost in translation: Methodological considerations in cross-cultural research. *Child Development, 78*(4), 1255–1264.

Peña, E.D., Kester, E.S., & Sheng, L. (2012). Semantic development in Spanish–English bilinguals: Theory, assessment, and intervention. In B.A. Goldstein (Ed.), *Bilingual language development and disorders in Spanish-English speakers* (pp. 131–152). Baltimore, MD: Paul H. Brookes Publishing Co.

Perez, A.M., Peña, E., & Bedore, L.M. (2010). Cognates facilitate word recognition in young Spanish-English bilinguals' test performance. *Early Childhood Services Journal, 4*, 55–67.

Pettito, L.A., Levy, B., Guana, K., Tetrault, K., & Ferraro, V. (2001). Signed and spoken language acquisition from birth: Implications for mechanisms underlying bilingual acquisition. *Journal of Child Language, 28*(2), 1–44.

Roberts, T. (2008). Storybook reading in primary or second language with preschool children: Evidence of equal effectiveness for second-language vocabulary acquisition. *Reading Research Quarterly, 43*(2), 103–130. doi:10.1598/RRQ.43.2.1

Roberts, T., & Neal, H. (2004). Relationships among preschool English language learner's oral proficiency in English, instructional experience and literacy development. *Contemporary Educational Psychology, 29*, 283–311.

Rolstad, K., Mahoney, K., & Glass, G. (2005). The big picture: A meta-analysis of program effectiveness research on English language learners. *Educational Policy, 19*, 572–594.

Santos, R., Cheatham, G., & Durán, L. (Eds.) (2012). *Supporting young children who are dual language learners with or at-risk for disabilities* (Young Exceptional Children Monograph Series No. 14; pp. 164–173). Missoula, MT: Division for Early Childhood.

Shanahan, T., & Beck, I. (2006). Effective literacy teaching for English-language learners. In D. August & T. Shanahan (Eds.), *Developing literacy in second language learners: Report of the national literacy panel on language-minority children and youth* (pp. 415–488). Mahwah, NJ: Lawrence Erlbaum Associates.

Slavin, R.E., & Cheung, A. (2005). A synthesis of research on language of reading instruction for English language learners. *Review of Educational Research, 75,* 247–284.

Teaching Strategies. (2010). *The creative curriculum system for preschool.* Washington DC: Author.

The Nation's Report Card. (2012). *Average scale scores for long-term trend reading, age 9 by status as English language learner.* Retrieved from http://nationsreportcard. gov/ltt_2012/age9r.aspx#0-5

Tsybina, I., & Eriks-Brophy, A. (2010). Bilingual dialogic book-reading intervention for preschoolers with slow expressive vocabulary development. *Journal of Communication Disorders, 43,* 538–556.

U.S. Census Bureau. (2010). *Overview of race and Hispanic origin: 2010.* Retrieved from http://www.census.gov/prod/cen2010/ briefs/c2010br-02.pdf

U.S. Department of Education. (2007). *Research summary on dialogic reading.* Retrieved from http:ies.ed.gov/ncee/ wwc/interventionreport.aspx?sid=135

U.S. Department of Health and Human Services. (2008). *Dual language learning: What does it take?* Retrieved from http://eclkc.ohs.acf.hhs.gov/hslc/ecdh/ eecd/Individualization/Learning%20 in%20Two%20Languages/DLANA_ final_2009%5B1%5D.pdf

U.S. Department of Health and Human Services. (2013). *Report to Congress on dual language learners in Head Start and Early Head Start programs.* Retrieved from http:// www.acf.hhs.gov/sites/default/files/opre/ report_to_congress.pdf

Wackerle-Hollman, A., Durán, L., & Rodriguez, M. (2014). *Spanish individual growth and development indicators.* Minneapolis, MN: Center for Early Education and Development, University of Minnesota.

Whitehurst, G.J., Arnold, D.S., Epstein, J.N., Angell, A.L., Smith, M., & Fischel, J. (1994). A picture book reading intervention in day care and home for children from low-income families. *Developmental Psychology, 30*(5), 679–689.

Whitehurst, G.J., Galco, F.L., Lonigan, C.J., Fischel, J.E., DeBarshe, B.D., Valdex-Menchaca, M.C., & Caulfield, M. (1988). Accelerating language development through picture book reading. *Developmental Psychology, 24,* 552–559.

Whitehurst, G., & Lonigan, C. (2001). *Get ready to read!* Washington, DC: National Center for Learning Disabilities.

Wong Fillmore, L. (1991). When learning a second language means losing the first. *Early Childhood Research Quarterly, 6,* 323–346.

Family Language Questionnaire

Child's name: _____

Today's date: _____

About your child

1. What is your relationship to the child?
   - ☐ Mother   ☐ Other relative
   - ☐ Father   ☐ Foster parent
   - ☐ Grandparent   ☐ Other—*Please describe:* _____

2. What languages are spoken in your home? _____

3. What languages do **you** use when you talk to your child? *(Check one)*
   - ☐ English   ☐ Home language   ☐ Both

4. What languages do **other people at home** use with your child? *(Check one)*
   - ☐ English   ☐ Home language   ☐ Both

5. What languages does **your child** use when talking at home? *(Check one)*
   - ☐ English   ☐ Home language   ☐ Both

6. With what language is your child **most comfortable** now? *(Check one)*
   - ☐ English   ☐ Home language   ☐ Both

7. From the ages of 0 to 1 year, was English, your home language, or both spoken to your child at home?
   - ☐ English
   - ☐ Home language
   - ☐ Both

Current language use

We are interested in how much English and home language your child hears and speaks. First, think about weekdays (Monday through Friday) and then think about weekends (Saturday and Sunday).

8. What languages does your child **hear** Monday through Friday?

Morning routine (awake to 9 a.m.)	Late morning/midday (9 a.m. to 1 p.m.)	Late afternoon (1 p.m. to 4 p.m.)	Evening (4 p.m. to bedtime)
☐ Home language ☐ English ☐ Both	☐ Home language ☐ English ☐ Both	☐ Home language ☐ English ☐ Both	☐ Home language ☐ English ☐ Both

(page 1 of 2)

9. What languages does your child **hear** Saturday and Sunday?

Morning routine (awake to 9 a.m.)	Late morning/midday (9 a.m. to 1 p.m.)	Late afternoon (1 p.m. to 4 p.m.)	Evening (4 p.m. to bedtime)
☐ Home language ☐ English ☐ Both	☐ Home language ☐ English ☐ Both	☐ Home language ☐ English ☐ Both	☐ Home language ☐ English ☐ Both

10. What languages does your child **speak** Monday through Friday?

Morning routine (awake to 9 a.m.)	Late morning/midday (9 a.m. to 1 p.m.)	Late afternoon (1 p.m. to 4 p.m.)	Evening (4 p.m. to bedtime)
☐ Home language ☐ English ☐ Both	☐ Home language ☐ English ☐ Both	☐ Home language ☐ English ☐ Both	☐ Home language ☐ English ☐ Both

11. What languages does your child **speak** Saturday and Sunday?

Morning routine (awake to 9 a.m.)	Late morning/midday (9 a.m. to 1 p.m.)	Late afternoon (1 p.m. to 4 p.m.)	Evening (4 p.m. to bedtime)
☐ Home language ☐ English ☐ Both	☐ Home language ☐ English ☐ Both	☐ Home language ☐ English ☐ Both	☐ Home language ☐ English ☐ Both

About you and your family

12. What is the highest level of education that you have completed? *(Check one)*

☐ 6th grade or less ☐ Some education after high school/vocational program
☐ Less than 12th grade ☐ Associate degree (AA)
☐ GED ☐ College degree (BA/BS)
☐ High school diploma ☐ Graduate/professional degree

13. What is the **country** of each parent's birth? *(Fill in for all applicable guardians)*

Mother: _____   Father: _____   Other guardian: _____

14. How many years has each lived in the United States? *(Fill in for all applicable guardians)*

Mother: _____   Father: _____   Other guardian: _____

(page 2 of 2)

Blended Practices for Teaching Young Children in Inclusive Settings, Second Edition,
by Jennifer Grisham-Brown and Mary Louise Hemmeter with Kristie Pretti-Frontczak and invited contributors.
Copyright © 2017 by Paul H. Brookes Publishing Co., Inc. All rights reserved.

Directions for use

Teachers can choose questions from this list that are relevant to the particular family they are serving and the context of intervention. These questions are meant as a guide to conduct an informal interview to gather more information from the family to assist in screening, eligibility determination, or intervention planning. *Note:* Insert the child's name instead of saying "your child."

Section I: Family constellation

1. Who is in your family?
2. Who lives with you and *your child*/children?
3. Explain how a big decision is made in your family.
4. Tell us about who helps you take care of your children.

Section II: Cultural beliefs and child-rearing practices

Child expectations

1. Describe how you think *your child* learns new things.
2. What things do you think are important for *your child* to learn now?
3. Do you think *your child* might need help with learning new things or with talking?
4. Is *your child* able to get around the house and get around outside like other children you know?
5. What do you think *your child* needs to be successful and have the opportunities you would like to see him or her have?

Views on disability

1. Describe what special gifts *your child* brings to your family.
2. What worries or concerns do you have for *your child*?
3. Describe the services or the people who help you with *your child's* learning and/or medical problems.
4. Describe the future you see for *your child*.
5. How do you expect *your child* will do in school?

Section III: Family routines

Mealtimes

1. Describe a mealtime. Who eats together? Where do you eat? What are some of your family's favorite foods?
2. What are the mealtime rules?
3. Are there any foods that your family does not eat for religious reasons?

Sleeping

1. Where does *your child* sleep? What happens when *your child* wakes up during the night?
2. Does *your child* have a bedtime?
3. Tell me about naptime. Does *your child* fall asleep?
4. How can you tell when *your child* is sleepy?

Child behavior

1. Describe what you consider to be good behavior.
2. Do you have any concerns about *your child's* behavior?
3. Describe a time when *your child* misbehaved. What did you do?
4. Who is responsible for disciplining children in your family?

(page 1 of 2)

Section IV: Family and community

Family support systems

1. Does your family mostly rely on friends and family members or different agencies in the community for assistance?
2. Does your family get support from any community organizations such as public health, social services, other community groups, or church groups?
3. How does your family get help when you need it?
4. Do you feel like you have a good connection to your community?

Family strengths and needs

1. What do you see as the strengths of your family?
2. How does your family get through difficult times?
3. What current difficulties is your family facing?
4. Do you have any unmet needs that would help you in raising *your child*/children?

Section V: Level of knowledge of U.S. school systems

1. How long have you and your family been in the United States?
2. Did you attend school in the United States? If not, where did you go to school?
3. Describe what school was like in your home country.
4. How familiar are you with Head Start, early intervention, or early childhood special education?
5. Did you have special education services in your home country? Did you have preschool?
6. Is it okay for male home visitors or other specialists to come to your home if necessary?

Sources: Barrera and Kramer (2009) and Lynch and Hanson (2011).

(page 2 of 2)

Resource	Source	Content
	Books	
Paradis, J., Genesee, F., & Crago, M.B. (2011). *Dual Language Development & Disorders: A Handbook on Bilingualism & Second Language Learning, Second Edition*	Paul H. Brookes Publishing Co.	Bilingual development Reading and academic considerations for dual language learners Bilingual development of children with cognitive disabilities International adoption
Barrera, I., & Kramer, L. (2009). *Using Skilled Dialogue to Transform Challenging Interactions: Honoring Identity, Voice, and Connection*	Paul H. Brookes Publishing Co.	Culturally responsive practice Family interviewing and information gathering
Castro, D.C., Ayankoya, B., & Kasprzak, C. (2011). *The New Voices-Nuevas Voces Guide to Cultural and Linguistic Diversity in Early Childhood*	Paul H. Brookes Publishing Co.	Training resources on the topics of bilingual development, home language maintenance, working with interpreters, and culturally responsive practice
Goldstein, B.A. (Ed.). (2012). *Bilingual Language Development and Disorders in Spanish-English Speakers, Second Edition*	Paul H. Brookes Publishing Co.	Semantic, syntactic, and phonological development Language loss Recommended interventions Language socialization
Tabors, P.O. (2008). *One Child, Two Languages: A Guide for Early Childhood Educators of Children Learning English as a Second Language, Second Edition*	Paul H. Brookes Publishing Co.	Stages of second language acquisition Recommended classroom practices Bilingual assessment
Santos, R., Cheatham, G., & Durán, L. (Eds.). (2012). *Young Exceptional Children Monograph No. 14: Supporting Young Children Who Are Dual Language Learners with or At-Risk for Disabilities*	Division for Early Childhood	Autism and dual language learning Indigenous populations and native language maintenance and revitalization Special education evaluation and screening Bilingual development Family perspectives

(page 1 of 2)

Resource	Source	Content
Web sites		
Hennepin County Library	http://www.hclib.org/BirthTo6/EarlyLit.cfm	Family resources for early literacy in multiple languages
¡Colorín Colorado!	http://www.colorincolorado.org	A bilingual site for families and educators of dual language learners
Washington Learning Systems	http://www.walearningsource.org/	Handouts in English and Spanish as well as other languages on learning activities in natural environments
ZERO TO THREE	http://www.zerotothree.org/early-care-education/early-language-literacy/songsengspan.pdf	Songs, rhymes, and fingerplays in Spanish
PACER Center	http://www.pacer.org/translations/index.asp	Parent handouts on child development available in multiple languages
Parents Know	http://helpmegrowmn.org/HMG/index.htm	Information on different disabilities and child development in Spanish, Hmong, and Somali
Talk With Me manual: A resource guide for speech-language pathologists and educators working with young children who are linguistically diverse and their families	http://www.msha.net/?page=talk_with_me_manual	A comprehensive guide to special education and speech-language evaluations and intervention
Challenging common myths about young English language learners	http://fcd-us.org/sites/default/files/MythsOfTeachingELLsEspinosa.pdf	A short article that addresses the common myths associated with second language acquisition

(page 2 of 2)

## CHAPTER 12

Blended Practices for Promoting Early Math Skills

Jessica K. Hardy, Sarah Hawkins-Lear, Mary Louise Hemmeter, and Jennifer Grisham-Brown

Miss Leticia teaches in a blended preschool classroom with 16 children between the ages of 3 and 5 years. Half of the children have identified disabilities/delays and half are typically developing who have qualified for public preschool based on their family income. Miss Leticia uses an emergent, project-based curriculum in her class. Her classroom recently completed a shoe project. While observing the children working on the project, she became aware of the fact that her student's math abilities varied widely. Some of the children in her class understand basic math concepts and need to be challenged with more difficult math content. Other children, however, are having difficulty with basic math skills such as counting and one-to-one correspondence. Another student in Miss Leticia's class has significant disabilities and is struggling to differentiate a number and a letter. Miss Leticia really wants to support all of the children in her classroom as they work toward important math standards, but she is not sure where to begin.

The purpose of this chapter is to provide support to teachers like Miss Leticia who are working in highly diverse classrooms, want to address important early learning standards, and want to do so within the context of a developmentally appropriate environment. This chapter includes information on issues and trends related to early math development and instruction, an explanation of early math skills, recommended practices for early math instruction, information on how to provide a mathematically rich environment, and how to design and implement blended practices for teaching math skills. The chapter concludes by demonstrating how Ms. Leticia uses her knowledge of teaching math and the curriculum framework to support all children in her classroom.

ISSUES AND TRENDS IN MATH DEVELOPMENT

Blended practices in early math instruction must be informed by research. Recent research points to the importance of early math knowledge in predicting later achievement. It also demonstrates the need for high-quality instruction to positively impact children's development and ameliorate disparities among young children's math knowledge.

Importance of Early Math Instruction

Mathematical competence is critical for success in school, adulthood, and many careers. Educators and other stakeholders are increasingly recognizing the importance of early experiences and education in developing mathematical competence (e.g., National Association for the Education of Young Children [NAEYC] & National Council of Teachers of Mathematics [NCTM], 2010). One example of this can be seen in the movement toward STEM (science, technology, engineering, and math) in early childhood education (ECE) (e.g., Aronin & Floyd, 2013; Moomaw & Davis, 2010). Thus, it is essential that teachers understand the importance of early math skills and be prepared to provide instruction to young children.

One of the reasons for the increasing focus on math in ECE is that research suggests that early math performance is predictive of later achievement. Perhaps most notably, early math skills were more predictive of later school achievement than other skills, including early reading, early attention, and early social-emotional skills, in a meta-analysis of six longitudinal studies (Duncan et al., 2007). In addition, early number sense was found to be correlated with performance in first grade and third grade (Jordan, Glutting, & Ramineni, 2010; Jordan, Kaplan, Locuniak, & Ramineni, 2007; Jordan, Kaplan, Ramineni, & Locuniak, 2009). Math skills in kindergarten have been found to be correlated with math skills in first grade (Denton & West, 2002).

Disparities in Early Math Knowledge

Research also suggests that there are differences in math achievement among children based on socioeconomic status, race, and ability. Denton and West (2002) analyzed data from the Early Childhood Longitudinal Study, Kindergarten Class of 1998–99 (ECLS-K), and found that there were discrepancies in math achievement between children from low socioeconomic status backgrounds and those from higher socioeconomic status backgrounds. Discrepancies based on socioeconomic status were also found in an analysis of the Pre-Elementary Educational Longitudinal Study (PEELS) data (Markowitz et al., 2006). Disparities related to race also were found when the ECLS-K data was analyzed. Caucasian and Asian children outperformed African American children on measures of math achievement (Denton & West, 2002). Caucasian children outperformed African American and Latino children on math measures when the PEELS data were analyzed (Markowitz et al., 2006). Thus, intervention in early math skills is critical for addressing the achievement gap between children from diverse socioeconomic and racial backgrounds. Although there is less research around disparities in math achievement according to ability, there is evidence that disparities exist. For example, researchers analyzed the PEELS data and found differences between children with and without disabilities on measures of math knowledge, especially for children with more significant disabilities (Markowitz et al., 2006).

Prevalence of Early Math Instruction in Preschool Classrooms

Evidence suggests that little math instruction occurs in preschool classrooms, despite the importance of early math skills. For example, 652 preschool programs in 11 states were analyzed, and only 8% of the day included mathematics instruction (Early et al., 2010). The frequency and type of teacher math talk have also been measured. Researchers found that the frequency varies widely among teachers, but variety in the type of math talk does not, with most math talk relating to cardinality (Ehrlich, 2007; Klibanoff, Levine, Huttenlocher, Vasilyeva, & Hedges, 2006) or the number of items in a group.

Based on the research, it is clear that 1) math is an important and valued subject in ECE; 2) young children need instruction in early math skills to support their learning and reduce disparities based on race, socioeconomic status, and ability; and 3) teachers need support in how to best provide math instruction in preschool classrooms.

EARLY MATH SKILLS

Mathematics includes both content skills and process skills (NCTM, 2000). The content skills are categorized into the following areas: 1) number sense and counting, 2) number relationships and operations, 3) algebra, 4) geometry, 5) measurement, and 6) data analysis. Definitions and examples for skills in each category are provided in Table 12.1.

Mathematic process skills help children learn math content skills and are further developed as young children engage in mathematics learning (NCTM, 2000). The process skills are categorized as follows: 1) problem solving, 2) reasoning and proof, 3) communication, 4) connections, and 5) representation. Problem solving is the crux of mathematics and involves "finding a way to reach a goal that is not immediately attainable" (NCTM, 2000, p. 116). Children can solve problems naturally in their everyday environments, such as rotating a puzzle piece until it fits correctly into the puzzle. They can also solve math problems that are presented intentionally to them, such as, "You have three apples and then you give me one. How many apples do you have now?" The reasoning and proof process skill occurs when children "are encouraged to make conjectures, are given time to search for evidence to prove or disprove them, and are expected to explain and justify their ideas" (NCTM, 2000, p. 122). The communication process skill involves children being able to talk or write about their mathematical thinking with others (NCTM, 2000). The connections process skill involves making links between intuitive and formal mathematics, between math concepts, and between math and other content areas (NCTM, 2000). The representation process skill is similar to the communication process skill; it involves children representing their thinking through pictures, symbols, gestures, and drawing (NCTM, 2000). Consider this example:

> Miss Leticia's preschool classroom is engaging in a unit of study about shoes. They have visited a shoe store and have created a shoe store in their dramatic play area. The children have noticed that the shoes in their shoe store are different sizes and they don't fit every person in the classroom. Miss Leticia asks, "How can someone know if a pair of shoes is the right size?" The children share a few ideas, and one of them has the idea to measure each child's foot and compare each child's foot size with the size of the shoe. Later that day, they talk about their solution in a large-group discussion. Miss Leticia asks another question, "How can we show the size of a pair of shoes?" One child suggests writing the length of each pair of shoes on the box holding the shoes. Miss Leticia replies, "That's a great idea!" and helps the children label the shoes during their next centers time.

The children are demonstrating several math process skills in this example. First, they are problem solving as they try to answer Miss Leticia's questions.

Table 12.1.   Early math skills

Skill	Definition	Example
Number sense and counting	Understanding number, quantities, and the rank order of numbers (Office of Head Start, 2010)	
Numeral identification	Associating the names of numbers with their corresponding numerals (Office of Head Start, 2010)	Saying the number name that corresponds to a numeral
Rote counting	Reciting numbers in the correct order (Sarama & Clements, 2009)	Saying, "1, 2, 3, 4, 5, 6, 7, 8, 9, 10" out loud, but without counting anything
Functional counting	Counting actual objects using one-to-one correspondence	Counting the number of cookies in a bowl
One-to-one correspondence	Matching one object to a corresponding number or object (Bricker et al., 2002; Kostelnik et al., 2011)	Putting a napkin next to each plate at a table
Cardinality	Understanding that "the number name of the last object counted [represents] the number of objects in the set" (Office of Head Start, 2010, p. 16)	Counting a group of five objects and then saying, "There are five!"
Subitizing	Identifying the number of objects by looking at them, but without counting them (Sarama & Clements, 2009)	Saying there are two children at the sensory table by looking at them without counting
Ordinality/number line	Knowing the correct order of numbers or numerals on the number line (Clements & Sarama, 2009)	Putting numbers in order from 1 to 5
Number relationships and operations	Understanding the relationships between numbers and how numbers can be used to solve problems (Office of Head Start, 2010)	
Whole and parts	Understanding that a whole is made up of different parts and parts can be combined to make a whole (Campbell, 1999)	Saying there is one apple before and after it has been cut into two parts
Addition and subtraction	Identifying "the new number created when numbers are combined or separated" (Office of Head Start, 2010, p. 16)	Identifying the number of orange slices left when a peer takes one off a plate
Comparing quantities	Using a range of strategies, such as counting, subitizing, or matching, to compare quantity in two sets of objects and describ[ing] the comparison with terms, such as more, less, greater than, fewer, or equal to" (Office of Head Start, 2010, p. 16)	Saying there are more blue blocks than red blocks
Algebra	Understanding patterns and relationships (Benson, 2003)	
Classification and sorting)	"Sorting and grouping objects by a common attribute or properly, such as color or size" (Benson, 2003)	Putting all the big bears in one container, the medium bears in another, and the small bears in another

(continued)

Table 12.1.   *(continued)*

Skill	Definition	Example
Seriation/ordering	Putting items in a sequence based on a particular attribute, such as size (Benson, 2003; Charlesworth & Lind, 2010).	Lining up teddy bears by how big they are
Patterning	Finding regularities in how things are ordered (Charlesworth & Lind, 2010), duplicating and extending observed patterns, and creating patterns (Office of Head Start, 2010).	Cutting and pasting pictures to form an AB pattern
Geometry	Identifying and manipulating shapes and understanding concepts related to directionality and spatial sense (Clements & Sarama, 2009; NCTM, 2000)	
Shape identification and manipulation	Recognizing, naming, constructing, comparing, and analyzing shapes (Clements & Sarama, 2009; Office of Head Start, 2010), as well as combining and separating shapes to make other shapes (Clements & Sarama, 2009; Office of Head Start, 2010)	Putting pattern blocks together to form a sailboat
Directionality and spatial sense	Understanding directionality and position of objects, such as up, down, in front, behind, etc. (Office of Head Start, 2010)	Putting objects on top of, inside, and next to a box when directed
Measurement	"[A]ssigning a number to a magnitude of some attribute of an object, such as its length, relative to a unit" (Clements & Sarama, 2009, p. 163)	
Measuring	Using standard and nonstandard tools to measure objects' length, weight, or volume (Clements & Sarama, 2009)	Using a string to measure how long a car is
Comparing sizes	Comparing objects according to size attributes and using terms to describe them such as bigger, taller, longer, and heavier (Charlesworth & Lind, 2010; Office of Head Start, 2010)	Saying that Jonathan runs faster than Omar
Data analysis	Organizing, displaying, and understanding data (NAEYC & NCTM, 2010)	
Graphing	Making simple graphs to represent information (Charlesworth & Lind, 2010)	Filling in a graph to indicate a favorite food
Data analysis	Using graphs to make comparisons, draw conclusions, and answer questions (Clements & Sarama, 2009)	Looking at a class graph and using it to say that more kids in the class have a dog as a pet than a cat

From Hardy, J.K., & Hemmeter, M.L. (2014). Assessing early academic skills. In M. McLean, M.L. Hemmeter, & P. Snyder (Eds.), *Essential elements for assessing infants and preschoolers with special needs* (pp. 280–282). Boston, MA: Pearson Education; reprinted by permission.

Second, they are engaging in representation as they write the size numbers on the boxes. Third, they are communicating their thinking about the concept of size in a large-group discussion. It is important to provide rich experiences and instruction so children can demonstrate math process skills.

It is also important for teachers to understand how mathematical concepts develop. The learning trajectories approach developed by Clements and Sarama (2009) is one resource for understanding how math concepts develop. Learning trajectories contain the developmental progression involved in learning a particular skill, along with the ages children typically move through the progression. There are learning trajectories for a variety of skills, including 1) counting, 2) comparing and ordering numbers, 3) recognizing numbers and subitizing, 4) composing combinations of numbers, 5) adding and subtracting, 6) measuring, 7) recognizing geometric shapes, 8) composing geometric shapes, 9) patterning and early algebra, and 10) classifying and analyzing data (Clements & Sarama, 2007, 2009). See Table 12.2 for an example of a learning trajectory for patterning and early algebra.

Table 12.2. Learning trajectory for patterning and early algebra

Age Range	Level Name	Level	Description
2	Pre-Patterner	1	A child at the earliest level does not recognize patterns. For example, a child may name a striped shirt with no repeating unit a "pattern."
3	Pattern Recognizer	2	At this level, the child can recognize a simple pattern. For example, a child at this level may say, "I'm wearing a pattern" about a shirt with black and white stripes.
4	Pattern Fixer	3	At this level the child fills in missing elements of a pattern.
4	Pattern Duplicator AB	4	A sign of development is when the child can duplicate an ABABAB pattern, although the children may have to work alongside the model pattern. For example, given objects in a row, ABABAB, the child may make his or her own ABABAB row in a different location.
4	Pattern Duplicator	5	At this level, the child is able to duplicate simple patterns (not just alongside the model pattern). For example, given objects in a row, ABBABBABB, the child may make his or her own ABBABBBABB row in a different location.
5	Pattern Extender	6	A sign of development is when the child can extend simple patterns. For example, given objects in a row, ABBABBABB, he or she may add ABBABB to the end of the row.
6	Pattern Maker from *n*	7	As a child develops patterning, he or she is able to fill in a missing element of a pattern. For example, given objects in a row with one missing, ABBAB . . . ABB, he or she may identify and fill in the missing element.
7	Pattern Unit Recognizer	8	At this level, a child can identify the smallest unit of a pattern. For example, given objects in a row with one missing, ABBAB . . . ABB, he or she may identify and fill in the missing element.

Understanding the range of early math skills relevant to young children is the first step in providing high-quality early math instruction. Providing an environment rich in opportunities to engage in math skills is the next step. The next section includes specific recommendations for how to set the stage for mathematics learning in the classroom.

Recommended Practices in Early Childhood Education Mathematics Instruction

Recommended practices in ECE mathematics instruction derive from two main sources. The first is a position statement developed by the NAEYC and NCTM (2010). The second source is a report on early mathematics learning by the National Research Council (NRC, 2009). The recommended practices are summarized in Table 12.3.

Building on children's interests, background knowledge, and experiences is the first recommended practice. Children are exposed to mathematics from a young age and can demonstrate beginning mathematical thinking. For example, a young child might request "more" of a desired snack or notice a pattern in the floor as he or she walks. This natural interest should be capitalized and built on to enhance children's mathematical thinking. It is also important to remember that children also have different background knowledge and experiences in early mathematics. For example, one child might come from a home in which there is little talk of mathematical concepts, and another might come from a home in which the parents often engage in math talk (e.g., "You are getting taller! Let's measure how much you've grown!").

Providing mathematically rich environments for children is the second recommended practice. This includes providing materials and toys that allow children to practice mathematical skills, such as manipulatives or small collections of items that can be counted, sorted, and organized into patterns. Providing mathematically rich environments also includes engaging in talk about mathematical concepts. For example, when a teacher is

---

Table 12.3.   Recommended practices in early childhood math instruction

1. Build on children's interests, background knowledge, and experiences.

2. Provide mathematically rich environments for children.

3. Encourage children to explore and learn mathematical concepts through play.

4. Base curriculum and instruction on developmentally appropriate practices.

5. Base curriculum and instruction on what is known about how mathematical concepts develop.

6. Provide systematic and intentional opportunities for children to learn math concepts using a variety of activities and evidence-based teaching strategies.

7. Integrate math learning throughout the curriculum.

8. Use assessment strategies to understand and support children's learning.

helping a child put crackers on his or her plate, the teacher could say, "Let's count them as you put them on your plate. One, two, three! You have three crackers!" The teacher can also embed mathematical concepts in everyday activities, such as having children name different shapes while they wash their hands or by talking about whole and parts when cutting an apple for children to share at snack.

Encouraging children to explore and learn mathematical concepts through play is the third recommended practice. Play provides natural opportunities to engage in mathematical thinking. For example, children who are engaging in a grocery store play scenario might sort food by category (e.g., fruits and vegetables, meat, canned goods) and count out money. Children often naturally engage in these activities, but adult encouragement can and should be used as well.

Basing curriculum and instruction on developmentally appropriate practices is the fourth recommended practice (e.g., Copple & Bredekamp, 2009). This means that practices should be based on what is age appropriate, culturally and socially appropriate, and individually appropriate. This recommendation helps a teacher plan what types of experiences to provide. For example, a teacher who has a strong understanding of what is developmentally appropriate would not expect 3- and 4-year-olds to complete 30 minutes of math worksheets. Rather, the teacher might provide manipulatives for children to use as the teacher implements instruction around math concepts.

Basing curriculum and instruction on what is known about how mathematical concepts develop is the fifth recommended practice. Teachers must understand the range of early math skills and processes relevant to young children, and they must also understand how concepts develop. For example, young children learn to count in a predictable sequence (Clements & Sarama, 2014). Understanding this sequence will help teachers plan instruction around counting.

Providing systematic and intentional opportunities for children to learn math concepts by using a variety of activities and evidence-based teaching strategies is the sixth recommended practice. Providing a mathematics-rich environment and helping children learn math through play is important, but it may not be sufficient for helping all children learn the full range of early math skills. Teachers must also provide intentional instruction to all children, based on their specific learning needs. Evidence-based teaching strategies should be used, and instruction should be individualized to meet the needs of all children.

Integrating math learning throughout the curriculum is the seventh recommended practice. Mathematics does not exist in a vacuum—it is intrinsically related to other areas of the curriculum and other developmental domains. Consider, for example, an activity in which children clap the syllables of their names. This is a literacy activity, but it also includes math skills such as counting and one-to-one correspondence. In addition, children's understanding can be deepened if their learning is integrated across curricular areas and developmental domains. Consider the classroom described earlier in which children are engaged in an in-depth exploration of shoes. They could engage in activities in which they compare and contrast different shoes, categorizing them along multiple dimensions (e.g., their color, how they fasten, how they are used). The children could poll the teachers in their school to find out what type of shoes the teachers are wearing, and then they could graph and analyze the data. The children are learning math concepts as they are deepening their understanding of the topic they are investigating.

Using assessment strategies to understand and support children's learning is the eighth recommended practice. Instruction must be based on children's individual needs, which requires ongoing assessment. Teachers can use strategies such as math screeners, checklists, and anecdotal records to understand children's mathematical thinking in order to plan additional learning opportunities.

These recommended practices form the basis of this chapter, and several of the recommended practices are addressed in further depth throughout the chapter.

BLENDED PRACTICES FOR TEACHING MATH SKILLS

Implementing blended practices in early math skills has three components: 1) assessing children's skills, 2) providing a high-quality universal curriculum, and 3) using evidence-based interventions. Each of these components will be addressed separately. These components, however, should be implemented concurrently as part of a cohesive program.

Assessment

Ongoing assessment is a critical component of a program of instruction around math. Ongoing formative assessment can be used to determine children's progress and refine the instruction being provided. Assessment can also be used to identify children who need more targeted support beyond the universal curriculum.

Teachers can assess children using published, standardized measures, such as the Tools for Early Assessment in Math (Clements, Sarama, & Wolfe, 2011), which is a universal screening tool. There are also Individual Growth and Development Indicators developed for early numeracy (Hojnoski & Floyd, 2004), which are used for universal screening and progress monitoring. Math assessments that can be used for universal screening are listed in Table 12.4.

Teachers may also use informal assessment strategies such as anecdotal records, checklists, rating scales, rubrics, and trial recordings. Informal assessment strategies can be used in a performance assessment or authentic assessment (Hardy & Hemmeter, 2014). Performance assessment

Table 12.4.   Math assessments

- Tools for Early Assessment in Math (Clements, Sarama, & Wolfe, 2011)

- Test of Early Mathematics Ability, Third Edition (Ginsburg & Baroody, 2003)

- Early Mathematics Diagnostic Assessment (The Psychological Corporation, 2002)

- Individual Growth and Development Indicators of Early Numeracy (Hojnoski & Floyd, 2004)

- Assessment, Evaluation, and Programming System for Infants and Children (AEPS®) Test: Birth to Three Years and Three to Six Years, Second Edition (Bricker, 2002)

- Teaching Strategies GOLD Birth Through Kindergarten Assessment Toolkit (Heroman, Burts, Berke, & Bickart, 2010)

is teacher-directed and involves a child answering questions or performing specific tasks in response to a teacher request (e.g., the teacher presents the child with eight bears and says, "Put the bears in groups by color"). Authentic assessment occurs as children are performing real-life tasks (e.g., the teacher notes the accuracy of a child's patterning as the child alternates colored blocks as he or she constructs a tower). An example of a checklist used to assess a child's patterning skills is presented in Figure 12.1, and an example of trial recording system used to assess a child's quantity comparison skills is presented in Figure 12.2. In the example in Figure 12.2, a teacher would use a response prompting procedure, such as the system of least prompts (described in a later section), to provide instructional trials. The form would be used to record the type of response the child makes (unprompted correct, prompted correct, or prompted error).

Informal assessments are often developed by teachers to assess particular skills. Informal assessments, however, can also be used to provide a more comprehensive measure of children's early math skills. One such assessment is the reproducible Early Math Screening Instrument (Hardy, 2013), which is presented in Appendix 12A. The Early Math Screening Instrument was developed for use in research to identify skills to target

Child: _____

Directions: Mark + if child demonstrates the behavior independently, 0 if child does not demonstrate the behavior, and P if child demonstrates the behavior with adult help.

Behavior	Date:	Date:	Date:
Duplicates AB pattern			
Duplicates ABB pattern			
Duplicates ABC pattern			
Extends AB pattern			
Extends ABB pattern			
Extends ABC pattern			

Figure 12.1.   Checklist example—patterning.

Child: _____   Date: _____

Directions: Present two sets of items of differing amounts. Ask the child, "Which has more?" or "Which has less?" Mark X under the child's response.

Beh. 1	More				Beh. 2	Less		
Trial	UC	PC	PE		Trial	UC	PC	PE
1					1			
2					2			
3					3			
4					4			
5					5			

Figure 12.2. Trial recording example—quantity comparison. (Key: UC = unprompted correct; PC = prompted correct; PE = prompted error)

for instruction. It was designed to be a comprehensive screening and progress monitoring tool and, as such, is appropriate for use by teachers. The Early Math Screening Instrument can be used to determine which skills a child has already learned, which skills are emerging, and which skills are unknown. For example, if a child can sort by color but not any other dimension (e.g., shape, size, function), that skill would be considered emerging and instruction should be planned accordingly. It can also be used over time to measure children's acquisition of skills.

High-Quality Universal Curriculum

Teachers have several options when choosing a universal curriculum. There are published curricula that can be purchased for use in the classroom. A curriculum can be comprehensive, meaning it includes content for all of the curricular areas, or it can be math specific. See Table 12.5 for a summary of many early childhood curricula with a math focus or math components.

Teachers do not have to use published curricula, however. A curriculum has three elements: 1) learning goals, 2) scope and sequence, and 3) activities. Learning goals can be based on learning standards such as the Head Start Early Learning Outcomes Framework: Ages Birth to Five (Office of Head Start, 2015) or local or state standards. Learning goals can also be created from the math skills listed in Table 12.1. For example, a math goal related to algebra could be that children can extend and create at least three different types of patterns.

After determining math goals, it is necessary to determine the skills that make up that goal (scope) and the order in which the skills typically develop (sequence). For the learning goal related to patterning, this might include 1) duplicating an AB pattern, 2) duplicating an ABB pattern, 3) duplicating an ABC pattern, 4) extending an AB pattern, 5) extending an ABB pattern, 6) extending an ABC pattern, 7) creating an AB pattern, 8) creating an ABB pattern, and 9) creating an ABC pattern.

Table 12.5.   Math and comprehensive curricula

Curriculum	Focus	
	Comprehensive	Math
Big Math for Little Kids (Ginsburg, Greenes, & Balfanz, 2003)		X
Numbers Plus Preschool Mathematics Curriculum (Epstein, 2009)		X
Building Blocks—SRA Real Math, Grade Pre-K (Clements & Sarama, 2007)		X
Everyday Mathematics (University of Chicago School Mathematics Project, 2012)		X
Mathematics Their Way (Baratta-Lorton, 1995)		X
Pre-K Mathematics Curriculum (Klein, Starkey, & Ramirez, 2004)		X
Connect4Learning: The Pre-K Curriculum (Sarama, Brenneman, Clements, Duke, & Hemmeter, 2016)	X	
Creative Curriculum for Preschool (Dodge, Bickart, Colker, & Heroman, 2010)	X	
Assessment, Evaluation, and Programming System for Infants and Children (AEPS®): Curriculum for Three to Six Years, Second Edition (Bricker & Waddell, 2002)	X	

After establishing the scope and sequence, teachers must then determine the activities that will be used to help children move through the scope and sequence and reach the learning goal. Teachers can use a variety of resources to help them create activities as part of a universal curriculum, including books, web sites, and published curricula. Teachers must always use their best professional judgment when evaluating activities to ensure that they are of high quality and are developmentally appropriate.

Instructional Considerations

Teachers designing high-quality math instruction need to consider how to 1) create a mathematically rich environment, 2) design developmentally appropriate activities, 3) deliver complete learning trials, and 4) select and implement specific instructional procedures that have been found to be effective in teaching math skills to young children. Details for how to address each of these considerations are provided in this section.

Create a Mathematically Rich Environment   Instruction in early math skills should begin with an environment rich in opportunities to engage in and learn about math. Teachers can provide a mathematically rich environment in two ways: 1) preparing the physical environment to support children's use of math skills and 2) engaging in math talk. First, teachers should carefully consider the materials provided in the physical environment. Children should be provided with materials that support their use of mathematics in play, routines, and intentional activities.

The classroom environment can be arranged to support children's use of math as they engage in play or routine activities such as cleaning up or washing hands. For example, items in the dramatic play center can naturally support sorting. As children put the materials away during clean-up time, the teacher can help them place items in the correct baskets (e.g., for food, dishes, utensils). In addition to having a visual of the letters of the alphabet at the writing center, a visual of numerals can also be posted, which encourages children to incorporate numerals into their writing. The teacher can include materials such as rulers in the block center to help children incorporate measurement into their play (e.g., measuring the length of a road constructed of blocks). The classroom environment should also include materials specifically related to math. The number of manipulatives available for early childhood classrooms is virtually limitless. Examples of such items are provided in Table 12.6, along with the math skills for which the items may be used.

Engaging in mathematical talk is the second way teachers should provide a mathematically rich environment. Teachers should model language related to mathematics throughout the day. Teachers should also ensure

Table 12.6. Math manipulatives

Materials	Math skills for which items may be used
Pattern blocks and picture cards	Shape manipulation
Interlocking plastic straws	Measurement
Rulers	Measurement
Collections of items with different attributes (e.g., different colored plastic bears, different size shells)	Counting, quantity comparison, addition, subtraction, cardinality, subitizing, sorting
Tangrams	Shape manipulation
Interlocking cubes	Patterning, counting, quantity comparison, addition, subtraction, cardinality, subitizing, sorting
Puzzles and stacking toys that incorporate shape, size, numerals, and quantities	Shape identification, numeral identification, seriation, quantity comparison
Numeral cards	Numeral identification, ordinality
Balance scale and weights	Measurement, size comparison
Wooden cubes	Counting, quantity comparison, addition, subtraction, cardinality, subitizing, sorting
Small items and pattern cards	Patterning
Bowls or trays	Sorting
Beads and string	Patterning, counting

Table 12.7. Math talk examples

Example of math talk	Math skills addressed
"I am going to cut this apple into pieces so we can each have a slice."	Whole and parts
"Put a napkin next to each plate."	One-to-one correspondence
"How many children are here today? 1, 2, 3, 4, 5, 6, 7, 8, 9, 10, 11, 12. There are 12 children here today!"	Counting and cardinality
"That piece of pizza looks like a triangle."	Shape identification
"Let's put all blocks on this shelf and the vehicles on that shelf."	Classification and sorting
"You have made a big block tower. It is taller than my tower!"	Comparing sizes
"You both are making a lot of dots on your paper. Who has less dots on his or her paper?"	Comparing quantities
"The puzzle piece you're looking for is behind you."	Directionality and spatial sense
"Let's line up the playdough pieces from smallest to biggest."	Seriation
"You had two dolls, but then you shared one with Jamie. Now you have one doll."	Subtraction
"I see a pattern in my drawing. First there is a red square, then a blue square, then a red square, and then another blue square."	Patterning

they provide math talk related to a range of skills. For example, math talk related to counting might come more naturally to teachers, but math talk related to other skills might be more difficult to produce, especially in the moment. This could result in neglecting math talk related to other skills. It is important that teachers incorporate the range of math skills into their math talk. For example, as he or she plays with children at the block center, a teacher could say, "You have made a big block tower. It is taller than my tower!" Additional examples of math talk are provided in Table 12.7, along with the types of math skills being addressed. Teachers must thoughtfully plan ways to engage in math talk throughout the day.

Providing a mathematically rich environment is a necessary component of providing high-quality math instruction. It is not sufficient to provide materials and engage in math talk, however. Even within a high-quality math environment, children will need intentional, systematic instruction to acquire, generalize, and maintain early math skills. The next section includes information on how to plan instruction in early math skills.

Design Developmentally Appropriate Activities   It is important to consider the context in which the instruction is provided when planning intentional instruction in early math skills. Instruction can be embedded in other activities such as classroom routines, play activities, or project work. For example, a teacher could embed instruction on patterning during a music activity or embed instruction on measurement in a cooking activity. Although embedding instruction is a recommended practice in ECE, many math skills are difficult to embed naturally in other activities. In addition, there are often not sufficient opportunities to embed instruction around a particular skill. Thus, it is important to consider other activities that allow for intentional, repeated instruction in early math skills. Two such activities are games and teacher-directed activities.

Games, which can be played with other children or an adult, generally have an overarching goal to accomplish (e.g., filling the basket, reaching the finish line). Games can be developmentally appropriate, engaging tasks in which to provide instruction in early math skills. A variety of types of games can be used. For example, the teacher could create a simple board game in which children move cars around a race track by rolling a die and moving the number of spaces on the die. This teaches counting and one-to-one correspondence. High Card (also known as War) is another math-related game in which two children show a card and the person with the highest card gets to keep both cards. This game teaches the number line and numerical magnitude comparisons. See Table 12.8 for a list of resources for creating games to teach early math skills.

The teacher instructs the child to use materials, usually manipulatives, in a particular manner during teacher-directed activities. For example, an adult provides miniature vehicles of different colors and works with the child to sort them. Teacher-directed activities conducted with enthusiasm and using interesting materials can be engaging activities in which children can receive instruction in many math skills. The advantage of teacher-directed activities is that they provide an ideal context for delivering instruction in a range of math skills.

Complete Learning Trials　Complete learning trials should be used, regardless of the type of activity (e.g., routines, play, games, teacher-directed activities). Complete learning trials involve an antecedent, behavior, and consequence. An antecedent is a cue that sets the occasion for the child to respond. Examples include the following task directions: "Put the food in

---

Table 12.8.　Resources for creating games

- Charlesworth, R., & Lind, K.K. (2010). *Math and science for young children.* Belmont, CA: Cengage Learning.

- Cutler, K.M., Gilkerson, D., Parrott, S., & Browne, M.T. (2003). Developing math games based on children's literature. *Young Children, 58*(1), 22–27.

- Kamii, C. (1982). *Number in preschool and kindergarten.* Washington, DC: National Association for the Education of Young Children.

- Kamii, C., & Housman, L.B. (2000). *Young children reinvent arithmetic: Implications of Piaget's theory* (2nd ed.). New York, NY: Teachers College Press.

- Moomaw, S., & Hieronymus, B. (2011). *More than counting: Math activities for preschool and kindergarten* (Standards edition). St. Paul, MN: Redleaf Press.

one basket, and put the dishes a different basket." "Tell me how long the pencil is using the inchworm manipulatives." "Has it been sunny or rainy more days this week?" An antecedent also includes the assistance the child needs to correctly perform the skill. This assistance can be in the form of a gestural or verbal model of the task (e.g., "This is a hot dog. A hot dog is food, so it goes in the food basket") or a prompt with directions about how to perform the skill (e.g., "Count how many blocks are colored in under the rainy picture and how many blocks are colored in under the sunny picture. Which has more?")

The child's behavior is what the child actually does—how he or she performs the task. The child will either correctly perform the task, incorrectly perform it, or fail to respond. The consequence is a logical outcome of the child's behavior (e.g., the child is done cleaning up and can move to the next activity) or a planned teacher response. The consequence varies depending on whether the child's behavior is correct or incorrect. Teachers should always reinforce the child for a correct response or acknowledge the response was correct (e.g., "You're right, red comes next in the pattern!"). Teachers can also reinforce or acknowledge the child's effort in performing a skill, even if the child is incorrect (e.g., "I could tell you were working hard to count those blocks"). The consequence can also be used to inform the child if he or she incorrectly performed the response (e.g., "You almost had it—let me help you fix it"). The teacher can help the child fix an incorrect response by performing the skill with the child or modeling the correct response and having the child repeat it. The first strategy is more appropriate for complex skills such as sorting, whereas the second strategy is more appropriate for discrete skills such as naming numerals. Performing the skill with the child ensures that the child will be successful.

Specific Instructional Procedures

Specific Instructional Procedures Specific instructional procedures also can be used to teach early math skills to individual or small groups of children who need instruction on targeted or individual outcomes. These instructional procedures include the system of least prompts, constant time delay, and the demonstration-practice procedure (see Chapter 7 for detailed information about these and other systematic teaching strategies). The system of least prompts is a response prompting system that involves providing a task direction and a response interval. If the child does not respond correctly, then more intensive prompts (from a pre-established prompt hierarchy) are increasingly provided until the child produces the correct response. After producing the correct response, whether it was prompted or unprompted, the child is reinforced. For example, if a teacher wanted to teach a child to give out one item to each child in a small group (e.g., cup, marker, piece of paper), the teacher might complete the following steps:

1. Ask the child to give a cup (or other material) to a child during snack time and wait for the child to independently give each peer a cup.

2. If the child does not give a cup to each peer, then the teacher models what the child is supposed to do and waits to see if the child follows the model.

3. If the child still does not give a cup to each peer, then the teacher provides a physical prompt to the child so that the child can perform the expected behavior.

Constant time delay is another response prompting procedure that involves providing two types of trials—zero-second delay trials and time delay trials. In zero-second delay trials, a task direction is provided and then the controlling prompt (i.e., the prompt that reliably elicits the correct response by the child) is immediately provided. The child should then respond and is reinforced for correct responses. Time delay trials are used after a period of using zero-second delay trials (usually a few sessions or days). In the time delay trial, the task direction is provided and is followed by an interval in which the adult waits for the child to respond (usually 3–5 seconds). If the child responds correctly, it is considered an unprompted correct and the child is reinforced. If the child does not respond, then a prompt is provided. If the child responds correctly to the prompt, then it is considered a prompted correct and the child is reinforced. If the child responds to the task direction with an incorrect response, then an error correction procedure can be used or the child can be directed to wait for the prompt if he or she is unsure of the correct response. For example, if a teacher is trying to teach a child the names of shapes, the teacher might complete the following steps:

1. Ask the child to make a square (or other shape) playdough "cookie" with cookie cutters.

2. Wait 4 seconds.

3. If the child does not pick the square cookie cutter, pick up the cookie cutter and say, "This is a square—I'm going to make a square cookie. Now you do it!"

The demonstration-practice procedure (Hardy, 2014) is an approach that combines the use of modeling and complete learning trials and can be used in the context of play activities or teacher-directed tasks. In the demonstration-practice procedure, the teacher demonstrates the skill and then provides several opportunities for the child to practice the skill, interspersing additional teacher demonstrations of the skill as necessary. For example, if a teacher wants to teach shape manipulation using the demonstration-practice procedure, he or she might complete the following steps:

1. While playing with blocks, the teacher says, "I'm going to put the blocks together to make a picture."

2. The teacher then says, "I need to fit the blocks together like a puzzle so the whole picture is covered. I make sure the blocks stay in the lines,"

and then models the task and acknowledges what he or she did: "I did it—I made the picture!"

3.   Teacher tells the child to "Put the blocks together to make the picture" and waits for the child to respond.

4.   If the child does not respond correctly, the teacher interrupts the error and provides a prompt (verbal, gestural, or physical) for the child to complete the task correctly. The teacher then acknowledges that the child performed the task (e.g., "You put the blocks together to make the picture").

Providing blended practices in early math skills is a complex process that requires careful planning to ensure that a high-quality curriculum is in place, ongoing assessment is used, and evidence-based interventions are used. The next section includes a case study of designing a program of instruction around math in a blended preschool classroom.

MISS LETICIA'S CLASSROOM: A CASE STUDY

Assessment

Miss Leticia decides to create a checklist to assess her children's math skills. She decides to focus on math skills Teaching Strategies GOLD assessment (Heroman, Burts, Berke, & Bickart, 2010), which she uses to assess all of the children in her classroom. These skills include counting, cardinality, quantity comparison, sorting, and patterning. These math skills lend themselves to being assessed in the natural environment as children participate in everyday routines or hands-on activities. Miss Leticia decides to assess children's counting and cardinality skills during snack preparation. She specifically assesses whether children can count to three by asking each child to count the cups on the snack table, of which there are three. If the child does that correctly, then Miss Leticia then asks the child to count the plates on the snack table, of which there are 10. She records whether each child can perform the task on the checklist shown in Figure 12.3. Miss Leticia assesses cardinality by counting the number of cups and then asks, "How many are there?" Miss Leticia is able to collect data on multiple children during this routine. She also plans to continue collecting data during snack time for the rest of the week to ensure that she collects data on all of her children.

Miss Leticia determines that most of her children need further instruction in cardinality and patterning. Some of her children need further instruction in counting, quantity comparison, and sorting. She uses this information to plan the scope and sequence of her math curriculum.

Scope and Sequence

The next step is to determine the scope and sequence of the curriculum. Miss Leticia decides to focus specifically on the math concepts on which she assessed her children. She uses the following early learning standards

Directions: Mark + if child demonstrates the behavior independently and 0 if child does not demonstrate the behavior.

Child's name	Date	Counts three items correctly	Correctly identifies how many in set	Counts 10 items correctly	Correctly identifies how many in set

Figure 12.3. Counting and cardinality checklist.

from the Creative Curriculum Objectives for Development and Learning (Heroman et al., 2010), which are aligned with Teaching Strategies GOLD, to guide her scope and sequence:

- *Counts using one-to-one correspondence (i.e., one number name for each object)*

- *Uses the number name of the last object counted to represent the number of objects in the set (cardinality)*

- *Compares sets and identifies which sets has more, less, or the same (equal)*

- *Sorts and classifies objects using attributes such as color, shape, or size*

- *Recognizes, copies, and extends simple patterns*

Miss Leticia further delineates the sequence that children can use to meet each early learning standard. For example, the standard related to sorting and classifying objects can be broken down into the following steps:

1. *Identifies which object is different when presented with a group of three objects/pictures of one color and one object/picture of a different color*

2. *Puts an object/picture in an already-formed group based on its color*

3. *Sorts six or more objects/pictures into different groups by color*

4. *(Repeat previous steps for shape and then size attributes)*

Miss Leticia uses the assessment data she gathered to hypothesize which children will respond to universal instruction, which children will benefit from targeted instruction, and which children will need systematic instruction. She uses this assessment information, along with the scope and sequence, to determine the activities and instruction she will provide for her children.

Activities and Instruction

After a teacher has assessed the children and developed target math goals, the next step is to create activities to address the math goals and match the activities and instruction to the needs and preferences of the children. The teacher must plan teaching activities and instruction for children working on universal outcomes, those working on targeted outcomes, and those working on individualized outcomes.

Miss Leticia begins to think about how to design activities that allow her to embed instruction on counting, cardinality, quantity comparison, sorting, and patterning. Examples of universal activities and instruction may include counting and comparing the number of children present and absent during circle time; counting and comparing cups, plates, and napkins during snack time; counting the number of jumping jacks children do during gross motor time; counting the beats to a song while using a musical instrument; providing manipulatives that encourage children to sort and pattern; providing large-group activities in which children are asked to sort pictures on a chart based on their size, shape, or color; and encouraging children to notice patterns in clothing (e.g., striped shirt, plaid shorts). Children may participate in these activities on a daily basis. Miss Leticia uses modeling and embedding complete learning trials throughout these activities.

Miss Leticia notices, however, that some children can count to five but need additional support when counting to 10 during large-group times. She also observes some children skipping numbers, saying numbers out of order, or saying some numbers more than once when they are counting. Some children are able to sort by color but not by any other attribute. She also observes that some children do not ever use the manipulatives to copy or extend patterns. She determines that these children need targeted instruction.

Targeted activities and instruction typically occur in a small-group format. Miss Leticia focuses on providing multiple complete learning trials for each student using prompts. For example, Miss Leticia provides verbal prompting to each child as he or she counts the 10 insects under the large magnifying glass during a science activity. She supports children in counting correctly and identifying the cardinal number of the set. She also provides opportunities for children to compare quantities by putting insects into two different group and embedding instruction on "more" and "less." In addition, Miss Leticia creates an art activity in which the children have multiple opportunities to count 10 items. The children can count the number of paper scraps to use, the number of markers or crayons to use, or the number of glue dots to use before gluing the paper scraps to a larger piece of paper. Multiple embedded learning opportunities within this art activity allow the children to practice counting and cardinality. Miss Leticia uses modeling and prompting at the manipulatives center to help children sort and pattern. She creates an art activity in which children use stamps and ink pads to make patterns on paper.

Miss Leticia observes that a few children in her classroom are not acquiring their math goals, even after universal and targeted instruction. She decides that these children need systematic instruction, which will occur in a one-to-one format in which Miss Leticia will plan intentional, intensive, and individualized instruction to address the math goals.

Miss Leticia designs activities to use while embedding instruction on the skills in which more systematic and intensive instruction is needed. Miss Leticia decides to use constant time delay to provide instruction on these skills. Miss Leticia knows that the children in her classroom who need systematic instruction on counting enjoy the book and block centers. Therefore, Miss Leticia intentionally places counting books in the book center and adds trucks and cars to the block center. Now, when she observes target children playing in either center, she can join them and embed intensive instruction while participating in a preferred activity. For example, while reading a book together, Miss Leticia asks one child, Oliver, to count the number of bugs on the page. While playing with blocks, she directs Oliver to count the number of blocks in the tower or the number of cars that will drive under the tower. There is not a specific start or stop time within both activities, so she can provide multiple intensive and individualized opportunities over a longer duration. For example, while Miss Leticia and Oliver participate in a shared reading time, she asks Oliver, "How many bugs are on this page?" and then waits 3 seconds for him to reply. If Oliver correctly counts the 10 bugs, then she says, "Great, you counted 10 bugs!" If he does not count the 10 bugs, then she provides hand-over-hand assistance and verbally models as she counts the 10 bugs with him. This occurs throughout the shared reading time. See Figure 12.4 for an example of an intervention plan for counting.

Progress Monitoring

Progress monitoring is used to determine whether children are responding to instruction and to revise instruction if necessary. Progress monitoring must be directly linked to the scope and sequence of the curriculum and the activities and instruction provided to children to determine whether the instructional goals and instruction are appropriate for the children. Miss Leticia must determine how she is going to monitor the progress of the children in her classroom across all types of instruction.

Miss Leticia decides to use the checklist she developed to assess her children's math skills while she implements universal instruction. She will be able to determine what math skills the children have mastered, what math skills are emerging, and what math skills the children have not made any progress toward acquiring. She decides to do this once every 2 months. She also decides to add a component to the checklist to allow her to record the level of assistance her children need to complete a task correctly (e.g., verbal prompt, gestural prompt, physical prompt).

Child: _____   Outcome: <u>Counts 10 items</u>

Skill	Antecedent	Wait time: 3 Seconds	Behavior + Correct behavior − Incorrect behavior	Consequence	Modification/ adaptation
Count 10 items	"Look at the bugs on the storybook page; let's count them."	Give the child 3 seconds to begin counting.	+ correct within 3 seconds	Descriptive verbal praise: "Great, you counted the bugs!"	
			− incorrect after 3 seconds	Provide hand-over-hand assistance while counting 10 bugs.	
Count 10 items	"Let's count the blocks in the tower we just built."	Give the child 3 seconds to begin counting.	+ correct within 3 seconds	Descriptive verbal praise: "You are right; there are 10 blocks in our tower!"	
			− incorrect after 3 seconds	Provide hand-over-hand assistance while counting 10 blocks.	

Figure 12.4.   Intervention plan for counting.

Miss Leticia decides to readminister the checklist on a weekly basis for specific targeted outcomes while she implements targeted instruction. For example, Briana needs targeted instruction around sorting and patterning but not counting, cardinality, and quantity comparison. Thus, only the sorting and patterning items will be assessed on a weekly basis for Briana. Miss Leticia will use the weekly data collection to determine the progress her children have made on two math goals after receiving targeted instruction.

Miss Leticia will collect data on a daily basis when implementing systematic instruction on individualized outcomes. She will create a data collection form for each child that will allow her to monitor the child's progress on his or her individualized math goals. See Figure 12.5 for an example of a data collection form.

Miss Leticia monitors children's progress and uses the information she gathers to further refine the instruction she provides to children. She also uses the information to determine if children need more or less intensive instruction. For example, Briana has made significant progress after several weeks of targeted instruction. Thus, Miss Leticia determines that she can be moved from targeted to universal instruction for all of her math goals. This process of data-based decision making is a critical component of providing instruction using the curriculum framework.

Miss Leticia continues to use the curriculum framework throughout the year, and she is pleased to see the improvement her children are making

Child: _____   Outcome:_____

Instructional procedure: _Constant time delay_

Directions: Present two sets of items of differing amounts. Ask the child, "Which has more?" or "Which has less?" Mark X under the child's response.

Embedded learning opportunity	Response			
	UC	UE	PC	PE

Figure 12.5. Sample data collection form for systematic instruction. (Key: UC = unprompted correct [performs the skill correctly before a prompt is provided]); UE = unprompted error [performs the skill incorrectly before a prompt is provided]); PC = prompted correct [performs the skill correctly after a prompt is provided]); PE = prompted error [performs the skill incorrectly after a prompt is provided])

in demonstrating math skills. She also knows this process has helped her improve the quantity and quality of math learning opportunities she provides to her children.

SUMMARY

As the field of ECE continues to recognize the importance of early math instruction for setting a high trajectory for achievement for young children, it is critical that teachers use recommended and evidence-based practices. Teachers must always provide a mathematically rich environment with authentic opportunities to engage in mathematical thinking. However, teachers must also be equipped to provide systematic instruction to meet the needs of all learners. The practices described in this chapter can be used to support all children, including those with disabilities.

LEARNING ACTIVITIES

1. A unit of study about shoes is discussed on page 314. Choose a unit of study or project that could be explored in an early childhood classroom. Make a list of three to five ways math instruction could be incorporated into the unit of study.

2. Recommended practices in early childhood math instruction are outlined on pages 315–316. Choose one of the recommendations and write about a time you saw the recommendation being followed well or a time when the recommendation was not followed well.

3. Choose a math skill and design an activity in which you could assess children's use of the skill. Then design a data collection sheet that could be used to record children's behavior.

4. Choose a math skill and outline the sequence for how that skill develops (see example on page 330 for sorting and classifying objects). Then choose an instructional procedure mentioned in the text and provide instruction in that skill to a child.

REFERENCES

Aronin, S., & Floyd, K.K. (2013). Using an iPad in inclusive preschool classrooms to introduce STEM concepts. *Teaching Exceptional Children, 45*(4), 34–39.

Baratta-Lorton, M. (1995). *Mathematics their way: An activity-centered mathematics program for early childhood education.* Parsippany, NJ: Dale Seymour Publications.

Benson, H.S. (2003). Glossary of math terms. In D. Koralek (Ed.), *Spotlight on young children and mathematics* (p. 43). Washington, DC: NAEYC.

Bricker, D., (Series ed.) (2002). *Assessment, Evaluation, and Programming System (AEPS®) for Infants and Children* (2nd ed.). Baltimore, MD: Paul H. Brookes Publishing Co.

Bricker, D., & Waddell, M. (2002). *Assessment, Evaluation, and Programming System for Infants and Children* (AEPS®): *Curriculum for Three to Six Years* (2nd ed.). Baltimore, MD: Paul H. Brookes Publishing Co.

Campbell, P.F. (1999). Fostering each child's understanding of mathematics. In C. Seefeldt (Ed.), *The early childhood curriculum: Current findings in theory and practice* (3rd ed.) (pp. 106–132). New York, NY: Teachers College Press.

Charlesworth, R., & Lind, K.K. (2010). *Math and science for young children* (6th ed.). Belmont, CA: Wadsworth Cengage Learning.

Clements, D.H., & Sarama, J. (2007). *Building blocks—SRA real math, grade pre-K.* New York, NY: SRA/McGraw-Hill.

Clements, D.H., & Sarama, J. (2009). *Learning and teaching early math: The learning trajectories approach.* New York, NY: Routledge.

Clements, D. H., & Sarama, J. (2014). *Learning and teaching early math: The learning trajectories approach* (2nd Ed.). New York, NY: Routledge.

Clements, D.H., Sarama, J., & Wolfe, C.B. (2011). *TEAM—Tools for early assessment in math.* New York, NY: McGraw-Hill Education.

Copple, C., & Bredekamp, S. (2009). *Developmentally appropriate practice in early childhood programs.* Washington, DC: National Association for the Education of Young Children.

Cutler, K.M., Gilkerson, D., Parrott, S., & Browne, M.T. (2003). Developing math games based on children's literature. *Young Children, 58*(1), 22–27.

Denton, K., & West, J. (2002). *Children's reading and mathematics achievement in kindergarten and first grade.* Washington, DC, U.S. Department of Education.

Dodge, D.T., Bickart, T.S., Colker, L.J., & Heroman, C. (2010). *Creative Curriculum for Preschool.* Bethesda, MD: Teaching Strategies.

Duncan, G.J., Claessens, A., Huston, A.C., Pagani, L.S., Engel, M., Sexton, H.,...Duckworth, K. (2007). School readiness and later achievement. *Developmental Psychology, 43,* 1428–1446.

Early, D.M., Iruka, I.U., Ritchie, S., Barbarin, O.A., Winn, D.-M.C., Crawford, G.M.,...Pianta, R.C. (2010). How do pre-kindergartners spend their time? Gender, ethnicity, and income as predictors of experiences in pre-kindergarten classrooms. *Early Childhood Research Quarterly, 25,* 177–193.

Ehrlich, S.B. (2007). *The preschool achievement gap: Are variations in teacher input associated with differences in number knowledge?* (Unpublished doctoral dissertation). University of Chicago, Chicago, IL.

Epstein, A.S. (2009). *Numbers plus preschool mathematics curriculum.* Ypsilanti, MI: High/Scope Press.

Ginsburg, H.P., & Baroody, A.J. (2003). *Test of early mathematics ability* (3rd ed.). Austin, TX: PRO-ED.

Ginsburg, H.P., Greenes, C., & Balfanz, R. (2003). *Big math for little kids.* Parsippany, NJ: Dale Seymour Publications.

Hardy, J.K. (2013). *Math Screening Instrument* (Unpublished instrument). Vanderbilt University, Nashville, TN.

Hardy, J.K. (2014). *Systematic instruction of early math skills* (Unpublished doctoral dissertation). Vanderbilt University, Nashville, TN.

Hardy, J.K., & Hemmeter, M.L. (2014). Assessing early academic skills. In M. McLean, M.L. Hemmeter, & P. Snyder (Eds.), *Essential elements for assessing infants and preschoolers with special needs* (pp. 271–315). Boston, MA: Pearson Publishing.

Heroman, C., Burts, D.C., Berke, K., & Bickart, T.S. (2010). *Teaching strategies GOLD: Objectives for development and learning: Birth through kindergarten.* Bethesda, MD: Teaching Strategies.

Hojnoski, R., & Floyd, R. (2004). *Individual Growth and Development Indicators of Early Numeracy (IGDIS-EN).* St. Paul, MN: Early Learning Labs.

Jordan, N.C., Glutting, J., & Ramineni, C. (2010). The importance of number sense mathematics achievement in first and third grades. *Learning and Individual Differences, 20,* 82–88.

Jordan, N.C., Kaplan, D., Locuniak, M.N., & Ramineni, C. (2007). Predicting first-grade math achievement from developmental number sense trajectories. *Learning Disabilities Research and Practice, 22,* 36–46.

Jordan, N.C., Kaplan, D., Ramineni, C., & Locuniak, M.N. (2009). Early math matters: Kindergarten number competence and later mathematics outcomes. *Developmental Psychology, 45,* 850–867.

Kamii, C. (1982). *Number in preschool and kindergarten.* Washington, DC: National Association for the Education of Young Children.

Kamii, C., & Housman, L.B. (2000). *Young children reinvent arithmetic: Implications of Piaget's theory* (2nd ed.). New York, NY: Teachers College Press.

Klein, A., Starkey, P., & Ramirez, A.B. (2004). *Pre-k mathematics curriculum.* Glenview, IL: Scott Foresman.

Klibanoff, R.S., Levine, S.C., Huttenlocher, J., Vasilyeva, M., & Hedges, L.V. (2006). Preschool children's mathematical knowledge: The effect of teacher "math talk." *Developmental Psychology, 42,* 59–69.

Kostelnik, M.J., Soderman, A.K., & Whiren, A.P. (2011). *Developmentally appropriate curriculum: Best practices in early childhood education* (5th ed.). Upper Saddle River, NJ: Pearson Education.

Markowitz, J., Carlson, E., Frey, W., Riley, J., Shimshak, A., Heinzen, H.,...Klein, S. (2006). *Preschoolers' characteristics, services, and results: Wave 1 overview report from the Pre-Elementary Education Longitudinal Study (PEELS).* Rockville, MD: Westat.

Moomaw, S., & Davis, J.A. (2010). STEM comes to preschool. *Young Children, 65*(5), 12–14.

Moomaw, S., & Hieronymus, B. (2011). *More than counting: Math activities for preschool and kindergarten* (Standards edition). St. Paul, MN: Redleaf Press.

National Association for the Education of Young Children & National Council of Teachers of Mathematics (NAEYC & NCTM). (2010). *Early childhood mathematics: Promoting good beginnings. Joint position statement.* Washington, DC: NAEYC and Reston, VA: NCTM. Available from www.naeyc.org/positionstatements/mathematics

National Council of Teachers of Mathematics. (2000). *Principles and standards for school mathematics.* Reston, VA: Author.

National Research Council. (2009). *Mathematics learning in early childhood: Paths toward excellence and equity.* Washington, DC: National Academies Press.

Office of Head Start. (2015). *Head Start Early Learning Outcomes Framework: Ages Birth to Five.* Washington, D.C.: U.S. Department of Health and Human Services.

Office of Head Start. (2010). *The Head Start child development and early learning framework: Promoting positive outcomes in early childhood programs serving children 3–5 years old.* Arlington, VA: Office of Head Start, Administration for Children and Families, U.S. Department of Health and Human Services.

Sarama, J., Brenneman, K., Clements, D.H., Duke, N.K., & Hemmeter, M.L. (2016). *Connect4Learning: The pre-k curriculum.* Lewisville, NC: Connect4Learning.

Sarama, J., & Clements, D.H. (2009). *Early childhood mathematics education research: Learning trajectories for young children.* New York, NY: Routledge.

The Psychological Corporation. (2002). *Early Mathematics Diagnostic Assessment.* San Antonio, TX: Author.

University of Chicago School Mathematics Project. (2012). *Everyday mathematics.* New York, NY: McGraw-Hill Education.

Early Math Screening Instrument

Early Math Screening Instrument

Child: _____

Session 1 date: _____

Session 2 date: _____

Session 3 date: _____

Data collector: _____

Data collector: _____

Data collector: _____

Directions: Present the materials and give the task direction. Mark C, E, or NR for each item.

Counting and Number Sense

#	Category & directions	Item	Materials	Task direction	Session 1	Session 2	Session 3
1	Verbal counting	5	n/a	Count as high as you can, starting with 1.			
2	Verbal counting	10	n/a				
3	One-to-one correspondence	n/a	5 animals and 5 blocks	Give each animal a block.			
4	Counting	5 objects	5 blocks	Count the blocks.			
5	* Complete 5 only if 4 was correct	10 objects	10 blocks	Count the blocks.			
6	Cardinality	n/a	4 blocks	[After counting blocks aloud for child]: How many blocks are there?			

Blended Practices for Teaching Young Children in Inclusive Settings, Second Edition,
by Jennifer Grisham-Brown and Mary Louise Hemmeter with Kristie Pretti-Frontczak and invited contributors.
Copyright © 2017 by Paul H. Brookes Publishing Co., Inc. All rights reserved.

From Hardy, J.K. (2013) *Early Math Screening Instrument.* Unpublished instrument.

Counting and Number Sense

#	Category & directions	Item	Materials	Task direction	Session 1	Session 2	Session 3
7	Numeral identification—expressive	1	1 number card	What number is this?			
8		2	2 number card	What number is this?			
9		3	3 number card	What number is this?			
10		4	4 number card	What number is this?			
11		5	5 number card	What number is this?			
12		6	6 number card	What number is this?			
13		7	7 number card	What number is this?			
14		8	8 number card	What number is this?			
15		9	9 number card	What number is this?			
16		10	10 number card	What number is this?			
17	Numeral identification—receptive * Complete only if expressive (7–16) were <u>incorrect</u>	1	5 number cards, including 1	Point to the 1.			
18		2	5 number cards, including 2	Point to the 2.			
19		3	5 number cards, including 3	Point to the 3.			
20		4	5 number cards, including 4	Point to the 4.			
21		5	5 number cards, including 5	Point to the 5.			
22		6	5 number cards, including 6	Point to the 6.			
23		7	5 number cards, including 7	Point to the 7.			
24		8	5 number cards, including 8	Point to the 8.			
25		9	5 number cards, including 9	Point to the 9.			
26		10	5 number cards, including 10	Point to the 10.			

(page 2 of 7)

Blended Practices for Teaching Young Children in Inclusive Settings, Second Edition,
by Jennifer Grisham-Brown and Mary Louise Hemmeter with Kristie Pretti-Frontczak and invited contributors.

From Hardy, J.K. (2013) *Early Math Screening Instrument.* Unpublished instrument.

APPENDIX 12A **Early Math Screening Instrument** (continued)

Counting and Number Sense

#	Category & directions	Item	Materials	Task direction	Session 1	Session 2	Session 3
27	Ordinality * Complete 28–30 only if 27 was <u>correct</u>	1-5	Number cards 1-5	Put the numbers in order.			
28		1-10	Number cards 1-10	Put the numbers in order.			
29		Insertion, 1-5	Number cards 1-5 (insert 2)	Put this number in the right spot.			
30		Insertion, 1-10	Number cards 1-10 (insert 7)	Put this number in the right spot.			
31	Comparing numerical magnitudes * Complete 33 & 34 only if 31 & 32 were <u>correct</u>	Large difference, bigger	2 and 8 number cards	Which is bigger?			
32		Large difference, smaller	1 and 7 number cards	Which is smaller?			
33		Small difference, bigger	3 and 4 number cards	Which is bigger?			
34		Small difference, smaller	6 and 7 number cards	Which is smaller?			

Number Relationships and Operations

#	Category & directions	Item	Materials	Task direction	Session 1	Session 2	Session 3
35	Comparing quantities	Large difference, more	3 and 7 blocks	Point to the one that has more.			
36		Large difference, less	2 and 8 blocks	Point to the one that has less.			
37		Small difference, more	3 and 4 blocks	Point to the one that has more.			
38		Small difference, less	4 and 5 blocks	Point to the one that has less.			
39	Addition * Complete 40 only if 39 was <u>correct</u>	Adding 1	2 blocks	You have 2 and I give you 1. How many do you have?			
40		Adding 2	3 blocks	You have 3 and I give you 2. How many do you have?			
41	Subtraction * Complete 42 only if 41 was <u>correct</u>	Taking away 1	2 blocks	You have 2 and I take away 1. How many do you have?			
42		Taking away 2	5 blocks	You have 5 and I take away 2. How many do you have?			

Blended Practices for Teaching Young Children in Inclusive Settings, Second Edition,
by Jennifer Grisham-Brown and Mary Louise Hemmeter with Kristie Pretti-Frontczak and invited contributors.

From Hardy, J.K. (2013) *Early Math Screening Instrument.* Unpublished instrument.

Algebra

#	Category & directions	Item	Materials	Task direction	Session 1	Session 2	Session 3
43	Sorting * Complete 46 only if 43–45 were <u>correct</u>	Color	Miniature objects of 3 different colors	Put all the ones that are the same color together.			
44		Shape	3 different shapes of multicolored foam shapes	Put all the ones that are the same shape together.			
45		Size	Foam shapes of 3 different sizes	Put all the ones that are the same size together.			
46		Function	Same color miniature objects of 3 different categories	Put all the same types together.			
47	Oddity	Color	3 miniature objects the same color and category and 1 of a different color	Which one is different?			
48		Shape	3 foam shapes (the same shape) and 1 of a different shape	Which one is different?			
49		Size	3 foam shapes the same size and 1 of a different size	Which one is different?			
50		Function	3 miniature objects of the same category and color and 1 of a different category	Which one is different?			
51	Seriation * Complete 52 & 53 only if 51 was <u>correct</u>	Smallest to largest	3, 4, 5, 6, 7, and 8 Unifix cube towers	Put them in order from smallest to largest.			
52		Largest to smallest	3, 4, 5, 6, 7, and 8 Unifix cube towers	Put them in order from largest to smallest.			
53		Insertion	3, 4, 5, 6, 7, and 8 Unifix cube towers (insert 7)	Put this one where it goes in order.			

Blended Practices for Teaching Young Children in Inclusive Settings, Second Edition,
by Jennifer Grisham-Brown and Mary Louise Hemmeter with Kristie Pretti-Frontczak and invited contributors.
Copyright © 2017 by Paul H. Brookes Publishing Co., Inc. All rights reserved.

From Hardy, J.K. (2013) *Early Math Screening Instrument.* Unpublished instrument.

341

					Session 1	Session 2	Session 3
		Algebra					
#	Category & directions	Item	Materials	Task direction			
54	Patterning * Complete 58–59 only if 54–57 were <u>correct</u>	Duplicating AB	Blocks of 2 different colors arranged in an AB pattern	Make the same pattern with your blocks.			
55		Duplicating ABB	Blocks of 2 different colors arranged in an ABB pattern	Make the same pattern with your blocks.			
56		Extending AB	Blocks of 2 different colors arranged in an AB pattern	Keep going with the pattern.			
57		Extending ABB	Blocks of 2 different colors arranged in an ABB pattern	Keep going with the pattern.			
58		Abstracting AB	Blocks of two different colors arranged in an AB pattern and other manipulatives of different colors	Look at these blocks. Make the same pattern you see with these new materials.			
59		Identifying unit AB	Blocks of 2 different colors arranged in an AB pattern	What do you see repeating over and over again?			

Blended Practices for Teaching Young Children in Inclusive Settings, Second Edition, by Jennifer Grisham-Brown and Mary Louise Hemmeter with Kristie Pretti-Frontczak and invited contributors.

From Hardy, J.K. (2013) *Early Math Screening Instrument.* Unpublished instrument.

APPENDIX 12A   **Early Math Screening Instrument** (continued)

#	Category & directions	Item	Materials	Task direction	Session 1	Session 2	Session 3
				Geometry			
60	Shape identification—expressive	Circle	Circle shape card	What shape is this?			
61		Square	Square shape card	What shape is this?			
62		Rectangle	Rectangle shape card	What shape is this?			
63		Triangle	Triangle shape card	What shape is this?			
64		Rhombus (diamond)	Rhombus shape card	What shape is this?			
65		Oval	Oval shape card	What shape is this?			
66	Shape identification—receptive * Complete only if expressive (60–65) were incorrect	Circle	6 shape cards	Point to the circle.			
67		Square	6 shape cards	Point to the square.			
68		Rectangle	6 shape cards	Point to the rectangle.			
69		Triangle	6 shape cards	Point to the triangle.			
70		Rhombus (diamond)	6 shape cards	Point to the rhombus (or diamond).			
71		Oval	6 shape cards	Point to the oval.			
72	Shape manipulation * Complete 74 & 75 only if 72 & 73 were incorrect	Matching picture with 3 shapes	Pattern blocks and small picture	Put the shapes together to make this picture.			
73		Matching picture with 6 shapes	Pattern blocks and large picture	Put the shapes together to make this picture.			
74		Matching in picture	Pattern blocks, small picture with shape outlines	Match the shapes on the picture.			
75		Matching shapes	Pattern blocks, shape outlines	Match the shapes on the picture.			

APPENDIX 12A **Early Math Screening Instrument** (continued)

#	Category & directions	Item	Materials	Task direction	Session 1	Session 2	Session 3
			Measurement				
76	Comparing sizes	Bigger	Two different sized pictures or shapes	Point to the one that is bigger.			
77		Smaller	Two different sized pictures or shapes	Point to the one that is smaller.			
78		Longer	Two different sized Unifix cube towers	Point to the one that is longer.			
79		Shorter	Two different sized Unifix cube towers	Point to the one that is shorter.			
80		Heavier	Balance scale, heavy item, and light item	Point to the side that is heavier.			
81		Lighter	Balance scale, heavy item, and light item	Point to the side that is lighter.			
82	Measuring	Length	Pencil and blocks for measuring	How long is the pencil? Use the blocks to measure.			
83		Weight	Balance scale, heavy item, colored blocks	How much does the heavy item weigh? Use the colored blocks to measure.			

(page 7 of 7)

344

Index

References to tables and figures are indicated with a *t* and *f*, respectively.

345